INTERPRETING DUNS SCOTUS

John Duns Scotus is commonly recognized as one of the most original thinkers of medieval philosophy – indeed, of Western philosophy *tout court*. His influence on subsequent philosophers and theologians is enormous and extends well beyond the limits of the Middle Ages. His thought, however, might be intimidating for the non-initiated because of the sheer number of topics he touched on and the difficulty of his philosophical style. The eleven essays collected here, especially written for this volume by some of the leading scholars in the field, take the reader through a variety of topics, including Duns Scotus's life and intellectual environment, his argument for the existence of God and his conceptions of modality, order, causality, matter and form, freedom, and human nature and its dignities. His views on the way human beings become aware of practical principles, on the extent and limits of their knowledge in this life, and on the concept of being and the notion of analogy are also analyzed. This volume provides a reliable entryway to the thought of Duns Scotus while giving a snapshot of some of the best research that is now being done on this difficult but intellectually rewarding thinker.

GIORGIO PINI is Professor of Philosophy at Fordham University in New York City. He is the author of *Categories and Logic in Duns Scotus* (2002), *Scoto e l'analogia* (2002), and the critical edition of a previously unedited work by Duns Scotus, *Notabilia super Metaphysicam* (2017). He has published numerous essays on later medieval metaphysics and theories of cognition.

T0371093

INTERPRETING DUNS SCOTUS

Critical Essays

EDITED BY

GIORGIO PINI

Fordham University

Shaftesbury Road, Cambridge CB2 8EA, United Kingdom

One Liberty Plaza, 20th Floor, New York, NY 10006, USA

477 Williamstown Road, Port Melbourne, VIC 3207, Australia

314–321, 3rd Floor, Plot 3, Splendor Forum, Jasola District Centre, New Delhi – 110025, India

103 Penang Road, #05–06/07, Visioncrest Commercial, Singapore 238467

Cambridge University Press is part of Cambridge University Press & Assessment,
a department of the University of Cambridge.

We share the University's mission to contribute to society through the pursuit of
education, learning and research at the highest international levels of excellence.

www.cambridge.org
Information on this title: www.cambridge.org/9781108411387

DOI: 10.1017/9781108328975

© Giorgio Pini 2022

First published 2022
First paperback edition 2023

A catalogue record for this publication is available from the British Library

Library of Congress Cataloging-in-Publication data
NAMES: Pini, Giorgio, editor.
TITLE: Interpreting Duns Acotus : critical essays / edited by Giorgio Pini.
DESCRIPTION: Cambridge, United Kingdom : Cambridge University Press, 2021. |
Includes bibliographical references and index.
IDENTIFIERS: LCCN 2021024843 (print) | LCCN 2021024844 (ebook) |
ISBN 9781108420051 (hardback) | ISBN 9781108411387 (paperback) |
ISBN 9781108328975 (epub)
SUBJECTS: LCSH: Duns Scotus, John, approximately 1266-1308. | Philosophy, Medieval. |
BISAC: PHILOSOPHY / History & Surveys / Medieval | PHILOSOPHY /
History & Surveys / Medieval | LCGFT: Essays.
CLASSIFICATION: LCC B765.D74 I58 2021 (print) | LCC B765.D74 (ebook) | DDC 189/.4–DC23
LC record available at https://lccn.loc.gov/2021024843
LC ebook record available at https://lccn.loc.gov/2021024844

ISBN   978-1-108-42005-1   Hardback
ISBN   978-1-108-41138-7   Paperback

Contents

Acknowledgments

When this volume was still in the planning stages, Marilyn McCord Adams, who had agreed to contribute to it, passed away. Before being admitted to the hospital, with her characteristic generosity she sent me her chapter on Duns Scotus on the dignities of human nature. This might be the last essay she completed in her wonderfully productive life. It is an essay that perfectly reflects her penetrating intellect and her mastery of—and admiration for—Duns Scotus's thought. It is a great honor to have it in this collection. While expressing my gratitude to her, for the lasting mark she left on philosophy, medieval scholarship, and the lives of those who were so fortunate as to cross paths with her, I also wish to extend my deepest thanks to her husband, Robert Merrihew Adams, who checked and authorized the small changes necessary to adjust Marilyn's essay to the editorial norms of this series.

I carried out part of the work on this volume in 2018–2019, thanks to a Faculty Fellowship from Fordham University and a Solmsen Fellowship from the Institute for Research in the Humanities (IRH) at the University of Wisconsin-Madison. I wish to thank both institutions for their unflagging support of scholarship. I owe a special debt of gratitude to many people both at Fordham and IRH for many inspiring conversations as well as many laughs. Finally, I wish to thank my graduate assistants at Fordham University, Brenton Smith, Ciarán Coyle, and especially Emma Emrich for her tireless and skillful work on the index.

Notes on contributors

MARILYN MCCORD ADAMS held numerous academic appointments over the course of her career, including Professor of Philosophy at UCLA, Horace Tracy Pitkin Professor of Historical Theology at Yale Divinity School, and Regius Professor of Divinity at the University of Oxford.

RICHARD CROSS is Rev. John A. O'Brien Professor of Philosophy at the University of Notre Dame.

STEPHEN D. DUMONT is Professor of Philosophy at the University of Notre Dame.

GLORIA FROST is Professor of Philosophy at the University of St. Thomas in St. Paul, Minnesota.

WOUTER GORIS is Professor of Philosophy at the University of Bonn.

MARTIN PICKAVÉ is Professor and Canada Research Chair of Medieval Philosophy at the University of Toronto.

GIORGIO PINI is Professor of Philosophy at Fordham University.

GARRETT R. SMITH is Research Fellow (Akademischer Rat) at the University of Bonn.

CECILIA TRIFOGLI, FBA, is Professor of Medieval Philosophy at the University of Oxford.

THOMAS M. WARD is Associate Professor of Philosophy at Baylor University.

THOMAS WILLIAMS is Professor of Philosophy and Catholic Studies at the Universisty of South Florida.

Introduction

Giorgio Pini

Since their first formulation, many of John Duns Scotus's views have attracted the attention of philosophers and theologians alike. Responses have ranged from admiration to opprobrium, including (perhaps most memorably) ridicule: in the sixteenth century, Duns Scotus gained the dubious distinction of entering the English language as a common noun—through the word 'dunce'. In the relatively tolerant and sedate environment of contemporary academia, a mention of his name might still be met with a smirk, often on account of his alleged obscurity, or even provoke an occasional outburst of hostility, especially from those who are partial to interpreting the history of philosophy as a fight between abstractions (realism *versus* nominalism, voluntarism *versus* intellectualism, transcendence *versus* immanence, the Secular *versus* the Sacred, and so forth). For mysterious reasons—probably connected to the alleged opposition between two of those abstractions, Thomism and Scotism—it is not rare to see the name of Duns Scotus associated with some vague and ghastly philosophical catastrophe.[1] It is high time for Duns Scotus to be considered *sine ira et studio*. It is also high time for his thought to be better known, and not just among the specialists of medieval philosophy.

The originality of Duns Scotus's views is beyond question and his influence was pervasive well into the modern era.[2] It is equally undeniable, however, that Duns Scotus *is* a difficult thinker, and easy to misunderstand, as the French historian of philosophy, Étienne Gilson, dismally remarked.[3] In particular, three factors seem to have acted as stumbling blocks for even the most well-intentioned among his interpreters. First, Duns Scotus had a tendency to consider any given topic from different

---

[1] On the use of Duns Scotus as a villain in some recent philosophical narratives, see Horan 2014: 15–58; O'Regan 2015. On previous views on the place of Duns Scotus in the history of philosophy, see Pomplun 2016.

[2] Ariew 2000; Honnefelder 2005; Leader 1984; Schmutz 2002; Schmutz 2008.   [3] Gilson 1952: 8.

points of view—to proceed *collative*, by way of contrasting opposite positions, as one of his first followers put it.[4] As a result of this way of doing, he changed his mind over time about several significant issues. But even when no change of mind occurred, a proclivity to approach an issue from many perspectives and a certain reluctance to simplify what is complex make it difficult, and probably inadvisable, to identify a "Scotistic" system—an aspect that was again stressed by Gilson[5] but has been curiously and repeatedly missed by many of Duns Scotus's friendly and less friendly interpreters, often eager to reduce his thought to a string of few bold claims.

Second, Duns Scotus's language and arguments are technical and at times idiosyncratic. These technicalities and idiosyncrasies are not an accidental feature of his thought. Rather, they must be taken fully into account if one wants to grasp the exact nature of the claims Duns Scotus is making. Clearly, this requires much time and effort.

Third, Duns Scotus kept crossing the boundaries between philosophy and theology in a way that might strike some of his readers as excessively nonchalant. As a result, any attempt to separate a philosophical core from a theological background might lead to frustration: more often than not, Duns Scotus's most original philosophical insights occur when he is dealing with strictly theological issues. In the past, this aspect of his thought has led to a charge of "theologism," namely the claim that Duns Scotus reduced philosophy to a part of theology. Although some interpreters have tried to defend him, this suspicion lingers.

This collection of essays intends neither to present Duns Scotus's thought in a simplified way nor to guide the reader through all the niceties of Duns Scotus's many and varied positions. Nor does it provide a comprehensive introduction to all his main views. Other books have already done so, some of them in an excellent way.[6] Rather, each of the following chapters offers a specific example of how a scholar who has devoted much time and effort to interpreting Duns Scotus engages with key aspects of his work and thought—some of them still little explored by scholars, other ones more familiar but approached from a fresh perspective.

The result is a snapshot of some of the best research that is now being done on this extremely original thinker. It is also a concrete illustration of how some of the best scholars working on Duns Scotus now deal with the

---

[4] The expression is by Peter Thomae. See Petrus Thomae, *Quaest. de ente* (Smith, 398); Dumont 1988: 200–201.
[5] Gilson 1952: 7–8.   [6] See notably Williams 2003a.

three difficulties I have mentioned above. Although each author treats his or her subject in the way he or she thinks most appropriate, it is perhaps possible to identify a common trait in the following essays: they all positively *embrace* the challenging nature of Duns Scotus's views and style of thinking. Specifically, with regard to the first difficulty, the following essays refrain from any attempt to reduce Duns Scotus's thought to a few formulas. Rather, they offer a nuanced understanding of his positions and arguments by paying attention to the precise wording of his arguments, the most recent acquisitions of textual scholarship, the historical context in which he developed his views, and the way some of his positions evolved over time. In other words, the multifaceted nature of Duns Scotus's thought is emphasized rather than disguised. Similarly, with regard to the second difficulty, the authors of these essays make no attempt to conceal the technical character of Duns Scotus's claims. But this technicality—an unavoidable consequence of the difficulty of the issues Duns Scotus was dealing with—is explained as clearly as possible, and, if some interpretive difficulties remain, this is stressed and accepted as a characteristic aspect of serious scholarship. Finally, with regard to the third difficulty, the authors of the following essays take a more relaxed attitude towards the thorny issue of the relationship between philosophy and theology than much of the scholarship pursued by previous generations of Duns Scotus's interpreters did. It must now be acknowledged that theological concerns are everywhere, and not just in Duns Scotus but in most medieval thinkers, and not just in medieval thinkers but also in many modern ones. An exaggerated preoccupation with drawing a clear-cut separation between philosophical and theological issues risks to have a distorting effect when applied to much of the history of Western thought, and it leaves too many interesting things out of the picture. It also distracts from what really matters, namely the presence of good arguments and of original solutions to deep problems—and there is no dearth of either in Duns Scotus, as the readers of this collection will find out.

The volume begins with a presentation of Duns Scotus's life. Stephen Dumont reconsiders the biographical data known to scholars in light of recent advancements in textual criticism and the considerable amount of information about the medieval educational system that has become available in the last couple of decades. As a result, Dumont sheds new light on several aspects that had so far perplexed interpreters, including Duns Scotus's possible stay in Cambridge, the way he commented on the *Sentences* in Oxford and Paris, and the precise dates of his Paris regency. It was long customary to start a treatment of Duns Scotus's life by stressing how little was known about him. After Dumont's careful analysis, we can conclude that much more can be known than we used to think.

The following seven chapters are devoted to key themes in two areas to which Duns Scotus made some of his most original contributions, namely metaphysics and philosophical theology, starting with God and then moving to a consideration of a few key aspects of the created world.

In his contribution, Richard Cross examines Duns Scotus's celebrated modal argument for the existence of a first cause in the light of the most extensive *ex professo* discussion of modality that he offers: namely, the account of the senses of 'potency' in his questions on Aristotle's *Metaphysics*, book IX, qq. 1–2. Cross holds that it is possible to give two alternative reconstructions of Duns Scotus's argument for the existence of a first cause depending on which of two alternative interpretations is given to the term 'potency'. First, 'potency' can be taken as what is metaphysically possible. In this interpretation, the potential is co-extensive with 'being'. Second, 'potency' can be taken to mean what is opposed to the actual. In this second interpretation, being in potency is a kind of non-being. Cross concludes that, contrary to what might first appear, it is the second interpretation of 'potency' that should be preferred if we want Duns Scotus's argument for the existence of a first cause to work.

In Chapter 3, Thomas Ward focuses on a concept that plays a central role in Duns Scotus's metaphysics—essential order. Ward starts with Duns Scotus's presentation of essential order in the *De primo principio*, where essential order is said to obtain between two beings, x and y, where x is essentially prior to y and y is essentially posterior to x. But, as Ward observes, Duns Scotus makes use of essential order in several other contexts as well, including his hylomorphism, chemistry, action theory, metaethics, and even ecclesiology. In these other contexts, the notion of essential order is not clearly defined, and it is not always obvious how its deployment is supposed to map onto the canonical definition of essential order offered in the *De primo principio*. Ward takes a step toward this systematization by analyzing Duns Scotus's use of essential orders outside of the *De primo principio*, letting the *De primo principio* discussion both inform and be informed by these other contexts.

In the next chapter, Gloria Frost moves to considering the way the first cause's action relates to the action of created causes, with a particular focus on the action of created wills. As Frost notes, since medieval thinkers considered God an active causal source of all existents, they believed that God must in some way actively cause the actions of created causes, including the acts of the will. Duns Scotus's thought on this matter is particularly interesting because, as is widely recognized, he was committed to a robust understanding of the created will's freedom. Frost argues that Duns Scotus struggled to figure out how God could be involved in causing the operation of such a spontaneously and autonomously operating cause. He wrestled with two different theories, and ultimately could not make up his mind. This chapter reconstructs Duns Scotus's analysis of competing positions while tracking the developments in his thought.

The next chapter focuses on the notion of the created agents' will not in relation to God's causality but in order to refine our understanding of what Duns Scotus meant by 'freedom'. As Martin Pickavé observes, John Duns Scotus's teaching on freedom and the will has been the object of much attention and has rightly been praised as a radically new approach to human agency. Unlike most of his predecessors, Duns Scotus considered a "synchronic" power for opposites as fundamental to human free will and set out to give a detailed account of the metaphysical makeup of the power through which we possess free will. Pickavé, however, argues that this cannot be the full story, because Duns Scotus also maintained that freedom is compatible with necessity. To get a clearer picture of Duns Scotus's overall understanding of freedom, Pickavé begins by focusing on how Scotus engaged with Anselm of Canterbury's definition of freedom. Although Duns Scotus did not seem to accept Anselm's account, he followed Anselm in the quest for an understanding of freedom that applies to both God and creatures. After addressing the exact nature of the power for opposites that Duns Scotus frequently associated with freedom, Pickavé turns to the "formal concept" (*ratio formalis*) of freedom and how it is common to God and creatures. Pickavé concludes that freedom is for Duns Scotus fundamentally a power for self-determination rather than a power for opposites.

The examination of human agency takes us naturally to the metaphysical makeup of human beings considered in light of their place in the order—both natural and providential—established by God. In her contribution, Marilyn McCord Adams shows that Duns Scotus firmly believed in the dignities (plural) of human nature—both the natural human dignity celebrated by Aristotle, who maintained that the material world was made for the sake of rational animals, and the supernatural dignities paid to humankind by God in the Incarnation and to particular human beings by predestining them to glory. When it comes to identifying more concretely the features in which such dignities consist, Duns Scotus's metaphysical views—about essential powers and about what is essential to powers—combine with his theological conviction that, when it comes to patterns of Divine concurrence with or obstruction of natural powers, God has different policies for different states of human history—to complicate his method.

An essential characteristic of human beings is that they are composed of form and matter. Like any good Aristotelian, Duns Scotus held that human beings share this feature with a large section of the created world. In her chapter, Cecilia Trifogli provides an in-depth presentation and assessment of some crucial aspects of Duns Scotus's contribution to the later medieval debate on hylomorphism, including his views on the existence and nature of prime matter, the plurality of substantial forms in a material substance, and the nature of animate substances.

The following chapter shifts the focus to metaethics and, even more specifically, to some epistemic concerns characteristic of Duns Scotus's approach to metaethics. In his contribution, Thomas Williams turns again to the will, but from a perspective different from the one adopted in some of the previous essays. The will is the key component of Duns Scotus's moral theory, both because Duns Scotus held (quite uncontroversially) that we are morally responsible only for our free choices and their outcomes and because (more controversially) he thought that most principles detailing what is morally good and what is morally bad depends on God's free decisions. For Williams, then, the key question is how we know contingent practical principles. He offers an account of our knowledge of such principles that is (a) consistent with what Duns Scotus says about the relationship of the moral law to the divine will and to human nature, (b) consistent with what he says more generally about our knowledge of contingent truths, and (c) consistent with his actual argumentative practice in dealing with contingent practical principles. Williams's examination of Duns Scotus's argumentative practice uncovers a third, hitherto unnoticed, sense of 'natural law'. Williams suggests that the core unifying sense of 'natural law' for Duns Scotus is precisely the epistemic status of the precepts of natural law as non-inferentially evident.

The next three chapters keep an epistemic focus but move away from the will to examine the nature of the most basic concepts through which human beings grasp the way the world is structured. In his contribution, Wouter Goris focuses on the very notion of "object of the intellect." He argues that the distinction between "natural object of inclination" (*obiectum naturale inclinabile*) and "natural reachable object" (*obiectum naturale attingibile*) is at the basis of a fundamental reorientation in the doctrine of the first adequate object of the intellect in Duns Scotus's later works. In the absence of any direct intellectual intuition of the soul and its potencies in this life, natural reason has no epistemic access to the first adequate object of the intellect except by way of abstraction of the *per se* objects it attains effectively. This insight induces Duns Scotus to revise his criticism of the position that he ascribes to Aristotle and Thomas Aquinas, namely that the "quiddity of material things" is the first adequate object of the intellect. Although Duns Scotus claims consistently that this position cannot be maintained by a theologian, he comes to accept it in his later works as correctly expressing the philosopher's view of the first adequate object of the intellect in this life.

In my chapter, I consider Duns Scotus's arguments against the so-called semantic analogy—the view according to which a term can signify two or more things according to relations of priority and posteriority. I argue that this view was commonly adopted in Paris but was rejected by a group of late thirteenth- and early fourteenth-century English thinkers, which included Duns Scotus. Since supporters of semantic analogy held that 'being' was the foremost example of a term signifying according to priority and posteriority, the implications of this debate on metaphysics are profound. I argue that Duns Scotus's rejection of semantic analogy should be considered as preliminary to his famous claim that being is a univocal concept.

Duns Scotus's views sparked much discussion among both followers and opponents. The last essay in this collection considers the different attitudes that a number of Duns Scotus's followers took with regard to the analogy of being. Taking a position different from the one I defend in the previous chapter, Garrett Smith holds that there is room in Duns Scotus's thought not only for *things* related to one another by a relation of dependence but also for analogous *concepts*, namely concepts that capture those real relations in the way they represent things in the world. Smith, however, grants that Duns Scotus's statements on the analogy of being are fragmentary. They were reworked into a coherent theory by three Franciscans in Barcelona during the 1320s, namely, Aufredo Gonteri, Peter of Navarre, and Peter Thomae, who proposed three different ways to balance the analogy of being with the rival thesis of univocity and offered an early example of how Duns Scotus's thought could be developed in different directions.

The essays in this collection will hopefully provide an entryway to some key positions of one of the most daring and rigorous thinkers in the history of Western philosophy. Readers will find no shortcut through Duns Scotus's thought but will be able to rely on the assistance of expert guides, who will take them along a challenging but rewarding intellectual journey.

CHAPTER I

John Duns Scotus's life in context

Stephen D. Dumont

Numerous detailed surveys of Scotus's life and writings have appeared over the course of modern scholarship, but the most standard of these is now nearly 20 years old.[1] In that time, major works of Scotus have been published and advances made in our understanding of his academic career. These include the completion of the monumental edition of Scotus's Oxford commentaries and a more accurate understanding of the institutions and procedures governing the stages of Scotus's studies and teaching. An updated account of Scotus's life and works highlighting these more recent advances is certainly warranted.

Aside from Scotus's works themselves, only a few, scattered documents yield precise information about his life and career. This situation has been aggravated by historical myth and scholarly misunderstanding. Most notably, an earlier scholarship took otherwise unknown details of Scotus's family and early life from an eighteenth-century chronicle known as the *Monasticon Scoticanum*. Unfortunately, this work was subsequently shown to have been an elaborate and deliberate fabrication of Scottish history by its erratic compiler, Marianus Brockie.[2] On the other hand, recent findings have improved upon Scotus's standard biography. These include a corrected understanding of the relationship between the academic programs in religious houses and universities, the dissolution of the myth of Scotus's

---

[1] Williams 2003. The recent and extensive biographical study by Vos 2019 should be used with care. Still useful, despite having relied on the Brockie material at places, is Little 1932. On Alan Wolter's biographies of Scotus, which remained standard until that of Williams, see below.

[2] Ephrem Longpré announced his discovery of the Brockie manuscripts in Longpré 1929b. A summary of the Brockie material relevant to Scotus's early life was published almost immediately in Callebaut 1931. These were universally accepted in the literature for some 40 years until the fabricated character Brockie's *Monasticon* was demonstrated in Docherty 1968. Unfortunately, the widely used biography of Scotus by Allan Wolter in Duns Scotus 1962 was reprinted without modification until 1980, thereby propagating the Brockie account given by Callebaut. Not until a second edition of this work in 1987, some 25 years after Docherty originally published his findings, did Wolter omit the Brockie material (see n. 8 below).

Cambridge lectures, and a reassessment of the canonical assumption that bachelors of theology at Paris lectured for 2 years.

I EARLY LIFE

Except for a short manuscript colophon discussed below, no documents exist concerning Scotus's early life, entry into the Order, or pre-university education. To supply this information, much of twentieth-century scholarship turned unwittingly to the detailed fabrications of the Brockie forgeries and then attempted to correlate them with the cryptic regulations of the Orders and universities. The resulting picture of Scotus's career was a mix of historical fiction and scholarly speculation that has yet to be fully sorted out. To begin with what is certain, Scotus's nationality was Scottish, as attested by manuscripts as well as by a royal census taken during his theologate in Paris.[3] His surname 'Duns' refers to the Scottish town near the English border. As discussed below, it is estimated that Scotus was born in 1265 or early 1266 based on the record of his ordination to the priesthood. Where or at what age he entered the Franciscan Order is not known, since previously reported details depended entirely upon Brockie. Judging from his contemporaries, it is likely that Scotus entered the Order young, possibly at the minimal age of fifteen set by the Narbonne constitutions of 1260.[4] A number of notable Franciscan theologians in England contemporary with Scotus are attested to having entered the Order even as *pueri*, that is, thirteen or younger, and Scotus himself makes a remark that suggests this might have been common practice.[5] Although Scottish in nationality, Scotus as a Franciscan belonged to the province of England, a fact specified in manuscripts of his works.[6] That is, in this early period of

[3] Città del Vaticano, Biblioteca Apostolica Vaticana, ms. Vat. lat. 876 f. 226r: "Iohannes hic *Scotorum*, in ordine Minorum, in scholis profecit *Anglorum*, fuit doctor Parisinorum." For other such testimonies that Scotus was *natione Scoti*, see Balić 1965: 3 n. 7. The census of Philip the Fair in Paris of 1303, in which Scotus is listed as Scottish, is discussed below pp. 31–32.

[4] The Narbonne constitutions of 1260 set the minimum age at eighteen, with fifteen allowable in exceptional cases. See Cenci and Mailleux 2007: 70. Despite this rule, it seems the practice of recruiting the young continued. For example, the same year that the Narbonne regulation came into effect, Peter John Olivi entered the Order at twelve. See, Erhle 1887: 410–11. On the disparity between recruitment and regulations in this period, see Roest 2014: 57–58 n. 13.

[5] According to William Woodford in his *Defensorium Fratrum Mendicantium contra Richardum Armachanum*, c. 62, William of Ware, Robert Cowton, Walter Chatton, and William of Ockham all entered the Order as *pueri*. See Little 1926: 866. For Scotus's remark, see *Ord.* IV, d. 25 n. 81 (Vat. XIII.355), cited by Wolter 1993: 8, n. 26.

[6] Thus, in the *explicit* of his Parisian commentary contained in Todi, Biblioteca Comunale, ms. 12, f. 192va: "Explicit summa fratris Iohannis Duns *provinciae Anglicanae* super primum librum *Sententiarum* secundum lecturam suam Parisiensem."

its history, the Order treated its convents in Scotland as falling within the northern custody of Newcastle of its English province, a fact once again obscured by the fabrications of Brockie.[7] Thus, wherever Scotus entered the Franciscans, he passed into the Order's educational network of *studia* for England, thereby opening a path to his degree studies in theology at Oxford and, ultimately, to being sent to Paris for his doctorate.

While, as mentioned, we have no direct information concerning Scotus's entrance into the Order and early education, one commonly cited account should be abandoned. After the Brockie forgeries had been exposed, scholars sought out another historical chronicle for information about Scotus's earlier formation. In this case, they turned to the sixteenth-century *History of Great Britain* by John Major, the Scottish theologian who printed Scotus's Parisian lectures for the first time.[8] In his *History*, Major gives a short account of Scotus's early life that has been generally taken up in the literature:

> When no more than a boy, but having begun grammar, Scotus was taken by two Scottish Franciscan friars to Oxford, because at that time there existed no university in Scotland. By the favor of those two friars he lived in the Franciscan convent at Oxford and entered into the Order of Blessed Francis.[9]

Despite an impression of authenticity imparted by its details, Major's above story is entirely anachronistic. As just indicated, in Scotus's lifetime Scotland fell within the Franciscan province of England as part of its

---

[7] Scottish Franciscan convents were placed under control of the English province as part of the reorganization of the Order after Elias of Cortona was deposed as Minister General in 1239. A subsequent attempt to establish a separate provincial minister for Scotland was rejected in 1260 at the general chapter of Narbonne under Bonaventure. Independence of the Scottish houses does not seem to have come before 1329 under Robert the Bruce. See Bryce 1909: 1.8–10. Little 1932: 570 recounts an agreement reached in 1278 at Haddington between King Alexander III of Scotland and the Franciscan Minister General, Jerome of Ascoli, to grant the Scottish provinces independence. This purported meeting is also a fabrication by Brockie. Despite noting its anachronisms, Little accepted the account of this meeting from summary of the Brockie chronicle made by Callebaut 1931: 315–316.

[8] As indicated above, Allan Wolter included the Brockie account of Scotus's early life in his 1962 anthology of Scotus's writings, which was reprinted unchanged until a second, revised edition in 1987. Here Wolter modified his earlier introduction, noting the unreliability of Brockie sources and substituting the John Major account. Wolter republished this material in a 1993 article, after which the Major account became standard in biographies of Scotus. See Wolter's introduction to John Duns Scotus 1987: xii–xiv and Wolter 1993: 5–7.

[9] Major 1521: IV.16, p. 170: "Hunc puellum in grammaticis initiatum ad Oxoniam duo fratres Minores Scoti duxerunt, quia tempore illo in Scotia nulla erat universitas, et in Minorum conventu gratia istorum duorum fratrum Oxoniae conversatus, beati Francisci religionem professus est." Translation modified from that of Constable 1892: 206.

northern custody of Newcastle. That is, despite his Scottish origin, Scotus as a Franciscan belonged to the province of England. He thus had access to Oxford University by way of the Order's *studia* system of its English province. Major's explanation for why Scotus was taken as a boy directly to Oxford—that there was no university in Scotland—is thus wholly irrelevant. Moreover, the early education of young entrants into the Order during Scotus's time occurred at their local convent or custodial school, not at a *studium generale*. In particular, there is no evidence that in the thirteenth century the Oxford convent had a school for young boys.[10] Finally, it is hardly plausible that in the 1280s the Order would have given a boy still in grammar school consideration for the exceedingly rare case of a degree at a university. It is therefore obvious that Major, writing two centuries after the fact, had no historical understanding of the Order's *studia* system into which Scotus entered or its relationship to Oxford University proper. Major's credibility is further eroded by his ensuing, fictional account of Scotus's teaching career. According to Major, Ockham heard Scotus lecture at Oxford and then accompanied him to Paris![11] Finally, as discussed below, Major's account is also contradicted by the only known, contemporary reference to Scotus's early academic career. It asserts that Scotus went to Oxford not as a boy (*puellus*) but as an adult (*floruit*) and not directly but only after having first gone to Cambridge. The biographical testimony of Major concerning Scotus, therefore, cannot be considered any more reliable than that of Brockie.

II STUDIA AND UNIVERSITIES

The Franciscan educational system into which Scotus entered, and to which all of our direct knowledge of his life is tied, comprised two distinct institutions.[12] The first was the Order's own network of schools or *studia* that operated at both the local (*studia particularia*) and provincial (*studium generale*) levels. In this way, the Order provided and regulated the education needed to achieve its pastoral missions, train its teachers, and, at the highest level, produce leaders for the Order and church. At the local or "custodial" level, younger entrants would be instructed in Latin grammar,

---

[10] Little 1892: 43.

[11] Major 1521: IV.21, p. 188: "Per id tempus in Anglia aliqui erant eruditi viri, quorum duo Doctoris Subtilis auditores erant, scilicet Guillelmus Ockham et Gualterus Burlaeus ... Hic [sc. Ockham] cum Doctore Subtili de Anglia Parisium venit ..."

[12] This very general overview of Franciscan education depends upon Roest 2000. See also Noone 2007.

logic and some elementary theology. More capable students were sent for advanced instruction in philosophy.[13] The highest level of education within the mendicant system, to be achieved by a few, was training as a lecturer in theology. This instruction was given at a *studium generale*, that is, a school serving its entire home province as well as other provinces of the Order. In Scotus's time, the most important places for this advanced level of training in theology were the Order's houses of study in Paris, Oxford, and Cambridge. Of these, the Parisian *studium generale* was the most international and important, with the Order providing for two students from *every* province to study there for 4 years in its lectorate program.[14] The Parisian lectorate program was important for two reasons. First, it ensured a supply of well-trained instructors and administrators back to the various provinces. Second, as discussed in more detail below, it enabled a few, very select friars to qualify for a degree program in theology at the University of Paris proper. The Oxford *studium generale* was next in importance, having developed quickly under the initial guidance of a series of renowned university masters beginning with Robert Grosseteste. The Cambridge Franciscan *studium*, while also important, was slower to develop and relied on Oxford-trained theologians into the fourteenth century.[15] As we shall see, Scotus was exceptional in having studied or taught at all three of these major *studia generalia*.

The system of education described above was internal to and regulated by the Franciscan and other mendicant Orders. Separate from these mendicant networks of *studia* were universities in the strict sense of a corporation of masters and students comprising the faculties of arts, theology, law, and medicine, each with their own stringent regulations for admission, degrees and obligations.[16] These two distinct—and often contentious—educational institutions interacted when the Orders would send a very few from their *studia* programs to universities for doctoral degrees in theology, who would then become themselves regent masters in that faculty. Such advancement to a university degree was a rare outcome of mendicant *studia*. When it did occur, it was typically after the friar had first taught or served in the Order for several years, demonstrated

---

[13] Training in these disciplines appears to have been in place by the general chaper of Strasbourg (1282), which would have roughly corresponded to Scotus's early years in the Order. See Roest 2014: 56 note 10.

[14] On the lectorate program and its evolution, see Roest 2000: 87–97.

[15] For the history of the Franciscans at Oxford and Cambridge respectively, see: Little 1892 and Moorman 1952.

[16] For an overview of universities during Scotus's time, see Leff 1968.

conspicuous talent, and had an influential promoter. In Scotus's time, obtaining a doctoral degree in theology meant going either to the University of Paris or Oxford, where in each case the Franciscans had already secured a faculty chair. Unlike their secular counterparts, however, mendicant masters of theology would hold their university chairs for only 1 or 2 years to allow for the promotion of the next friar and to assume teaching posts in the *studia* or high offices in the Order and church.

All of our hard, documentary evidence bearing on the life of Scotus comes from his later, university years at Oxford and especially at Paris, where he became master of theology. It is his earlier life and education—roughly the 10 years or so prior to his verified presence at Oxford for which we have no documentation—that has been the object of speculation and historical fabrication of Brockie and Major. There are, however, two pieces of evidence that enable a more consistent and well-founded reconstruction of Scotus's earlier life and education. The first is the recent, more accurate understanding of the Franciscan lectorate program described above. The second is a short *curriculum vitae* of Scotus entered into one of the oldest manuscripts of his works surviving at Oxford.

III LECTORATE PROGRAM

As indicated above, the Order provided the cost for every province to send two friars to its convent in Paris to study in its lectorate program and further allowed an additional two at the expense of the province itself.[17] (Again, this internal program was entirely separate from the Order's decision to send a candidate to the University of Paris for a degree in theology, which rotated yearly among the provinces and was determined by the Minister General.) The Parisian lectorate program was perhaps the oldest, largest, and most expensive educational initiative undertaken by the early Order. Already in existence in the 1240s, the administrative particulars of the 4-year Parisian lectorate were formally set out in the Narbonne constitutions of 1260 under Bonaventure and then reasserted in nearly identical terms in the subsequent legislation of Assisi (1279), Strasbourg (1282), Milan (1289) and Paris (1292).[18] That is, this program was in existence and remained unchanged across Scotus's lifetime.

---

[17] For its role in relation to university degrees, see Courtenay 1999.
[18] Successive statements of the program are found edited and collected in Cenci and Mailleux 2007 under rubric IV.12–13, 19 for the following general chapters: 58 (Pre-Narbonne), 83–84 (Narbonne), 125–126 (Assisi), 181–183 (Strasbourg), 240–241 (Milan) and 315–316 (Paris).

> Those to be sent to the general *studium* in Paris should have studied for two
> or three years after the novitiate in a *studium* of their own or neighboring
> province, unless they have been so well educated that they could be sent
> directly after their novitiate. However, they should be sent only on the
> authority of the provincial minister with the advice and consent of the
> provincial chapter. ... Those sent to Paris should study for at least four
> years, unless they make such progress that they are rightly judged capable of
> performing the duties of a lector.[19]

The above statute stipulates that the selected friar is to be sent to Paris
after the 2 or 3 years of schooling in his province following his novitiate
year, i.e., the preliminary period of study and reflection prior to a final
decision to enter the Order.[20] Since the regulation allows for sending an
already educated candidate to Paris immediately (*continuo*) after the novitiate, the apparent intent of the Order was to enroll a qualified friar in the
lectorate program while still young. This implies, given the Order's admission of younger members, that a friar in the lectorate would normally be
sent to the Order's Parisian convent in their early twenties and would
typically remain at Paris until their mid or late twenties.[21] As the above
statute states, the purpose of the Parisian program was to render the
candidate qualified to carry out the duties of a lector, i.e., to return to
his home province and teach in its *studia*.[22] That is, at this stage, there
would be no thought of a friar going from his lectorate years at Paris
immediately into doctoral studies in theology at the University. Indeed, as
mentioned, if a degree at Paris came at all, it would be the decision of the
Minister General made only after the candidate had returned for service in
his home province.

How does this fit with what little we know of Scotus's early life? As it
turns out, whether or not Scotus studied at Paris prior to pursuing his
doctorate at the University has long been a disputed point of his biography. Nearly a century ago both André Callebaut and A. G. Little held that
Scotus likely had a pre-doctoral period at Paris, with Little arguing that

---

[19] "Item, mittendi Parisius ad studium generale primo exerceantur tribus vel duobus annis post
noviciatum, in aliquo studio provincie sue vel vicine, nisi adeo fuerint litterati quod post
noviciatum continuo possint mitti. Non mittantur tamen nisi de auctoritate ministri cum
consilio et assensu capituli provincialis. ... Illi autem, qui mittuntur Parisius studeant quatuor
annis ad minus, nisi adeo provecti fuerint quod merito iudicentur idonei ad doctoris officium
exequendum." Cited according to the Assisi statute (see previous note). The statutes alternate
between the designations *doctoris officium* and *lectoris officium*, the latter of which was the
original formula.
[20] On the novitiate year, see Roest 2000: 238–250.   [21] See Roest 2000: 91–92.
[22] See Roest 2000: 92–93.

such was necessary to satisfy Parisian requirements to lecture on the *Sentences*. They both dated this earlier Parisian period from the mid to late 1290s.[23] Against this view, C. K. Brampton, joined by Allan Wolter, later argued that nothing in the statutes required Scotus to have studied earlier at Paris and discounted that he went there prior to beginning his doctorate in 1302.[24] Fortunately, recent advances in our understanding of the Franciscan lectorate program have provided some clarity on its application to Scotus, generally concluding that he had an earlier Parisian period.

Building on observations made by A. G. Little, William Courtenay has shown in a seminal study that the Franciscan lectorate program at Paris did not merely provide training for lectors in the Order.[25] It also played a crucial role in enabling prospective candidates to meet the Parisian residency requirements for the university degree in theology. The statutory prerequisite at the University of Paris for lecturing on Lombard's *Sentences*—the last major step before proceeding to the doctoral exercises—was indeed formidable: some 7 or 8 years of theological study and lecturing on the Bible.[26] Understandably, the mendicant Orders sought exceptions to this onerous requirement given that their candidates would have already spent years studying and teaching theology in their provincial *studia*. Why should they have to repeat their previous years of theological study at Paris? About 1290, Giles of Rome, while regent master at Paris, secured just such an exception for the Augustinians. It allowed the theological residency requirement to be fulfilled by theological study in the Order's *studia* as long as at least 4 years of it were carried out in Paris. As Courtenay argues, it does not seem that the younger Augustinian Order—Giles of Rome was its first Parisian master of theology—would have been granted such a privilege unless it had already been allowed for the larger and more established Franciscans and Dominicans.[27] Indeed, some years later, Giles of Rome reminded John of Murrovalle, a Parisian master himself and former Franciscan Minister General, that this exception had been granted to his

---

[23] Callebaut 1924 and Callebaut 1929: 73; Little 1932: 571–572.

[24] Brampton 1964 and Wolter 1993: 8–9. More recent scholars agreeing with Brampton are Vos 2019: 28–30 and, it would seem, Williams 2003: 1–2, who omits any mention of an earlier Parisian period. William J. Courtenay was originally inclined to Brampton's view but, as discussed presently, he subsequently argued for an earlier Parisian lectorate. For Courtenay's earlier view, see Courtenay 1995: 157.

[25] Courtenay 2012.

[26] For cautions on how to interpret and apply these regulations based on later statutes, see Courtenay 2012: 4–5.

[27] Courtenay 2012: 6–7 and n. 14.

Order during his time at Paris. That is, by about 1290 the Franciscans had obtained a privilege that allowed the 4 years of their Parisian lectorate program, which the Order had in place since the mid-thirteenth century, to fulfill the residency requirement in theology for admission to read the *Sentences* at the University of Paris. Against this background, Courtenay concludes with Little that, although there is no direct evidence attesting to an earlier period for Scotus in Paris, it nevertheless "rests on safe inferences".[28]

The present consensus, then, is that Scotus participated in the lectorate program at Paris. Indeed, as shown below, Scotus began lecturing on the *Sentences* immediately upon his arrival at Paris in the fall of 1302. Therefore, absent some unknown privilege, he must have previously fulfilled the Parisian residency requirement by spending 4 years in the lectorate under the agreement secured by the mendicants more than a decade earlier. Given all of this is the case, when was Scotus's lectorate period in Paris?

As mentioned, Callebaut and Little had placed Scotus's earlier Parisian stay from the mid-1290s to as late as 1297.[29] They, however, were unaware of Scotus's earlier lectures at Oxford on the *Sentences*, the *Lectura*, which he would have given in the late 1290s. Moreover, the lectorate does not appear to be intended for friars already in their thirties. More recent scholarship has moved the period of Scotus's lectorate to about 1286–90, just prior to his documented presence in Oxford in March 1291. This dating was supported by Scotus's apparently early acquaintance with Gonsalvus of Spain, who was himself in Paris during this time as a bachelor of the *Sentences*. It would therefore account for Gonsalvus's later statement, examined below, that he knew Scotus "from long experience" as well as Scotus's apparent use of material from Gonsalvus in the construction of his own questions on the *De anima*.[30]

A further, and perhaps more significant, circumstance supports the mid to late 1280s as the likely period for Scotus's Parisian lectorate. As stated, the selection of a friar to read the *Sentences* and pursue the doctorate in theology at Paris was not made by the province, as was the case with the lectorate, but by the Minister General. Since only one candidate from all

---

[28] Courtenay 2012: 14.   [29] See n. 23 above.
[30] Courtenay 2012: 12–13 and n. 29; John Duns Scotus, *QDA*, 123*–127*, 139*–143*. Gonsalvus, however, had probably read the *Sentences* at Paris by 1286 and had already returned to Spain by 1288, at the latest, serving as papal legate and then minister of the Santiago province. See Gonsalvus Hispanus, *Quaest. disp. et de Quodl.*, xxii–xxv, where the date "1296" on p. xxv is a misprint for "1286."

the provinces was sent to Paris for the doctorate each year, selection in practice required having come to the attention of the Minister General.[31] John of Murrovalle was the Minister General who sent Scotus to Paris to read the *Sentences*. What connection, if any, did he have to Scotus? Murrovalle was one of the most prominent Franciscans in the later thirteenth century. He read the *Sentences* at Paris about 1283 and quickly ascended in the Order. While still a bachelor of theology in 1284 he was one of the authors of the so-called *Letter of the Seven Seals* that resulted in the censure of Peter John Olivi. Promoted to master in 1288, he was regent until 1290, when he was made lector of the Sacred Palace. Having followed an established path for advancement in the Order, Murrovalle was elected Minister General in 1292, an office he held until 1304.[32]

Based on the above reconstruction of Scotus's lectorate, the mid-to-late 1280s would have coincided exactly with John of Murrovalle's period as a bachelor and promotion to master. Scotus presumably would have attended Murrovalle's lectures, disputations, sermons and other academic functions obligatory for a senior bachelor of the *Sentences* and regent master. In fact, in his Oxford *Sentences* Scotus cites Murrovalle's distinctive position on free will held by him and publicly attacked at Paris in 1287/88.[33] All of this is consistent with placing Scotus's Parisian lectorate about in the mid to late 1280s.

Current scholarship accepts, with refinements, a biographical fact about Scotus that was noted more than a century ago, namely, that he took part in the Order's lectorate program at Paris prior to pursuing theological studies at Oxford. Such a prior lectorate at Cordeliers accounts for two factors necessary for a Franciscan of the period to have become a master of theology at Paris. It enabled Scotus to fulfill the Parisian residency requirement for lecturing on the *Sentences* and brought him to the attention of the two Minister Generals responsible for such decisions within the Order: John of Murrovalle, who selected Scotus to read the *Sentences* at Paris, and Gonsalvus Hispanus, who recommended his subsequent promotion to master. Disturbing this coherent account is the only piece of direct evidence we possess of Scotus's early life. It is a statement that prior to his theologate at Oxford, he was at Cambridge, not Paris.

---

[31] Courtenay 1993: 160 and Courtenay 1999: 85: "With one or two possible exceptions, only those who had been trained in the lectorate at Paris and who had come to the attention of the leadership of the order were viable candidates for selection as *sententiarii*."

[32] For the biography of Murrovalle, see Emili 2010.

[33] Scotus, *Lect.* II, d. 25, q. unica, nn. 51–3 (Vat. XIX, 244–245). On Murrovalle's theory of the will, see Alliney 2013.

IV   CAMBRIDGE

The only surviving document concerning Scotus's life before he went for
doctoral studies at Oxford is a brief biographical statement identified nearly
a century ago. This is the famous annotation in Oxford, Merton College,
ms. 66 that asserts Scotus was at Cambridge before going to Oxford:[34]

> These are from the *Ordinatio* of venerable brother John Duns of the
> Franciscan Order, who flourished at Cambridge, Oxford and Paris and
> died in Cologne.[35]

Merton College, ms. 66 contains books I and IV of Duns Scotus's great
Oxford commentary on the *Sentences* known as the *Ordinatio* and is one of
the oldest surviving copies of that work.[36] The manuscript was owned in
succession by two early fourteenth-century Mertonians from whom it
passed into the College library.[37] From the dates of its owners, the
manuscript can be estimated to have been produced in Oxford about
1325. The above statement terminates a table of questions for book IV
inserted by the same scribe, but different from the one who wrote the main
text. Nevertheless, this later scribe has inserted numerous corrections and
passages into the margins from other authoritative copies of the
Ordinatio.[38] In one case, the scribe of the above annotation adds text he
says he found among the quaterns of Scotus's own copy of the *Ordinatio*
itself.[39] Thus, the antiquity and Oxford provenance of the manuscript, as
well as the authority of its scribe, support the accuracy of the above
statement. It clearly asserts in chronological order the principal stages of
Scotus's advanced education and teaching career: Cambridge, Oxford,

---

[34] Attention was first drawn to this colophon in Callebaut 1928.

[35] F. 120vb: "Haec de *Ordinatione* venerabilis fratris I. Duns de Ordine fratrum minorum, qui floruit
Cantabrigiae Oxonii et Parisius et obiit in Colonia."

[36] On this manuscript, see Powicke 1931: 168 n. 538; "Disquisitio historico-critica" (Vat. I, 32*–34*);
Thomson 2009: 68–69.

[37] The Mertonians were John Burcote and the famous William Reed, who was so important for the
establishment of the college libraries at Oxford. On Burcote, from whose estate Reed obtained the
codex in 1349, see Emden 1957: 306. On Reed, see Thomson 2010.

[38] For the many annotations, see the description of the codex in "Disquisitio historico-critica" (Vat.I,
32*–34*). According to the Vatican editors, Reed was the source of the above biographical
annotation. Thomson, however, shows that Reed did not annotate the volumes he purchased.
"Disquisitio historico-critica" (Vat. I, 33*, n. 1) and Thomson 2010: 291.

[39] Thus, for example, the scribe of the colophon asserts that he took an addition placed in the lower
margin of f. 32rb from the *Liber Scoti* itself: "Illud invenitur in quaterno, qui fuit scriptus post
quaternum fratris Ioannis Duns." It was this added passage that helped secure the authenticity of
the *Lectura*. See "Prolegomena" (Vat. XVII, 8*) and I *Ord.* d. 3 n. 61 (Vat. III, 42–43, apparatus to
line 21). This same hand has also made an interlinear insertion to the *explicit* of the first book
adding the information "de Ordine fratrum minorum, natione Scotus." (f. 120va)

Paris and Cologne. This seemingly straightforward statement of Scotus's academic life has nevertheless been the object of much confusion and speculation ever since its first identification.

André Callebaut, who first drew attention to the annotation, postulated that Scotus taught at Cambridge in the mid-1290s, but that conflicts with our present knowledge that Scotus was in theological studies at Oxford during that period.[40] Further confusion arose when the Vatican editors argued that Scotus had a Cambridge commentary on the first book of the *Sentences*, a so-called *Lectura Cantabrigiensis*, which they explicitly connected to the above Merton remark.[41] This alleged Cambridge commentary, however, turned out to be a fiction. In reality, it was simply a version of Scotus's *Parisian* lectures, a fact explicitly asserted in both of its surviving manuscripts but inexplicably ignored by scholars.[42] Finally, the Merton statement has also been invoked to refer to a later Cambridge stay during Scotus's expulsion from Paris for the academic year 1303–04, which period is discussed below.[43] This, however, arbitrarily violates the chronology itself given in the annotation, which is otherwise accurate.

Even apart from all the previous scholarly confusion, the Merton statement appears to pose a further difficulty for our above reconstruction of Scotus's Parisian lectorate. It seems to place Scotus at Cambridge between his lectorate at Paris and the start of his Oxford theologate in 1290/1291. This would not seem likely given the commonly accepted facts about his age, making Scotus too young for the lectorate. Nevertheless, an intervening period at Cambridge is possible, if two further facts are considered. First, as shown below, Scotus's ordination record indicates that he was almost certainly older by a few years than traditionally accepted. This would allow Scotus's Parisian lectorate to be shifted somewhat earlier, say about 1283/84–1287/88. The second consideration is the obligation of the returning friar to his home province after his lectorate.

As indicated, after their lectorate in Paris, friars were called back to their home province to render an account of their activities and expenditures and undertake the *officium lectoris*, i.e., begin teaching.[44] Allowing that

[40] Callebaut 1928: 610.
[41] This argument was first set out in the volume four of the Vatican edition: "Adnotationes" (Vat. IV, 2*).
[42] The fiction of the so-called Cambridge Lecture, which is in reality a version of Scotus's Parisian *Reportatio*, was definitively demonstrated by Rödler 2005: 92*–111*.
[43] Wolter 1993: 10.
[44] Teaching needs in the provinces were so pressing that friars were often recalled before they had completed their lectorate. See Roest 2000: 92–3.

Scotus was slightly older than generally assumed, his 4-year Parisian lectorate would have ended about 1287 or 1288. As shown below, Scotus was certainly in the Oxford convent by early 1291 to begin his doctorate in theology. Given all of this, the above colophon, if accurate, appears to indicate that when Scotus returned to his home province of England from his Parisian lectorate, he was not sent directly to Oxford to begin his doctoral studies. Rather, he was sent first to Cambridge for a 2- or 3-year period as a lector or, perhaps, further studies. If this was the case, what could Scotus have been teaching or studying at Cambridge?

It seems unlikely that Scotus was teaching or studying theology at Cambridge. He certainly did not teach theology, since he is not among the list of Cambridge lectors, all of whom were older, more experienced academics with doctoral education.[45] Nor do we have evidence of Scotus studying theology at Cambridge. He did so twice at a *studium generale*: at Oxford in the 1290s and again at Paris beginning in 1302. In both cases, he left enormous commentaries in several versions on the required theological text of the schools, Peter Lombard's *Sentences*. As just indicated, Scotus has no commentary on the *Sentences* from Cambridge, despite a tortured tradition of imputing one to him.[46] On the other hand, some theological study at Cambridge cannot be absolutely ruled out, since there is evidence of requiring lectures on the *Sentences* at other English *studia* before doing so at Oxford. Such was the case with Wodeham, who read the *Sentences* at Norwich before doing so to Oxford. There is also the possibility that Scotus could have met part of his Oxford "auditor" requirements in theology (see below) at the Order's Cambridge studium. We have no firm evidence, however, for either of these possibilities.

Rather, several considerations make it more likely that, if Scotus was at Cambridge, he was lecturing on philosophy. First, his question style commentaries on Aristotle's logic are generally thought to be early works and are indebted to English sources.[47] By comparison to his later, theological works, Scotus's treatment of questions in these logical commentaries is brief and straightforward, which is to say, suitable for teaching. Second, it was during the late 1280s and early 1290s—roughly the period of Scotus's Cambridge stay—that the Order began expanding its teaching of philosophy. Thus, the Paris chapter of 1292 ordered that every province

[45] The list of lectors is contained in Eccleston 1951: 58–61.
[46] Positing a Cambridge commentary on the *Sentences* for Scotus, Allan Wolter holds that he could not have been studying philosophy at Cambridge. See Wolter 1993: 10.
[47] See, for example, the introductions to Scotus's logical works for dating and sources (OPh I, xxix–xxxiv, xli–xlii; OPh II, 33–35, 265–266).

was to have a *studium* in arts, and such general statutes usually normalize the emerging practice.[48] It does not seem merely coincidental that, at the precise period when the Order was starting its expansion of instruction in the arts, Scotus would be the first Franciscan to write commentaries on nearly the entirety of Aristotle's logic, the largest area of need within the arts curriculum.[49] Finally, about 1290 Scotus began theological studies at Oxford University, admission to which required a prior regency in a faculty of arts. Since friars were prohibited from becoming masters of arts, mendicant candidates seeking admission to theology at Oxford had to attest to 8 years of study in philosophy, unless an exception (*gratia*) was granted.[50] Thus, a prior period of studying and lecturing on Aristotle at the Cambridge *studium* would have contributed to Scotus meeting the Oxford admission requirement for theology. At the same time, however, it should be stressed that Scotus would not have produced *all* of his Aristotelian commentaries at Cambridge. His commentary on the *Metaphysics*, for example, shows revision over the course of his career and remained incomplete. Similarly, certain questions of his *De anima* show influences from his later theological works.[51]

For nearly a century, scholarship has accepted the authority of the brief biographical statement of Oxford, Merton College, ms. 66 that asserts a Cambridge period of study or teaching for Scotus, only then to ignore its chronology and arbitrarily assign it to a later stage in his career. This was done in part to accommodate a purported Cambridge commentary on the *Sentences* that in reality never existed. To the contrary, an early Cambridge period as asserted in the Merton biography is consistent with Scotus's lecturing there on the arts. This agrees with his responsibilities owed to the province upon returning from the Parisian lectorate, the needs of the Order arising from its late thirteenth-century expansion of arts *studia*,

---

[48] See Roest 2000: 65–72 on the expansion of the teaching of arts in the Order. For the 1292 statute, see Cenci and Mailleux 2007: 58.

[49] It is seldom noted that Scotus was the first major Franciscan commentator on Aristotle and the most prolific. Earlier notable commentators, such as Roger Bacon and Richard Rufus, had in fact written their Aristotelian works as masters of arts well before entering the Franciscans. It is only after Scotus that we find major theologians in the Order regularly producing commentaries proper on Aristotelian works, all of whom belong to the first quarter of the fourteenth century: Alexander of Alessandria (*De anima, Metaphysics*), Francis of Marchia (*Physics, Metaphysics*), Francis of Meyronnes (*Isagoge, Categories, Perihermenias*), William of Ockham (*Isagoge, Categories, Perihermenias, Elenchi, Physics*) and Gerald Odonis (*Ethics*).

[50] The prohibition against regency in arts does not occur in mendicant constitutions, but it was the stated practice. See Little 1926: 823.

[51] On Scotus's revision of his *Metaphysics*, see Pini 2005 and Dumont 1995. On his *De anima*, see its parallels to Scotus's theological works illustrated in *QDA*, 128*–133*.

the early dating of Scotus's logical commentaries on Aristotle, and the statutory requirements for admission to his degree studies in theology at Oxford, to which we now turn. At the same time, it must be stressed that there is no independent corroboration that Scotus taught or studied at Cambridge after his lectorate. If, however, the Merton *explicit* is accepted as authentic, which seems generally assumed in the literature, then this would be the most probable explanation.

V   OXFORD

It is not until the 1290s that we have any historical documents naming Scotus. The first is the record of his ordination to the priesthood by Oliver Sutton, Bishop of Lincoln, at Northampton on March 17, 1291.[52] This document is important for two reasons. First, it indicates that by this time Scotus had arrived at Oxford to pursue theological studies. This is clear because Oxford fell in the diocese of Lincoln. There is no record, however, that Sutton ever carried out an ordination at Oxford, and so members of that convent had to travel to the bishop. The presence of two other Franciscans ordained with Scotus at Northampton further attests to his Oxford residency at the time. Sutton's register indicates that he ordained members of the same religious orders together. Scotus was the first of five Franciscan priests ordained at Northampton, and he was followed immediately by William of Shirebourne. Also among the Franciscans at Northampton, that day was John Stapleton, who was ordained a deacon. Shirebourne, Stapleton and Scotus were all associated with the Oxford convent. As discussed below, they are found together 9 years later as a part of a distinguished group of Franciscan academics presented by the English provincial to Sutton's successor, John Dalderby, for the privilege to hear confessions at the Oxford house. Thus, there can be little doubt that Scotus was already at Oxford when ordained in 1291, presumably to begin his work toward a degree in theology.

The second detail yielded by Scotus's ordination record is an approximation of when he was born. It is generally stated that the minimum age for the priesthood was in practice twenty-five.[53] Assuming that Scotus

---

[52] Record of Scotus's ordination was first published in Longpré 1929a. Sutton was bishop 1280–1299, but only the second half of his ordination register from the years 1290–1299 survives. It has been published in its entirety in Hill 1975.

[53] The ancient law of the church was that ordination to the priesthood required having completed (*inpleverit*) one's 30th year, since this was the age at which Christ began his public ministry. Ordination at twenty-five was permitted for exigency, but this was not set as the canonically

would have been ordained as soon as canonically eligible, it is then inferred that he was born before March 17, 1266. Given that Sutton held an ordination at Hertford a year earlier on May 27, 1290, to which the Oxford convent sent the above-mentioned Stapleton for ordination as a subdeacon, it is also inferred that Scotus must not have been eligible for the priesthood at that time. It is accordingly concluded that Scotus was probably born between May 1265 and March 1266.[54]

While this account has been accepted for most of the modern scholarship, Sutton's ordination register actually indicates that Scotus was somewhat older than the canonical minimum for ordination. As mentioned, Scotus was the first of five Franciscans ordained by Sutton and immediately ahead of his Oxford colleague, William of Shirebourne. Since ordination was almost certainly by seniority, Scotus must have been older than Shirebourne. This is in fact confirmed by their academic careers. Shirebourne is listed as the thirty-eighth lector of the Oxford convent and documented as regent in 1312 together with the secular master Henry of Harclay and the Carmelite regent, Robert Walsingham.[55] Scotus, however, belonged to the scholarly cohort at Oxford prior to these figures. He was an exact contemporary of Richard of Conington, who was the thirty-fourth lector at Oxford and the Franciscan regent in theology 1305/6.[56] As indicated below, Conington and Scotus debated in a series of *Collationes* about 1300 and are recorded as respondents in various disputations the same year. Moreover, Scotus was Parisian master by 1305, some 7 years before Shirebourne's regency, and this despite having to read the *Sentences* for a second time at Paris and incurring a disruption of his program in the academic year 1303–04. Clearly, Scotus was older than Shirebourne and thus past the canonically minimal age when ordained. Allowing that Scotus was even 2 or 3 years older than commonly asserted provides some flexibility in the above reconstruction of his career in the 1280s and accommodating, as indicated, a Cambridge period before coming to Oxford.

minimum age until Clement V at the Council of Vienne in 1311. See Friedberg 1959: I, 276; II, 1140. The Franciscans formally forbade ordination before completion of the 25th year in their Paris constitutions of 1292. See Cenci and Mailleux 2007: I, 348.

[54] See, for example, Williams 2003: 2.

[55] See Eccleston 1951: 55 and Hastings 1890: 213–214, where "Magistrum Willelmum de Schireburn, Magistrum fratrum Minorum," Harclay, and Walsingham are all mentioned as regent masters in the Dominican action against the University in 1312. On Harclay and Walsingham, see respectively Emden 1957: II, 874–75 and Xiberta 1931: 111–137.

[56] On Richard of Conington, see Doucet 1936.

Here it may be objected that if Scotus were already past canonical minimum for ordination, then he would have been ordained by Bishop Sutton at one of his two other ordinations within the previous year.[57] On the present account, however, Scotus would still have been either in the lectorate at Paris or possibly at Cambridge for the 1289–1290 academic year. Cambridge, of course, was not in the diocese of Lincoln but rather of Ely, which in fact lacked a consecrated bishop for most of 1290.[58] That is, the reason Scotus that was not ordained by Sutton the previous year was not because he had yet to reach canonical age. Rather, it was because he had yet to reach Oxford. Accordingly, we can place Scotus's arrival at Oxford in the Fall of 1290, sometime after September.

To resume, our first fixed point in Scotus's career is his presence in Oxford during the 1290–1291 academic year, presumably to undertake studies in theology. There cannot be, however, any precise mapping of Scotus's theological studies onto regulations at Oxford. Surviving statutes are too vague, often anachronistic, and in the case of mendicants too often excepted. Nevertheless, the general stages and length of degree requirements correspond quite well to known points of Scotus's period at Oxford.

The Oxford curriculum in theology was generally similar to that of Paris; both were lengthy and comprised several stages.[59] (1) The first was an initial period of 5 years of attending lectures (*auditio*) on the Bible and Lombard's *Sentences*. Admission to this stage required having been regent as master of arts, which, as noted, was forbidden by the mendicants. In that case, the statutes stipulated 8 years of prior study in the arts for admission and then an additional program year spent in this auditor stage of theology. Although in the 1310s the secular masters at Oxford began strict enforcement of the arts requirement for admission to theology, in

---

[57] These were at Hereford on May 27, 1290, where, as mentioned, John Stapleton was sent from Oxford to be ordained subdeacon, and Stamford on September 23, 1290. Sutton also held an ordination at Wycombe on December 23, 1290, but no Franciscans were present. See Hill 1975: 1–10.

[58] The Bishop of Ely during the period in question was John de Kirkeby, who was consecrated by John Peckham on October 22, 1286. He fell ill early in 1290 and died on March 26. His successor, William de Luda (Louth), was not installed until October. Ordination records for Ely survive only from 1348, but these show that the diocese held only one per year. It is unlikely that Kirkeby held them more often. During his episcopacy, he remained treasurer to Edward I and was attested as neglecting his diocese. In addition to his considerable royal duties, Kirkeby held so many benefices that Peckham had blocked his earlier appointment as bishop of Rochester. See Prestwich 2008.

[59] For this outline of the Oxford program, see Rashdall 1942: III, 158–159, which summarizes the surviving statutory evidence in Gibson 1931: 48–55 and Anstey 1868: II, 388–398. For excellent overviews of how university requirements aligned with mendicants working towards degrees, see Little 1926: 825–829, Courtenay 1987: 66–69 and Roest 2000: 97–115.

Scotus's time there was a more cooperative attitude by the University and exceptions seem to have been granted. (2) This "auditor" period was a prerequisite for the second stage called "opponency". This was an additional 2 years of study but now added participation in disputations as an opponent (*opponens*), that is, lodging arguments in opposition to the position taken.

(3) The above 7 years of preparatory study would have taken place at the Order's convent at Oxford—or even partially at another convent with a theological *studium*—under the supervision of the Franciscan regent. At this point, the candidate would then be presented by the Franciscan masters or guardian to the Chancellor and other regents of the University for an examination of credentials and admission as a bachelor of theology, i.e., to lecture on the *Sentences*.[60] At Oxford, bachelors lectured first on the *Sentences* and then on the Bible, the reverse of Parisian order. Surviving statutes stipulate that lectures on the *Sentences* were to be completed within the three terms of a single academic year.[61] Lectures on one book of the Bible were to be done during the 2 years of subsequent residency or, with permission, during the summer vacation. As a bachelor, the candidate would also participate in disputations as a *respondens*, i.e., replying to objections made by the opponent. (4) After completing his lectures, the candidate would be deemed a "formed bachelor" (*baccalaureus formatus*), i.e., one who had fulfilled all baccalaureate requirements. A formed bachelor had to maintain residency for two more years to continue as a respondent in disputations and preach. Some mendicants—certainly Scotus—used this residency period to revise their lectures on the *Sentences*. (5) Finally, promotion to master of theology comprised two separate academic acts: a granting by the chancellor of the license to teach (*licentia docendi*) followed by a complex ceremony called 'inception' at which the new master was inaugurated. The mendicants typically remained regent masters of theology at Oxford and Paris for a year.

The above-mentioned stages of the University program in theology correspond well with the known dates of Scotus at Oxford, indicating that he was in degree studies. First, consider Scotus's year as bachelor of the *Sentences*. His original Oxford lectures on the *Sentences*, known as the

---

[60] Cf. Anstey 1868: II, 389.

[61] Although statutes from Oxford are clear that lectures on the *Sentences* are to be completed in 1 year (Anstey 1868: II, 395), scholars have long held that, as at Paris, lectures were over 2 years. See Schabel 2020: especially 99.

Lectura, can be confidently assigned to the 1298–1299 academic year. His *Lectura* must postdate the academic year 1297–1298 since its prologue reports Godfrey of Fontaines's distinctive view on the nature of theology from his *Quodlibet* XIII, q. 1.[62] On the other hand, the surviving books I and II of the *Lectura* must both be before mid-1300. First, Scotus himself attests to having begun the great expansion of the *Lectura* into his *Ordinatio* by June 1300.[63] Secondly, Walter Burley's *Quaestiones De anima*, which were disputed while he was still a bachelor of arts at Oxford in 1300, appropriates Scotus's question on free will found only in *Lectura* II, d. 25.[64] As just outlined, admission as a bachelor of the *Sentences* at Oxford required 7 years (or eight for mendicants without an exemption) of prior auditing and opposing. Thus, the dating of Scotus's bachelor's lectures in the *Lectura* means that he must have begun theological studies in the 1290–1291 academic year, depending on exceptions. This aligns well with Scotus's presence in Oxford for that year documented by his ordination recorded by Bishop Sutton in March, 1291.

As indicated, at Oxford bachelors lectured on the Bible after the *Sentences*. Does any evidence survive of Scotus lecturing on the Bible as a bachelor of theology? Generally speaking, the lectures of bachelors on the Bible have not survived. It is possible, however, that a vestige of Scotus's biblical lectures and disputations remains in his prologue to the *Ordinatio*. It contains a question on the sufficiency of sacred scripture that is found neither in the earlier *Lectura* nor in later Parisian *Sentences*.[65] This question title is atypical for topics taken up in prologues to the *Sentences* during this period, which are usually devoted to problems connected to construing theology as a science, rather than questions concerning scripture as such. Moreover, in this one prologue question alone Scotus quotes and discusses more scriptural passages than in the rest of his enormous *Ordinatio*

---

[62] *Lect.* I prol. p. 4, qq. 1–2, nn. 161–162 (Vat. XVI, 53–54). Godfrey's *Quodlibet* XIII is dated to 1297–98; see Wippel 1981: xxviii.

[63] See Scotus, *Ord.* I prol., p. 2 q. un., n. 112 (Vat. I, 77), where Scotus mentions the defeat of the sultan of Egypt by Mongol and Christian forces that occurred on December 23, 1299. News of the victory had reached Canterbury (or Cambridge) by June 6, 1300. Balić 1927: 41–44 and Little 1932: 573.

[64] Burley 1997: xi, 138–146. Burley adopts Scotus's position that the object and will are essentially ordered co-causes of volition. Burley's dependency on Scotus is extensive and verbatim at places. See Scotus, *Lect.* II, d. 25, q. un. (Vat. XIX, 229–263). Since Scotus never wrote the corresponding distinction of the *Ordinatio* and held a different view on the will at Paris, Burley had to be using the *Lectura* question. This dependency was not noticed by Synan or the literature. On the whole issue in Scotus, see Dumont 2001.

[65] "Utrum cognitio supernaturalis necessaria viatori sit sufficienter tradita in sacra Scriptura," in *Ord.* I, prol., p. 2, q. un. (Vat. I, 59–88).

prologue combined.[66] It is possible that Scotus had disputed this question as part of his required biblical lectures and then inserted it into his revised prologue for the *Ordinatio*. Such a practice among mendicants is not unknown. Robert Holcot published his disputed questions from his bachelor's lectures on the Gospel of Matthew among his *Quodlibeta*.[67] As noted above, Scotus himself dated this question as so revised in his *Ordinatio* prologue to the summer of 1300, thus indicating that his required bachelor's lectures on the Bible had taken place in the previous academic year of 1299–1300, subsequent to his *Sentence* lectures as stipulated by statute.

Finally, there is firm evidence of Scotus in mandatory residence as a "formed bachelor" after having given his lectures of the *Sentences*. He is found responding at the "vesperies" of the inception of Philip Bridlington, who was the incoming Franciscan regent master for the academic year 1300–1301.[68] As indicated, responding at an inception exercise is one of the obligations during residence as a bachelor, so this dating again fits precisely with the course of university studies outlined above. Other indications that Scotus was still at this stage in the 1300–1301 academic year are his disputations with Richard Conington in his Oxford *Collationes*, which were mandatory exercises conducted in the convent among bachelors.[69] During this period, he also continued the revision of his original lectures on the *Sentences* into an *Ordinatio*, which, as noted, was a mendicant practice during the "formed bachelor" period.

That Scotus was in Oxford as an advanced bachelor at the end of the 1299–1300 academic year is confirmed by a singular document that provides a survey of the Franciscan convent for that year.[70] On July 26, 1300, the Provincial Minister, Hugh de Hertepol, himself a master of theology, personally presented twenty-two friars from the Oxford convent to Bishop John Dalderby in Dorchester seeking permissions for them to hear

---

[66] Cf. Index entries for "Biblia Sacra" in Vat. I, 287–288.   [67] Courtenay 1980.

[68] Little and Pelster 1934: 255–56, 345.

[69] On the *Collationes Oxonienses* see the recent edition and study by Alliney and Fedeli in Duns Scotus, *Coll. Ox.* (Alliney and Fedeli), especially p. clix for dating these exercises to Spring, 1301. For an analysis of one of the *collatio* debates at Oxford between Scotus and Conington, see Dumont 1996, although the dating there proposed for the *collatio* should be corrected to 1300–1301. By 1310, the Order had specified that *collationes* were one of the three academic exercises—together with lectures and ordinary disputations—that excused liturgical obligations. See Cenci and Mailleux 2010: 11, n. 20d and 84, n. 29. This academic sense of *collatio* as a *disputatio* should be strictly distinguished from other, older senses of the term, such as sermons or monastic practices.

[70] Edited in Little 1943: 235.

confessions.[71] This group of friars included the convent's academic elite, headed by the two current masters of theology, Adam of Howedon as regent and the above-mentioned Philip Bridlington as incoming. Also found in this group were the next two provincial ministers of England, six of the Order's future masters in theology at Oxford, and the province's next master of theology at Paris, Duns Scotus. Among those with Scotus were his fellow bachelor, Richard of Conington, as well as the more junior, William of Shirebourne.

This entry in Dalderby's register is the last dated mention of Scotus at Oxford prior to his departure for Paris. Although at the time Scotus was a formed bachelor of theology, awaiting his licensing, inception and regency, he was never promoted at Oxford. Rather, at some point, presumably after the meeting with Dalderby, Hertepol advanced Scotus as the province's nominee to lecture on the *Sentences* at Paris. While the Order's statutes gave the minister general the determination of the next Parisian bachelor of the *Sentences*, they also required provincial ministers to submit in writing suitable candidates during a general chapter of the Order.[72] Accordingly, Hertepol must have recommended Scotus as the Order's Parisian bachelor of the *Sentences* to the minister general, John of Murrovalle, at the next general chapter, which was held at Genoa in June 1302.[73] Consequently, Scotus must have arrived at Paris in time for the academic year 1302–1303 and, as shown below, began lecturing on the *Sentences* immediately, a fact consistent with the above observations on his prior Parisian lectorate.[74]

---

[71] The impetus for this face-to-face meeting was Boniface VIII's bull *Super cathedram* of February 18, 1300, which required the mendicants to present selected friars to local bishops for permission to hear confessions. Dominican and Franciscan provincials immediately overwhelmed their ordinaries with such petitions, as Dalderby's register attests. See Little 1943: 230–31.

[72] This provision was enacted at the Paris General Chapter of 1292, with the instruction that it should be "renewed in every General Chapter." See Cenci and Mailleux 2007: 314, n. 11f–h.

[73] The Genoa Chapter and its date are mentioned in Glassberger 1887: 109 and 111. The acts of the chapter do not survive. John of Murrovalle held only one other General Chapter, namely, at Lyon in 1299. Thus, Murrovalle must have sent Scotus to Paris at the Genoa Chapter. See Ehrle 1892: 66–67. That June would not have been too late to send Scotus to Paris for the 1302 academic year is clear from the parallel case of William Peter Godinus. At their General Chapter in Toulouse, May 25, 1304, the Dominicans absolved Godinus as Provincial of Toulouse and sent him to Paris, where he was licensed and regent that year. See n. 113 below.

[74] Vos surmises that Scotus arrived in Paris during the academic year 1301–02, prior to starting his lectures on the *Sentences* in the fall of 1302, in order to hold his Parisian *Collationes*. See Vos 2019: 117–124 and note 107 below.

VI PARIS

As might be expected, more documentation exists for Scotus's Parisian theologate than for any other period of his life. Nevertheless, the literature has long disputed the precise dating and duration of key stages of his career there. Fortunately, a recent re-evaluation of a central part of the theology program—the reading of the *Sentences*—cleanly resolves several points of uncertainty previously left to speculation. As indicated, Scotus began his period as a bachelor of the *Sentences* immediately upon arrival at Paris in 1302. This is known from two explicits in a copy of a report (*reportatio*) of Scotus's lectures contained in the famous manuscript, Worcester, Cathedral Library, ms. F 69. The first terminates a table of questions for Book I of Scotus's Parisian *Sentences*; the second occurs at the end of the question lists for all four books. They read respectively as follows:

> Here end the questions on the first book of the *Sentences* given by Brother John Duns Scotus of the Friars Minor at Paris in A.D. 1302 near the beginning of 1303 (*intrante tertio*).

> Here end the questions on the *Sentences* given by the above-mentioned John Duns Scotus in the *studium* at Paris in A. D. 1303.[75]

The precious information contained in these seemingly straightforward statements has been variously interpreted and contested. The first problem is the meaning of the phrase *intrante tertio* in the first *explicit*.[76] While not an expression usual in scholastic colophons, its intended sense is clear. The participle *intrante* and its correlate *exeunte* are used in medieval dating. Most frequently they reckon days relative to the middle of a month, which obviously does not apply here.[77] The word *intrante* is also found when dating by regency to indicate proximity to the start of the next regnal year, signifying a period of up to two months.[78] Usage matching that of the above *explicit* can be found in English documents contemporary with the Worcester manuscript.[79]

---

[75] F. 158v: "Expliciunt quaestiones super primum Sentenciarum datae a fratre I. Douns et Scoto ordinis fratrum minorum Parisiis anno domini millesimo tricentesimo secundo intrante tercio;" f. 160v: "Expliciunt quaestiones Sentenciarum date a fratre I[ohanne Duns (*over erasure*)] antedicto in studio Parisiis Anno Domini MCCCIII." Cf. Thomson 2001: 430.

[76] Little 1932: 575: "... what 'A.D. 1302 *intrante tercio*' exactly means is doubtful." For discussion of difficulties with the phrase, see Courtenay 1995: 159–161.

[77] Cheney and Jones 2000: 15.   [78] Vincent 1893: 153–155.

[79] Hartshorne 1862: 146: "Hic incipit Rotulus Ospitii Dominae anno regni Regis Edwardi vicesimo tertio *intrante quarto*." [= 1295], i.e., the twenty third year of King Edward near the beginning of the twenty-fourth. This matches the syntax of the above *explicit*: "anno Domini millesimo tricentesimo secundo *intrante tercio*."

The *explicit* accordingly means that Scotus lectured on the first book of the *Sentences* in 1302 until near the start of 1303 as would be reckoned by the medieval calendar. That is, given that lectures on the *Sentences* at Paris commenced in October, 1302, the first *explicit* asserts that Scotus finished reading the first book near the start of 1303. Given that the manuscript was probably written at Oxford, and in any case certainly by an English scribe, the calendar year is being reckoned from the Annunciation (March 25).[80] Thus, the expression *intrante tertio* means that Scotus finished his first book on the *Sentences* about late January. This reading, however, raises a second difficulty when taken with the second *explicit*.

The second *explicit*, which seems to state plainly that Scotus completed his lectures at Paris in 1303, appears to pose a further problem. Together with the first *explicit*, it implies that Scotus read the *Sentences* in the single academic year of 1302–1303. This would contradict the long-accepted conviction that, prior to about 1320, bachelors at Paris lectured on the *Sentences* over the course of two academic years, not one. In an important study, however, William Duba and Christopher Schabel have shown that the canonical "two-year rule" is supported neither by statute nor by surviving *Sentences* where the dating of books and the sequence of bachelors are otherwise established.[81] Rather, their findings indicate that already in the late thirteenth-century lectures on the *Sentences* at Paris were given in a single academic year, including those of Scotus.[82] Thus, the long presumed 2-year cycle for reading the *Sentences* at Paris in this period poses no difficulty for the above two *explicits*. Indeed, as shown below, other facts of Scotus's Parisian career can only be explained on the assumption of a 1-year reading for his *Sentences*.

In sum, Scotus read the *Sentences* at Paris in a single academic year from October 1302 until June 1303. Cross references in the Worcester manuscript show that Scotus lectured on the books in the customary teaching sequence of I–IV–II–III, although, as is typical, they have been copied and assembled in numerical order.[83] The actual order in which they were taught is important, because the commentary ends roughly halfway through book III at distinction 17, indicating that Scotus terminated his

---

[80] See Thomson 2009: 43: "Most of the cursive hands are anglicana . . . Probably written by monks at Gloucester College [i.e., Oxford] . . . ."

[81] Duba and Schabel 2017.

[82] Duba and Schabel 2017 argue this in particular for Scotus at 165–173.

[83] Thus, book II refers to book IV as having already been completed. See, "Prolegomena," (Vat. XXI, 9*).

Parisian lectures at this point.[84] While *Sentences* commentaries of the period generally compress or truncate Book III in a rush to finish by the end of the academic year, another reason explains Scotus's incomplete lectures. At just this moment, royal agents arrived at the Parisian convents to record declarations of adherence or non-adherence to King Philip the Fair's campaign against Pope Boniface VIII.[85] The royal census of the Franciscan house was made on June 24 and 25, 1303, that is, precisely when Scotus was nearing the end of his lectures on *Sentences* III. Scotus, like most of the foreign friars at Cordeliers, did not adhere to the King's case against Boniface and, consequently, was under a royal edict to leave France within three days. Thus, in the last week of June 1303, Scotus stopped his Parisian lectures on the *Sentences* at book III, distinction 17, never to be completed.[86]

The royal census of Cordeliers records some 173 friars present at the convent, who were separated into two lists as either adherent or non-adherent to Philip's case against Boniface.[87] This fortuitously surviving document provides a rare, detailed picture of Scotus's environment during his time as a Parisian bachelor. Scotus is grouped with the other English non-adherents, where his status as a bachelor lecturing on the *Sentences* is inferred from being listed first among the English friars and having an assistant (*socius*), whose name is given only as Thomas. The document then names four other English theologians present with Scotus at Cordeliers, who would themselves go on to form a future series of regent masters at the Oxford convent.[88] Most notable among them was William of Alnwick, who is listed among the adherents, and so could remain in Paris. Apart from his own substantial contributions, Alnwick was an important redactor of Scotus's works. He would himself eventually be licensed at Paris and become the forty-second lector in theology at Oxford.[89] Listed immediately after Scotus and his *socius* among the non-adherents were three others: a certain John, John Crombe, and Thomas of

---

[84] Duba and Schabel 2017: 172 cite several examples to show that, roughly speaking, if Scotus's lectures stopped in the last week of June, they would have ended about where they in fact do terminate, namely, at book III, distinction 17.

[85] For an analysis of the dispute and its impact on the religious houses of Paris, see Courtenay 1996.

[86] All known manuscripts of the third book of Scotus's Parisian *Sentences* end at distinction 17, although, as indicated below, some supply the omitted distinctions 18–40 by appending the corresponding Oxford material. See Hechich 2008: 73–74.

[87] For the census and an analysis of it, see Courtenay 1993, which is then revisited with corrections in Courtenay 2011.

[88] See Courtenay 2011: 188.

[89] See William of Alnwick, *Quaest. disp. de esse intelligibili et de Quodl.* (Ledoux, x–xlvi).

England. 'John' and 'Thomas of England' can almost certainly be identified as the friars John of Wylton and Thomas of St. Dunstan.[90] These identifications are quite likely since these names correspond, in the precise order of seniority, to the fortieth, forty-first, and forty-fourth lectors in theology at the Oxford convent, with Alnwick as the forty-second lector listed separately among the adherents. There can be little doubt, then, that this group of friars comprised the English province's four allowable candidates in the Parisian lectorate program, i.e., two funded by the Order (*de gratia*) and two by the province (*de debito*). This piece of information provides rare details on the early fourteenth-century lectorate at Paris.[91] Among other insights, it explains why John of Wylton and Alnwick both, in the end, adhered to the royal appeal. They were probably the two *de gratia* candidates at Paris so that their return to Oxford would have meant the loss of two "academic scholarships" to the English province.

Also listed among the non-adherents was Gonsalvus Hispanus as the outgoing regent master of theology, who would be elected Minister General the following spring. His letter in November 1304 to the guardian of the Paris convent recommending Scotus for promotion is considered below. Among the adherents, who were thus able to remain at Cordeliers, were the incoming regent master, Alan, and the current formed bachelor, Giles of Longny.[92] The recording of these two theologians is significant. Scotus would later, upon his return to Paris, function as the respondent at Giles's own inception as master, presided over by Alan as the current regent. This ceremony is preserved in an additional, rare text considered below.

After Philip's expulsion of non-adherents at the end of June 1303, Boniface VIII retaliated on August 15 by recalling the power to confer the license, effectively suspending the granting of degrees at the

---

[90] On Crombe, Wylton and St. Dunstan, see respectively Emden 1957–1959: I, 516; III, 2053; III, 1624. For their regencies as lectors at Oxford, see Eccleston, *Tractatus de adventu fratrum* (Little, 55). Wylton originally was a non-adherent, but then like Alnwick, joined the adherents, and thus remained in Paris for that year, for the reasons surmised. On the identifications, see Courtenay 2011: 188–191, 226 n. 112.

[91] For example, it shows that of the four in the Parisian lectorate only one, Alnwick, would proceed to reading the *Sentences* and licensing at Paris. These identifications also reveal something of the ages and careers of those sent to the Parisian lectorate. The case of St. Dunstan, who was the youngest of the four, is instructive. Since he was at least 20 years old when ordained subdeacon by Bishop Sutton in 1293, he was no younger than twenty-nine when beginning his Parisian lectorate in 1302. He was not lector at Oxford until about 1317, immediately preceding John of Reading, and thus would have been about forty-four. For his dates, see Eccleston, *Tractatus de adventu fratrum* (Little, 55–56), where in note '3b' the year should read "1293." St. Dunstan's case would indicate both a somewhat older age for the Parisian lectorate than typically estimated and a period of more than 15 years between starting the lectorate in Paris and promotion.

[92] See Courtenay 2011: 221–222.

University.[93] Although Boniface died a short time later in October, his successor, Benedict XI, did not return the authority to grant degrees to the University until a letter to King Philip dated April 18, 1304. The King ordered this and other conciliatory letters from the Pope formally proclaimed at a public meeting of officials at Notre Dame on June 28.[94] That is, Boniface's ban on degrees at Paris remained in force until the very end of the 1303–1304 academic year. The expulsion of scholars by Philip and the suspension of degrees by Boniface had very real impacts on Scotus and his fellow bachelors. Thus, as mentioned below, Albert of Metz, a nonadherent, was a formed bachelor who was older than Scotus and should have been promoted ahead of him.[95] Albert, however, expelled from Paris, had not yet returned by Scotus's own promotion. Similarly, Alexander of Alessandria, the future minister general of the Order, was also a formed bachelor at the time. At his expulsion, he returned to Italy. He prevailed upon Pope Benedict to grant him the license at the Lateran, where he then incepted as master of theology under the Franciscan Cardinal Gentile da Montefiore.[96] The Order then sent him to Bologna as lector until he returned to Paris to succeed Scotus as regent in 1307.[97] As these cases show, there can be little doubt that Scotus, having been expelled from France at the end of June 1303, similarly left for his home province of England.

It is generally supposed that upon leaving Paris Scotus returned to the Oxford convent, and in fact there is evidence to support this. For example, Scotus appears as an opponent in the *Quodlibet* of the Dominican Nicholas Trivet held at Oxford in December 1303.[98] Confirmation that Scotus returned to England comes from a Barcelona manuscript containing book III of his Paris lectures, which, as mentioned, terminated at distinction 17. While this codex contains a full set of all forty distinctions for book III, it nevertheless inserts exactly at the transition from distinction 17–18, the following annotation: "Up to this point brother John Duns

---

[93] *CUP*, II, 104 n. 636.

[94] *CUP*, II, 113–14 n. 645. For the public proclamation ordered by Philip, see Guillaume de Nangis, *Chronique latine* (Géraud, I, 342): "Vigilia apostolorum Petri et Pauli, Parisius in ecclesia cathedrali, praelatis et clero praesentibus ad hoc specialiter evocatis, lectae sunt, ex parte regis Franciae, litterae continentes inter alia, quod papa Benedictus ... auctoritatem licentiandi magistros in decretis et theologia, quam sibi dicebat papa Bonifacius reservasse, more solito cancellario Parisiensi restaurans."

[95] On Albert of Metz, see Glorieux 1933: II, 204 n. 343.

[96] On Montefiore, who had been master at Paris, see Glorieux 1933: II, 142 n. 322.

[97] *CUP*, II, 105–106, n. 639; Piana 1970: 9.

[98] Hechich 1958: 21–22 nt 65. Trivet's question has been edited in Hauke 1967: 7*–16*.

lectured at Paris; the rest is from England."[99] That is, the Barcelona manuscript appends to Scotus's Parisian lectures on Book III the missing distinctions 18–40, which it has supplied, as the annotation says, from an English version of his commentary. The English source of these additional distinctions is now known as Scotus's Oxford *Lectura*.[100] Indeed, Scotus's Oxford *Lectura* for book III is posterior to his Parisian lectures, since it explicitly cites and quotes his Paris commentary.[101] In sum, upon his exile from Paris, Scotus returned to Oxford, where he lectured a second time on the third book of the *Sentences*. His Oxford *Lectura* on book III, unlike his corresponding lectures at Paris, covered all forty distinctions and was used by some manuscripts to supply the missing distinctions from the incomplete Parisian version. In fact, this later *Lectura* III from Oxford is Scotus's only complete commentary on the third book of the *Sentences* in any version.[102]

When did Scotus return to Paris from Oxford? The answer to this question has long vexed scholarship owing to the presumed "two-year rule" for reading the *Sentences*. That is, if Scotus read the *Sentences* over 2 years, as had been generally assumed, then he would have left Paris in June 1303 having lectured only on books I and IV. He thus would have required a second academic year to finish reading books II and III. This, however, seemed contradicted by the two documents considered below that presuppose Scotus was a "formed bachelor," i.e., had completed his lectures on the *Sentences*, upon his return to Paris in the Fall of 1304. Moreover, the "two-year rule" also contradicts the more recent evidence given above: during his exile from France Scotus gave a second set of lectures on the third book of the *Sentences* at Oxford that cites his corresponding—and hence *earlier*— Parisian commentary. On the other hand, a 1-year reading of the *Sentences* by Scotus at Paris in 1302–03, as actually attested in the Worcester manuscript itself, is consistent with all these facts.

That Scotus was back in Paris for the start of the 1304–1305 academic year as a formed bachelor—i.e., had completed his lectures on the *Sentences*—is confirmed by two documents. The first is the famous letter of commendation by the Minister General, Gonsalvus of Spain, which is

---

[99] This is Barcelona, Arxiu de la Corona d'Aragó, ms. Ripoll 53, f. 34rb: "Usque huc legit frater Iohannes Parisius; aliud de Anglia," written at end of *Rep. par.* III d. 17. See Longpré 1935.

[100] See in particular "Prolegomena," (Vat. XXI, 7*–12*).

[101] Thus, in the Oxford *Lectura* at *Lect.* III d. 5, Qq. 1–2, nn. 14–20 (Vat. XX, 161–163) Scotus introduces his position (161, l. 63) with *Dixi Parisius*—"I said at Paris."

[102] The *Ordinatio* is incomplete in Book III, missing all of distinctions 18–25, which in many manuscripts were supplied by inserting the corresponding material from the *Lectura* III. See "Prolegomena" (Vat. X, 42*–52*).

the only known historical record concerned specifically with Scotus.[103] As indicated, Gonsalvus was the Franciscan master during Scotus's sentential year at Paris and was subsequently elected Minister General in May 1304. His letter, dated November 18, 1304, is addressed to the guardian and masters of the Paris convent and replies to their notification of the advancement (*expeditio*) of Giles of Longny to licensing by the Chancellor.[104] As mentioned, Giles appeared as a formed bachelor on the royal adhesion list of June 1303 in support of King Philip's petition. Giles thus would have remained in Paris, but could not be promoted owing to Boniface's embargo on degrees that remained in force for all of the subsequent 1303–04 academic year. Judging from the date of Gonsalvus's letter, Giles must have been licensed by October 1304 at the latest. These details are relevant, since, as discussed below, Scotus was himself the responding bachelor in Giles's promotion ceremony after licensing, a duty by statute assigned to a *baccalaureus formatus*. After acknowledging Giles's promotion, Gonsalvus proceeds in his letter to nominate Scotus as the next candidate both by rule and on merit. By rule, Scotus meets the requirement that the next master must come from outside the province of France. As to merit, Gonsalvus famously praises Scotus for his "laudable life, superb knowledge, most subtle intellect, and other fine qualities, about which I am fully informed, partly by long experience and partly by his reputation, which has spread everywhere." Gonsalvus's appeal to "long experience" has generally been taken to mean that Scotus was in the Parisian lectorate when Gonsalvus himself was there reading the *Sentences* in the mid-1280s. All of this indicates that Scotus had completed his lectures on the *Sentences* by his return to Paris in the Fall of 1304 since Gonsalvus could not have otherwise put him forward for promotion.

Further detail in Gonsalvus's letter confirms this beyond any doubt. After having recommended Scotus, Gonsalvus recalls that Albert of Metz, who is older than Scotus, should be promoted if he can be returned to Paris. But Gonsalvus adds that Albert should be advanced only if the Chancellor would license both him and Scotus at the same time, an unlikely scenario except for the suspension of degrees at Paris for the past year. In that case, Albert could incept first, and Scotus immediately under him. Gonsalvus's plan shows beyond doubt that Scotus must have already

---

[103] *CUP* II, 117–118, n. 652. Translated in Little 1932: 577–578.

[104] The terms *expeditio/expedire* in academic contexts indicate that a bachelor has been advanced to licensing by the Chancellor. Correspondingly, *impedire* means that advancement has been blocked. Thus, Gonsalvus's letter shows that the licensing of Giles has occurred. I thank Christopher Schabel for alerting me to this academic usage.

been a formed bachelor at the time of his letter. Otherwise, Gonsalvus would not have ordered that Scotus should be licensed at the same time as the older Albert.

The second important document of Scotus's bachelor period at Paris is the actual transcript of his participation in the promotion exercises of Giles of Longny acknowledged in the above letter of Gonsalvus. Texts of such promotions rarely survive, and this case is particularly significant given the figures involved. The process of "promotion" involved two separate ceremonial acts: licensing and inception, both of which Gonsalvus mentions in his above letter nominating Scotus.[105] Licensing was the conferral of the ancient "permission to teach" (*licentia ubique docendi*), which was conferred by the chancellor. It was this capacity that Pope Boniface reserved to himself in his response to King Philip. After receiving the license, the candidate advanced to inception, a series of ceremonial disputations that marked his entrance into the guild of masters. Of these, the disputation in the bishop's hall—the *aula*—was the most significant, for here the candidate was, for the first time, vested with the regalia of a master and exercised the privilege of determining a question. The first question debated in the *aula* was posed by the incoming master, but the initial response fell to a formed bachelor (*baccalaureus responsivus*), who assumed most of the burden of debate. The senior bachelor had to defend his response against objections posed in turn by the incoming master, his presenting master, and other senior masters on the faculty, and finally the chancellor. The new master would then give his determination, which he then fully defended in a separate session called the 'resumption'. In the present case, the incoming master was Giles of Longny, the presenting master was Alan, and the responding bachelor was Scotus. The senior master, possibly representing the chancellor, was Godfrey of Fontaines. That is, the inception document of Giles not only establishes that Scotus was a formed bachelor by October 1304 but also records a live debate between him and Godfrey of Fontaines that ultimately turned to a famously contentious issue, whether there were virtues in the will. The significance of this document had long been overlooked because from the sixteenth-century it had been printed as belonging to the *Sentences* of Scotus himself.[106]

---

[105] On these exercises, see Bazàn 1985: 109–122.

[106] Giles of Longny's inception was printed in early editions as if it were Scotus's *Rep. par.* III, d. 18, qq. 2–3 (Vivès XXIII, 391–400). Balić discovered a manuscript in which the original disputation was preserved and properly identified. See Balić 1959: 97–101.

To summarize, after having spent at least part of the previous academic year in exile at Oxford, Scotus had returned to Paris by the Fall of 1304 to resume his theologate as a formed bachelor. In that capacity, he discharged one of its main responsibilities by responding at the inception of Giles of Longny, which occurred in October at the latest. He was nominated that November as the next master by the Minister General. It seems likely that Scotus spent most of the 1304–1305 academic year as a formed bachelor, given his absence from Paris the previous year. During his period as a formed bachelor, Scotus likely participated in his Parisian *Collationes* at Cordeliers, just as he had when at the same stage of his program at Oxford.[107]

Although we possess a contemporary citation of Scotus's inception by William of Alnwick, no document survives that firmly dates his promotion or regency.[108] Nevertheless, the years in which these occurred can be reliably inferred once certain facts are recognized. First, it is necessary to correct a longstanding historical error. Nearly a century ago, a set of three quodlibetal disputations by the Franciscan Peter of England were identified, which Palémon Glorieux subsequently dated to 1303–1305 owing to their citation of *Inter cunctas sollicitudines* issued by Pope Benedict XI on

---

[107] As noted above (n. 74), Vos 2019: 117–124 argues that Scotus held his Parisian *Collationes* during the academic year 1301–1302, prior to starting his lectures on the *Sentences* in the fall of 1302. Citing Scotus's own reference to his "last Parisian *Collatio*" at *Ord.* I d. 10 n. 36 (Vat. IV, 354), Vos surmised that Scotus must have already disputed all of his Parisian *Collationes* by this early point in his composition of the *Ordinatio*. Vos concludes that this chronology required Scotus to have been at Paris during the academic year 1301–1302 in order to have held all of these *Collationes* prior starting his Parisian lectures on the *Sentences* the following Fall. But this does not follow. Assisi, Biblioteca comunale, ms. 137 (the so-called A manuscript), at f. 157ra, records this reference by Scotus to his last Parisian *Collatio* as occurring within an addition made "*extra manu Duns*" (cf. Vat. IV, 353 *apparatus criticus* to line 1). This scribal expression means that Scotus added the passage containing this reference in the margins or on sheets inserted into his already existing draft of *Ordinatio*. That is, this reference to the *Collationes Parisienses* is one of Scotus's later annotations and additions to his working copy of the *Ordinatio* that he brought with him to Paris. Scotus's last Parisian *Collatio* therefore postdated his original draft of *Ordinatio* I, d. 10. Moreover, as indicated, Scotus participated in *Collationes* at Oxford as a formed bachelor after having already completed his lectures on the *Sentences*. Thus, it does not seem plausible that Scotus would have held his *Collationes* at Paris before having even started the *Sentences* there. Finally, as indicated above, Scotus was only selected by Morrovalle at the General Chapter in 1302 to lecture at Paris. In part, Vos's chronology followed his view that Scotus read the *Sentences* at Paris over 2 years rather than one, which combined with his exile to Oxford in June 1303, would have left no other time to dispute his Parisian *Collationes* than the academic year 1301–1302.

[108] In his *Quaestiones de esse intelligibili*, William of Alnwick summarizes what he says are two arguments that Scotus himself made at his inception, presumably at the *aula*: "... duo argumenta quae ipse facit in quaestione sui Principii." See William of Alnwick, *Quaest. disp. de esse intelligibili et de Quodl.* (Ledoux, 158).

February 17, 1304.[109] Glorieux then inferred that this Peter of England must have been a regent master at Paris during that period, succeeding Gonsalvus of Spain, at the end of the 1302–1303 academic year. Glorieux's identification, however, cannot be correct. If this Peter of England had succeeded Gonsalvus as a regent master at Paris, he would certainly have appeared on the royal census of June 1303. But the royal list contains no 'Peter' from the English province. Rather, this individual must instead be Peter of Baldeswell, who was regent not at Paris but at Oxford precisely at this time as the thirtieth Franciscan lector, succeeding the above-mentioned Philip of Bridlington.[110] Without this correction, it would be difficult to place Scotus in the Parisian sequence of masters according to the apparent rotation used by the Franciscans, as described below.

Secondly, Scotus participated in a well-known disputation concerning the principle of individuation with his Dominican colleague, William Peter Godinus.[111] This disputation records the inception exercise known as the "debate between the masters" (*disputatio magistrorum*) that formed the second half of the proceedings held in the bishop's hall (*aula*), as discussed above. Unfortunately, the incepting master is not known, but regulations dictated that the *disputatio magistrorum* begin with a formal answer to the question by the most junior master, who is identified as Scotus, with responses from a senior master, who was Godinus, in an exchange that went for several turns.[112] Since Godinus was licensed at Paris in the Fall of 1304, and then sent to the papal court as lector in 1306, his disputation with Scotus must have taken place within the 1305–06 academic year.[113] That is, Scotus had been promoted as a new master by this time.

Finally, it seems that in this period Franciscans typically had two masters of theology in a given year at Oxford and Paris. Since Franciscans had only a single chair in the faculty at either university, it seems that one master was regent, under whom a formed bachelor would be promoted in order to take over as the next regent in the following year.

[109] These questions were first noted by Castagnoli 1931 and the identification of Peter of England made by Glorieux 1935: 212–215. See also Duba 2007: 572–579.
[110] This identification was first suggested by Emden 1957–1959: I, 96. On Baldeswell, see also Little and Pelster 1934: 248.
[111] Edited in Stroick 1974: 581–608, but see next note.
[112] Pelster 1922: 368–369, with Parisian inception procedures quoted. Erfurt, Bibliotheca Amploniana, ms. F.369, identifies in the margins the arguments and responses of Scotus and Godinus, which identifications, unfortunately, are omitted in the above edition of Stroick.
[113] On Godinus, see Quétif and Échard 1719: 591–592; *Acta capitulorum generalium Ordinis Praedicatorum: ab anno 1304 usque ad annum 1378* (Reichert I n. 1; 6, ll. 8–10).

This seems clear from the surviving list of lectors at Oxford, in which masters turn over roughly every year. The practice must have been the same at Paris, where the pressure on the sole Franciscan university chair was even greater since it rotated among the provinces. This seems confirmed from the adhesion list of 1304, which records both Gonsalvus and Alan as masters.

Given the above, the sequence of promotions and regents during Scotus's Parisian stay can be reconstructed as follows. It indicates that he was promoted in the academic year 1305–1306 when he functions as a "junior master" in his debate with Godinus and then becomes regent the following year when he probably disputed his quodlibet.

1302–1303: Gonsalvus regent; Alan listed as master in June 1303, has already been promoted.

1303–1304: Alan becomes regent; no promotions this year owing to ban by Boniface VIII.

1304–1305: Alan still regent; Giles of Longny is promoted. Alan still regent since he is the *magister aulator* in the inception of Giles in Fall, 1304. Letter of Gonsalvus arrives at Paris in January 1305 putting Scotus next in line for a promotion.

1305–1306: Giles of Longny becomes regent; Scotus is promoted. Presumably, Scotus's licensing and inception occurs in the Fall, 1305 on the model of Giles's promotion. Scotus is the *magister iunior* in debate with Godinus, who is the *magister senior*, in an inception exercise during this year.

1306–1307: Scotus becomes regent. Alexander of Alessandria, who had already been licensed and promoted in the Lateran in the Fall of 1303, is in line to be the next regent. As regent, Scotus holds his *Quodlibet* in Advent or Lent of this academic year.

1307–1308: Scotus has left Paris and is in Cologne *studium* as *lector*. Alexander of Alessandria, having returned from Bologna, is regent.

Given the above, Scotus probably held his one quodlibetal disputation as regent master, either in Advent of 1306 or Lent of 1307. This enormous work contains twenty-one questions and is one of the great examples of that literary genre.[114] As a magisterial disputation, it is perhaps the most carefully redacted and polished of Scotus's writings, although its revision

---

[114] See Noone and Roberts 2007.

was not completed.[115] Perhaps also as master Scotus disputed his famous Parisian question on the formal distinction entitled *De formalitatibus*, cited by contemporaries as the *Logica Scoti*.[116] During his time at Paris, Scotus no doubt continued to revise his great *Ordinatio*, large sections of which he never completed. Indeed, Scotus himself noted that he had failed to dictate its final questions.[117]

VII   COLOGNE

As indicated, Alexander of Alessandria was a non-adherent to Philip the Fair's call against Boniface VIII and departed the Paris convent at the end of June 1303. After his promotion in Rome and subsequent lectorship in Bologna, Alexander returned to Paris as the regent master in the Fall of 1307. His presence at Paris is attested by his seal on an opinion letter sent by the theologians in March 1308 to King Philip concerning his prosecution of the Templars.[118] This almost certainly means that Scotus had left Paris by the beginning of the 1307–08 academic year for the *studium* in Cologne, where he is listed as lector in a provincial document dated February 20, 1308.[119] Older literature construed Scotus's transfer to Cologne as abrupt and hasty, made by the Order out of concern for reprisals against him for his positions, particularly his defense of the Immaculate Conception.[120] The reality was more mundane. The Order routinely moved its masters out of Paris after about a year of regency, both to make room for incoming promotions and to place these highly trained academics in upper-level positions of the Order or Church. In Scotus's case, he was sent as a lector to Cologne no doubt to raise the level of teaching in the convent school, which served as the *studium generale* for the province.[121] Nor was there anything peculiar in sending someone from the English province to Cologne. Indeed, shortly after Scotus's death, Peter of England, probably to be identified with Scotus's slightly older colleague at

---

[115] A scribal note to the last question indicates that it had not been finally revised by Scotus. See Noone and Roberts 2007: 140–143.

[116] Dumont 2005; Emery and Smith 2014.

[117] *Ord.* IV d. 49 p. 1 q. 6 "Editorum monitus" (Vat. XIV, 394).

[118] *CUP* II, 127 n. 664 note. On the letter, see Courtenay 2016.   [119] Willibrord 1931: 304.

[120] See examples adduced by Wolter 1993: 12–13.

[121] Roest 2000: 128 n. 43: "The presence of a brilliant scholar (like the short presence of Scotus in Cologne) could significantly change the level of teaching in these schools [i.e., provincial *studia generalia*]." The provincial document cited in note 119 shows that theology was being taught at the Cologne *studium*, since a certain 'Gaulterus' is named immediately after Scotus as lecturer on the *Sentences*.

Oxford, the above mentioned Peter Baldeswell, was made provincial of Cologne in 1309, remaining in office until 1316 before being returned to England.[122] The assignment of Scotus to Cologne thus fell entirely within ordinary practices of the Order.

Scotus, however, was only in Cologne for little more than a year before he died on November 8, 1308. This date is reported by Matthew Ferkić, who had in 1620 witnessed the book of the dead in the sacristy of the medieval convent of Cologne before it was destroyed.

> Chained to the altar in the sacristy is an ancient manuscript containing all the names of both members of the Order and secular benefactors for whom Masses of atonement are to be offered. For the day November 8, this book reads: "Brother John Scotus, a famous doctor of theology and lector at Cologne, died." To this was added a short time later: "Who died in 1308 A.D. on the eighth day of November."[123]

On the traditional dating of his birth, Scotus died at the age of forty-two; accepting the above evidence that he was somewhat older, he was closer to forty-five. In either case, Scotus lived only 1 year after his university period, with the result that he left many of his works unfinished or in draft form. The consequences of this for the transmission and integrity of his writings, and thus for their accurate interpretation, were truly catastrophic. This was particularly evident in his great work, the *Ordinatio*, where long lacunae in books II and III were posthumously filled in with earlier Oxford material or, even more problematically, with a mélange of Parisian texts. Moreover, this literary contamination occurred at the earliest stage of a very large textual transmission, only then to be set permanently into type at the start of the printing era and passed on to modernity. The recovery of Scotus's original *Ordinatio* required nearly a century of scholarship. At the same time, the rapid and large dissemination of Scotus's works is testimony to the power and inventiveness of his thought, which, like his life itself, straddled both the thirteenth and fourteenth centuries, both Oxford and Paris.[124]

---

[122] In addition to notes 109 and 110 above, see Glorieux 1933: II, 197–198.

[123] Ferchius, *Apologiae pro Joanne Duns Scoto*, I.8, pp. 9–10: "Praeterea. In altari sacrarii ferrea cathena est alligatus liber membranaceus satis antiquus omnia nomina, tum religiosorum tum benefactorum saecularium, pro quibus propitiatorium Missae sacrificium offerendum est, continens, quo in libro sub die octava Novembris legitur: 'Obiit Fr. Ioannes Scotus Sacrae Theologiae Doctor eximius, Lector Coloniensis.' Mox subditur, 'Qui obiit anno Domini 1308 sexto idus Novembris'."

[124] I am grateful to William J. Courtenay and Christopher Schabel for their extensive comments and corrections.

Biographical Summary of Duns Scotus
(Documented dates in bold.)

1263/1266	1266 is commonly assigned year of birth on assumption that Scotus was the canonically minimum age of 25 when ordained a priest on March 17, 1291. His ordination record in fact indicates that he was very likely born a few years earlier.
1280	Estimated entry into Franciscans at a minimum age of 15 years old. Again, Scotus's entry could be somewhat earlier given the above indication about his age at ordination.
1286–1290	Approximate period of his lectorate program in Paris, but see below.
1288–1290	A statement in a nearly contemporary manuscript asserts that Scotus taught (*floruit*) at Cambridge immediately before Oxford, presumably in philosophy. If so, then the above Parisian lectorate is proportionally earlier.
March 17, 1291	Scotus is ordained a priest by Bishop Oliver Sutton at Northampton. Indicates Scotus is present at the Oxford convent, likely to begin theology. Ordination register shows that Scotus is very likely past the canonically minimum age of 25, since he is older than his fellow Oxford friar, William of Schirebourne, ordained the same day.
1298–1299	Bachelor of theology at Oxford. Gives his first lectures on the *Sentences* known as the *Lectura*.
Academic Years 1299–1301	Gives required lecture on a book of the Bible to complete his bachelor's degree in theology, i.e., to become a *baccalaureus formatus*. Participates in disputations known as *collationes* with Richard of Conington, responds in promotion exercises of the incoming Franciscan master of theology, Philip Bridlington, and by early 1300 has begun revision of his *Lectura* into his *magnum opus*, the *Ordinatio*.
July 26, 1300	In a group of prominent Oxford friars presented by the English Provincial, Hugh Hertlepol, to Bishop John Dalderby at Dorchester for permission to hear confessions. This same group includes Richard of Conington and William of Shirebourne.
June 1302	At the General Chapter in Genoa, Scotus is selected by the Minister General, John Murrovalle, as the Order's next lecturer on the *Sentences* at Paris, where he begins that Fall.
October 1302– June 25, 1303	Scotus is a bachelor of theology at Paris, lecturing for a second time on the *Sentences*, which are known as the *Parisian Reports* (*Reportationes Parisienses*). His lectures ended on June 25 or 26, 1303, when he and most of the other foreigners at the convent were expelled from France for refusing to support Philip the Fair's petition against Pope Boniface VIII. Scotus terminated his Parisian lectures on the *Sentences* halfway through Book III, the last book in the teaching order.

(cont.)

August 15, 1303	In retaliation for King Philip's expulsion of non-adherents to his cause, Pope Boniface recalls the authority of the Chancellor at Paris to award degrees in theology, effectively halting promotions in the University. Boniface dies on October 11.
Academic Year 1303–1304	After expulsion from Paris at end of June, Scotus is presumed to have returned to Oxford, where he intervenes in a quodlibetal disputation of the regent Dominican master, Nicholas Trivet. During this Oxford period, he lectures for a second time on Book III of the *Sentences*, which he did not complete in Paris.
June 28, 1304	Letter of Pope Benedict XI restoring the authority of licensing to the Chancellor of the University is publicly promulgated at Paris by order of King Philip.
Academic Year 1304–1305	Scotus returns to Paris as a "formed bachelor." As at Oxford, he participates in *collationes* at the convent and the inception of the incoming Franciscan master. (See below)
October 1304	Promotion of Giles of Longny as next Franciscan master of theology at Paris. Duns Scotus functioned as the responding bachelor at the *aula* of his inception ceremony.
November 18, 1304	Gonsalvus of Spain, the Franciscan Minister General, writes the Guardian and masters of the Paris convent acknowledging the above promotion of Giles of Longny and selecting Duns Scotus as the next master of theology.
Academic Year 1305–1306	Promotion of Scotus as incoming master of theology while above-mentioned Giles of Longny is regent. Scotus disputes as the *magister iunior* with the Dominican regent, William Peter Godinus, in the "masters' debate" portion of an inception ceremony. In either this or ensuing year Scotus holds a disputed question on the formal distinction known as the *Logica Scoti*.
Academic Year 1306–1307	Regent master of theology at Paris and holds his *Quodlibet*.
Fall, 1307	Alexander of Alessandria transferred from the Bologna *studium* to Paris as regent master, and Scotus is sent to the Cologne convent, where he is listed as *lector* on February 20, 1308.
November 8, 1308	Scotus dies at Cologne, according to tradition at the age of 42. In line with the above remarks about his age, he was more likely about 45.

CHAPTER 2

The modal framework of Duns Scotus's argument for the existence of a first cause

Richard Cross

In what follows, I want to examine Scotus's modal argument for the existence of a first cause in the light of the most extensive *ex professo* discussion of modality that he offers, namely, the account of the senses of 'potency' in his questions on Aristotle's *Metaphysics*, book IX, qq. 1–2. I shall offer two different interpretations of Scotus's argument for the existence of a first cause, one more evident, one less evident, in line, respectively, with two relevant senses of 'potency' in the Aristotelian questions. I shall argue that the more-evident interpretation turns out to be incompatible with the discussion of modality in the *Metaphysics* questions. And I shall show that the less-evident interpretation itself can cast some light on aspects of the *Metaphysics* discussion that are otherwise opaque.

I THE ARGUMENT

Scotus lays out his arguments as a premise and sequence of conclusions. At each stage, he shows how the conclusion follows from the previous one:

(P)   "[Among beings], some nature can be caused (*est effectibilis*)."[1]
(C1) "Among beings (*in entibus*), some nature can cause (*est effectiva*)."[2]
(C2) "Something [viz. among beings, some nature] that can cause is simply speaking first."[3]
(C3) "[Among beings], the [nature] that is simply speaking the first cause is uncausable."[4]
(C4) "[Among beings], the [nature] that is simply speaking the first cause is an actual existent."[5]

Natures here could be individual-natures (determinate individuals independent of any actual existence they may or may not have) or

---

[1] Duns Scotus, *DPP*, 3.5 (Wolter, 43).   [2] *DPP*, 3.4 (Wolter, 43).   [3] *DPP*, 3.7 (Wolter, 44).
[4] *DPP*, 3.16 (Wolter, 51).   [5] *DPP*, 3.18 (Wolter, 51).

kind-natures. Scotus accepts both, and on the face of it, the argument does not force us to restrict its domain to one or the other, as we shall see.[6]

The argument is modal. Scotus comments that he could have proposed a non-modal argument to a first cause—arguing not from the possibility of an effect but from the actuality of an effect directly to the actuality of a first cause—but that the modal version is more powerful: it infers actuality from possibility; its premise (P) is necessary, not contingent; and its conclusion tells us not only about the existence of a first cause but something about its nature too.[7]

So Scotus understands (P) to be necessary, in a sense that I will spell out later. It is clearly not *a priori*. Although Scotus does not say so, I assume that, even if necessary, it is known by us merely *a posteriori*, inferred from the existence of actual effects. (C1) is derived from it "through the nature of correlatives:" what it means to be an effect is to be caused. So, if there is a nature that can be caused, there must be a nature that can cause.

(C2) is derived from (C1) by noting that some causal series are transitive—specifically, those in which a cause causes an effect to cause a further effect.[8] According to Scotus, such transitive causal series always have a causation-deficit: each member of such a series is "dependent,"[9] and thus "the whole totality of dependents depends on something that is not part of this total-ity."[10] Scotus does not mention the impossibility of an infinite regress of causes in this totality: so presumably he holds that the overall dependence claim obtains whether the series has a beginning or is beginningless.[11] So if there is a nature that can cause, there must be a nature or natures that are first causes in this sense—things on which "the whole totality" of a set of dependents depends. (C2), then, establishes the possibility of a first cause. (Note, again, that Scotus has said nothing about the number or kind of such first causes. The claims he makes at this stage in his argument are quite weak.)

(C3) is derived from (C2) by arguing disjunctively: either such a nature is such that it can be caused (or such that its activity results from the

---

[6] Scotus comments that he uses 'nature' so as not to prejudge the view that there could be more than one first cause: Scotus, *DPP*, 3.3 (Wolter, 43). But individuals, in Scotus's metaphysics, include both some common features (a feature shared in common with other things of the same kind) and an individuating feature. And no nature could be actual without being actualized in one (or more) singular (on these points, see *Ord*. II, d. 3, p. 1, q. 6, n. 175 [Vat. VII, 477–478]).

[7] *DPP*, 3.6 (Wolter, 43).   [8] See *DPP*, 3.11 (Wolter, 47).   [9] *DPP*, 3.13 (Wolter, 47).

[10] *DPP*, 3.13 (Wolter, 47–49).

[11] Scotus rejects the possibility of an infinite sequence given that such a sequence is *simultaneous*, on the grounds that "no philosopher assumes" a temporally simultaneous infinite set (see Scotus, *DPP*, 3.13 [Wolter, 49]).

activity of some other cause) or not. If it is such that it can be caused, then there must be a nature that can cause it—and thus it not be first—just as in the move from (P) to (C1). So, it is not such that it can be caused. And this is (C3).

Here is how Scotus argues for the move from (C3) to (C4):

> [Among beings], the [nature] that is simply speaking the first cause is an actual existent, and some actually existing nature causes in this way. This is proved: [Maj] that to whose nature (*rationi*) being-able-to-be-from-another (*posse esse ab alio*) is repugnant can exist of itself if it can exist (*si potest esse, potest esse a se*). Being-able-to-be-from-another is simply speaking repugnant to the nature of the first cause.[12]

If we give full weight to the role of (Maj) in the argument from (C3) to (C4), the final stages of the argument go something like this:

(C3) A first cause is something to whose nature being-able-to-be-from-another is repugnant.

(Maj) If that to whose nature being-able-to-be-from-another is repugnant can exist, then it exists.

(C2) A first cause can exist.

(C4) A first cause exists.

Why think that (Maj) is true? In what follows, I will attempt to describe some possible ways in which Scotus might understand this premise, and why he thinks that it has some degree of plausibility. As we shall see, the discussion of modality in the *Metaphysics* questions offers two such ways, incompatible with each other. On both of them, the argument just given is valid. But only one of them is compatible with some other claims Scotus makes about modality in the *Metaphysics* questions.

II THE MODAL FRAMEWORK

As commentators have pointed out, the modal notions Scotus presupposes are only tangentially related to assumptions made in contemporary modal logic. We sometimes partition the modal universe along the following lines: take the domain of the possible (everything that does not include a contradiction) and divide it into the actual and the non-actual. Scotus proposes something rather different. For him, the most general category, into which everything extramental falls, is not the possible but *being*,

---

[12] *DPP*, 3.18–3.19 (Wolter, 51–53).

defined (modally) as "that to which existence is non-repugnant."[13] And *being* is further divided into act and potency:

> The first distinction of being seems to be into being outside the soul and being in the soul, and this [being] outside the soul can be distinguished into act and potency (of essence and existence), and each of these existences (*esse*) outside the soul can have existence in the soul, and that existence in the soul is other than every existence outside the soul.[14]

Ignore the first division (into being "outside the soul" and "in the soul"), since these senses of 'being' are probably not univocal.[15] The primary division of real being—the most general predicate, under which everything extramental falls—is into act and potency. And each of these is divided into essence and existence—which here mean something like a kind-nature and there being an actual instantiation of that nature's. So, both potential and actual things fall under the scope of *being*. The topic of this section is the distinction between act and potency: what is actual and what is it to be actual? And what is potential and what is it to be potential?

Scotus's fundamental distinction is between potency considered as power (dispositional property, as we would say) and potency considered as a mode of being.[16] Since he is searching for a notion of potency that is either coextensive with being, or that is incompatible with actuality, Scotus immediately dispenses with the notion of potency as power, since 'a principle is no less real when it actually principiates than when it does not principiate but can principiate'.[17]

So the relevant potency is a non-dispositional feature of something real or extramental. In line with this, Scotus excludes two other senses: the "metaphorical potency that is in mathematics,"[18] according to which "lines [are] *able to be* in squares, and numbers *able to be* in other numbers as their square roots,"[19] and the "logical potency" attaching to non-contradictory propositions (which Scotus takes to be mental items).[20] (I will return to

---

[13] *Ord.* IV, d. 8, q. 1, n. 23 (Vat. XII, 5).   [14] *Ord.* I, d. 36, q. un., n. 36 (Vat., VI, 285).
[15] See *Rep.* I-A, d. 29, q. un., n. 9 (Wolter and Bychkov, II, 238). See too Scotus, *Quodl.*, q. 3, n. 2 (Wad. XII, 67; Vivès XXV, 113–114): "Being or thing... taken wholly generally, extends itself to everything that does not include a contradiction, whether it is a being of reason (that is, precisely having existence in the thinking intellect), or a real being, having some entity outside the intellect's thought... [In this sense] every conceivable thing that does not include a contradiction is called a being or thing (whether that commonness is that of analogy or univocation I do not now care)."
[16] See *QMet.* IX, qq. 1–2 nn. 14–15 (OPh IV, 512).   [17] Ibid., n. 15 (OPh IV, 512).
[18] Ibid., n. 16 (OPh IV, 513).
[19] Santogrossi 1993: 57; see Scotus, *QMet.* IX, qq. 1–2, n. 17 (OPh IV, 513).
[20] Ibid., n. 18 (OPh IV, 514).

logical potency in a moment, since it turns out to be important to the senses of 'potency' relevant in the argument for God's existence.)

Scotus discerns three senses of 'potency' as a feature of the real—kinds of potency that he labels 'metaphysical potency':

> [Metaphysical potency] is taken in three ways: in one way, it is opposed to the impossible, not as it implies the mode of a composition (as in the second member of the distinction [i.e. logical potency]), but as a disposition of something incomplex ... And in this way, the possible (*possibile*) is convertible with the whole of being, for there is nothing that is a being whose notion includes a contradiction.
>
> In another way, potency is taken as it is opposed to the necessary... And in this way the necessary is said to be that which has indefectible entity, and possible being that which has defectible being.
>
> In a third way, metaphysical potency is said most strictly, as it does not stand with act in relation to the same thing ... Only metaphysical potency taken in the last way is opposed to act, because [opposites] have to do with the same thing,[21] and cannot be simultaneously ... Potency thus understood signifies an order to an act, and this order is essentially a relation to act.[22]

The second sense here captures a sense of 'possible' as *defectible*, and Scotus makes no further use of it. (Neither do we use the term in that sense.) The first and the third, however, are relevant, since, as I shall argue, (Maj) can be read in line with either of these senses, and on either reading the argument for the existence of a first cause can be shown to be valid. The first—Scotus's broadly metaphysically possible—is a sense of 'possible' that makes the possible co-extensive with *being*. The contrast is with logical possibility: the possibility attaching to a proposition (a 'complex') about such an essence or instantiation. But note that this broad metaphysical potency corresponds to logical possibility as just outlined: for every metaphysical potency there corresponds a true proposition that is logically possible.[23]

The third sense of 'potency' is incompatible with actuality. The actual is the existent—what is or has been in the actual world.[24] What is the corresponding potency—the potency such that *being* is exhaustively divided into the actual and the potential? It is the "end term of a power:"

---

[21] Scotus is here alluding to Aristotle, *Cat.* 5, 4a11–12.
[22] Scotus, *QMet.* IX, qq. 1–2, n. 21 (OPh IV, 515).
[23] See *QMet.* IX, q. 13, n. 10 (OPh IV, 622).
[24] See *QMet.* IX, qq. 1–2, nn. 27, 36 (OPh IV, 518, 523).

> Something is said to be in potency ... because it is the end term of a power, or that to which there is a power, and this thing is said to be in potency objectively, like the soul of the Antichrist is now said to be in potency, and whiteness that is to be produced [is] likewise [said to be in potency].[25]

So we can label this kind of potency 'objective potency', and the domain of being is divided into the actual and the objectively potential. According to this passage, it includes both substances (the Antichrist) and accidents (this white patch).[26]

We can run the argument for the existence of a first cause in accordance with either of these two senses of 'potency'—broad metaphysical potency, and objective potency. Take the first, the more-evident interpretation. Here the possible coincides with what is expressed in logically possible propositions, and modalities are more or less those current in contemporary thinking on modal logic. On this reading, the final stages of the argument go like this:

(C3′) Any first cause is uncausable.
(Maj′) If it is possible that what is uncausable exists, then what is uncausable exists.
(C2′) It is possible that a first cause exists.
(C4′) A first cause exists.

This, I think, is the standard interpretation of the argument.[27] But we can run the argument in line with the third sense of 'metaphysical potency' from the questions on the *Metaphysics* too—the less-evident interpretation just mentioned. Recall that (C1) is "Among beings (*in entibus*), some nature can cause (*est effectiva*)," and note the very first noun: "among *beings*," implicit in (P) and all the other conclusions too. The division of *being* is into the actual and the potential: so among those things that are actual or potential, some nature can cause. Here are the final stages of the argument, set out using the language of objective potency in place of 'can be caused' and cognates:

(C2″) Among beings, some essence is simply speaking a first cause.
(C3″) Among beings, some essence lacks objective potency.
(Maj″) Among beings, if some essence lacks objective potency, then that essence is actual.
(C4″) Among beings, that essence is actual.

And to be actual, of course, is to be a particular.

---

[25] *Lect.* II, d. 12, q. un., n. 30 (Vat. XIX, 80); see too *QMet.* IX, qq. 1–2, nn. 40, 57 (OPh IV, 524, 530).
[26] See Figure 1. [27] I described the argument more or less in these terms in Cross 1999: 19–21.

The point of (Maj″), and thus of the crucial move from (C3″) to (C4″), is just that the domain of being—of the metaphysically possible in Scotus's widest sense—is exhausted by the objectively potential and the actual: by the causable and the actual. So, if something belongs in the domain of being and lacks objective potency, that being is actual. And this is (Maj″).

The argument requires that objective potency is a feature of some of the things included in the domain of being. But Scotus offers a reason for this:

> It seems necessary to posit, for every active potency, some corresponding possible thing, because there is no active potency with respect to that which is not in itself possible. But God is creative before he creates, therefore the creatable is able (*possibile*) to be created, not only by logical potency (because that, as it is of itself, can be without any active [power] ...). On account of this, therefore, this metaphysical potency is posited in a possible essence (some entity which is not in a chimera). But there is a great difficulty about its foundation—what type of entity it has before it exists— and neither is this to be expanded on here; perhaps it would seem more diffuse and prolix than the principal topic.[28]

On the face of it, this reason is not semantic (to secure reference to non-existents) but metaphysical: if something can cause, something can be caused; and this latter potency belongs to beings that are not—that are non-actual. Causation requires an effect-shaped space or hole, as it were. (I return to this argument below.) As Scotus puts it,

> This potency ... does not require that the subject actually exists, since it is not an actual accident. And it should be conceded that what is founded in something non-existent is not existent; neither is the potency something existent, because then it would be act or in act.[29]

The subject of the potency is a being, but non-existent. Scotus admits that there is a question of ontological commitment here, and although he says that he will forebear from discussing it on the grounds of its difficulty, he nevertheless provides a contrasting case, as we shall see. And we need to posit the subject of the relevant potency, in this sense, because if there were no such subject, there would be nothing that can be caused.

III   INTERPRETATIVE APORIAS

It turns out that the scope of objective potency set out in the *Metaphysics* questions is susceptible to two interpretations, and these interpretations, in

---

[28] *QMet.* IX, qq. 1–2, n. 33 (OPh IV, 520–521).   [29] Ibid., n. 30 (OPh IV, 520).

turn, affect how we should understand Scotus's notion of the broadly metaphysically possible—the notion underlying the argument to (C4′). And this is the first problem I shall discuss. But there is a second one too: namely, what is the ontological status of objectively potential items? What ontological commitment, if any, does the theory involve? The discussion in the *Metaphysics* leaves the question open (suggesting but apparently not deciding between two possible views). It turns out that the answer to the first problem casts light on this one as well.

On the first issue, then, the actual is what is or has been in the actual world. But what is the objectively potential? Scotus says things that suggest one or other of two quite different options, one very narrow, one very broad. The very narrow option would make the objectively potential that which is not but will be in the actual world. Call this (ever-changing) group of things 'O'. This option gives us a straightforwardly temporal interpretation of the modal term. The very broad option would make the objectively potential O along with anything caused in any non-actual but possible world—construing 'possible world' in the modern sense, as any maximal non-contradictory state of affairs. Call this (ever-changing) group of things 'P'. Let the set of Scotus's broadly metaphysically possible essences, co-extensive with being, be 'M'. On the narrow view, $M = A + O$; on the broad view, $M = A + P$.[30]

It is not possible to solve the first of these problems decisively simply on the basis of Scotus's own reflections on the nature of objective potency.[31] What I will do is present the evidence on the two sides, first in favour of identifying the objectively potential as P (i.e. that which is not but that will be in the actual world, along with anything caused in any non-actual but possible world—again, construing 'possible world' in something like our modern sense; this is the very broad sense of 'objectively potential' just mentioned).

First, Scotus's main argument in favour of objective potency, outlined at the end of the previous section, appeals to divine power. And this immediately suggests the broader interpretation of metaphysical potency just adumbrated: on the face of it, God's causal power ranges over infinitely many possible natures. Thus, Scotus holds that the scope of God's power ranges over what can be expressed by propositions with logical potency: and the constraint on such propositions is merely semantic consistency. So, the argument seems to require that all of these have objective potency

---

[30] The options are made clear in the right-hand branch in Figure 1.
[31] Santogrossi notes this fact, but offers no further comment: see Santogrossi 1993: 63.

too. If they did not, God could only create what he creates—which Scotus would believe to be false.

Furthermore, secondly, the definition of 'being' as 'that to which existence is not repugnant' likewise suggests that it is internal consistency—lack of internal contradiction or semantic incompatibility—that is at stake. Again, this seems to require that the objectively potential is P, not O.

Indeed, thirdly, elsewhere Scotus is explicit that having being metaphysically possible in Scotus's broad sense is antecedent to objective potency, suggesting that the internal coherence of an essence is something distinct from, and prior to, its possessing objective potency, supposing it to possess objective potency:

> Neither should we think that [being something—*esse aliquid*] is not repugnant to man because it is a being in potency, and is repugnant to chimera because it is not a being in potency; rather, it is the other way round, because it is not repugnant to man, therefore it is possible by logical potency, and because it is repugnant to chimera, therefore it is impossible by the opposed impossibility. And objective potency follows this possibility, and this if we suppose the omnipotence of God, which regards every possible thing (while that is other of itself), even though this logical possibility, absolutely, from its own notion, can stand even though *per impossibile* no omnipotence relates to it.[32]

The broadly metaphysically possible (in Scotus's sense) corresponds to the logically possible (in his sense): there are true propositions about every metaphysically possible essence, and these propositions are all logically possible. The idea in this passage is that the broadly metaphysical and logical potency (in Scotus's senses) attaching to *man* is independent of, and prior to, a human being's having objective potency. Thus, it is not the case that *being* 'is repugnant to man because it is a being in potency'—which is to say because it can be the end term of a causal power. Rather, true propositions about *man* are logically possible because *man* is internally non-contradictory—because *man* has metaphysical potency in Scotus's broad sense. And what makes *man* causable—what explains its objective potency—is its being such as it is and belonging to the domain of being. Scotus maintains that these features belong to an essence quite independently of any causal considerations ("this logical possibility . . . can stand even though . . . no omnipotence relates to it").[33] This suggests that the

---

[32] *Ord.* I, d. 36, q. un., n. 61 (Vat. VI, 296).
[33] The impossibility involved here is not semantic; hence Scotus believes he can reason without deductive explosion: see Martin 2004.

constraints on the possibility of an essence are merely semantic, antecedent to any questions of causal powers and possibility. And I take it that the point about chimeras is not just that there are not, as a matter of fact, chimeras: it is that their existence is logically impossible in our sense. This argument, then, provides manifold reasons for holding that objective potency ought to attach to any causable essence whose being involves no internal contradiction. So P seems to be the correct interpretation.

This, incidentally, helps us understand the modality in the premise (P) of Scotus's argument for God's existence: it is not part of the nature of (e.g.) a human being that that being needs to be caused, but it nevertheless follows in some way from the nature, or somehow supervenes on it: there could not be a self-existent human being. Scotus thus accepts iterated modalities: it is necessary to the being in question that if it exists it is caused to exist: it is necessary that it has objective potency.

There is, however, a powerful argument in favour of identifying the objectively potential as O—the very narrow view of the objectively potential outlined above. Put very simply, Scotus says as much in the questions on the *Metaphysics* (and elsewhere). As Scotus generally understands the objectively potential, objective potency is a *relation* that has as its end term the (future) actually existent individual essence.[34] So what grounds objective potency is something actual: the actually existent individual essence. But on the face of it, relations cannot be free-floating: they must inhere in some entity. So there is a relation in what is potential—the relation of *being potential*—that has as its other *relatum* the *actual existent*. So the only items that have objective potency are those that are not but will be actual in the actual world. This explains the permissibility of quantifying over non-existents: their identity is fixed by their (future) actuality.

Now, the more-evident version of the argument requires that the objectively potential be identified as P. This is because in this argument M must comprise all actual and possible objects, where the modalities are construed in terms of semantic consistency. If the objectively potential is merely O, the scope of M is greatly diminished, and the restrictions on the possible are more than merely semantic. In other words, the *prima facie* sense of the *ex professo* discussion of modality in the Aristotelian questions is incompatible with the more-evident interpretation of the argument from *De primo principio*.

Suppose, then, that the less-evident version of the argument is the intended version. We can use this claim, in turn, to cast light on the

---

[34] See *QMet.* IX, qq. 1–2, n. 28 (OPh IV, 518).

second question, one that the discussion in the *Metaphysics* questions raises but leaves open: that of ontological commitment. Scotus considers two possible accounts of the reality of the objectively potential. The first includes the potential in the domain of being;[35] the second excludes it, maintaining that both the possible essence and the relation to the future actual existent are simply non-beings.[36]

Here is the first view, according to which the domain of being includes A along with the objectively potential:

> It should be understood that metaphysical potency taken precisely, namely, as it abstracts from every natural power, is founded precisely in the essence that is said to be possible, and is an order of that essence to existence as to its end term, just as in the essence of the Antichrist there is founded a potency to his existence. But this potency that is between two things can denominate both of them: one as the quasi-subject, and the other as the quasi-end-term . . . And the foundation is possible by a potency founded in it; and the end term is possible by the same potency, since the same [potency] is directed to the end term (*eadem est ad ipsum terminum*). But most properly and fully the whole is spoken of when it is said "the essence is a possible existent" or "can be," because then the relation of both of them is expressed. Whence this proposition "it is possible for this to be" expresses more than "this is possible," because the first includes the foundation and the end term.[37]

The idea is that objective potency is a relation had by a possible essence to its own future actualization. So here we have further clear evidence that the objectively potential is to be identified as O, and the domain of being thus comprises A + O. We can speak about it in two ways: as a relation had by the essence to its existence (at some time distinct from that at which it exists; and supposing an actually existing thing to be in some sense a composite of the individual essence and its existence); and as the potency of the actually existing object—the whole thing. In this case, 'of', in "potency of," should be construed as what has the actually existing object as the end term of the relation—clearly, the whole point of the discussion is that the actually existing object cannot be the *subject* of any such relation, since actuality and potency are contradictorily opposed.

Scotus is happy to quantify over non-existent particulars, provided that those particulars are related in the way described to actually existent

---

[35] See ibid., n. 27 (OPh IV, 518–519).
[36] See ibid., n. 35 (OPh IV, 522–523). I represent the first view in Figure 1, and the second in Figure 2.
[37] Ibid., n. 27 (OPh IV, 518–519).

particulars—i.e. to *themselves* at some time later at which they exist. As he puts it elsewhere, following a suggestion from Averroes, there is a sense in which actual existence "increases perfection, but not multitude:"[38] we can think of something's coming into existence as that thing's having first potential existence and then actual existence.[39] So here quantification over *possibilia* requires a relation to their future selves, so to speak.

The second view, the one that excludes the objectively potential from the domain of being, seems to me to be more problematic, despite its ontological parsimony:

> In another way, it is said that being in potency is simply speaking non-being, and consequently that a relation founded in it is simply a relation of reason.
>
> And the division of being into being-in-act and being-in-potency is as it were a division by contradiction—not simply speaking, because then being-in-potency would be convertible with non-being, and would be said of the impossible. But just as a privation does not imply more entity than a negation does, even though it is a negation contracted to a subject (and thus division by having [*habitum*] and privation is by some kind of contradiction), so in the case at hand being-in-potency does not imply anything other than a certain non-being—namely, that which being can come after (*succedere*).
>
> And we should understand that as it were the same thing comes after itself— as it were that it first founds the potency, and then is the end term of a power—even though this is merely according to the intellect that conceives of the same thing. For when there is nothing in reality, there is nothing the same or different, since these things [viz. the same and different] are differences of being. In this way, therefore, a difference of being (to the extent that a being is conceived) determines to itself a conceived essence as foundation, which thing, the same thing, will be later on, whereas non-being, whether in reality or in the intellect, does not determine any subject. And to this extent being-in-potency is more a being than the negation of being is, just as a privation seems to be more a being than negation is. Whence privation is said to be the end term of a natural movement, and negation not. Thus being is understood to come after being-in-potency, and not after non-being absolutely, according to those who posit that an essence has no entity at all other than when it exists actually.[40]

There is no relation of objective potency on this view, and items lacking actual being are simply speaking nothing—they do not belong in the

[38] Averroes, *In Met.* VIII, com. 15 (Iunt. VIII, 224aA).
[39] Scotus, *Lect.* II, d. 12, q. un., n. 63 (Vat., XIX, 93); see too n. 59 (Vat., XIX, 92).
[40] *QMet.* IX, qq. 1–2, n. 35 (OPh IV, 522–523).

domain of being, and are parasitic on nothing. Saying that the relation of objective potency is "a relation of reason" means simply that the future item can be thought of. So the modal world here is very different from what we have seen thus far: the whole domain of being—that to which existence is not repugnant—is identified as the actual; the objectively potential is simply non-being, a subdivision of a category that also includes *impossibilia*. Thus, claiming that "the division of being into being-in-act and being-in-potency is as it were a division by contradiction" is just a way of saying that being-in-potency falls outside the scope of *being*; "as it were" because the domain of non-being includes not only being-in-potency but also *impossibilia*. There is no difference in ontological thickness between being-in-potency and the impossible. But they are differently related to the actual—since the one does and the other does not include the notion that it is followed, temporally, by being.

The third paragraph (the one beginning "And we should understand . . .") apparently affirms some difference in ontological thickness, but only if ontological thickness is construed in terms of the presence or absence of a possible relation (of reason) to some future existent. So it does not in fact contradict what Scotus has just said in the second paragraph. The "differences of being" that Scotus is talking about are relations of sameness or distinction: since the essences Scotus is talking about do not belong to the domain of being, we cannot truly say that they are either the same as or different from their future selves. We can, of course, think about the future existents, and to this extent, we can talk as though there are essences related to their future selves—even though there are not. And this is what Scotus means, I think, in the sentence beginning "In this way, therefore, a difference of being . . ."

If Scotus does intend to exclude the objectively potential from the domain of being, what does he think he should say about the metaphysical claim that underwrites the need for objective potency, namely, "It seems necessary to posit, for every active potency, some corresponding possible thing, because there is no active potency with respect to that which is not in itself possible," quoted above? Simply that objective potency belongs to some future thing, in principle identifiable. For a future thing to be causable, it is sufficient simply that the relevant future thing is not necessary, but will be: "The relation [of causing] is a relation of reason, and it suffices that there correspond to it a relation of reason."[41]

---

[41] Ibid., n. 37 (OPh IV, 523).

Scotus says that this more parsimonious view "is probable, and maximally so if it is posited that essence and existence differ merely in reason."[42] This has led some commentators to suppose that Scotus accepts this second view.[43] But I think there is good reason to doubt this. The term 'probable' simply means that there are plausible arguments for it—not that those arguments necessarily trump those for the opposite position. And Scotus himself does not accept the view that essence and existence differ merely in reason.[44] But as well as undercutters, there are rebutters for this view. First of all, the Averroes-inspired passage that I just mentioned seems to be incompatible with it. (But the passage is early; so perhaps Scotus changed his mind between that passage and the apparently very late book IX of the *Metaphysics* questions.) Secondly, the view is incompatible with the modal framework required for the argument for God's existence, supposing the less-evident interpretation is the correct one. For the second view, the objectively potential is not included in the scope of *being*. So as stated premise (P) would be false—indeed, it would be flatly contradictory, because the domain of being is restricted to what is actual, and (P) is about the objectively potential. It would need to be re-formulated as "some individual-nature can be caused." (C1) could stand, but it would be understood not *de possibili* but *de facto*—contrary to Scotus's express intention—since the domain of being includes only the actual. The modal argument would thus be reducible to the non-modal one. So, this less-evident reading of Scotus's argument for the existence of a first cause (the one that interprets the modalities in the argument in line with objective potency, not metaphysical potency in the broad sense), if correct, would show us that the second view in the questions on Aristotle's *Metaphysics*, book IX, qq. 1–2 is not Scotus's own, and that he accepts the first.

One disadvantage of the less-evident interpretation is that the argument does not get us a God whose existence is sufficiently grounded, from a modal point of view. The modalities Scotus employs do not get him a non-contingent God (in our sense). But as the discussion in the *Metaphysics* questions makes clear, Scotus is a modal pluralist, and he has the resources to allow for God's being a necessary existent in something like our sense.

---

[42] Ibid., n. 36 (OPh IV, 523).

[43] Marrone 1996: 188; Boler 1996: 153, and Santogrossi 1993: 74, are agnostic. But note that Marrone's view presupposes that the text is early, and that Scotus later (in his *Sentences* commentaries) accepts the second theory: both claims that are false.

[44] See Cross 2013.

But if the less-evident interpretation is correct, this is not the modal notion operative in the argument for the existence of a first cause. We have to look elsewhere for a stronger account of divine necessity in Scotus: specifically, in his account of God's essence as identical with his *esse*. I have dealt with this identification elsewhere.[45]

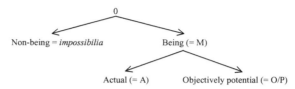

Figure 1   (*QM* IX, qq. 1-2, n. 27)

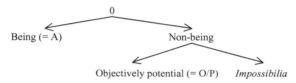

Figure 2   (*QM* IX, qq. 1-2, n. 35)

[45] See Cross 2013. Versions of this chapter were read at the Princeton philosophy department colloquium, the Franciscan University of Steubenville (as the annual St Edith Stein Lecture), the 2018 Boulder Medieval Philosophy Conference, and a 2018 conference on late Scholasticism held at the Notre Dame London Centre. I am grateful to many for helpful comments and questions, including Robert Adams, Mark Johnston, Peter King, Lukáš Novák, Chris Shields, and Paul Symington.

CHAPTER 3

Duns Scotus on essential order in *De Primo Principio* and elsewhere

Thomas M. Ward

I ESSENTIAL ORDER, AT HOME AND ABROAD

In his magisterial work of natural theology, *De Primo Principio* (*DPP*), Duns Scotus describes a species of order he calls *essential order* before putting essential orders to heavy use in a series of dense arguments which purport to establish that there exists a first efficient cause, a first final cause, and a most eminent being, and that these three are one and the same: the divine essence.[1] Essential orders are deployed more frequently, more centrally, and are characterized more systematically in this treatise than in any other part of Scotus's *opera*.[2] For this reason, it makes good methodological sense to turn to *DPP* to get the skinny on what Scotus means by essential order. But, Scotus frequently turns to essential order in other aspects of his theological and philosophical work. Some of these uses of essential order give us a fuller picture of this central concept in Scotus's metaphysical toolbox. So in this essay, I explicate some key aspects of essential order, making use (mostly) of *DPP*, along with some other important texts.

In addition to offering a general outline of essential order, I argue for three main theses. First, from Scotus's claim that it is *contradictory* that something posterior in an essential order of dependence should exist without its prior, I think one of two results follow, both of which would be unwelcome to Scotus on other grounds: *either* the divine essence is the only essence on which any creaturely essence essentially depends *or* some creatures really are essentially prior in an essential order of dependence to other creaturely essences, and therefore God cannot actualize any

---

[1] *DPP* is generally assumed to be a very late work. Likely it is a compilation of writings taken from *Ord.* I. For discussion, see the introduction to Duns Scotus, *DPP* (Wolter, ix–xiii). I use Wolter's text in this essay.

[2] Pithy treatments of essential orders in *DPP* may be found in King 2003: 38–42; Adams 2010; Cross 2005: 21–28.

creaturely essence without also actualizing every other creaturely essence essentially prior to it.

Second, I argue that while *DPP* does not offer an explicit definition of *essential* order, it does strongly *imply* that to be an essential order is to be an order which obtains among its *relata* in virtue of their essential features *only*, and I discuss a non-*DPP* text which confirms and makes explicit that this is indeed what it is to be an essential order. Third, I argue that based on Scotus's use of essential order in a non-*DPP* text, there is at least one type of essential order which is not listed in the inventory of types of essential orders given in *DPP*.

II ESSENTIAL ORDER IN DPP

II.1 *Properties of being*

Scotus opens his little book with a prayer, seeking, like his theological forebear, Anselm, a powerful argument for God's existence (*DPP* I.1–2).[3] He postulates that focusing on the *passiones entis* is a helpful way forward and identifies essential order as among the *passiones entis* (I.3). These "properties of being" are special insofar as they characterize any being whatsoever, whether actual or merely possible. Some of these properties are well-known transcendentals such as truth and goodness.[4] Others, however, are the so-called disjunctive transcendentals, which are transcendentals that come in pairs, F or G, such that for any being, x, (Fx or Gx) and not (Fx and Gx).[5] Perhaps the most famous of the disjunctive transcendentals is "finite or infinite," which divides all being with creatures on the left and God on the right.[6]

Scotus identifies essential order as one of the disjunctive transcendentals (I.3) since any being is either essentially ordered to another being or it is that to which another being is essentially ordered. Thus, every being stands in a relation of essential order to at least one other being. (Ultimately, Scotus holds that every being stands in a relation of essential order to every other being, but this does not follow merely from the fact that essential order is a disjunctive transcendental.) For reasons which, I presume, are supposed to become clear only by the end of the book,

---

[3] Hereafter, for the sake of brevity, whenever I cite *DPP*, I will give the chapter number and paragraph number in parentheses, for example (I.1–2).
[4] *Ord.* I, d. 8, p. 1. q. 3, n. 114 (Vat. IV, 206).   [5] *Ord.* I, d. 39, qq. 1–5, n. 13 (Vat. VI, 414).
[6] Helpful studies include Aertsen 2012: 371–432; King 2003: 26–28; Wolter 1946: 82–89.

essential order is deemed the "more fruitful" way of deriving a conclusion for God's existence (I.3).

II.2   *The relation of essential order*

In *DPP*'s order of exposition, the divisions and types of order are given before the definition of the relation of order. It may seem problematic to make these distinctions before giving the reader a sense of what it is that is being divided, but Scotus tells us very early that, whatever else order is, it is a relation by which things are arranged with regard to *priority* and *posteriority* (I.5), such that if two things, A and B, are *ordered*, then A is prior to B and B is posterior to A, or B is prior to A and A is posterior to B. But priority and posteriority alone clearly underdetermine the relation of order. Not every instance of priority and posteriority counts as an order, still less as an essential order. For example, temporal relations (e.g., before, after, simultaneous) and quantitative relations (e.g., greater than, less than) involve relations of priority and posteriority but are not relations of order, in the intended sense.

Additionally, the relation of order is irreflexive (II.2), asymmetrical (II.4), and transitive (II.6). It is an interpretive question whether these properties *define* the relation of *essential* order or merely order. In favor of these three properties being definitive of essential order (such that some relation R is an essential order if and only if R is irreflexive, asymmetrical, and transitive) is that after listing these properties in II.2–7, Scotus turns his attention, starting in 2.8, to proving various theorems about individual types of *essential* orders and about relations between types of essential orders. The irreflexive-asymmetrical-transitive trio presented in II.2–7 therefore appears in context to be all Scotus has to say by way of definition of essential order *as such*.

Against this reading, however, is that Scotus evidently thinks that some instances of *order* exhibit these three properties and yet are not *essential orders*. This is clear from the distinction between accidentally ordered causes and essentially ordered causes, a distinction drawn in III.9–11. Scotus tells us there are three differences between these two types of causal series. A and B are essentially ordered causes of some effect C if and only if (i) A is the cause of B's causing of C, (ii) A is prior to B in the order of eminence, and (iii) A's causing B's causing is simultaneous with B's causing C (III.11). If A and B fail to satisfy (i), (ii), and (iii) in their joint causing of effect C, they would constitute an accidentally ordered series. But even if merely accidentally ordered, it would still be the case that

A could not be its own cause (irreflexivity), that if A is a cause of B, then B is not a cause of A (asymmetry), and that if A is a cause of B and B is a cause of C, then A is a cause of C (transitivity).

The evidence from Scotus's discussion of accidentally ordered causes seems to me compelling in favor of the reading of II.2–7 in a way in which, if Scotus defines anything, he defines only the relation of *order*, but not *essential order*. This means, however, that nowhere in *DPP* does Scotus define the relation of essential order as such.[7] We get rich and rigorous description of various types of essential orders and how they relate to each other, but no *definition* of the genus to which these various types belong.

II.3   The divisions and types of order

II.3.1   The order of eminence
Scotus makes four "divisions" of order, which result in seven types of order. Essential order may obtain in any of these seven types of order. The first division is between *eminence* and *dependence*. In an essential order of eminence which obtains among some pair, A and B, where A is prior to B, A is "more perfect and more noble" than B (I.7).

II.3.2   The order of dependence
In an essential order of dependence, B (the posterior) depends on A (the prior). In Scotus's explication of the essential order of dependence in I.8, he makes a subtle interpretation of (and, arguably, an innovation to) a notion of order he finds in Aristotle's *Metaphysics*. There, Aristotle identifies a type of priority and posteriority in which A can *exist* without B but B cannot *exist* without A (*Metaphysics* V, 1019a2–4). On Scotus's reading, dependence relations may obtain even if A (the prior) *cannot in fact exist* without B (the posterior). A, reasons Scotus, may produce its effect, B, necessarily. In this case, A could not exist without B. But an order of dependence may nevertheless obtain among A and B, if B depends on A and not the other way around. But if A and B go together, so to speak, no matter what, then we cannot include *ability to exist without the other* in a definition of *what it is* for A to be prior in the order of dependence to B.

Scotus, therefore, says instead that the mark of dependence is that, without A, B's existence "includes a contradiction" while, without B, A's existence does not include a contradiction, and these logical modalities hold whether or not B's existence follows (metaphysically) necessarily

---

[7] Michael Gorman noticed this omission in Gorman 1993.

from A's existence, such that in fact A (metaphysically) could not exist without B (I.8).

It is not clear to me what are the full ramifications of Scotus's view that B's existence and A's nonexistence include a contradiction, while A's existence and B's nonexistence do not include a contradiction (even if, metaphysically, necessarily, if A exists, then B exists). But, it's worth saying at least a bit about these ramifications. To "include a contradiction" is in Scotus's terminology to be logically impossible, and to be logically impossible is for two or more things (things in the broadest possible sense) to stand in relations of *repugnance* to each other. Relations of repugnance (and non-repugnance as the case may be) obtain independent of any causal power, including God's. Scotus elsewhere offers white and black as examples of repugnant things; presumably, these are repugnant because no subject can be white and black at once in the same way.[8] Why this repugnance obtains is mysterious. The point that needs to be made here, however, is that whatever explanation there might be for the repugnance of white and black, that explanation emphatically is *not* that there is no causal power which can cause white and black to compose a unity. Instead, the reason why no causal power can unite these is that they are, formally, of themselves, repugnant, un-unitable.

Thus, returning to the dependence of B on A, we can say that Scotus's interpretation of Aristotle here makes dependence relations (or, at least, the dependence relations most relevant to the task of *DPP*) fully explicable in the order of essences, rather than existence. This is crucial for the success of the God-arguments of *DPP*. In chapter III, after the essential-order framework has been explicated to a satisfactory level of detail in chapters I and III, Scotus announces that his God-arguments will reason from premises about the possible rather than the actual since all true (non-tensed) propositions about the possible are *necessary*, while true propositions about (contingent) actual things are only contingently true (III.6). Unlike Aquinas in his famous Five Ways, Scotus's arguments in *DPP* do not rely on the actual existence of any concrete thing; instead, they rely on relations of repugnance, non-repugnance, and entailment, which obtain necessarily among essences. Therefore, whatever else may be the case about an order of dependence, we can say that *dependent on A* is included in or entailed by *what it is to be* B, whereas *that on which B depends* is neither included in nor entailed by *what it is to be* A – even if, given the existence of A, the existence of B follows.

---

[8] *Rep.* I-A, d. 43, q. 1, n. 23 (Wolter and Bychkov, II, 527).

II.3.2.1   Non-causal dependence

The second division of order is a division of the order of dependence: *causal dependence* and *non-causal dependence* (I.9). The third division of order is a division of the order of non-causal dependence into two: proximate non-causal dependence and remote non-causal dependence (I.13). The fourth and final division is a division of the order of causal dependence into four: final causality, efficient causality, formal causality, and material causality (I.15). The four divisions yield seven types of order:

1.   Order of eminence
2.   Order of proximate non-causal dependence
3.   Order of remote non-casual dependence
4.   Order of final causal dependence
5.   Order of efficient causal dependence
6.   Order of formal causal dependence
7.   Order of material causal dependence.

In the summary of chapter I, Scotus confusingly says that the investigation has yielded six types of order, where the two types of non-causal dependence are counted as one (I.16). I do not know why he did this.

II.3.2.1.1   Proximate non-causal dependence   In general, an order of non-causal dependence obtains among two things, A and B, which are non-causally related to each other but which are causally related, proximately or remotely, to some one common cause, C, which is a (proximate or remote) cause of A and a (proximate or remote) cause of B. In an order of *proximate non-causal dependence*, C is a cause of A and C is a cause of B, and C could not cause B unless C first caused A. A is therefore prior in the order of non-causal dependence to B because A is not a cause of B but A's existing is a necessary condition for B's existing. This relation can be helpfully illustrated in the following figure:

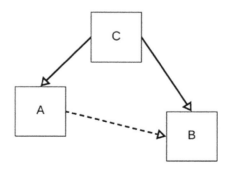

The solid arrows represent causal dependence of the lower (A and B) on the higher (C), and the dashed arrow represents a proximate non-causal dependence of B on A. Scotus himself offers at least one example of an order of proximate non-causal dependence. When some efficient cause (C) produces some material substance, that material substance receives both a quantitative form (A) and a qualitative form such as a color form (B). A color form does not causally depend on a quantitative form, but being quantified is (let us assume, plausibly) a necessary condition for being colored (II.36).

II.3.2.1.2 *Remote non-causal dependence*   In an order of *remote non-causal dependence*, D is a cause of A and D is a cause of C, and C is a cause of B, and C could not cause B unless D first caused A. A is therefore prior in the order of non-causal dependence to B because A is not a cause of B but A's existing is a necessary condition for C's causing B. This relation can be helpfully illustrated in the following figure:

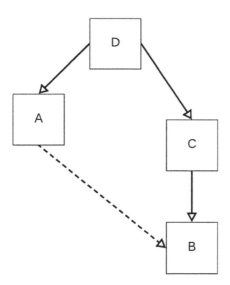

Here, the solid arrows represent causal dependence of the lower on the higher (A and C on D and B and C on D), and the dashed arrow represents a remote non-causal dependence of B on A. Scotus does not give an example of a remote non-causal dependence, but we can concoct one which is in the spirit of his example of a proximate non-causal dependence. When some efficient cause (D) produces a material substance, that material substance receives both a quantitative form (A) and a qualitative form such as a form of color (C). In the presence of a subject which has the appropriate sensory power, a colored object causes the presence of the "species" or representation of color (B) in the sensory organs of the sensing subject.[9] Since the color (C) of the substance could not exist without the quantity (A) of the substance, and since the color of the substance causes the color species (B) in the sensitive subject, we can say that B is both causally dependent on C and non-causally dependent on A. The non-causal dependence of B on A is, in this case, remote rather than proximate, simply because while both A and B are effects of D, B is an effect of D further down the causal chain than A.

II.3.2.2   Causal dependence

The four types of causal dependence correspond to the four types of Aristotelian causes: final, efficient, formal, and material (I.15). The four relations of order corresponding to these four causes are as follows:

1.   Final cause/thing ordered to an end (*finitum*)
2.   Efficient cause/thing brought about (*effectum*)
3.   Material cause/thing made of matter (*materiatum*)
4.   Formal cause/thing formed (*formatum*)

In each case, the cause is prior and the effect is posterior. This point may seem trivial, but in the case of final causality, this leads to an innovative view about how an end can be a cause. An end can be a cause, according to Scotus, only if it is *loved* by some intelligent agent and, so loved, "moves" the intelligent agent to effect that end; or, more perspicuously, the end is a cause if and only if it is among the intelligent agent's *reasons* for efficiently causing some effect which is specifically similar to that end (II.14–18).[10]

The material and formal causes are called *intrinsic* causes because they cause a thing precisely by being parts of it (II.26). The final and efficient causes are called *extrinsic* causes since any final- or efficient-caused thing is not a final or efficient cause of itself (II.26).

Scotus tells us that any material substance essentially depends on at least one cause in each type of cause and that the four causes are themselves

---

[9] Scotus, *Ord.* I, d. 3, p. 3, q. 1, n. 334 (Vat. III, 202), cited in Pasnau 2003: 289.
[10] See also the important discussion in *QMet.* V, q. 1 (OPh III, 395–411).

essentially ordered in their joint production of a material substance: the final cause moves the efficient cause to give form to matter (II.33). For this reason, the *finitum, effectum, materiatum,* and *formatum* are one and the same substance, where each term picks out the substance in relation to one of its four (types of) causes. Note that the *cooperation* of the four causes in their production of a single effect must be one of the *non-causal* essential orders of dependence since each type of cause has a different sort of causality, and therefore, they do not compose a *causal series* when they produce their joint effect. This is the point of Scotus's distinction between causes which are essentially ordered in their causing, on the one hand, and, on the other hand, essentially ordered things which are causes (II.33). The four causes are essentially ordered in the latter way. The efficient causal and final causal series which Scotus eventually argues terminate in God are essentially ordered in the former way.

Not every causal dependence is essentially ordered in this former way. As we have already had occasion to note (Section II.2), Scotus distinguishes between essentially ordered causal series and accidentally ordered causal series. Both sorts of series equally satisfy the conditions for order, but an essentially ordered series meets three additional criteria. To repeat what was mentioned in Section II.2, A and B are essentially ordered causes of some effect C if and only if (i) A is the cause of B's causing of C, (ii) A is prior to B in the order of eminence, and (iii) A's causing B's causing is simultaneous with B's causing C (III.11). It follows from this that a series of essentially ordered causes really is a series *only* of *causes*: if A is in an essentially ordered causal series with B, then A is the cause of *B's causing*, not (*qua* member of essentially ordered series of causes) B as such. In our example, C would not be part of the series of essentially ordered causes which comprises A and B, and this is because (in the example) C is the terminus of the series – it is C, and not C's causing (e.g., some further term, D) which is the joint effect of A's causing B's causing. Of course, C is still essentially ordered to A and B, as *effectum* to efficient causes (or *finitum* to final cause, as the case may be). In short, the series A-B is a series of causes which are essentially ordered in their causing, while the series A-B-C is a series of essentially ordered things, two of which are causes.

II.4   *The relata of essential order*

One interpretive challenge of *DPP* concerns exactly what are the *relata* of essential orders. Given that essential order is identified early on as a property of being (I.3), and therefore, the essentially prior and the essentially posterior disjunctively transcend all being, we should expect that *anything whatsoever*, taking *thing* in the broadest possible sense, is essentially ordered in at least one way to at least one thing distinct from it. And this is, in fact, the case, as it turns out. However, there are two complicated moments elsewhere in *DPP* worth thinking about in connection with the question about the *relata* of essential order.

The first focuses only on essential orders of causal dependence. Here there appears to be an inconsistency between the *relata* given in Scotus's introduction of the four types of causal essential order (I.15) and the *relata* given in Scotus's later distinction between essentially and accidentally ordered causal series (III.9–11). In I.15, the essential order is between cause and effect, for example, between the efficient cause and its *effectum*. But, in III.11, the essential order is between cause and cause, or, strictly, between a cause and another cause's causing. Here, the appearance of inconsistency can be resolved if we simply take all essentially ordered causal series as instances of the canonical cause/effect division, where *causings* are the *relata* of the series. An essentially ordered series of causes orders things' causings and only things' causings. Thus, in an essentially ordered series A–B–C–D, where A–B–C are essentially ordered in their causing, A's causing B's causing's C's causing is the causal series which brings about D, where A's causing is a cause (of B's causing C's causing) but not an effect, B's causing is both a cause (of C's causing) and an effect (of A's causing), and C's causing is an effect (of A's causing B's causing). Therefore, there is no inconsistency between I.15 and III.9–11 on the question of the *relata* of essential orders of causal dependence.

The second complication focuses on the beginning of Scotus's argument for a first efficient cause. Scotus says that his goal, here in chapter III, is to demonstrate that in the three essential orders of efficient causality, final causality, and eminence, there is "some one *nature* which is simply first" (III.3, my emphasis). The first theorem of III.4 is given a few lines down: "Some *nature* among beings can produce an effect" (III.4, my emphasis). The proof of the theorem argues that if something can be produced, then something can be productive; but something can be produced; therefore, something can be productive. In his proof of the antecedent, he asserts that something is contingent and glosses contingency as being "possible to exist after not existing." But anything which exists after not existing exists because of something other than itself since it is not the case that there is a contingently existing x but no existing y such that y causes x. Therefore, something can be productive (III.5).

In the following paragraph (III.6), Scotus makes clear the significance of his use of "nature" in the first theorem and its proof. In his God-arguments, he prefers not to rely on premises about *actual* contingent things, which are "evident" but not "necessary," but prefers instead to use premises and conclusions about the *possible* since these, if true, are necessarily true. Making natures the *relata* of the essential orders invoked in the God-arguments stays neutral between actually existing and merely possible things, allowing Scotus to argue from "some nature is producible" to "there actually exists a nature which is the first efficient cause" (III.18).

The details of this or the other two "primacy" arguments need not detain us here. The point is that Scotus's argumentative strategy demands that the *relata* of essential orders are natures rather than concrete things. Given the way Scotus actually deploys, in chapter III, the apparatus of essential order developed in chapters I and II, it is plausible to think that not just in the God-arguments but anywhere there is essential order, the *relata* are natures and not *concreta*. Where actually existing things are essentially ordered, plausibly it is an order which obtains because of the *natures* of the actually existing things—perhaps what makes these *essential* orders is that they are orders due to essence or nature. On this broad picture, when concrete things are in essential orders, they are there not *qua concreta* but because they are attached, so to speak, to the natures they instance.

This is speculative, of course, but the speculation is grounded a bit by the consideration that essential orders of eminence explicitly obtain among natures (essences) (I.7). Natures or essences are not explicitly identified as the *relata* of essential orders of dependence, but reading the *relata* of these essential orders of dependence in this way helps to make some sense out of a difficult passage considered earlier. In I.8, Scotus says that what is posterior to the prior in an essential order of dependence may or may not follow necessarily from the prior, but whether it does or not, positing the prior without the posterior includes no contradiction whereas positing the posterior without the prior does include a contradiction. Earlier on, I reasoned on Scotus's behalf that this use of the language of contradiction suggests that Scotus is trying to make essential orders of dependence fully explicable independent of the causal power of actually existing things. Given this project, it makes sense that the *relata* of essential orders of dependence, like essential orders of eminence, would obtain among natures, or among concrete things insofar as they instance the natures they do. This interpretation of Scotus finds support in *QMet.* VII, q. 1, n. 17, where Scotus says that the essential order of an accident to a substance is founded on the essences (quiddities) of each, and not their concrete instances. This interpretation is also the view we find in *Quodl.*, q. 19, which I discuss later.

II.5   *Priority, posteriority, and contradiction*

Before leaving *DPP* behind, I would like to offer an argument that Scotus's account of essential orders of dependence implies a startling result, one which Scotus himself would have been unlikely to welcome: for any x and for all y, if x is essentially dependent on y and y is not God, then not even God could produce x without producing y. Given *DPP*'s explication of the dependence of the posterior on the prior in terms of the *contradiction* which ensues if we posit the posterior without the prior (I.8), it seems to follow that, if everything in the world is essentially *dependently* ordered to everything in the world—as Scotus himself says at III.49—then anything at all to which God is prior in any essential order of dependence, but which is also posterior in any essential order of dependence to anything other than God, requires the existence of *every* created prior on which it depends, *on pain of contradiction*. This entails that if God wants to make a particular giraffe currently living at the Cameron Park Zoo, he must also make, on pain of contradiction, everything which is essentially prior, in any order of dependence, to that giraffe. This would leave only those things which God makes immediately, without any secondary causes, free to occupy other possible worlds without the baggage of essentially prior members of this world. This seems like a severe restriction on divine power.

I see no reason to *attribute* this view to Scotus; I only claim that it seems to *follow from* things Scotus says in *DPP* I.8. If in fact it does *not* follow, I think it would be for roughly the following reasons. Return to our particular giraffe. Since it exists in the actual world and is not itself a First (uncaused) Cause, we know that it is essentially dependent on at least one prior term in an essentially ordered efficient causal series. But remember, the *relata* of essential orders are not, strictly speaking, actual things but the *essences* of actual things. So we need to be very careful in identifying what it is exactly upon which the giraffe is essentially dependent. And we need to be very careful in identifying what exactly about the giraffe makes the giraffe essentially dependent upon whatever it is essentially dependent upon. Given that essences are the *relata* of essential orders, we may be forced to say something like this: in a highly general sense, the giraffe is a *producible individual essence*, and this means it is essentially ordered to at least one *efficient cause*. But, at this highly general level, it does not follow that, say, the actual giraffe's actual parents are among its efficient causes. All we need, so to speak, to get this particular giraffe, is *some efficient cause or other* with power sufficient for bringing about this particular giraffe—actualizing this particular individual essence. And for all the *DPP* framework tells us, this could be some other giraffes, or an angel, or God directly. If so, then if we imagine this particular giraffe on the scene without having the particular giraffe parents it in fact has, we are *not* imagining something contradictory; we are in fact imagining some alternative route to the production of this particular giraffe. And in this case, the "startling result" I mentioned above would not in fact follow from the *DPP* framework.

Perhaps this is right. I confess I do not know. In favor of this reading which blocks the startling result is the obvious fact that Scotus would deny that God can make this particular giraffe only by making everything else by which he has in fact brought about this giraffe. Nevertheless, against this reading which blocks the startling result, I'd like to say that if this really is the teaching of the *DPP*—namely, that this giraffe is not essentially dependent on its parents strictly speaking but on any essence at all with power to produce this giraffe—then it is not clear to me how to identify any essential orders of dependence other than the essential dependence of all things (except God) upon God. Consider the giraffe. If it essentially depends not on its parents but on anything with giraffe producing power—which its parents in fact had but which many other things have or might have, and which God has necessarily—then the giraffe might turn out to be *essentially* dependent on just one thing, God, or God *insofar as* he is able to produce the giraffe. If it is essentially dependent on anything besides God, then of course it is still also essentially dependent on God. But I see no reason for supposing that it would in fact be essentially dependent on anything besides God. God, so to speak, is sufficient all on his own for the production of this giraffe, precisely under the aspect of—or the characterization of his essence as—able to produce this giraffe. If God in fact ropes in secondary causes to produce this giraffe, then this is a contingent fact about the world he decided to make, and not a necessary fact about what it would take to produce this giraffe. But somehow I don't think the *DPP* essential orders framework was intended to eliminate creaturely efficient causes from the realm of essential orders of efficient causal dependence.

III ESSENTIAL ORDER ABROAD

Leaving aside, unresolved, this question about Scotus's I.8 claim that the essentially posterior considered without the essentially prior includes a contradiction, I turn now to consider two non-*DPP* texts, one of which clarifies one unclear aspect of *DPP* and the other of which complicates the essential orders framework given in *DPP*.

III.1   Essential order in the Incarnation

In *Quodl.*, q. 19, Scotus asks whether the unity of Christ's human and divine natures consists in the dependence of the human nature on the Word (or the Son, the second person of the Christian Trinity of Father, Son, and Holy Spirit). His affirmative answer is that the human nature essentially depends on the Son and therefore the unity of the divine and human natures is a unity of order.

According to Scotus, the terms of this union are, properly speaking, an individualized human nature (and not a concrete human person) with the Son. The Son has numerically the same divine nature as the Father and the Holy Spirit, but each divine person has its own distinguishing, "incommunicable" feature, i.e., a feature which cannot in principle be in common between two or more things. So there is a question about how exactly this individualized human nature can be united with just the Son and not with the whole Trinity, or the divine nature itself.

Michael Gorman has offered a clear explication of Scotus's answer, which clarifies an important point about the *relata* of essential orders, and on which I here rely.[11] The gist of the answer is that, in hypostatic union, the individualized human nature and the Son stand in an essential order of dependence in which the human nature is dependent on the Son, but the Son is the prior *relatum* of this essential order of dependence in virtue of its incommunicable feature and not in virtue of the divine nature (and there is nothing else to the Son in virtue of which it could be the *relatum* of an essential order).[12]

An objector objects that the Son cannot be the term of an essential dependence in virtue of his incommunicable feature, because this feature is that in virtue of which the divine nature is concretized in the individual person

---

[11] Gorman 1993.
[12] *Quodl.*, q. 19, n. 3 (Vivès XXVI, 260–262); English translation in Duns Scotus, *God and Creatures*, nn. 10–11 (Alluntis and Wolter, 420–421).

of the Son, but essential orders have to do with essence.[13] The objection trades on the claim that essential order obtain only among (*inter*) essences.

Scotus's reply does not deny the crucial claim that essential orders obtain among essences. His move is to distinguish a narrow and broad sense of essential order, and argue that the Son can be the term of an essential order of dependence in the broad sense. In the narrow sense, essential order does indeed obtain only among essences. But in the broad sense, which Scotus also calls "*per se* priority," essential order may obtain both among quidditative and among hypostatic entities.[14]

As Gorman glosses the distinction, Scotus does not here deny that essential order obtains among essences or natures. Instead, the key move is to distinguish between communicable and incommunicable *essential* features and argue that, at least in a broad sense, even an incommunicable feature of a hypostasis (or concrete substance) can be that in virtue of which a thing stands in an essential order to some other thing. Consider the following distinction: on the one hand, the Son, who is incommunicable, is a term of an essential order; on the other hand, the Son, in virtue of his incommunicable feature, is a term of an essential order. Gorman's reading of Scotus sides with the latter. Gorman concludes, "Thus, something is in an essential order in the broad sense whenever it is in an ordering relation by virtue of some essential feature that it has [whether communicable or incommunicable]; it is in an essential order in the narrow sense whenever it is in an ordering relation by virtue of some *communicable* essential feature that it has."[15]

The upshot of the *Quodl.*, q. 19, deployment of essential order is that we get some confirmation about the speculative conclusion in Section II.4, above: a relation R is a relation of essential order if and only if R is a relation of order (a relation defined by irreflexivity, asymmetry, and transitivity) *which obtains among or in virtue of essences/natures*.

III.2   Essential order in human procreation

The second text to consider, in *Ord.* I, d. 3, p. 3, q. 2, introduces what appears to me to be a type of essential order additional to the seven types outlined in *DPP*. The topic of the question is whether the intellect is the

---

[13]   *Quodl.*, q. 19, n. 5 (Vivès XXVI, 265–266); English translation in Duns Scotus, *God and Creatures*, n. 19 (Alluntis and Wolter, 423).

[14]   *Quodl.* q. 19, n. 9 (Vivès XXVI, 469–470); English translation in Duns Scotus, *God and Creatures*, n. 29 (Alluntis and Wolter, 426).

[15]   Gorman 1993: 467, emphasis mine.

total cause of knowledge in the soul. Scotus thinks it is not, and develops his own view, which is, roughly, that the intellect and the object of understanding concur in the production of knowledge. In the context of explaining this concurrence, Scotus offers an example taken from human procreation.[16] The example is easier to explain than the topic it is designed to illustrate, so I concentrate on the example in order to show that Scotus recognizes an additional type of essential order not captured in *DPP*.[17]

In this text, Scotus distinguishes two types of essential orders. The first is straighforwardly an essential order of causal dependence: "a higher cause 'moves' a lower cause in such a way that the lower does not act unless moved by the higher."[18] The example here is the causality a human hand exerts when it moves a mortar and pestle to grind wheat.

The second type of essential order offered in this text is the one that interests us. In this type, "the higher does not move the lower, nor does it give the latter the power by which it moves."[19] Yet the higher and lower concur in the production of some effect. Consider a mother and father. Neither alone can produce offspring. Embryology as understood in Scotus's time held that the father contributes the seed and the mother contributes auspicious conditions for the seed to develop into a human fetus. Given this embryology, Scotus identifies the father as the more perfect agent in human procreation and the mother as the less perfect. Nevertheless, in an act of procreation, the mother does not receive her causality from the father, the way the mortar and pestle receive its motion from the hand. Moreover, the father cannot procreate all on his own. (The father's cooperation with the mother is not like God's cooperation with creatures in many creaturely effects, in which God *could* but *does not* produce the whole effect all by himself.) Instead, father and mother each contributes something without which the procreative effect would not come about. It is not merely the case that "two causes do the job better than could one cause alone."[20] Instead, the effect, a new human life, is a "more perfect" effect than either father or mother could produce on his or her own.[21] As Michael Fatigati says, "The mother and father could each

---

[16] For a similar use of the example, see *Lect.* II, d. 25. q. un., n. 73 (Vat. XIX, 254).
[17] *Ord.* I, d. 3, p. 3, q. 2, nn. 496–498 (Vat. III, 293–295). The entire distinction has been translated recently in Duns Scotus, *On Being and Cognition* (van den Becken).
[18] *Ord.* I, d. 3. p. 3. q. 2, n. 496 (Vat. III, 293–294); English translation in Duns Scotus, *On Being and Cognition* (van den Bercken, 225).
[19] Ibid.   [20] Pasnau 2003: 292.
[21] *Ord.* I, d. 3, p. 3. q. 2, n. 496 (Vat. III, 293–294); English translation in Duns Scotus, *On Being and Cognition* (van den Bercken, 225).

produce things apart from one another (chopped wood, cooked food), but nothing they produce apart from one another is quite as perfect as what they are able to cause *together* (a child)."[22]

Efficient (and final) causal series are very "top-down" in *DPP*. God's causing causes the causing of every created efficient (or final) cause all the way down to some creaturely effect which is not itself a causing. In this top-down way, efficient causes are always cooperating in the production of joint effects. The single example we have in *DPP* of causes cooperating for some joint effect in such a way that the causes are not themselves ordered top-down in a causal series, is the cooperation of the four causes in the production of a material substance. But in this instance, the four causes are not themselves causally ordered to each other. (Recalling an earlier distinction, discussed in Section II.3.2.2, above, they are essentially ordered things which are causes, but not causes which are essentially ordered in their causing.) But in Scotus's procreation example, it appears that we have two efficient causes which together produce a common effect, but which are not themselves essentially ordered in such a way that the prior (the father) is an efficient cause of the causing of the posterior (the mother). If there is any *DPP*-typical essential order here, it is an essential order of eminence: Scotus identifies the father as the "more perfect" cause than the mother. But a mere essential order of eminence is insufficient to explain their cooperatively efficiently causing a human life, nor does the text suggest that this order is sufficient.

I do not myself see a way of mapping this particular example of a causal essential order of dependence onto the framework of *DPP*. What I would like to suggest is that we have here a hybrid type of essential order of dependence. In a straightforward essential order of efficient causation, A and B produce their effect C by A's causing B's causing of C. But this does not obtain in the present example. In a straightforward essential order of *non-causal* dependence, A is essentially prior to B because their common cause C, must produce A in order to produce B. But in the mother-father-offspring case, it looks like we have a hybrid, in which the father's efficient causality stands in an essential order of efficient causation terminating in God, and the mother's efficient causality stands in an essential order of efficient causation terminating in God, and the father is essentially prior to the mother (at least in the order of eminence), but their joint effect, the offspring, is *efficient-causally* essentially ordered to both mother and father. With reference to the earlier figures used to represent essential orders of

---

[22] Fatigati 2013: 9. In the same vein, see Cross 2014: 128–131.

non-causal dependence, we could illustrate this hybrid case in the following way:

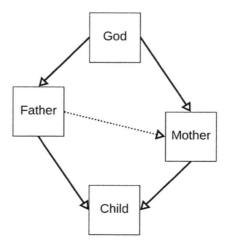

Recall that dashed arrows in the figures for non-causal dependence represented a non-causal dependence of the lower on the higher, while solid arrows represented a causal dependence of the lower on the higher. Here, the dotted arrow represents neither causal nor non-causal dependence. It is instead what we might call an *ordered co-causal dependence*, where the lower is posterior to the higher but both are required for the production of their joint effect. Despite the lack of causal dependence of one upon the other, the mother and father's joint production of their offspring offers no fundamental *counterexample* to the *DPP*'s top-down approach to efficient causality, insofar as mother and father each is connected up, ultimately, to God, in an essentially ordered efficient causal series which efficiently causes each parent's individual causal contribution to their joint offspring. Nevertheless, what this picture requires is a supplementation of *DPP*'s account of essential order, a type of essential order, represented by the thick arrow, which is not captured by any of the seven essential orders distinguished in *DPP*.

IV CONCLUSION

There are many other places in Scotus's *opera* in which he deploys essential order. Most of these are easily assimilable to the *DPP* framework. For example, Scotus argues that God is worthy to be loved the most because he is first in the essential order of eminence, and love (by nature) ought to be in proportion to the goodness of the lovable object.[23] He thinks the Church is essentially ordered to Christ in a way analogous to the world's essential orders to God and thinks each of the seven clerical orders of the Church is essentially ordered to the celebration of the Eucharist; these orders are plausibly construed as (at least) final causal orders.[24] He thinks that the body parts of a fetus, prior to that fetus's reception of an animal soul, compose efficient- and final-causal essential orders to each other and to the organism whose parts they will become.[25] And he thinks a human act of will is essentially ordered to the divine will, and this order is plausibly construed as an essential order of efficient causation.[26]

The two non-*DPP* examples of essential order I have considered here tell us something about essential order which we don't learn from *DPP*. The *Quodl.*, q. 19, text confirms and makes explicit something which is at best only implicit in *DPP*, namely that essential orders are orders which obtain among their *relata* due to essential features of the *relata*. And the *Ord.* I.3.3.2 text gives us a new, hybrid sort of essential order which cannot be explained fully in the terms of any of the seven orders distinguished in *DPP*.

---

[23] *Ord.* III, d. 27, q. un., n. 47 (Vat. X, 68–69).

[24] *Rep.* IV, d. 24, q. un., n. 14 (Wad. XI.2, 778; Vivès XXIV, 357). The text printed as *Rep.* IV in the Wadding and Vivès editions is currently being edited by Oleg Bychkov, who kindly shared his collation of mss of the text to confirm the authenticity of this part of Wadding's *Rep.* IV.

[25] *QMet.* VII.20.48. For an argument that efficient causing and final causing are the two orders which obtain here, see Ward 2014: 103–106.

[26] *Rep.* II, d. 37, q. 2, n. 6 (Wad. XI.1, 401; Vivès XXIII, 193–194).

CHAPTER 4

Duns Scotus on how God causes the created will's volitions

Gloria Frost

Medieval thinkers in the Christian, Jewish, and Islamic traditions believed that God's causality was all-pervasive.[1] God created everything which exists and his constant causal activity sustained his creatures in existence. Furthermore, medieval thinkers conceived of God's causality as supremely efficacious. His will was infallible and his power extended to all things possible. Nevertheless, it was standard in the medieval Christian tradition to deny that God was the *only* active cause. The majority of Christian figures held that creatures also had active causal powers through which they were agent causes of certain effects and events in creation.[2] When coupled together, these beliefs about God and creatures' causality led to a variety of interesting questions and debates.

One of the most fundamental questions regarded how divine causality relates to the very actions of created causes. Since God was considered an active causal source of all existents, it was believed that God must in some way actively cause the very actions of created causes. Yet, there was much debate about *how* God was a cause of creatures' actions. Did he cause creaturely actions in only a mediate way by sustaining the creatures who in turn acted solely through their own powers? Or did God more immediately cause creaturely actions by causally aiding creatures in eliciting their actions? The most interesting and controversial discussions centered upon the created will. Though there was much debate about how to understand the operation of the created will and the nature of its freedom, all agreed that in some respect the created will elicited its actions contingently. Thus, questions arose about how the operation of the created will could be both

---

[1] When possible I cite Scotus's texts from the Vatican edition.
[2] By contrast, many medieval Islamic thinkers defended occasionalism which denied active powers to creatures. See Perler and Rudolph 2000.

contingently caused by the creature and also caused by a God whose will cannot be impeded.

This chapter explores Duns Scotus's intriguing theories about how God causes creaturely volitions. Scotus's thought on this matter is particularly interesting because, as is widely recognized, he was committed to a robust understanding of the created will's freedom. In his celebrated account of the will's synchronic contingency, he argues that the will must retain the power to will the opposite of what it wills in the *very moment* when it elicits its volition.[3] In his view, freedom would be compromised if the will were only open to willing alternatives prior to its actually willing something. Furthermore, he maintained that the will caused itself to begin to will something new.[4] Unlike several others of his time, he rejected the view that the will was moved to its operation by an extrinsic cause. In light of his beliefs about the nature of the created will, Scotus struggled to figure out how God could be involved in causing the operation of such a spontaneously and autonomously operating cause. Throughout his career, he wrestled with two different theories about God's causation of created volitions. He ultimately could not make up his mind. Others have noted that, while Scotus accepted in his earlier works that God immediately produced the created will's volitions, he later doubted this view in favor of the position that God merely sustains the created will in being without directly producing its acts.[5] The goal of this chapter is to advance understanding of Scotus's shifting thoughts about God's production of the created will's actions. The chapter first provides some historical context for Scotus's discussion. Then it moves to Scotus's analysis of the main positions while tracking the developments in his thought. Though Scotus had reservations about how to best conceive of God's causation of the will's act, his discussion of this topic was nevertheless important in its own time and remains of enduring interest today. He went beyond others of his time by recognizing that there was more than one way in which the causality of a superior and inferior cause could be intertwined in the production of a joint effect. Scotus's main contribution lies in his development and analysis of alternative models of causal cooperation.

---

[3] See *Lect.* I, d. 39, qq. 1–5, n. 5, (Vat. XVII, 495); *Ord.* I, dd. 38–39, qq. 1–5, nn. 16–17, (Vat. VI, 417–419); *Rep.* I-A, dd. 39–40, qq. 1–3 n. 43 (Söder, 251). See Pickavé's chapter in this volume.
[4] Scotus provides the will as an example of a self-moving power in *QMet.*, q. 14, (OPh IV, 625–673).
[5] See Wolter 1994. In a previous paper, I suggested that Scotus's reservations about whether God immediately produces the actions of created causes may have led him to reject his early account of God's knowledge of contingents. See Frost 2010.

I EARLIER MODELS OF GOD'S CAUSAL COOPERATION WITH CREATURES

Late thirteenth- and fourteenth-century thinkers typically discussed God's causal cooperation with the created will in their commentaries on Book II, distinction 37 of the *Sentences* where Lombard asks whether the act of sin is from God insofar as it is an action.[6] To understand God's relationship to sinful actions, many thinkers first discussed God's causal relationship to all volitions and in some cases, created actions in general. Before turning to Scotus's own commentary on this distinction, it is useful to first see the landscape of positions which were debated in his time.

Lombard himself did not settle the question of the manner in which God was causally involved in producing acts of sin. One position which he entertained is "mere-conservationism" (MC). On this view, God merely sustains the creature in being while it actively and immediately causes its volition. Beyond sustaining the created cause and its power, there is nothing more which God does in the production of the volition. Though Lombard was open to MC, Bonaventure later reported that in his time (*i.e.* the mid-thirteenth century) the majority rejected MC. According to Bonaventure, the majority held that in addition to sustaining creatures and their powers in being, God also produced the very actions of created powers.[7] According to Bonaventure, no created power is sufficient to elicit its actions without some further causal help from God. He writes in his *Sentences* commentary (completed 1250–1252):

> For every *created power*, in so far as it is in itself, is *defective* and is not *purely active* : therefore, even in so far as it makes a small operation, it must necessarily have help from that power which is *pure act* on account of its being in every way unmixed with matter, and which alone suffices of itself and is in no way needing help from another cause. And for this reason that position which says that every action is from God, in so far as it is an action, must be held without any ambiguity.[8]

---

[6] Peter Lombard, *Sent.* I, d. 45, cap. 4 (II, 543–547). For reference to some disputed and quodlibetal questions on God's causal interaction with created causes, see Glorieux 1925: 345.

[7] Bonaventure, *In II Sent.* d. 37, a. 1, q. 1, "Utrum actio malitiae substrata sit a Deo" (*Opera omnia* II, 862).

[8] Ibid.: "Omnis etiam *potentia creata*, quantum est de se, *defectiva* est nec est *pure activa*: ergo quantumcumque faciat modicam operationem, necesse habet adiuvari ab ea potentia, quae est *actus purus* propter omnimodam impermixtionem cum materia, et quae sola sibi sufficit, nullo modo indigens iuvari a causa alia. Et ideo haec positio, quae dicit, omnem actionem esse a Deo, secundum quod actio est, absque omni ambiguitate tenenda est."

According to Bonaventure, no created power can elicit its operations by itself because created powers are by their very nature defective. Created powers are powers received in matter.[9] In Aristotelian philosophy, form is associated with act and active power, while matter is associated with passivity and receptivity for action. So, Bonaventure seems to suppose that since created powers are forms which inform matter, they are inherently defective. The only way they can elicit an operation is with the help of God's power. Since God's power is not received or limited by matter, it is an inherently different sort of power which is of itself sufficient for operation. I will refer to the position described by Bonaventure as the "augmentation of power" view (AP).

Albert the Great similarly claims that AP was the common view in the mid-thirteenth century. He writes in his Sentences commentary (completed 1249):

> Since the moderns had seen that it is more perfect to act than to exist (because that which is not of itself and not able to remain in being of itself, much less is able to act from itself); and since the sinful act according to its matter is simply an act arising from an active power perfected according to nature, they concluded, therefore, that it does not arise from the power unless it is moved by the first cause.[10]

Like Bonaventure, Albert maintains that created powers are intrinsically incapable of acting through themselves. Yet, he reasons to the conclusion by way of a different argument. He claims that since creatures do not exist through themselves we can be all the more certain that they are not able to act of themselves. Acting is a greater perfection than merely existing. So, we can be sure that just as creatures need God's assistance to sustain them in existence, they likewise require God's help to elicit their actions. Albert goes on to state that many thinkers of his time regarded MC as heretical. According to him, this was because they thought MC entailed that God was not the sole, unique source of all being. Created causes would also be sources of being in so far as they produced their operations in being without God's help.[11]

---

[9] Bonaventure maintained that even spiritual substances were composed of "spiritual matter" which like corporeal matter would cause a defect in power. See Sullivan 2010.

[10] Albert the Great, *In II Sent.*, d. 35, I, a. 7, "An omnis actus sit a Deo tam bonus quam malus" (Borgnet XXVII, 575): "Quia vero moderni viderunt, quod perfectius est agere quam esse, quod id quod non est a se, nec potest a se manere in esse, multo minus potest agere a seipso; et cum actus malus secundum conversionem ad materiam, sit simpliciter actus egrediens a potentia activa perfecta secundum naturam, ideo concluserunt, quod non egreditur ab ea nisi secundum quod movetur a causa prima. . ." I have modified Borgnet's punctuation accoding to modern standards.

[11] Ibid.: ". . . alioquin sequeretur duo principia esse, et haec est causa quare et alia opinio fere cessit ab aula et a multis modernorum reputatur haeretica." Giles of Rome similarly links the view that the

Aquinas likewise defended AP and one way in which he supports the position is by citing the impossibility of self-moving powers. Aquinas, like many others of his time, thought that it was contradictory for a power to initiate its own action. The central argument against self-moving powers went as follows: (1) Only a power which is in a state of act can change a power in a state of potency to a state of act and (2) only a power in a state of potency can be changed to a state of act. But (3) the same power cannot both be in potency and act at the same time, so (4) no power can move itself from potency to act, *i.e.* no power can be that which changes itself from not acting to acting.[12] In his *De Potentia* question about how God works in the operations of nature, Aquinas argues that one of the ways in which God causes the operations of created causes is by moving or applying them to their actions. He states that "[n]othing moves or acts through itself unless it is an unmoved mover."[13] He then goes on to explain how certain types of created causes are applied to their actions by higher types of created causes. To avoid an infinite regress, he thinks that the chain of creatures which are each in turn moved to their action by a prior created cause must terminate with God who is in actuality through himself and thus not moved to actuality by any prior cause.[14] Aquinas argued elsewhere that even the human will required an extrinsic cause to move it from not willing something to willing it.[15] Unlike other created causes, God did not move the will to act by moving other creatures which in turn moved the will. God moved the will directly.[16] According to Aquinas's view, one way God helps created powers to cause their actions is by moving them from a state of not acting to a state of acting.[17] In the passage quoted above, Albert similarly links God's production of created operations to his movement or application of created causes when he states that nothing arises from a created power "unless it is moved by the first cause."[18]

Though Bonaventure and Albert claim that in the mid-thirteenth century there is a majority consensus behind AP, at the end of the thirteenth century and in the early fourteenth century it was clear that

created will is the sole immediate cause of its act of sin with Manicheism: Giles of Rome, *II Sent.*, d. 37, q. 1. a. 3 (Ziletti, 551).
[12] See, for instance, Thomas Aquinas, *Summa theologiae* I, q. 2, a. 3.
[13] See *De Pot.*, q. 3, a. 7, (Pession, 20:) "Sed quia nulla res per se ipsam movet vel agit nisi sit movens non motum . . ."
[14] Ibid.   [15] See for instance *Summa theologiae* I-II, q. 9, a. 3.
[16] *Summa theologiae* I-II, q. 9, a. 6.
[17] In *De Pot.*, q. 3, a. 7, as well as other texts such as *Summa contra gentiles* III, 67, Aquinas identifies other respects in which God also causes creature's actions.
[18] See text quoted in note 10.

MC was still up for debate. Peter John Olivi was one prominent defender of MC who was known to Scotus.[19] Olivi thought that MC was the only theory of God's causality which secured the created will's freedom and moral responsibility. Yet, he also defended MC with respect to natural causes as well.[20] He denied that created powers were in need of help from God to operate beyond his sustaining them in being. For instance, he claimed that many natural powers were generated already "sufficiently applied to act."[21] Furthermore, Olivi did not think there was anything heretical about maintaining that creatures could operate without further assistance from God. Recall that Albert claimed that many of his contemporaries regarded MC as heresy since they thought it implied that there would be more than one source of being. Olivi, however, points out that even if God does not aid created causes in eliciting their acts, those actions and their effects nevertheless are entirely dependent on God's active causal power in virtue of his sustaining their causes in existence.[22] Were God to cease to sustain the creature or its power, everything which causally depends on the creature would likewise cease to be. With this background in place, we can turn to Scotus's own discussions of God's causation of creaturely actions. As we will see, Scotus gave serious consideration to MC in each of his discussions of God's causation of the created will's actions.

II SCOTUS'S ANALYSIS OF "MERE-CONSERVATIONISM" (MC)

As mentioned above, Scotus's most extensive treatment of God's causal involvement in creaturely operations occurs in his commentaries on Bk. II, d. 37. In all three of his commentaries, i.e. the *Lectura*, *Ordinatio*, and *Reportatio*, he raises a separate question on whether the created will is the total immediate cause of its volition.[23] An immediate cause of an effect *e*

---

[19] See Olivi, *In II Sent.*, q. 11, a. 6, "An Deus sit eius [i.e. peccatis] causa" (Jansen III, 333–347). For a recent discussion of Olivi's views, see Frost 2014.

[20] Henry of Ghent, who was well known to Scotus, defends MC regarding the created will's act in his *Quodl.* IX, q. 5 (Opera omnia XIII, 120–121, ll. 14–26); and *Quodl.* XII, q. 26 (Opera omnia XVI, 155–156, ll. 78–88).

[21] Olivi, *In II Sent.*, q. 11, a. 6, (Jansen III, 340): "... multae potentiae naturales sunt a sua creatione vel generatione sufficienter applicatae ad actum, ita quod non egent nisi solum praesentia patientis idonei."

[22] Ibid., p. 346: "Non enim minus indigent virtute et manutenentia primae causae illud quod exit mediate ab ea quam illud quod exit immediate. Unde ad cessationem totalis influxus Dei non minus deficerent a suo esse quam illa quae exeunt immediate."

[23] *Ord.* II, dd. 34–37, q. 5 (Vat. VIII, 408–447); *Lect.* II, dd. 35–37, q. 5 (Vat. XIX, 351–370); *Rep.* II-A, d. 37, q. 2 (Wad. XI.1, 400–405). It should be noted that some scholars believe that the

causes *e* directly and through itself (i.e. not in virtue of causing another cause which in turn causes *e*). By contrast, a mediate cause of *e* causes *e* in virtue of causing the existence of a distinct cause *c* which in turn causes *e* immediately. In effect what Scotus is asking is whether God is also an immediate cause of the created will's action together with the will itself. On AP, God is an immediate cause of the will's volition (and thus, the will is not the total immediate cause of its action) since God acts directly and through himself in the causal process through which the act of will is produced. By contrast, if the will is the *total* immediate cause of its action, then God can be only a mediate cause of that act in virtue of his sustaining the will in existence (MC).[24] We will see that Scotus identifies, along with AP, another model for how God might be an immediate cause of the will's volition. In each of his three treatments of the question, Scotus begins by considering the arguments in favor of MC.

There are two especially persuasive arguments for MC which Scotus repeats in the *Lectura, Ordinatio*, and *Reportatio*. The arguments aim to support MC by showing that the alternative is untenable. According to the arguments, if God were an immediate cause of the created will's act, then the created will would be robbed of its freedom and its ability to cause its act contingently.[25] The first argument assumes that at least part of what it is for a cause to be free with respect to an effect *e* is to have *e* in its power, i.e. the cause can control whether the effect is produced. To have some effect *e* in its power a cause must be able to produce *e* either by itself or in cooperation with other cause(s) which are under its control. The argument reasons that if MC is denied and it is instead maintained that God is an immediate cause of the will's volition, then the will would not have power over its volition. This is because God's causality would be required for its volition and the will has no control over God's exercise of causality.[26] Thus, it seems that God's immediate causality of the created will's act must be rejected in order to preserve that will's power over its act.

Wadding edition mistakenly prints William of Alniwck's *Additiones Magnae* for books I and II of the *Reportationes*. See Hechich 2008. The *Additiones* are believed to accurately reflect Scotus's thought and for especially crucial passages I also supply texts from the relevant manuscripts of the *Reportationes*. For scholarship on Scotus's position in these texts, see Frank 1992 and Wolter 1994. For a recent study which discusses Scotus's views in the context of earlier and later figures, see Toth 2017.

[24] Scotus thought that there were other causes which could possibly function as immediate causes of the will's act, such as the intellect. On the developments in his position on whether the intellect is an immediate cause of the will's act see Dumont 2001.

[25] *Lect.* II, dd. 35–37, q. 5, n. 106 (Vat. XIX, 352–353); *Ord.* II, dd. 34–37, q. 5, nn. 98–99 (Vat. VIII, 409–410); *Rep.* II-A, d. 37, q. 2 (Wad. XI.1, 400).

[26] *Ord.* II, dd. 34–37, q. 5, n. 99 (Vat. VIII, 409).

The next argument for MC is based on the will's contingency. It explains that no inferior cause can contingently cause an effect which has been determined by a superior cause. This is because inferior causes follow the determination of superior ones. The argument illustrates this with an example: If my will determines today that *I will write tomorrow* and it is assumed (counterfactually) that my will is immutable and unimpedible as God's will is, then it cannot be the case that *I will write tomorrow* remains indeterminate on account of my hand's ability to write or not write. This is because the hand is determined to write tomorrow in virtue of the will determinately willing that this will happen. Likewise, if God were to will that my will has a volition *v*, then on that condition I would be determined to will *v*.[27] It does not matter that apart from this condition, I have the power to will *v* or not *v*. According to the argument, it is evident that God's causality of a volition *v*, determines that *v* must obtain because it is not possible for God to will something and it not happen.[28] It may be the case in other pairs of superior and inferior causes that the superior cause's determination to produce the effect does not negate the inferior cause's capability to refrain from causing the effect. No other cause except for God is such that what it wills must happen. Scotus's point is that given the infallibility of the divine will, the created will cannot have the power to not cause a volition once God has willed it since this would make God's causality fallible. Thus, according to the argument, the only way to escape determinism with respect to the created will is to deny that God is an immediate cause of the created will's act and instead embrace MC.

Scotus not only repeats these and other arguments in favor of MC, but he also responds to two serious objections against MC. The first objection is that on MC it seems that God would not be the cause of the creature's merit since he is not an immediate cause of the will's act.[29] This consequence is theologically problematic since Christianity teaches that God is a cause of the meritorious actions performed by creatures. In response to this objection, Scotus argues that God can still be a cause of merit on MC by causing grace and charity in the created will. God need not immediately

---

[27] *Lect.* II, dd. 35–37, q. 5, n. 111 (Vat. XIX, 354): "Sed voluntas Dei aeternaliter vult fiendum aliquid aut volendum; et quando determinatur voluntas divina ad volendum illud, determinatur voluntas creata ad causandum idem; igitur etc."

[28] *Ord.* II, dd. 34–37, q. 5, n. 111 (Vat. VIII, 411): "determinationem huius causae necessario concomitatur determinatio voluntatis meae respectu eiusdem (alioquin simul starent 'Deum velle hoc' et 'hoc non fore'); igitur illud 'velle' non est contingens ad utrumlibet 'propter potestatem voluntatis meae'."

[29] *Lect.* II, dd. 35–37, q. 5, n. 121 (Vat. XIX, 357); *Ord.* II, dd. 34–37, q. 5, n. 114 (Vat. VIII, 416).

cause the will's act itself to be a cause of its choosing rightly. By giving the will the grace and charity which is required for it to perform a meritorious action, God can be judged to have caused good actions in a manner according to which he does not cause other non-meritorious actions.[30]

The second objection has to do with standard medieval beliefs about the type of causal relationship which obtains between God and creatures. Medieval thinkers distinguished between two types of relationships which could obtain between causes which cooperate to produce a joint effect: an essential order and an accidental order. Accidentally ordered causes are causes which *merely happen* to work together to produce an effect, though one cause could have in principle produced the effect on its own.[31] An example is two donkeys which together pull a cart. Though it may require more strength, one donkey alone can in principle pull a cart. Essentially ordered causes, by contrast, are causes which are by their natures ordered to co-operate with each other in such a way that neither can produce their common effect on its own. The male and the female, for instance, were thought of as essentially ordered causes in the generation of a child. Unlike the single donkey which could pull the cart on its own if only its power were stronger, no matter how much the male's power is strengthened he cannot produce a child without the female's help. Causes in an essential order were required to be each of a different nature since it is the difference in their natures that allows one to supply what the other lacks for producing the final effect. Medieval thinkers assumed that natures can be ranked hierarchically, so given that the causes in an essential order differ according to their natures, one cause was always of a higher nature and the other of a lower. Though neither cause can produce the final effect without the other's exercise of its causality, the lower cause (i.e. the secondary cause) was believed to depend on the higher cause (i.e. the primary cause) in the very exercise of its causality. Though the primary cause could not produce the final effect on its own, it was not aided in exercising its causality by the secondary cause. Both causes were thought to act together at the same time to produce the effect.[32] It was a standard belief among medieval thinkers that God and creatures must relate to each other as

---

[30] *Lect.* II, dd. 35–37, q. 5, n. 123 (Vat. XIX, 357); *Ord.* II, dd. 34–37, q. 5, n. 116 (Vat. VIII, 416).

[31] An accidental order also obtains between members of causal series which extend into the past. For instance, a grandfather who produces a father who then causes a son would be seen as an accidental co-cause of the son.

[32] For a discussion of Scotus's understanding of essentially and accidentally ordered causes see Marcil 1965: 46–62. For a discussion of different kinds of essential order, see Ward's chapter in this volume.

essentially ordered causes, rather than as merely accidentally ordered causes. God's causality was seen as absolutely necessary for creatures to cause their effects and creatures were seen as being essentially dependent on God in exercising their causality.[33]

Scotus considered the objection that MC is inconsistent with the view that God and creatures co-operate as essentially ordered causes with God being the primary cause of their joint effect. According to MC, the creature is the total immediate cause of its action. Thus, it appears that the creature's causality does not depend on God's causality in the way stipulated in an essential order since God is not an immediate cause of its effects. Scotus's response to this objection is quite interesting. Elsewhere in his works, he identifies two different ways in which a primary cause and a secondary cause can be essentially ordered to one another.[34] Here he comes up with a new third type of essential order to reconcile MC with the standard belief that God is a primary cause of creature's actions. In his *Lectura* discussion of God's causation of the will's action, he summarizes the three types of essential orders as follows:

> One is an order of causes in which one cause is principal and the other is less principal, but nevertheless they do not depend in their causality,—just as the object and the intellect with respect to the act of knowing, and each is a partial cause ... Another order of causes is such that one cause is superior and the other is inferior and the superior moves the inferior, neither is the total cause of the effect, but both integrate as one total cause, just as the sun and the parent with respect to the generated child. There is, however, a third order of causes in which each is a total cause of the effect, in such a way that one receives its total causality from the other ...[35]

---

[33] It was commonly held that God could in some respect produce the effects of creatures without their help. The 1277 Parisian condemnations, for instance, censured the position that God was unable to produce the effects of secondary causes himself. See Piché 1999: 100, prop. 63 (69): "Quod deus non potest in effectum cause secundarie sine ipsa causa secundaria." There was debate about whether God could produce the same numerical effects of creatures without their help or only effects of the same generic type. See Keele 2007.

[34] See for instance *Lect.* I, d. 3,p. 3, qq. 2–3, nn. 366–368 (Vat. XVI, 367–368) and *Ord.* I, d. 3, p. 3, q. 2, nn. 496–498 (Vat. III, 394–395).

[35] *Lect.* II, dd. 35–37, q. 5, nn. 124–126 (Vat. XIX, 358): "Unus est ordo causarum, quando una est principalis et alia est minus principalis, ita tamen quod non dependeant in sua causalitate,—sicut obiectum et intellectus respectu actus intelligendi, et utrumque est causa partialis... Alius est ordo causarum, quarum una est superior et alia inferior, et superior movet inferiorem; neutra tamen est totalis causa effectus, sed integrant unam causam totalem, sicut sol et generans respectu geniti. Est autem tertius ordo causarum, quarum utraque est causa totalis effectus, ita tamen quod una capit totalem causalitatem suam ab alia..." See also *Ord.* II, dd. 34–37, q. 5, n. 117 (Vat. VIII, 416–417) and *Rep.* II-A, d. 37, q. 2 (Wad. XI.1, 401).

These three types of essential orders delineate the three possible options (at least in Scotus's mind) for how God's causality might relate to creatures' causality. Scotus's brief words here require much unpacking. Scotus notes that in the first type of order the causes do not "depend in their causality." The central difference between the first and second type of order lies in how the exercise of the secondary cause's causality relates to the primary cause's causality.

On the first type of essential order, which others have referred to as "autonomous" or "independent" co-causes, both causes exercise their causality through themselves.[36] Each cause requires an exercise of the other's causality in order to cause the final effect. However, neither cause is moved to act by the other nor does either one cause the other cause's causality. One cause is considered primary only because its nature is superior, but even the secondary cause posits its causality autonomously. In the text above, Scotus gives the example of the intellect and object which cooperate to cause an act of intellection.[37] In Scotus's view, the intellect can only elicit its act of knowing if there is a suitable object to be known. Yet, the object does not cause the intellect to cause its act. The intellect posits its causal contribution to its act through itself. Another example which Scotus gives elsewhere is the cooperation between the male and the female in generating a child.[38] Unlike many medieval Aristotelians, Scotus thought that the female exercised an active power in the act of generation. The female's active power was viewed as inferior to the male's active power, i.e. she was the secondary cause and he was the primary, yet Scotus did not think that the female required the male to exercise any action directly on her to activate her causality. To exercise her causality, she only required the condition of the male also exercising his causality. This is the locus of the central difference between the first and second type of orders.

The second order noted in the passage above has been referred to as an order of "participative" or "dependent" causes.[39] In this sort of order, the

---

[36] Roy Effler refers to these first two types of essentially ordered causes as "independent" and "dependent," while William Frank refers to the two types of orders as "participative" and "autonomous" co-causes. See Effler 1962 and Frank 1992. Neither Effler nor Frank mention the third type of essential order which Scotus identifies in the passage quoted above.

[37] On the causation of intellect and object see *Ord.* I, d. 3, p. 3, q. 2, nn. 497–498 (Vat. III, 394–395) and *Quodl.*, q. 15, n. 10 (Vivès XXVI, 142–143; Wolter and Alluntis, n. 34, 351–351). For an illuminating discussion of Scotus's views on this topic see Cross 2014: 128–34.

[38] *Ord.* I, d. 3, p. 3, q. 2, n. 496 (Vat. III, 394); See also *Quodl.*, q. 15, n. 10 (Vivès XXVI, 142), English translation in *God and Creatures* (Wolter and Alluntis, n. 33, 351).

[39] See n. 36.

primary cause moves the secondary cause and the secondary cause exercises its power by acting through the power of the primary cause. A clear example of this sort of causal order is that of a person who uses a pen to write a poem. To cooperate in writing a poem, the pen must be acted on by the person. The pen must undergo a change (i.e. it must be moved) through the primary cause's agency in order to exercise its causality. Furthermore, the pen participates in causing the writing of the poem by acting through the person's power. The pen does not have of itself a power to write or to compose poems. Only the person has this power and it is in virtue of the person using the pen as an instrument that the pen causally contributes to writing a poem. By contrast agents in the first type of order, such as the male and female who generate a child, have in themselves the power by which they contribute to the joint effect. Neither acts through the other's power.

In this passage above, Scotus's main aim is to identify a type of essential order which corresponds to the relationship between God and created causes on MC. The third type of essential order is the relevant one for doing the job. The third order differs crucially from the first two: in the first two types of essential orders, the primary and the secondary cause is each seen as a partial immediate cause of the effect (i.e. the creature's action) and together they combine to constitute the total immediate cause of the effect. In the third order, by contrast, the primary *and* the secondary cause are *both* regarded as total causes of the effect—one is the total *immediate* cause and the other is the total *mediate* cause. In the case of God and creatures, the creature is the total immediate cause of its action, while God is the total mediate cause of that action (in virtue of being the total cause of the creature and its power). Scotus claims: "[I]t is not repugnant to a creature (such as fire) that it has total causality with respect to any of its effects (such as with respect to a small quantity of heat) …"[40] Scotus claims in this text that there is no fundamental incompatibility between being both a created cause and a total cause. For example, there is no contradiction in the notion of a fire being the total cause of some small quantity of heat. He explains that the reason why some created causes lack total causality with respect to certain effects is on account of a limitation in the cause. For instance, a fire cannot be the total cause of an immense quantity of heat. This is not, however, because of a contradiction between the notion of a total cause and its nature as a creature, but rather because

---

[40] *Lect.* II, dd. 35–37, q. 5, n. 126 (Vat. XIX, 358): "…non repugnat creaturae (ut igni) quod habeat totalem causalitatem respectu alicuius effectus (ut respectu parvi caloris)…"

its power is limited. If a creature does have total causality with respect to its proper effect, Scotus reasons that God cannot also be an immediate cause of that effect. He writes: "That cause [i.e. the created active cause] therefore will cause alone as the total cause of its proper effect and God will not cause it immediately, or otherwise the same effect will be caused twice."[41] If an active creature's own causality is sufficient to immediately produce its proper effect, then God cannot also immediately cause that effect because there is nothing left for God to cause. God must be only a mediate cause. God is the *total* mediate cause of the creature's act since no other cause helps him in producing creatures and their powers.

In other contexts where Scotus describes types of essential orders, he does not mention this third type of order between a total immediate cause and a total mediate cause which cooperate to produce a joint effect. It seems that he realized that some of his contemporaries may be skeptical of whether this third type of order really exemplifies the features of an essential order. In the *Ordinatio* and *Reportatio* Scotus explicitly raised the question of whether this third type of essential order is consistent with the first proposition of the *Liber de causis*. The theses advanced in this work about primary and secondary causes greatly influenced later medieval discussions of the causal relationship between God and creatures. Perhaps most influential was the very first proposition of the work which stated that the first cause is *more* of a cause of the effect than the second.[42]

It is hard to see how Scotus's third type of essential order is consistent with this proposition since in this type of order the primary cause does not immediately cause the final effect. In response to this worry, Scotus writes in the *Reportatio*: "I say that to cause more is not to cause immediately, but [a certain thing causes more] because it causes the cause of the effect, and, as a consequence, it is more noble than the secondary cause."[43] In this brief text, Scotus makes a significant conceptual move: he separates superiority of causal influence from causal immediacy and links it rather with onto-logical dependence. Since the primary cause's causality produces the cause which is immediately bringing about the effect, its causality is the ultimate foundation upon which the effect depends. Scotus, like others of his time, was concerned to save the essential order between divine and created

---

[41] Ibid.: "Illa igitur causa causabit sola, ut causa totalis, effectum proprium, et non Deus immediate, —vel idem effectus bis causabitur!"

[42] *Liber de causis* (Pattin, 134): "Omnis causa primaria plus est influens super causatum suum quam causa universalis secunda."

[43] *Rep.* II-A, d. 37, q. 2 (Wad. XI.1, 401): "Dico quod magis causare non est immediatius causare, sed quia causat causam effectus, et per consequens est nobilior, quam causa secunda."

causality, as well as God's primacy in the essential order with creatures. Yet, unlike others, he did not see MC as threatening God's role as the primary cause since he decouples causal primacy from causal immediacy.

Up to this point, we have seen Scotus present arguments for MC and solve objections against the position. Yet, in his *Lectura* and *Ordinatio* discussion of God's causal involvement in the will's act, he nevertheless definitively rejects MC because it is incompatible with divine foreknowledge and omnipotence. Regarding how God's foreknowledge requires the rejection of MC, he writes the following in the *Ordinatio*:

> God does not have knowledge of future contingents except because he knows with certainty the determination of his will with respect to those things about which his will is immutable and unimpedible. But if the created will were the total cause with respect to its volition, and it relates contingently with respect to that volition, therefore, no matter how the divine will is determined toward a future contingent which depends on the created will, the created will would be able to will otherwise, and so certitude would not follow from knowledge of the determination of the divine will.[44]

Scotus begins this passage by referencing his theory of how God knows future contingents. He then reasons that the theory would not work if the will were the total immediate cause of its act and God were not also an immediate cause of that act. On Scotus's theory of God's knowledge of contingents, prior to creating the world God's will freely determines the truth-values of propositions about contingent events and realities.[45] For instance, prior to creation, God wills the truth-value of the proposition "Creature *c* wills volition *v*." God then knows future contingents by knowing the determinations of his own will regarding the truth-value of contingent propositions. In the passage quoted above, Scotus explains that if the created will were the total immediate cause of its own volition, then God could not know with certainty future contingents which depended on

---

[44] *Ord.* II, dd. 34–37, q. 5, n. 120 (Vat. VIII, 418–419): "[N]on habet scientiam de futuris contingentibus nisi quia certitudinaliter novit determinationem voluntatis suae respectu eorum ad quae voluntas sua est immutabilis et inimpedibilis sed si voluntas creata sit totalis causa respectu sui 'velle', et ipsa contingenter se habet ad illud 'velle',—ergo quantumcumque voluntas divina ponatur determinate ad unam partem eorum quae dependent a voluntate creata, poterit voluntas creata aliter velle, et ita non sequitur certitudo ex cognitione determinationis voluntatis divinae." See also *Lect.* II, dd. 35–37, q. 5 (Vat. XIX, 351–370) and *Rep.* II-A, d. 37, q. 2 (Wad. XI.1, 400–401).

[45] The theory is summarized in *Rep.* I-A, d. 38, qq. 1–2, n. 37, (Söder, 233–34); *Lect.* I, d. 39, qq. 1–5, n. 62 (Vat. XVII, 500) and *Ord.* I, dd. 38–39, qq. 1–5, nn. 23–24 (Vat. VI, 428–429). There is much literature on Scotus's theory. A more recent book-length study is Langston 1986. For a challenge to the "deterministic" reading of Scotus's theory, see Wolter 1990.

the created will's causality since the created will would be able to act against the determinations made by God's will regarding the truth-values of propositions. For instance, God might will that it is true that *Lucifer does not sin in situation x*, but if Lucifer's will is the total, immediate cause of its acts and it elicits those acts contingently, then regardless of what God wills it nevertheless remains possible that Lucifer wills otherwise. Thus, God cannot know these future contingents with certainty based on knowing his own will.

Scotus then argues along similar lines that MC compromises divine omnipotence. An omnipotent being is such that whatever it wills happens. If the created will were the total immediate cause of its volition and it causes that volition contingently, then it would be possible for it not to cause that which God willed. Thus, God would not be omnipotent.[46] Not only would God not be able to make acts of the created will happen on MC, but he would also not be able to stop them. Scotus reasons that if God's immediate causality were not required for the will to act, as MC supposes, then the only way God could stop the will from willing something would be by doing violence to it. He then adds: "But for the will to be done violence includes a contradiction, therefore, God would not be able to impede my will."[47] Scotus claims that it is contradictory for the will to be moved by violence since by its very nature an act of will cannot be an act which goes against the will's inclination. Acting according to one's will is inherently opposed to acting on account of another's coercion.

Though Scotus finds MC consistent with the view that God is the primary cause in an essential causal order with creatures, these concerns about how God exercises sovereignty over the actions of free creatures and how he knows contingents drove him in the *Lectura* and *Ordinatio* to reject MC. In these works, Scotus concludes that God must be a partial immediate cause of created volitions.

III SCOTUS'S *LECTURA* AND *ORDINATIO* POSITION ON GOD'S CAUSAL COOPERATION WITH CREATURES' OPERATIONS

As we saw above in Scotus's discussion of the three types of essential orders which can obtain between primary and secondary causes, there were two

---

[46] *Lect.* II, dd. 35–37, q. 5, nn. 130–132 (Vat. XIX, 359–360); *Ord.* II, dd. 34–37, q. 5, nn. 121–123 (Vat. VIII, 419) and *Rep.* II-A, d. 37, q. 2 (Wad. XI.1, 401).

[47] *Ord.* II, dd. 34–37, q. 5, n. 122 (Vat. VIII, 419): "sed voluntatem violentari includit contradictionem; ergo Deus non potest voluntatem mea impedire."

different ways in which primary and secondary causes can co-operate as partial, immediate co-causes of a joint effect. On the "participative" or "dependent" model, secondary causes are moved by the first cause to cause their operations. This type of essential order corresponds to *AP*. By contrast, on the "independent" or "autonomous" model the secondary cause is neither acted upon by the first nor does it receive an influx of power from the first. While each cause can only exercise its causality on the condition that the other exercises its causality as well, nevertheless the causes together produce the effect without the first cause doing anything to the secondary cause. Since the secondary cause exercises its causality through itself without the first cause moving it I will refer to this model as the "independent cause" model (IC).

Scotus does not give a lengthy analysis of the *AP* model, yet it is not difficult to see why he would not have regarded it as a viable model for how God co-operates with the created will. We saw in the passages from Albert and Bonaventure that part of what motivated AP was a conception of created powers as intrinsically deficient for operation. Scotus takes a different view of created causal powers, particularly the created will. Unlike defenders of AP, Scotus explicitly rejected the axiom "Everything which is moved is moved by another." He refuted the arguments adduced by others to support this principle and he identified many examples of self-motion in nature (e.g. nutrition).[48] Regarding the will, he said that the view which sees it as passively moved to its act destroys human freedom.[49] As we saw earlier, Bonaventure reasoned that God must help the will elicit its act because in so far as it is a created power, the will is "defective" and not "purely active."[50] Scotus, however, thinks of the created will quite differently. In his view, the will has a "superabundance of actuality" on account of its not being limited to one determinate act as is the case with natural causes.[51] He writes: "The indeterminacy ... in the will ... is of excelling perfection and power, which is not restricted to a determinate act."[52] This superabundance of actuality is what enables the will to move itself.

---

[48] Scotus, *QMet.* IX, q. 14, (OPh IV, 625–673). For literature on this topic see Effler 1962 and King 1994.

[49] Scotus, *QMet.* IX, q. 14, n. 62 (OPh IV, 649). Scotus is here considering the position that the will is moved by its object.

[50] See n. 8.

[51] Scotus, *QMet.* IX, q. 15, n. 31 (OPh IV, 683): "superabundantis sufficientiae, quae est ex illimitatione actualitatis..." See also Pickavé's chapter in this volume.

[52] Scotus, *QMet.* IX, q. 14, n. 34 (OPh IV, 683–684): "Indeterminatio... in voluntate... est excellentis perfectionis et potestativae, non alligatae ad determinatum actum."

In light of Scotus's conception of the will as excelling in perfection and a self-mover, it is not surprising that he opts for IC as the best model to capture the causal cooperation between God and the will. To understand how this model applies to God and the created will's joint causality of the created will's volition, it is necessary to realize that a distinction must be drawn between the created will's own causal contribution to the action and the action resulting from the joint causal contributions of God and the created will. Scotus claims that, though the created will's volition is co-caused by God, the created will's necessary causal contribution to bringing its volition about is posited autonomously by the will and solely through itself. God does not move the created will to act or otherwise cause it to cause its act. Scotus explicitly compares the causal co-operation between God and created will in the production of the created volition to the cooperation between an active power such as the intellect and its object and the male and female which causally cooperate in generating a child.[53] In each of these pairs, the two causes are such that, though each requires the other's causality to cause the final effect, each cause in the pair posits its causal contribution to the final effect through its own power. Neither moves the other nor acts through the other's power.

It is worth noting that in Scotus's own time his account of "independent" or "autonomous" essentially ordered co-causes (IC) would have been controversial in so far as it contradicts several of the constraints on essential orders in the *Liber de causis*. This work, regarded by many Latin Christian authors as authoritative, outright rejected the possibility that a secondary cause contributes to an effect solely through its own power. Though Scotus was careful to reconcile MC with the *Liber*'s first proposition, elsewhere he explicitly denies the work's authority since it is based on the "erroneous views of Avicenna."[54] The sixteenth proposition of the *Liber* states that secondary causes cannot cause the final effect except by acting through the power of the primary cause.[55] This is precisely what Scotus's *IC* model denies: the secondary cause posits its causal contribution through its own power and the primary cause directly produces the effect without acting on the secondary cause. Furthermore, the third

---

[53] *Rep.* II-A, d. 37, q. 2 (Wad. XI.1, 401).

[54] See, for instance, *Ord.* II, d. 2, p. 1 q. 4, n. 185 (Vat. VII, 238): "... doctrina *De causis* tradita est secundam doctrinam Avicennae erroneam. ... Et ideo auctoritas illa non est habenda sicut auctoritas, quia tradita est secundum radicem erroneam." See also *Lect.* II, d. 2, p.1, q. 4, n. 163 (Vat. XVIII, 152).

[55] *Liber de causis* (Pattin, 137): "Et non figitur causatum causae secundae nisi per virtutem causae primae."

proposition of the *Liber de causis* taught that the primary cause acts before the secondary cause.[56] Aquinas is an example of a major figure who endorsed this position regarding God and the creature's causal cooperation on the grounds of the *Liber de causis*'s authority. He reasons that the primary cause must act before the secondary cause because the primary cause activates the secondary cause's causality.[57] Scotus, by contrast, takes care to note that though God is a superior cause to the created cause, God's exercise of his causality does not precede the creature's in the production of the effect. They cause the effect together at the same instant. He writes:

> [A]lthough one is more perfect and prior to the other according to nature, nevertheless with respect to a third [i.e. the effect] they are together according to nature in causing, so that the effect is understood to be produced by them at once. It is not that the more principal cause first causes the effect in one instant and then after the second causes it, but they are understood with respect to the effect to cause at once.[58]

In the opening line of this passage, Scotus affirms that the first cause has a higher nature than the second cause. According to its essence, the first is a superior kind of entity to the second. Yet, Scotus goes on to claim that with respect to the effect, the first and second cause produces the effect together at the same natural instant.

Scotus explicitly claims that the created will "has in its power to either co-cause or not co-cause with the primary cause."[59] He supposes that the created will posits its necessary co-causality of its volition contingently and freely. He emphasizes this to explain how God is able to be an immediate cause of the will's volitions without being a cause of sin. He writes: "I say that when two partial causes concur to produce a common effect of both, there is able to be a defect in the effect—in the production of the effect—on account of a defect in either of the concurring causes . . ."[60] Since the

---

[56] *Liber de causis* (Pattin, 134): "Quod est quia causa universalis prima agit in causatum causae secundae, antequam agat in ipsum causa universalis secunda quae sequitur ipsam."

[57] For instance, he cites propositions from the *Liber* with authority in his *De Pot.*, q. 3, a. 7 discussion of God's operations in nature (Pession, 20): ". . . nam virtus inferior non coniungitur effectui nisi per virtutem superioris; unde dicitur in *Lib. de Caus.*, quod virtus causae primae prius agit in causatum, et vehementius ingreditur in ipsum."

[58] *Lect.* II, dd. 35–37, q. 5, n. 148 (Vat. XIX, 364): ". . . licet una sit perfectior et prior secundum naturam alia, tamen respectu tertii simul sunt secundum naturam in causando, prout effectus intelligitur simul produci ab eis: non quod causa principalior primo causet in uno instanti et postea secunda causa causet, sed simul respectu effectus intelliguntur causare."

[59] *Ord.* II, dd. 34–37, q. 5, n. 145 (Vat. VIII, 430): ". . . in potestate sua habet concausare causae primae vel non concausare. . ."

[60] *Ord.* II, dd. 34–37, q. 5, n. 142 (Vat. VIII, 428): "dico quod quando duae causae partiales concurrunt ad effectum commune ambarum, potest esse defectus—in productione effectus—ex

creature's causality is not determined by God's causality, the creature is able to independently introduce a defect in the effect. Scotus elaborates on the details of this solution; however, they lie outside of the scope of this present chapter.

Scotus's claim that God and creatures produce their joint effect at the same instant raises a question about how two free causes can cooperate if one does not cause the effect prior to the other. Scotus writes of the divine and created wills: "[A]s two ordered efficient causes, they cause a common effect [i.e. the act of the created will] in one instant of nature, so that neither causes without the other."[61] If the created will does not begin to cause its act prior to God's co-causality of that act, how does God know whether he should posit his concurrence or not? According to William Frank, Scotus was "content to leave in silence what must have appeared to him the mystery of God's inner life."[62] Others claim that Scotus's theory of God's co-causation can only be salvaged by Luis de Molina's theory of "middle knowledge." This theory states that God has pre-volitional access to a body of knowledge comprised of all of the contingent truths about how every possible creature would cause in any possible situation.[63] If God had such knowledge, then he would know prior to creation how the created will would co-cause in any possible situation and he could adjust his own co-operation to fit with the creature's.

Scotus's *Lectura* and *Ordinatio* position on God's role in causing the created volition is best seen as an attempt to steer a middle course between two undesirable extremes. MC, on the one hand, gives God no role in immediately causing created actions—the created will is the total immediate cause of its volition. Scotus was not opposed to this view of created powers in principle. However, he saw that MC implied that the created will could act against God's determinations regarding future contingents and that God could neither produce nor impede acts of the created will. AP, on the other hand, gives God's causality so strong a priority over creaturely causality that it can only be maintained at the cost of rejecting

---

defectu utriusque causae concurrentis..." For a discussion of Scotus's views on God's causation of sin, see Frost 2010: 23–30.

[61] *Ord.* II, dd. 35–37, q. 5 n. 145 (Vat. VIII, 429–430): "ita duae causae efficientes 'ordinatae' in uno instanti naturae causant effectum communem, ita quod neutra tunc causat sine altera."

[62] Frank 1992: 164.

[63] See Molina, *Liberi Arbitrii cum Gratiae Donis, Divina Praescientia, Providentia, Praedestinatione et Reprobatione Concordia*. For a contemporary discussion of middle knowledge, see Flint 1998. For the claim that Scotus's theories require middle knowledge see the seventeenth-century Scotist John Pontius's commentary printed in Luke Wadding's edition of the *Ordinatio* (Wad. V.2, 1307 and Wad. V.2, 1339). For contemporary literature, see Dekker 1998; Wolter 1994: 283.

the will's self-motion and denigrating its power. IC is Scotus's best attempt to balance the created will's autonomy with God's immediate production of the will's volition. Though God immediately causes the created will's act, the creature contributes to bringing about its act through its own power. The will is not moved by God, nor is the created will caused in any other way by God to posit its causality. The created will is free to cooperate or not cooperate in causing its volition. Thus, the created will's act itself is elicited contingently. As Scotus explains elsewhere, the created will's volition is not contingent merely upon whether God causes it or not, but rather, it has a two-fold contingency—*both* of the created volition's causes could have possibly not caused it.[64]

While IC is an innovative attempt to chart a middle path between the "hands off" and the "overly involved" models of God's causality, it is nevertheless difficult to see how it succeeds in securing the *desiderata* which drove Scotus to reject MC. To some extent, IC also compromises God's omnipotence and is inconsistent with Scotus's standard account of divine foreknowledge. IC can certainly secure that the created will *does not elicit* any volitions which go against God's determinations regarding future contingents. God has control over which positive acts are elicited on account of his immediate co-causality being required for the will to elicit any act. If God determines that the proposition *Creature c will not will volition v* is true, God can ensure that *v* does not obtain simply by withholding his own concurrence needed to produce *v*. However, it seems that IC has no way of guaranteeing that creatures *do elicit* the positive acts of will which conform to God's determinations of future contingents. For instance, if God determines that the proposition *Creature c wills volition v* is true and creature *c* is an autonomously operating co-cause of *v*, God has no way of guaranteeing that *c* will supply the necessary causality for *v* to obtain. Thus, God would not be able to infer that *v* obtains from the fact that he willed that *Creature c wills volition v* is true.

Others have tried to defend the coherence of Scotus's account of foreknowledge and his theory of God's concurrence by claiming that though God is not the sole immediate productive cause of contingent realities, he can nevertheless know which contingent actions obtain on account of knowing his own causation of those actions. According to IC,

---

[64] See for instance *Rep.* I-A, dd. 39–40, nn. 36–37, (Söder, 249): "Sed aliquid potest dici dupliciter contingens ex parte suae causae, sicut actus voluntatis meae habet duplicem causam contingentiae, unam ex parte voluntatis divinae sicut causae primae et aliam ex voluntate mea ut ex secunda causa."

God can only cause a creature's volition on the condition that the creature causes it as well. Each cause requires the other to cause the effect. Thus, although God's causation of the action does not causally determine the creature's causation of it, the fact that God caused the action logically guarantees that the creature did as well. Since the creature's and God's causation are jointly sufficient for the production of the creature's act, from his knowledge that he caused a volition, God can infer that the created volition obtains.[65]

Though it is correct that Scotus's theory allows God to logically infer which contingents obtain from knowing his concurrence, this does not solve the worry Scotus had with regard to MC about creature's being able to act otherwise from how God willed regarding the truth-values of contingent propositions. Scotus's general account of God's foreknowledge is *not* that God knows contingents by knowing his concurrence with created realities. Rather, Scotus claims that God knows contingents by knowing *the determinations of the truth-values of propositions* about contingents. Scotus regarded God's determination of the truth-values of future contingent propositions as a distinct and naturally prior act from his concurring in the production of the contingent realities which the propositions are about.[66] The difficulty Scotus raised about foreknowledge against MC was that if the creature is the sole immediate cause of its volition the creature could subsequently will otherwise from how God determined regarding the truth value of the relevant propositions. This same difficulty clearly applies to IC. If God wills that *Creature c wills volition v* and it remains in creature *c*'s power to either posit or not posit its co-causality of *v*, then God's knowledge of how he determined the truth-value of the relevant proposition cannot guarantee knowledge of whether *v* will obtain. It does not matter that on IC God can know that created volition *v* occurs by knowing he concurs with it. On Scotus's general theory of God's knowledge of contingents, God is supposed to have knowledge of which contingents obtain prior to his concurring with created causes to bring those contingents into existence.

---

[65] Frank 1992: 163–164 and Wolter 1990: 332–333. Cross has argued against Wolter and Frank's solution. See Cross 1999: 54. See also Cross 2005: 58–59.

[66] Evidence that Scotus regarded these two as distinct is found in his treatment of other topics. For instance, in his *Ordinatio* discussion of God's permission of sin he denies that God wills the truth of propositions of form *Creature c wills sinful action s*. Yet, he affirms that God concurs in the production of sinful volitions. Thus, God's concurrence with actions must be distinct from his willing the truth of propositions about such actions. See *Ord.* I, d. 41, q.un, n. 38–40 (Vat. VI, 335–336).

IV SCOTUS'S *REPORTATIO* POSITION ON GOD'S COOPERATION WITH THE CREATED WILL

It appears that Scotus himself realized that IC was not an entirely satisfactory theory. In his latest discussion of God's causation of the created will's volition in his *Reportatio*, Scotus does not definitively reject MC in favor of IC. He writes, "It is said that both are able to be sustained."[67] He claims that the arguments for IC (namely that MC is incompatible with foreknowledge and omnipotence) are "stronger" (*firmiores*).[68] Yet, after this claim, he reiterates that "the other opinion is similarly able to be sustained."[69] In the *Reportatio*, Scotus concludes merely that God must be the primary cause of the created will's act, which is to say that an essential order must obtain between God and the created will's causality. Yet, he does not specify which type of essential order it is. He writes: "I hold therefore that the volition is from two essentially ordered causes, ordered essentially in either the first way or the second way."[70] By the first way and the second way, he means what I have referred to as MC and IC. As we saw above, Scotus took care to argue that even on MC God was the essentially ordered primary cause of the will's act. He identified a third type of essential order which obtains between a total immediate and total mediate cause of the same effect. Though Scotus remains neutral in the *Reportatio* between MC and IC, Scotus's secretary and close associate William of Alnwick later wrote in his *Determinationes* that Scotus "probably" held that God does not immediately co-cause the created will's action. According to Alnwick, Scotus held that God merely "conserves the will and permits it to act freely."[71]

Scotus's openness to (and possible preference) for MC at the end of his career goes hand-in-hand with another development in his thought at Paris. In his *Reportatio* discussion of God's permission of sin, he explicitly

---

[67] *Rep.* II-A, d. 37, q. 2 (Wad. XI.1, 400): "Dicitur quod utrumque potest sustineri."

[68] Ibid., 400–401.

[69] Ibid., p. 401: "Alia opinio similiter potest sustineri." The Worcester manuscript of the *Rep.* II-A contains a line omitted from the Wadding text which further emphasizes that Scotus did not make up his mind at Paris about God's causal involvement in the created will's act. *Rep.* II-A, d. 37, q. 2, Worcester, Cathedral Library, ms. F. 69, f. 128ra: "Dico ergo non determinando unam opinionem nec aliam quod. . ."

[70] *Rep.* II-A, d. 37, q. 2 (Wad. XI.1, 401): "Teneo igitur quod volitio est a duabus causis essentialiter ordinatis, sive ordinentur essentialiter primo modo vel secondo modo."

[71] Alnwick, *Determinationes*, Città del Vaticano, Biblioteca Apostolica Vaticana, ms. Pal. Lat. 1805, f. 98r: "Ad hoc potest uno modo dici, secundum viam quam probabiliter tenet Scotus, quod Deus non concurrit immediate ad causandum actum voluntatis, sed conservat voluntatem et permittit ipsam libere <agere>." I quote this text from Wolter 1994: 260, n. 19.

denies that God knows all contingents by knowing the determinations of his will.[72] Furthermore, before his untimely death, Scotus had apparently placed blank leaves in his personal copy of the *Ordinatio* at the point where his account of God's knowledge of contingents was to occur.[73] This indicates that he had intended to revise his account of God's knowledge of contingents. Did Scotus realize that even on IC, his standard account of God's knowledge of contingents could not work? As we have seen, even if God is an immediate co-cause of the created will's act, the creature could fail to posit its necessary co-causality for an act, and thus acts which corresponded to the propositions which God willed to be true might possibly not obtain. Or did Scotus have independent doubts about his theory of God's knowledge of contingents which in turn diminished his motivation to unequivocally affirm God's immediate causation of the will's act? As we saw, upholding this theory of foreknowledge was a central reason why he rejected MC. So, if he had doubts about this account of foreknowledge, he may not have been so adamant to reject MC. Perhaps we will never be able to know the exact progression of Scotus's thoughts on these matters. It is nevertheless clear that, at the end of his career, Scotus was struggling to integrate his robust conception of the created will's freedom into a world that is perfectly known and absolutely governed by an infallible God.

V   CONCLUSION

Though it appears that Scotus himself was never settled in his views on how God cooperates with the created will, he nevertheless made a lasting contribution to historical discussions of this topic. While many others of his time were adherents to the AP model both on account of their rejection of self-motion and their deference to the authority of the *Liber de causis*, Scotus developed a model of essentially ordered causes in which the secondary cause posited its causal contribution *autonomously* and at the *same instant* as the primary cause. He located the primacy of the primary

---

[72] *Rep.* I-A, d. 46, q. 2, Wien, Österreichische Nationalbibliothek, ms. lat 1453, f. 125rb–va: "Ad aliud, quando dicitur quod novit alteram partem contradictionis, ergo vult eam, nego consequentiam..." *Rep.* I-B, d. 46, q. 2, Worcester, Cathedral Library, ms. F. 69, f. 63rb–63v: "Videtur tamen quod contrarium illo dictum est supra, ubi dictum est quod scientia Dei non est determinata ad contingens nisi quia voluntas eius (eius] est *Balić*) prius est determinata ad hoc volendum, ergo si determinate scit aliquod contingens, illud determinate vult." (I am relying on Carol Balić's transcription in Balić 1927: 54, which I have corrected against the manuscript.) On the developments in Scotus's views on God's foreknowledge, see Frost 2010.

[73] See Vat. VI, 26*–30*.

cause in its superior nature alone, rather than also in its movement of the secondary cause. He applied this model to a range of co-causal pairs (such as the intellect and its object and the male and female in the act of generation) and, at least for much of his career, he thought it was clearly the best model for capturing the causal relationship between God and creatures. As we have seen, Scotus also developed a third model of essentially ordered causes to show that MC was able to uphold both the indispensability and primacy of the first cause's causality. At the end of his career, he became increasingly open to this view. Scotus's efforts to make MC palatable did not have an enduring role in later discussions of divine causality. Few major figures defended MC. Yet, up through the seventeenth century, Latin Christian thinkers continued to debate about whether God cooperated with created causes according to the model of AP or IC. Many who conceived of the will as a self-mover followed Scotus in opting for IC.[74]

---

[74] See, for instance, Molina, *Liberi Arbitrii cum Gratiae Donis, Divina Praescientia, Providentia, Praedestinatione et Reprobatione Concordia*, II, 26, 12. For Francisco Suárez's discussion of these models and his refutation of the *AP* model, see his *Disp.* 22, 2, in *Disputationes Metaphysicae* (*Opera Omnia* XXV, 809–826).

CHAPTER 5

Duns Scotus on free will and human agency

Martin Pickavé

John Duns Scotus's teaching on freedom and the will has been the object of much attention, and it has rightly been praised as a radical new approach to human agency. Unlike most of his predecessors, Scotus considers a synchronic power for opposites to be fundamental to human free will and he sets out to give a detailed account of the metaphysical makeup of the power through which we possess free will.

However, at least on the face of it, Scotus seems to maintain conflicting ideas on freedom of the will. For example, he maintains that our freedom, insofar as it is understood as such and not as including any imperfection, is "with respect to opposite objects" (*ad opposita obiecta*).[1] Yet he also famously holds that "freedom is compatible with necessity" (*stat libertas cum necessitate*),[2] which seems to rule out alternatives. Arguing that the latter characterization applies only to God and God's will has little chance of success in getting us out of this puzzle because Scotus is adamant that the same formal concept of freedom applies both to God and to free creatures such as human beings. It is therefore not surprising that some of Scotus's immediate followers were reluctant to adopt his teaching on freedom of the will. In fact, in the decades after his death, Scotus's views led to a lively debate over the concept of freedom (*ratio libertatis*).[3] Moreover, it doesn't seem to help that Scotus frequently uses the term "freedom" and its cognates to directly qualify a faculty of the soul, the will, and that he employs the adjective "free" to describe the will's native mode of operation. Is freedom not primarily a property possessed by full-blown agents, such as human beings or God, and the volitions such agents are

---

[1] See, e.g., *Ord.* I, d. 38, q. 2 and d. 39, qq. 1–5, n. 15 (Vat. VI, 416) and *Lect.* I, d. 39, qq. 1–5, n. 46 (Vat. XVII, 493–494).
[2] See, e.g., *Quodl.*, q. 16, n. 33 (Noone and Roberts, 176); *Rep.* I-A, d. 10, q. 3, n. 51 (Wolter and Bychkov, 402).
[3] Guido Alliney has published a series of important articles on this debate. See, e.g., Alliney 2005, 2008.

capable of bringing about? And if so, is Scotus committing a category mistake when he ascribes freedom primarily to the will understood as a faculty of the soul?

In what follows I hope to clear up some of these conundrums. Thomas Williams once lamented that "Duns Scotus . . . made his libertarianism the cornerstone of his system of ethics. Unfortunately, commentators have failed to show how his theory of freedom unites various elements of his thought."[4] Although I agree with Williams's assessment at the time of his writing, I think we need to take a further step back, for it is my contention that Scotus's "theory of freedom" too requires more scrutiny. There is still little scholarly consensus as to what precisely this theory amounts to.[5] To bring more clarity to Scotus's views, I shall start by approaching Scotus by looking at the historical background of his teaching on free will. But rather than comparing him to Thomas Aquinas, as is often done, I begin by focusing on how he engages with Anselm of Canterbury's famous definition of freedom, for this will allow us to identify some key tenets underlying Scotus's views. This will lead me in the next step to address the exact nature of the power for opposites that Scotus frequently associates with freedom before I turn to the "formal concept" (*ratio formalis*) of freedom and how it is common to God and creatures. I will close this chapter by exploring how Scotus's views on free will compare to positions held in the modern free will debate and by discussing two objections to my interpretation.

I   DUNS SCOTUS AND ANSELM'S DEFINITION OF FREEDOM

Medieval philosophers before the fourteenth century rarely attempt to give explicit definitions of the freedom (*libertas*) that is fundamental to understanding human agency. One famous and highly influential exception is Anselm of Canterbury, who devotes an entire work, the dialogue *On the Freedom of Choice*, to the question of what precisely freedom of the will is. The definition he settles on states that our fundamental freedom is "a power to preserve rectitude of the will for the sake of rectitude" (*potestas servandi rectitudinem voluntatis propter ipsam rectitudinem*).[6] By understanding freedom of the will as a power directed at what is morally good,

---

[4] Williams 1998a: 193.
[5] For a discussion of various interpretations and a previous attempt to bring some order to the debate, see Incandela 1992.
[6] Anselm, *De libertate arbitrii*, c. 3 (Schmitt I, 212).

Anselm is defending what Susan Wolf more recently has called an asymmetrical account of freedom.[7] This has some clear advantages. Most importantly, it makes clear why we think of freedom of the will as something positive and even a perfection. We wouldn't do so if it were, say, a power for sinning, and it is not clear why we would do so if freedom were merely a power to do or choose otherwise.

Duns Scotus is undoubtedly influenced by Anselm. For instance, he makes a great deal of Anselm's account of the two affections of the will, the so-called affections for justice and for the advantageous, a piece of doctrine that becomes a cornerstone of his understanding of the will.[8] But does it also mean that he endorses Anselm's definition of freedom? Some commentators have answered this question in the affirmative.[9] Most importantly, by not considering a power to do or choose otherwise an essential feature of freedom, Anselm's definition is not at odds with the idea that freedom is, at least in some cases, compatible with necessity, as Scotus seems to maintain.[10]

Anselm's definition raises an obvious worry that he himself addresses: If freedom is a power to preserve the rectitude of the will for the sake of rectitude, then evil acts do not seem to be committed or chosen freely. But if that is so, then no one seems to be responsible for their sins, and so they are not sins at all because choices resulting from and acts committed out of necessity are involuntary and not up to the agent. Like Anselm, Scotus is keen to defend the idea that freedom is not a power to sin. Nor is the "ability to sin" (*posse peccare*), as he states using Anselm's own words, "freedom or a part of freedom."[11] He notes that an ability to sin (*posse peccare*) involves two things, an ability (*posse*) or power (*potentia*) for acting or willing and a defect (*deficere*) because sinning is something defective, a failure to do or will what one ought to do or will. The ability to act or will obviously belongs to freedom, for without it there wouldn't be freedom in the first place. But the defect does not; otherwise, every exercise of free will

---

[7] See, e.g., Wolf 1980.

[8] See especially *Lect.* II, d. 6, q. 2, nn. 28–41 (Vat. XVIII, 378–383); *Ord.* II, d. 6, q. 2, nn. 40–62 (Vat. VIII, 42–56); and *Rep.* II, d. 6, q. 2 (Vivès XXII, 615–624).

[9] See, for example, Bonansea 1983: 61: "The Anselmian definition of freedom is accepted by both St. Bonaventure and Duns Scotus who make it their own and develop it further." For a critique of this view, see Langston 1996.

[10] In *Quodl.*, q. 16, n. 35 (Noone and Roberts, 178), Scotus explicitly turns to Anselm as authoritative support for this compatibility.

[11] *Ord.* II, d. 7, q. un., n. 4 (Vat. VIII, 70); *Lect.* II, d. 7, q. un., n. 4 (Vat. XIX, 1); *Rep.* II, d. 7, q. 2 (Vivès XXII, 625b); and d. 23, q. un. (Vivès XXIII, 101a). See Anselm, *De libertate arbitrii*, c. 1 (Schmitt I, 209).

would involve a defect. Still, this does not mean that the free will of this or that particular agent cannot be defective, and therefore that such a particular free will has the ability to will defectively (*potest velle defectibiliter*).[12]

However, despite the occasional references to Anselm's teachings on freedom, there is no evidence that Scotus actually adopts Anselm's definition as his own. His Anselm-inspired explanations for why the ability to sin is no part of freedom indicate in my view rather that he agrees with Anselm about the defensibility of asymmetrical accounts of freedom than that he endorses Anselm's particular version of it. Note that with few exceptions most of his treatments of Anselm's views on freedom are in response to initial opinions that have been brought up at the beginning of questions on human or angelic sin. In those contexts, Anselm is an authority to be reckoned with. It is less clear, however, what we can infer from this regarding Scotus's own considered views on freedom and free will. Moreover, to my knowledge, Anselm's explicit definition of freedom appears only on six occasions in his works and when it does it is, so to speak, never really presented in Scotus's voice.[13] One would expect Scotus to be a bit more overt if he really made Anselm's definition his own.

Tellingly, Scotus uses Anselm's teaching on freedom as an authority to support his signature view that there are concepts, such as the concept of being, that apply univocally to God and creatures.[14] It is Anselm's attempt to come up with a definition of freedom that applies to both God and creatures that is the most prominent feature that Scotus takes over from Anselm's approach. This is the background in *Ordinatio* II, d. 44, where a quotation from Anselm leads Scotus to declare:

> With respect to Anselm, I say that freedom taken in an absolute sense is a pure perfection (*perfectio simpliciter*). Therefore, it is formally posited (*formaliter ponitur*) in God, according to him. Freedom in us is limited, although it can be considered according to its formal concept (*rationem*

---

[12] *Ord.* II, d. 7, q. un., n. 82 (Vat. VIII, 113). See also *Lect.* II, d. 7, q. un., n. 40 (Vat. XIX, 13); d. 23, q. un., nn. 38–39 (216); dd. 34–37, qq. 1–5, n. 98 (Vat. XIX, 350–351); and d. 44, q. un., n. 2 (Vat. XIX, 405); *Ord.* II, d. 44, q. un., n. 9 (Vat. VIII, 493); *Rep.* II, d. 7, q. 3 (Vivès XXII, 635a); d. 23, q. un. (Vivès XXIII, 110a); and d. 44, q. un. (Vivès XXIII, 231b–232a).

[13] *Ord.* II, d. 7, q. un., n. 85 (Vat. VIII, 114): "Et si arguas secundum Anselmum quod 'liberum arbitrium est potestas servandi rectitudinem propter se' . . ."; *Ord.* II, d. 28, q. un., n. 4 (Vat. VIII, 293); *Lect.* II, d. 7, q. un., n. 40 (Vat. XIX, 13): ". . . et secundum Anselmum *De libero arbitrio*, 'Libertas est potestas servandi rectitudinem'"; *Lect.* II, d. 28, q. un., n. 4 (Vat. XIX, 273); *Rep.* II, d. 7, q. 1 (Vivès XXII, 625a); and d. 28, q. un. (Vivès XXIII, 137a).

[14] See, e.g., *Lect.* I, dist. 3, q. 3, p. 1, qq. 1–2, n. 33 (Vat. XVI, 237): "Item, Anselmus *De libero arbitrio* cap. 1: 'Postestas peccandi non est potestas libertatis, alioquin Deus non haberet libertatem'; sed hoc non sequeretur nisi libertas secundum se univoce conveniret nobis et Deo." See also *Ord.* I, d. 8, p. 1, q. 3, n. 72 (Vat. IV, 185–186); *Rep.* I-A, d. 3, q. 1, n. 35 (Wolter and Bychkov, 195).

eius formalem), i.e., without such a limitation. And then it is not a limited perfection, but a pure perfection.[15]

This raises the question: What is the "formal concept" (*ratio formalis*) according to which freedom is a perfection that applies to God and creatures such as human beings? And what exactly is the limitation that applies to human freedom?

II   FREEDOM AND THE POWER FOR OPPOSITES

It is often said that Duns Scotus changed how medieval philosophers and theologians thought about freedom, insofar he is one of the first authors who considered a power for opposites to be a fundamental feature of freedom. In fact, some commentators consider a power for opposites, or more precisely the ability to choose among alternatives, to be the above-mentioned formal concept of freedom common to God and creatures.[16] In a famous passage of the *Ordinatio*, Scotus writes about the power for opposites:

> I say that the will, insofar as it is a first act, is free with respect to opposite acts (*libera est ad oppositos actus*); by means of these opposite acts it is also free with respect to opposite objects (*ad opposita obiecta*), towards which it tends; and finally, it is free with respect to opposite effects (*ad oppositos effectus*), which it produces. The first sort of freedom (*prima libertas*) has necessarily some imperfection attached to it, for it comes with the passive potentiality and mutability of the will. The third sort of freedom is not the same as the second, for even if *per impossibile* it brought about nothing outside, the will can—insofar as it is a will—still tend freely (*libere*) towards the object. But the second sort of freedom is without imperfection—rather it is necessary for perfection—because every perfect power can tend towards all that which is apt to be an object of such a power. Therefore, a perfect will can tend towards all that which is apt to be willable. Thus, freedom without imperfection—i.e., insofar as it is freedom (*in quantum libertas*)— is with respect to opposite objects towards which the will tends. And it is accidental to this sort of freedom that the will produces opposite effects.[17]

[15] *Ord.* II, d. 44, q. un., n. 8 (Vat. VIII, 493). The first reference to Anselm is to *De libertate arbitrii*, c. 1, the second to *Monologion*, c. 15 (Schmitt I, 29), where Anselm develops his idea of *perfectiones simpliciter* (although he doesn't use this expression).

[16] See, for example, Langston 1996: 158–159: "[T]he texts reveal that Scotus's own view of freedom is more properly connected with what has been called 'basic freedom': the ability to choose among alternatives. This is the concept of freedom that is univocal to God and creatures."

[17] *Ord.* I, d. 38, p. 2 and d. 39, qq. 1–5, n. 15 (Vat. VI, 417). The editors of the Vatican edition published this text in an appendix to volume VI because, as a marginal note in Assisi, Biblioteca comuniale, ms. 137 (the famous ms. A of Scotus's *Ordinatio*) explains, Scotus left this section blank

An almost identical passage can be found in Scotus's earlier *Lectura*; and his later *Reportatio* repeats the same main points, although he there prefers to speak of indifference (*indifferentia*) towards opposites rather than of freedom (*libertas*).[18] The line of thought presented in the passage quoted is clear. For Scotus, we human beings are free because our will is free. This raises the question of what it means for the will to be free. Common sense seems to indicate that this freedom has to do with alternatives or opposites. I seem to be free to do x if I am also able to do the opposite of x, including refraining from doing x. Or applied to volitions (acts of the will, which precede bodily actions), I seem to be free to will x if I am also able to not will x. For Scotus, the openness to such alternatives is something we all can experience.[19] But of what kind are these alternatives or opposites with respect to which we are said to be free? Scotus distinguishes three types, which leads him to distinguish three types of freedom—freedom with respect to opposite acts, opposite objects, and opposite effects—and to explain how they are related.

The easiest case is the third type of freedom. Being free with respect to opposite effects is obviously something secondary. Being free to go to the library or to the theatre depends, among other things, on the freedom to tend or direct oneself towards different objects such as going to the library or going to the theatre. In other words, it depends on freedom with respect to opposite objects and is thus not fundamental. The relationship between the other two types of freedom is more complicated. On the one hand, human agents are, as Scotus notes, free with respect to opposite objects through opposite acts: our will's relationship to opposite objects is always in terms of willing or not-willing (or willing against). This makes it sound as if the second type of freedom depends on the first. But on the other hand, Scotus claims that the second type, the freedom with respect to opposite objects, is a perfection, whereas the first is imperfect.

Why does freedom with respect to different acts, i.e., different volitions, involve imperfection? Scotus points to a "passive potentiality" (*passiva potentialitas*) and to "mutability," yet this hardly amounts to an explanation. What he has in mind can best be understood when we compare

---

in his personal copy of the *Ordinatio*. But for our present purpose, there is no reason to doubt that the text expresses Scotus's own thinking, as can also be gathered from the parallel texts mentioned in the next footnote.

[18] *Lect.* I, d. 39, qq. 1–5, nn. 45–46 (Vat. XVII, 493–494) and *Rep.* I-A, dd. 39–40, qq. 1–3, n. 38 (Wolter and Bychkov, 475–476).

[19] See, e.g., *QMet.*, IX, q. 15, n. 30 (OPh IV, 682–683): "Experitur enim qui vult se posse non velle, sive nolle."

Scotus to his contemporaries and predecessors. One reason why most thirteenth-century thinkers rejected the idea that freedom involves a power for opposites is exactly that conceiving of freedom in this way would involve making mutability and fickleness a feature of freedom, which would not sit well with the idea that freedom is a perfection nor that freedom can be ascribed to God.[20] For an agent to be free with respect to opposite volitions, the agent must be able to undergo a change from one volition to its opposite. But being able to undergo change just means to possess a passive potentiality that allows it to be subject to those changes. Regardless of what one thinks of the force of this common objection, in distinguishing between freedom with respect to opposite objects and freedom with respect to opposite volitions, Scotus finds an elegant way to defuse its appeal. Yes, the objection applies if one thinks about opposite volitions, but it doesn't sting when one has opposite objects in mind. It is thus with respect to opposite objects that Scotus locates the core of freedom or, as he says in the passage above, "freedom . . . insofar as it is freedom."

Have we found the formal concept of freedom? It seems so. For unlike the freedom with respect to opposite volitions, which involves an imperfection and belongs to us due to a limitation of our will's nature, freedom with respect to opposite objects can also be found in God. Unlike us, however, God doesn't require different acts to tend to opposite objects. God can do so with one simple and unlimited volition.[21] That the formal concept of freedom cannot consist of freedom with respect to opposite effects is clear. Although this freedom applies to God as well, it is only secondary freedom, just as it is in us.[22]

The case of divine freedom allows us to grasp other important features of this formal concept of freedom. First, freedom must be an active power, since God is supremely active. Freedom with respect to opposite objects is thus nothing other than an active power with respect to opposite objects (as opposed to a passive power of being able to be affected by opposite

---

[20] See, e.g., Henry of Ghent, *Summa quaest. ord.*, a. 45, q. 3 (Opera omnia XXIX, 116–118) and earlier in the thirteenth century Philip the Chancellor, *Summa de bono* (Wicki, 183–184).

[21] *Ord.* I, d. 38, p. 2 and d. 39, qq. 1–5, n. 21 (Vat. VI, 425–426): "Nostra enim erat libera ad oppositos actus, ad hoc ut esset ad obiecta opposita, proper limitationem utriusque actus respectu sui obiecti; ergo posita illimitatione volitionis eiusdem ad diversa obiecta, non oportet propter libertatem ad opposita obiecta ponere libertatem ad oppositos actus... Remanet ergo libertas illa quae est per se perfectionis et sine imperfectione, scilicet ad opposita obiecta, ita quod sicut voluntas nostra potest diversis volitionibus tendere in diversa volita, ita illa voluntas potest unica volitione simplici illimitata tendere in quaecumque volita."

[22] Ibid. (Vat. VI, 426): "Ipsa etiam voluntas divina libera est ad oppositos effectus, sed haec non est prima libertas, sicut nec in nobis."

objects). Second, God is not subject to time and temporal succession and as a result God's freedom or power with respect to opposite objects cannot be such that, say, before tending towards one object, God could have tended towards its opposite. For there to be divine freedom, God must be able to tend—and thus have a real power—towards object x at the very same moment God tends to its opposite.[23] Note that having a power to tend towards an object at the moment one actually tends towards its opposite, is not the same as having a power to tend towards two opposite objects at the same time. The latter is impossible, even for God. This is of course Scotus's famous doctrine of synchronic—as opposed to diachronic—contingency. For something to be contingent means that it could have been otherwise, for instance, that it is possible for it not to exist (and for something else to exist in its stead). But such a possibility presupposes a real power in which it is grounded. It is thus God's freedom with respect to opposite objects, which comes with a synchronic divine power for opposites, that guarantees the contingency of the creation.

Something similar applies in the case of human freedom. Remember that human agents are free with respect to opposite objects by being free with respect to opposite volitions. Because human agents act in time, their wills possess what Scotus calls a "manifest power for opposites," in virtue of which their wills can will one thing after not willing the same (and vice versa). In other words, human wills possess a diachronic power for opposite acts. But according to Scotus, the human will also has another "not so manifest" power, which has nothing to do with succession, a power in virtue of which the will has an ability for opposite volitions in the sense that at the very moment it wills x, it has a real power to not will x or to will against x.[24] Due to this latter power, human actions are contingent and such that they could have been otherwise.

If this sounds as if it turns the will into something very special, then this is exactly the conclusion Scotus is happy to draw. Yes, wills are special two-way powers—Scotus uses the Aristotelian expression "rational powers"—because they are not powers determined to only one manifestation, but to

---

[23] Ibid., n. 22 (Vat. VI, 427); *Lect.* I, d. 39, qq. 1–5, nn. 53–54 (Vat. XVII, 496–497).

[24] *Ord.* I, d. 38, p. 2 and d. 39, qq. 1–5, n. 16 (Vat. VI, 417–419): "Dico quod istam libertatem concomitatur una potentia ad opposita manifesta. Licet enim non sit in ea potentia ad simul velle et non velle (quia hoc nihil est), tamen est in ea potentia ad velle post non velle sive ad successionem actuum oppositorum... Tamen est et alia (non ita manifesta), absque omni successione... Libertatem ergo voluntatis nostrae, in quantum est ad oppositos actus, concomitatur potentia tam ad opposita successive, quam ad opposita pro eodem instanti." See also *Lect.* I, d. 39, qq. 1–5, nn. 47–51 (Vat. XVII, 494–496). For more on this "non-manifest power" see the classic paper Dumont 1995.

opposite manifestations. They need to be distinguished from ordinary
natural powers, which are determined to be manifested in only one way.
Of course, there are cases when natural powers can give rise to opposites
too. Heat, for instance, usually produces heat, yet in the complicated setup
of a refrigerator, it produces cold. But regardless of the final effect, heat's
immediate manifestation, provided normal conditions apply and a suitable
heatable object is present, is always that it produces heat in something else.
By contrast, rational powers can immediately manifest themselves in
opposite ways "with no change in their nature" (*manens natura una*).[25]

III FREEDOM AS SELF-DETERMINATION

What we have seen in the previous section suggests that, according to
Scotus, the formal concept of freedom is this: freedom is an active power
for opposites. This applies to God as well as to human beings. The main
difference between divine and human freedom is that for us freedom is
primarily an active power for opposite volitions, whereas for God freedom
is primarily an active power towards opposite objects. Secondarily, for both
God and us, this active power for opposites also results in an active power
towards opposite effects. Not only does this result seem to accord with
Scotus's main texts, it also captures something of our common intuition
about our own freedom.

Scotus is ready to defend this understanding of freedom in cases that
suggest otherwise. One scenario frequently discussed by medieval theologians and philosophers concerns the state of ultimate happiness, which is
supposed to consist of the beatific vision where one sees God face to face
and seemingly cannot do otherwise than enjoy God. In particular, it seems
impossible in this instance that rational creatures are able to sin. However,
if freedom consists of a power for opposites then it appears that rational
creatures lose their freedom in this highest state they are capable of, which
seems odd. This is another reason why many of Scotus's contemporaries
and predecessors deny a straightforward relationship between freedom and
a power for opposites.[26] Remarkably, Scotus is sticking to his guns. For
Scotus the beatific vision does not change anything in the nature of the
agent; in particular, this condition does not affect any of the agent's

---

[25] *QMet.*, IX, q. 15, nn. 10–11 (OPh IV, 677). For the distinction between these kinds of power see
also *Ord.* I, d. 1, p. 2, qq. 1–4, n. 302 and nn. 345–352 (Vat. II, 306–307 and 332–335).
[26] See, e.g., Henry of Ghent, *Summa quaest. ord.*, a. 47, q. 5 (Opera omnia XXX, 34): "De ratione
enim libertatis simpliciter non est posse velle et non velle, ut quidam putant. . ."

intrinsic powers. But the condition plays the role of an extrinsic cause that interferes with the agent's ability to fully exercise her intrinsic powers. The best way to put Scotus's idea is maybe to say that the agent retains her capacity to choose/act otherwise, but face-to-face with God no longer has the opportunity to do so. For Scotus, there is nothing peculiar about this case; he points to our power of sight as providing us with uncontroversial examples. Imagine your sense of sight is fine, but you suddenly enter a room that is pitch black. Obviously, you don't lose your capacity for seeing, even if you no longer have the opportunity to exercise it due to the lack of light. Something similar happens to the power for opposites in the beatific vision.[27]

There is, however, one major problem: tying freedom to a power for opposites can't possibly be Scotus's final word on the formal concept of freedom. For in discussing another important theological case, the persons of the Trinity, Scotus holds that the Holy Spirit is generated freely from the Father and the Son. But, of course, Scotus is also committed to the view that there are necessarily three and only three persons of the Trinity. We are faced with a case where something is both free and necessary. God, understood as the Father, did not have a power for opposites regarding the third person of the Trinity, yet the generation (or "spiration") is a free one.[28] Either Scotus is inconsistent in his teaching on freedom or the above-mentioned understanding of freedom is incomplete.

There are good reasons to go with the second option. In fact, when Scotus explains in his *Questions on the Metaphysics* how freedom is rooted in a two-way or rational power, he hints at a further analysis of the power for opposites. To see this, we need to go back to the fundamental difference between rational and natural powers. What is essential for the latter is that they are determined towards one manifestation, whereas rational powers are not determined towards one outcome and are thus indeterminate. However, indeterminacy comes in two forms:

> There is indeterminacy of insufficiency (*indeterminatio insufficientiae*), namely from potentiality and lack of actuality, in the way matter without form is indeterminate with regard to carrying out the action of the form;

---

[27] *Ord.* IV, d. 49, p. 1, q. 6, nn. 350–351 (Vat. XIV, 377–378). Strictly speaking, Scotus speaks of "remote" and "proximate power"; in the beatific vision the agent loses only the proximate power to do otherwise/sin. The sight example is changed from Scotus's own.

[28] Scotus discusses this issue in *Quodl.*, q. 16. For the importance of Scotus's teaching on divine freedom for his general account of freedom, see also Frank 1982. For other texts in which Scotus treats the same issue, see *Ord.* I, d. 10, q. un. (Vat. IV, 339–378); *Rep.* I-A, d. 10, q. 3 (Wolter and Bychkov, 400–404); *Lect.* I, d. 10, q. un. (Vat. XVII, 115–126). See also Cross 2005: 137–142.

and there is the indeterminacy of superabundant sufficiency (*superabundantis sufficientiae*), which comes from the boundlessness of actuality (*ex illimitatione actualitatis*), be it in an unqualified or qualified sense. Now, what is indeterminate in the first sense is not reduced to actuality unless it first is determined to a form by something else (*determinetur ad formam ab alio*). But something indeterminate in the second sense can determine itself (*potest se determinare*).[29]

A wall or any other surface, for instance, is indeterminate with respect to its colour: it can either be white or blue or of whatever other colour. The surface's indeterminacy with respect to colour is the result of a lack or insufficiency; surfaces are things that by themselves are not determined to have a certain colour. If they are white or blue then this is because they are determined by something else to have a given colour, say by the action of a painter. According to Scotus, there are, however, entities that lack determination not because they are passively indeterminate, such as a surface, but because they possess by themselves and through their own actuality the power to determine themselves to this or that. God is one of these other beings, for God obviously does not require something else to be determined to create this or that. But human beings, or more precisely, their wills, are also of this kind.[30]

The above-mentioned passage suggests that for something to be able to determine itself is even more fundamental than having a power for opposites; or better: that the ability to determine itself grounds the power for opposites. Scotus seems to draw this conclusion explicitly in a later passage of the same text when he compares the will to the intellect:

And the will is concerned with opposites (*est oppositorum*), both as regards its own act and as regards the acts of inferior powers [of the soul]. And it is concerned with opposites (*est oppositorum*) not according to the mode of nature (*modo naturae*), in the way the intellect acts, which is unable to determine itself towards an alternative (*ad alterum*), but in a free mode, being able to determine itself (*modo libero potens se determinare*). And therefore it is a power (*potentia*), because it can do something, for it can determine itself. But the intellect is strictly speaking (*proprie*) not a power

---

[29] *QMet.*, IX, q. 15, nn. 31–32 (OPh IV, 683). See also *Ord.* I, d. 8, p. 2, q. un., n. 298 (Vat. IV, 324); *Lect.* I, d. 7, q. 1, n. 26 (Vat. XVI, 481–482); d. 8, p. 2, q. un., n. 278 (Vat. XVII, 105); *Lect.* II, d. 25, q. un., n. 92 (Vat. XIX, 260–261). Scotus is not the first to distinguish between active and passive indeterminacy; for background, see Boulnois 2011: 408–409.

[30] *QMet.*, IX, q. 15, n. 34 (OPh IV, 683–684): "Indeterminatio autem quae ponitur in voluntate non est materialis, nec imperfectionis in quantum ipsa est activa, sed est excellentis perfectionis et potestativae, non alligatae ad determinatum actum."

with respect to external things, because if it is about opposites, it cannot determine itself, and unless it is determined by something else it cannot bring about anything externally.[31]

The intellect can be about opposites too. I can think of this rather than that, or of one and the same object in this way rather than in that way, or not at all. But for Scotus, this is not due to the spontaneity or any self-determination of the intellect itself. It is due to external and internal stimuli, as well as the influence of the will, which determine our intellective powers to produce a certain output. The intellect fundamentally operates "according to the mode of nature" (*modo naturae*). By contrast, the will is a power for opposites in a completely different way, namely, "in a free mode" (*modo libero*), precisely insofar as the will is able to determine itself.[32]

If my interpretation is correct and the power for opposites is strictly speaking secondary to a more basic capacity for self-determination, then it makes sense to situate freedom in this more fundamental capacity. In most cases—especially in human freedom and in divine freedom with respect to creatures—the power for opposites and the capacity for self-determination go hand in hand. However, that they are not identical and the one is the result of the other explains how Scotus can insist that the intra-Trinitarian production of the Holy Spirit is free yet still necessary, for nothing indicates that the relevant sort of necessity is incompatible with self-determination.[33]

---

[31] Ibid., n. 41 (OPh IV, 686): "Et ipsa [sc., voluntas] est oppositorum, tam quoad actum proprium quam quoad actus inferiorum; et non oppositorum modo naturae, sicut intellectus non potens se determinare ad alterum, sed modo libero potens se determinare. Et ideo est potentia, quia ipsa aliquid potest, nam potest se determinare. Intellectus autem proprie non est potentia respectu extrinsecorum, quia ipse, si est oppositorum non potest se [se DHK; quis *ed.*] determinare; et nisi determinetur nihil extra poterit." Note that in the last clause, I am following the reading "se determinare" present in the three manuscripts Padova, Biblioteca Antoniana, ms. 186; Tortosa, Biblioteca Capitular de la Catedral, ms. 201; and Bruxelles, Bibliothèque Royale, ms. 2908 (14310–12).

[32] For the close connection between freedom and self-determination see also *Ord.* I, d. 13, q. un., n. 56 (Vat. V, 94).

[33] In *Rep.* I-A, d. 28, q. 3, n. 87 (Wolter and Bychkov, 218–219), Scotus states explicitly that the indeterminacy of boundlessness (*indeterminatio illimitationis*) is compatible with necessity, but he does not really provide an explanation for why this is so. There are of course some forms of necessity that are incompatible with self-determination, such as the necessity that is imposed on something due to coercion. But for obvious reasons, God cannot be under such necessity nor can God's intra-Trinitarian activity.

IV   FREEDOM AS A MODE OF CAUSATION

One might hold that we are able to determine ourselves with respect to our volitions and actions because we possess a power to do or choose otherwise, a power we have for opposites. In this picture, the power for opposites explains why we are capable of self-determination. As we have just seen, this is not how Scotus seems to think about the relationship between the two. For he suggests exactly the converse relationship between the two. This may, however, invite an objection: the capacity for self-determination is a complex capacity comprising not just agential capacities but also cognitive ones, such as the capacity to represent the agent him- or herself and various courses of action, and further cognitive capacities enabling the agent to weigh different options. For this and other reasons, we usually think that only complex beings are capable of self-determination because only such beings come with the relevant set of subcapacities. But if that is how we ought to think about a capacity for self-determination, then Scotus is straying away from the truth, since for him the capacity for self-determination seems to be something primitive and is, as the last quote shows, primarily applied to the will, a faculty of the soul, instead of the full-blown human agent.

There is no reason to suspect that Scotus would deny that some acts of human self-determination require all this complexity. But cognitive capacities and the like cannot ultimately account for self-determination, even as a bundle, since cognitive capacities, as we learned from his statements about the intellect, are natural powers that are capable of only one determined manifestation. Consequently, they determine us more than that they allow us to determine ourselves. Only because of our will are we genuinely capable of self-determination in the more complex sense of self-determination.[34] If self-determination is not something we should properly ascribe to the will on the basis that we commonly understand by self-determination something more complex and at a different level, then we could use the term "spontaneity" to capture Scotus's understanding of the role of the will. But Scotus's point remains the same: only because of this basic spontaneity of the will can we go beyond the determination by natural causes, only because of it can we be true sources of our own activities. Moreover, only because of this fundamental freedom at the level of the will can more complex substances such as human beings be free agents. And for the same reason, a volition is strictly speaking—or

---

[34] See also *Quodl.*, q. 18, n. 9 (Vivès XXVI, 241b).

"formally" (*formaliter*)—not free, but the will alone.[35] It is free only insofar as it results from a free will.

That Scotus is not speaking loosely or inadvertently when he attributes the capacity for self-determination directly to the will becomes clear when we turn to passages in other works, where he talks about freedom as a specific intrinsic mode of causation. In his *Quodlibet*, for instance, he notes that "'nature' (*natura*) and 'freedom' (*libertas*) are the primary differences of [the species of] 'agent' or 'principle of action'" and a will is a type of agent "that always has its proper mode of causing (*proprium modum causandi*), namely, freely (*libere*)."[36] This proper mode of causing is a primitive mode, i.e., one that cannot be further analyzed and explained by recourse to prior causes.[37]

Unfortunately, Scotus also invokes primitiveness when addressing the question of how it can be that freedom—understood as this primitive spontaneity of the will—is compatible with necessity, as in the case of the intra-Trinitarian processions. Using Aristotle's words, he remarks that one should not seek a reason where no further reason can be given. The compatibility simply follows from the nature of the will and the divine goodness.[38] That we can't explain how freedom and necessity are compatible—or in other words: how a free cause can bring about something with necessity—does not however mean that we can't prove that they are compatible. And, in fact, Scotus attempts three demonstrations of their compatibility. There is no space here to examine these in detail. The second demonstration states:

> Action with respect to the ultimate end is the most perfect action. In such an action firmness in acting (*firmitas in agendo*) contributes to the action's perfection. Therefore, necessity (*necessitas*) in this action does not take away, but rather contributes to that which belongs to its perfection, to which freedom belongs (*cuiusmodi est libertas*).[39]

[35] See, e.g., *Ord.* I, d. 13, q. un., n. 45 (Vat. V, 88): "Actio volendi in nobis non est formaliter libera, sed ipsa voluntas."

[36] *Quodl.*, q. 16, nn. 56 and 59 (Noone and Roberts, 188 and 190). See also ibid., n. 62 (Noone and Roberts, 192); *Ord.* I, d. 13, q. un., nn. 45 and 50 (Vat. V, 89 and 92). For *libertas* as *conditio intrinseca voluntatis* see *Rep.* I-A, d. 10, q. 3, n. 51 (Wolter and Bychkov, 402).

[37] *QMet.*, IX, q. 15, n. 24 (OPh IV, 681). See also *Quodl.*, q. 16, n. 65 (Noone and Roberts, 194): "[S]icut non est alia ratio quare hoc habet talem modum essendi, nisi quia est tale ens, sic non est alia ratio quare hoc habet talem modum agendi, puta libere..., nisi quia est tale principium agendi."

[38] *Quodl.*, q. 16, n. 39 (Noone and Roberts, 179–180), where he refers to Aristotle, *Met.* IV, 6, 1011a12–13. See also *Lect.* I, d. 8, p. 2, q. un., n. 279 (Vat. XVII, 105).

[39] *Quodl.*, q. 16, n. 37 (Noone and Roberts, 179).

The argument is bound to raise more questions than it settles and to defend it would go beyond the scope of this chapter. Here it is enough to notice that the necessity in question is "firmness" (*firmitas*). Obviously, this necessity results from the way in which the action is produced and is not a necessity imposed by extrinsic determination or coercion, which are clearly incompatible with freedom understood as self-determination.

Even if freedom is compatible with necessity understood as firmness, human beings are not capable of willing anything with this necessity so as to lose their power for opposites with regard to such an object.[40] It does not follow, however, that having a power for opposites is just the second best and a weakness; God too has a power for opposites with regard to any object other than himself. Whether a will relates to an object with necessity or contingently, i.e., with a power for opposites, has also to do with the object and its degree of goodness.

As a result of all this, it follows that according to Scotus the distinction between natural and free causes is not the same as the distinction between causes that bring something about with necessity and those that bring something about contingently. As there are free causes that act with necessity, as the divine case is meant to demonstrate, so there can be natural causes that bring about effects contingently, insofar as other causes can interfere with them and impede their causality.[41]

V SCOTUS'S LIBERTARIANISM

As we have seen, Scotus attempts to present a comprehensive theory of freedom of the will, a theory that proves to be quite complex. Before closing, I would like to go back to what now turns out to be part of a much larger picture, namely the case of human freedom. In particular, I would like to draw a connection between Scotus's understanding of human freedom and the modern debate about free will. We saw that the power for opposites plays an important role in Scotus's understanding of human

---

[40] *Quodl.*, q. 16, nn. 16 and 22 (Noone and Roberts, 168 and 170).
[41] *Quodl.*, q. 16, n. 40 (Noone and Roberts, 180): "[N]on est eadem divisio in principium naturale et liberum, et in principio necessario activum et contingenter; aliquod enim naturale potest contingenter agere, quia potest impediri; igitur pari ratione possibile est aliquod liberum, stante libertate, necessario agere." There is however a question whether Scotus is really permitted to say that natural causes can cause contingently. For in his various treatments of divine foreknowledge in dist. 39 of the first book of his various commentaries on the *Sentences*, he seems to say that contingency presupposes a will. For the claim that free vs. natural is more basic than the distinction between necessary and contingent, see also *Ord.* I, d. 1, p. 2, q. 2, n. 31 (Vat. II, 87–88) and *Rep.* I-A, d. 10, q. 3, n. 53 (Wolter and Bychkov, 402–403).

freedom, so it would be natural to consider him a libertarian about free will since libertarians usually insist that freedom is tied to a robust power to do otherwise. Some commentators, however, reject the idea that Scotus subscribes to a libertarian understanding of freedom and consider his views a version of compatibilism.

Settling the question as to whether Scotus was a libertarian or compatibilist about free will is not as straightforward as one might think. Scotus holds that human free will is compatible with divine foreknowledge; and since God's foreknowledge is necessary, he is a compatibilist of some sort. But this he shares with other medieval philosophers and theologians, and this is, in any case, not the sort of compatibilism that modern philosophers have in mind or are interested in. The latter frequently define determinism, roughly, as the thesis that every state of the world is the result of a previous state and the laws of nature. Compatibilism is then the idea that free will is compatible with determinism so defined. It seems as if no medieval author could be a compatibilist of this kind, since medieval authors lack the relevant notion of a law of nature. A reasonable strategy, albeit one a bit *ad hoc,* is thus to take ideas cherished by libertarians or compatibilists and to consider Scotus's attitude towards these.

Employing this strategy, Douglas Langston judges that "Scotus cannot hold a libertarian definition of freedom."[42] For Langston, the "core libertarian freedom is the notion that an agent freely performs an action *a* if the agent can perform *a* and can refrain from performing *a*." Yet libertarians insist that the 'can' in question does not designate a mere capacity, but a more robust ability that includes the opportunity to do so. The power for opposites that free human agents possess according to Scotus undoubtedly includes a power to perform and refrain from a certain action. However, God's foreknowledge, while not depriving the agent of the mere capacity to do/choose otherwise than he or she actually does/chooses, takes away the opportunity to do so and thus robs the agent of the relevant ability. "Many of those who continue to claim that Scotus endorses a libertarian view of freedom" fail, according to Langston, to notice the crucial distinction between capacities and abilities and are thus misled.[43] This analysis sounds plausible if we think back to the case of the beatific vision discussed in Section III. As we saw there, in the state of ultimate happiness the beatified agent has lost any opportunity to exercise her power to do/choose otherwise and thus to refrain from her current action, while still

---

[42] Langston 2010: 272. See also Langston 1986, chapters 2 and 3.
[43] Langston 2010: 270–272; see also Langston 1986: 36.

retaining a power to do so. But other texts seem to support Langston's conclusion. He points, for instance, to passages like this one, in which Scotus comments on the compatibility of God's foreknowledge and human freedom:

> But if it is the sort of necessity with respect to which we use to say "it is necessary that something be so or that something will happen in this way," one ought not fear that such necessity, if it is posited with respect to our foreknown action, takes freedom away from us (*nobis aufert libertatem*). For this necessity of foreknowledge or of the foreknown as foreknown (*necessitas praescientiae, vel praesciti ut praesciti*), even if it is a necessity of immutability (*necessitas immutabilitatis*), is not however absolutely a necessity of inevitability or of determination of every kind (*simpliciter necessitas inevitabilitatis sive omnimodae determinationis*). [The action] is only inevitable on the assumption that it is so foreknown [by God].[44]

Because divine foreknowledge does not impose determination of all kind, our wills "retain their powers to act or not act … but they act in accord with the orders of causes God has established."[45]

Langston presents, in my view, the strongest case for a compatibilist interpretation of Scotus's philosophy of action. Yet his interpretation is not without problems.[46] It is difficult to see why Scotus would be so adamant in insisting that not everything happens necessarily[47] if he were at the same time harbouring compatibilist intuitions. Moreover, if Langston were correct in assessing Scotus as a compatibilist, then it would be hard to see what Scotus's point would be in insisting as much as he does on the fact that the will is a special two-way power, distinct from natural powers.

Scotus's conception of the will is usually taken as evidence that he is a libertarian about free will.[48] Consider how he describes the will's "non-manifest" power for opposites:

> In the same instant (*in eodem instanti*), in which the will has one act of willing, in the same instant and for the same instant (*in eodem et pro eodem*) it can have an opposite act of willing.[49]

---

[44] *Quodl.*, q. 16, n. 67 (Noone and Roberts, 196). Langston discusses this case in Langston 1986: 39–44.
[45] Langston 2010: 277.
[46] For a discussion of Langston and other compatibilist interpretations, see Frank 1992.
[47] See, e.g., *Lect.* I, d. 39, qq. 1–5, n. 40 (Vat. XVII, 491).　　[48] See Williams 1998a.
[49] *Lect.* I, d. 39, qq. 1–5, n. 50 (Vat. XVII, 495). See also *Ord.* I, d. 38, p. 2 and d. 39, qq. 1–5, n. 16 (Vat. VI, 417–419); *Rep.* I-A, dd. 39–40, qq. 1–3, n. 42 (Wolter and Bychkov, 477).

Assume that when you make a decision, you form a volition to do *x*, whatever *x* turns out to be. In Scotus's view, in the very same moment—thus without any need of a change in the will—you possess, in virtue of your will, the power to form an opposite volition.[50] For if it were the case that something has to change in the will for you to be able to form an opposite volition, then we would no longer talk about the same moment or instant. This way of describing the will makes it sound as if the will is what modern metaphysicians and philosophers of action call an "agent cause." As the text makes clear, Scotus's wills are efficient causes that can start new and alternative causal chains and are not determined by prior events or conditions. There are of course important differences between Scotus and modern philosophers of action. Unlike classic modern libertarians such as Roderick Chisholm, for whom the human person ought to be considered an agent cause, Scotus locates agent causation in a particular power of the human soul. But this can hardly be a reason not to count him among the members of the libertarian camp.

Having said this, I agree with Langston that there is an important question as to what 'can' means in the context of the will's power for opposite volitions, given such cases as the beatific vision and, more globally, divine foreknowledge, which present cases in which the agent's ability to access opposite courses of action seems to be threatened or at least curtailed. And the plausibility of Scotus's metaphysics of action will of course depend on whether one can give meaning to the relevant sense of 'can'.[51] But regardless of whether Scotus's view is defensible or not, it strikes me as obvious that, on his understanding of the will's power for opposites, the 'can' in question is more robust than the conditional sense of 'can'—as in "would have willed otherwise, if the agent had desired/decided, etc. otherwise"—compatibilists are usually content with. All this means is that Scotus's view of the will's freedom is fundamentally a libertarian one, even if it is possible to conceive of stronger forms of the power for opposites, forms that he rejects for various reasons.

VI CONCLUSION

I wish to close this chapter by raising a final objection to my reading of Scotus's account of freedom. As we have seen, freedom is for Scotus

---

[50] See also the text above in n. 25.
[51] This has been denied by Scotus's critics from William of Ockham onwards.

nothing other than the fundamental spontaneity of the will, a spontaneity through which wills determine themselves, which in most cases means
that wills have a power for opposites. However, in a famous passage in
the second book of the *Ordinatio*, Scotus refers to Anselm of
Canterbury's affection for justice (*affectio iustitiae*) as "the will's innate
freedom (*libertas innata voluntati*), because it is the first moderator
(*prima moderatrix*) of the affection for the advantageous (*affectio commodi*)."[52] This seems to suggest that freedom is (a) not just spontaneity,
but more concretely an affection for justice, whatever this means; and (b)
that freedom is more strongly related to the moral good than
I previously indicated.

The first thing to note about remarks like the one just quoted is that
they cannot be meant to address the formal concept of freedom. The idea
of the two affections of the will applies only to the wills of created beings
and not to God's will. Second, limiting ourselves to creatures, we might be
tempted to explain these remarks away by pointing out that Scotus is here
merely commenting on an idea by Anselm of Canterbury, rather than
speaking for himself. Yet there's no need for such manoeuvres. As Peter
King has recently shown, Scotus is engaged in a radical reinterpretation of
Anselm's two affections that has little in common with Anselm's original
proposal.[53] According to this reinterpretation, the affection for justice is
nothing other than the will itself insofar as it is free, and the affection for
the advantageous nothing other than the will as an appetite. The two
affections are merely two aspects of the very same thing. Note, moreover,
that in Scotus's own words, the will "can moderate itself with respect to
willing through its freedom" (*per libertatem ipsam potest se moderari*)[54]—
this makes it sound as if the affection for justice is not something more
fundamental than the will's spontaneity. On the contrary, the will's
spontaneity makes it possible for the will to exhibit the affection for justice.

That the passage under discussion links freedom to justice and, by
extension, to moral goodness, should not surprise us here. If Scotus had
been asked why human beings possess freedom of the will, he would no
doubt have responded that we possess this power to bring about morally
good actions. In this sense, he maintains an asymmetric account of
freedom. However, even though the goal or final cause is important for a

[52] *Ord.* II, d. 6, q. 2, n. 49 (Vat. VIII, 49).   [53] King 2010.
[54] *Ord.* II, d. 6, q. 2, n. 51 (Vat. VIII, 51).

full-fledged account of something, it is necessary to distinguish it from the other types of causes and descriptions of the same thing. In this sense, it is complementary to conceive of freedom as the basic spontaneity of the will as well as something the will (and by extension, the agent) possesses for the sake of acting justly.[55]

[55] Research for this chapter was supported by an Insight grant from the Social Sciences and Research Council of Canada (SSHRC). All translations in this chapter are mine.

CHAPTER 6

Duns Scotus on the dignities of human nature

Marilyn McCord Adams

I REFLECTIVE EQUILIBRIUM AND THE ROBUSTNESS OF NATURES

Philosophical theologian that he was, John Duns Scotus was a believer in the dignities (plural) of human nature. Already Aristotelian philosophy celebrated human dignity (singular): human beings are rational animals; the material world mentioned here exists for the sake of humankind. Christian theology pointed beyond natural to the supernatural dignities, to the honor God pays to humankind in the incarnation and to particular human beings in predestining them to glory. For neo-Thomists, the method of investigating these dignities is straightforward. "Grace builds on nature," so look to philosophy for an analysis of natural human dignity, and then turn to theology for an account of further "upgrades." Scotus finds such approaches over-simple for a combination of philosophical and theological reasons.

I.I The robustness of natures

Philosophically, medieval Aristotelians are committed to the robustness of natural kinds. Neither Aquinas nor Scotus is a Humean: they believe in real and not merely nominal essences. They hold that the constitution of natural kinds is metaphysically necessary, independent of anyone's will, human or Divine.[1] Because what it is to be a thing of a given kind is metaphysically necessary, it is immutable. What it is to be human, what it is to be a cow, and what it is to be fire are the same whatever the situation in which they are instantiated. God can create humans or not. God can put human beings in highly favorable or desperately miserable circumstances. But not even God can change what human nature is essentially:

---

[1] Duns Scotus, *Lect.* I, d. 31, q. un., n. 33 (Vat. XVII, 456); *Ord.* I, d. 35, q. un., n. 32 (Vat. VI, 258).

not even God can bring it about that rational animal is not what it is to be a human being.[2]

Medieval Aristotelians understood substance natures causally. Substantial forms were supposed to "root" formal functional principles, which are naturally consequent upon them. Formal functional principles are distinguished into active efficient causal principles (such as active power to heat up nearby heatables) and passive receptive principles (such as the natural aptitude to be heated up). Here below, *natural kinds have characteristic combinations of active and passive causal powers essential to them—once again, the ones that underwrite their functional regularities.* It follows that *a natural kind cannot be instantiated without the specimen's possessing the active and passive causal powers that essentially belong to that natural kind.*

I.2   Metaphysics constraining narrative interpretation

Medieval Christian theology inherited the doctrine that humankind has not only a nature but also a history. The human condition is said to have been much better in Paradise, much worse after the fall and before judgment, to have been considerably enhanced in Christ even during His earthly career, to be going to be even better in heaven than in Paradise, and even worse in hell than in this present evil age. It is the business of philosophical theologians to analyze and explain such differences. Important here is that—for Scotus—metaphysics sets limits on what such variations can be. Whatever tradition hands down, *it cannot mean that what happens in the fall changes or corrupts the nature, so that it loses or changes functional powers that are essential to it* (i.e., the functional powers a thing cannot be human without). In the wake of Adam's fall, God could have brought the human race to an end. God could and can obstruct or restrict the natural functions of creatures (the way God keeps the fire from singeing the three young men in the fiery furnace). God could cease to obstruct internal and external causes that interfere with a creature's optimal functioning. But God cannot make a thing of a given kind without its essential active and passive causal powers nor could God change the active and passive causal powers that are essential to that kind. Looking forward to the dual destinies of the life to come, Scotus insists, not even God can vary the human condition by altering what are the essential human active and passive causal powers. Nor can God bring

---

[2] *Ord.* IV, d. 49, q. 12, n. 6 (Wad. X, 574; Vivès XXI, 442).

about these differences by adding to human beings active or passive causal powers that are formally incompatible with the powers that are essential to being human (any more than God could make an immaterial substance green).[3]

Two further metaphysical constraints loom large for Scotus as he charts the dignities of human nature. First, not only is a certain array of active and passive causal powers essential to a natural kind. For Scotus, *powers are essentially defined by their adequate objects, where the adequate object is a generic object that subsumes all of the possible objects to which the power extends.* For example, calefactive power is essentially power to heat; vision, essentially power to perceive light and color. Scotus infers that it would be metaphysical nonsense to suppose that the same power (or even the same power-kind) has different adequate objects in different states or at different times. Likewise nonsensical, he finds, is the notion that a power could at one time or in one state extend to an object that does not fall under what was its adequate object at another time or in another state (e.g., vision couldn't be made to extend to perceiving sounds). Second, habits can and do modify certain kinds of powers, but they do not do so by changing a power's adequate object. Rather, habits make it easier for the power to be exercised in relation to something that already fell under its adequate object.[4]

I.3   Narrative cautioning metaphysics

For Scotus, then, it will not do simply to read off the essentials of human nature from reason and experience of human beings in this present cradle-to-grave life and then turn to theology to survey what "upgrades" grace adds. Rather what theology hands down are additional data that must be taken into account in identifying the essentials of human nature in the first place. If it is true that human beings in Eden or heaven or hell have, if Christ in His human nature has a certain property or causal capacity, then it belongs essentially to human nature to have the *passive* capacity to be subject to that property or causal capacity. If their cognitive or appetitive powers extend to certain objects in other states, then it belongs essentially to human nature and to its cognitive and appetitive powers to have adequate objects that subsume those objects.

---

[3] *Ord.* I, d. 3, p. 1, q. 3, nn. 186–187 (Vat. III, 112–114); *Ord.* I, d. 44, q. un., nn. 7–12 (Vat. VI, 365–369).
[4] *Lect.* II, d. 26, q. un., nn. 18–19 (Vat. XIX, 269).

For Scotus, theological narrative complicates method in yet another way. Aristotelian science infers from observed functional regularities to powers in the functioning things to natures that account for why certain power-packs regularly go together. Scotus agrees—*pace* Hume—that observed regularities call for an explanation, but theology alerts us: natural powers are not the only candidate explainers. *The real reason for the regularities might lie in Divine policies, which are different for different states.* In this present evil age, God might be regularly obstructing powers, so that they do not exhibit their full natural range.[5] Alternatively, God might be regularly producing effects in creatures that are beyond the scope of any created active powers (e.g., grace in the soul on the occasion of sacramental participation or the real presence of Christ's Body and Blood when the eucharistic rite is performed).[6] Finally, God might simply create statutory categories that confer on creatures worth that cannot be explained by any merely natural dignity (the way laws confer worth on paper money).[7] To get the right results, metaphysics must use caution: before letting observed regularities set the scope of natural powers, it is necessary to check what theology reveals about Divine policies.

Thus, for Scotus, theological givens instruct us about what we might think unaided natural reason and experience were in the best position to discover: the essentials of human nature. At the same time, Scotus thinks that some *a priori* metaphysical principles are so entrenched, and some empirical assessments so rooted that these set firm limits on how some soteriological claims about the prequel and sequel to this mortal life should be understood. Nor does Scotus appear to follow any simple rule of thumb for where to let which prevail, for when to put philosophy to school to theology or the other way around. What we find in his texts is some sort of reflective equilibrium.

II   ANIMALITY *EX PURIS NATURALIBUS*

Scotus embraces the conclusion of Aristotelian science that rational animal is the real definition of humankind. Humans share the genus animal with the beasts. Scotus lets unaided natural reason and cradle-to-grave experience settle what belongs to animality essentially. Against some other

---

[5] *Ord.* I, d. 3, p. 1, q. 3, n. 187 (Vat. III, 113–114); *Ord.* IV, d. 49, q. 13, nn. 11, 14 (Wad. X, 587, 592; Vivès XXI, 465, 472); *Quodl.*, q. 14, n. 12 (Wad. XII, 373; Vivès XXVI, 46–47).
[6] *Ord.* IV, d. 1, p. 2, q. 1, nn. 188–211 (Vat. XI, 65–75); *Ord.* IV, d. 1, p. 3, q. 1–2, nn. 329–334 (Vat. XI, 117–118).
[7] *Quodl.*, q. 17, nn. 3–9 (Wad. XII, 461–466; Vivès XXVI, 205–211).

theologians, Scotus contends: even in humans, mortality and conflicting appetites are natural consequences of animality.[8]

II.1   Naturally mortal

Scotus takes Aristotelian hylomorphism for granted. He argues that in living things the soul is the dominant substantial form, and that it has a natural aptitude to unite with a body organized from matter by lower-level substantial forms to produce an essential unity. Following Aristotelian science, Scotus insists that souls and bodies are essentially "made for each other," so that souls are apt to perfect only bodies of a certain chemical composition, shape, and density—the ones required for exercising the vital and/or sensory functions essential to the living thing. Scotus follows Aristotelian science to its logical conclusion: it is natural that when plant and animal bodies lose too much of their required definition, they cease to be ensouled—which is what it is for the plants and animals to die. To be sure, human beings are essentially rational and intellectual. But because human beings are also essentially animal, *it is natural to human beings to die.*

Scotus elaborates. Human bodies are by nature alterable in many ways that induce death. Following then up-to-date medical opinion, Scotus identifies the chief and essential cause of death as dehydration: the drying up and inadequate replacement of core moisture by natural heat.[9] Likewise, bad air[10] or drowning in water[11] or extreme heat or cold[12] can wreck the human body. Various forms of violence inflicted by natural agents can also render the body unsuitable for ensoulment. Because the human body is essentially divisible, it is corruptible through dismemberment (say, decapitation or being torn by lions or bitten in two by sharks).[13] Again, the human body is essentially combustible, reducible to ashes by fire.[14] Like other bodies, the human body could simply be acted upon by contraries to the point that it was unfit for animation.[15] Since it is natural for animals (including humans) to exist in a world that contains such corrupting causes, it is natural for animals to die: here below eventual separation from its soul is a natural condition of an animate body.[16] What goes for animal bodies goes for human bodies too: it is natural for the

[8] *Ord.* II, d. 29, q. un., nn. 13–14, 19 (Vat. VIII, 310–312, 314).
[9] *Lect.* II, d. 19, q. un., nn. 10–11 (Vat. XIX, 183–184).   [10] Ibid., n. 10 (Vat. XIX, 184).
[11] Ibid. n. 7 (Vat. XIX, 183).   [12] Ibid., n. 14 (Vat. XIX, 185).
[13] Ibid., n. 15 (Vat. XIX, 185).   [14] Ibid., n. 7 (Vat. XIX, 183).   [15] Ibid., n. 7 (Vat. XIX, 183).
[16] Ibid., n. 19 (Vat. XIX, 186).

human body to be separable from the human soul and so to be mortal and so to have the power of dying.[17] To be sure, human souls are (because they are rational and intellectual) nobler than the souls of plants or beasts. But Scotus follows Aristotelian science against the witness of some church fathers and denies that the human intellectual soul is the kind of thing that could include sufficient intrinsic power to keep body and soul together and to avoid separation.[18]

What, then, of traditional theology's claim that death is a punitive consequence of Adam's fall? There are two strategies for explaining why death did not occur before the fall in Eden the way it does now. One is to say that the human soul and body are *naturally* immune to death, but that their natures were damaged. Scotus is resolute: this cannot be right because what human being is essentially is the same in every state. Scotus takes the other approach of appealing to special Divinely arranged death-preventing protections, which were removed as a punitive consequence of the fall. Thus, Scotus suggests that eating from the tree of life in Paradise would have prevented dehydration. God located Paradise in a temperate climate friendly to human life.[19] God gave *ante-lapsum* Adam dominion over the beasts. Before the fall, there was no sin, and so no human being was out to wreak death and dismemberment on the human body. If some had sinned and others not, the guardian angels would have protected their sinless charges from harm.[20] Scotus speculates: Divine policies were such that if Adam and Eve had not sinned, they would not have died. Whether or not their offspring would have died would have depended on whether or not those offspring sinned, etc.[21] So, considering what it is to be a human being, death is as natural to human beings as to sheep and no more a punishment for humans than for sheep. Considering that God had originally hedged the human race off from death by protective arrangements that were removed in consequence of the fall, death can be seen as a punitive handing us over to the consequences of our nature.[22]

II.2 *Appetites naturally at odds*

All material things have natural appetites or natural tendencies for forms or states that perfect things of their nature. Thus, the elements have natural appetites for their proper places (earth for the center, fire for the rim, water

---

[17] Ibid., nn. 6, 9 (Vat. XIX, 183). [18] *Lect.* II, d. 29, q. un., n. 16 (Vat. XIX, 287).
[19] *Lect.* II, d. 19, q. un., n. 14 (Vat. XIX, 185). [20] Ibid., n. 15 (Vat. XIX, 185).
[21] *Lect.* II, d. 20, q. 1, nn. 8–9 (Vat XIX, 190). [22] Ibid., n. 19 (Vat. XIX, 186).

and air in between). In animals, sensory appetites are triggered by
cognition: they are natural appetites to go for sensory goods insofar as
they are presented by the sensory powers. Because natural appetites are
natural, they act to the limit of their power—unless obstructed—in
pursuit of their object.[23] It is likewise natural for a sensory appetite to
delight in its object when reached and to be "sorry" when access is
denied.[24] Scotus insists that it is natural to human beings to have many
sensory cognitive faculties and many sensory appetites that pull in different
directions (e.g., when something looks good but smells bad). Human
nature functions well when reason intervenes to weigh competing claims
before action is taken by the will. Nevertheless, Scotus declares that it is
not native to will-power to be able to withdraw a sensory appetite from the
object of its delight without penalty.[25] Disharmony and frustration among
human appetites are our *natural* predicament, a consequence of what is
internal to animal nature and not an externally imposed punishment.
Before the fall, original justice made it possible for the will to deny sensory
appetites their objects without sorrow. Once again, loss of original justice
is a punishment that returns us to our natural state.[26]

II.3   Post-mortem dowries

Even theologians who were mind–body dualists maintained that because a
human's body is a partner in what s/he does or suffers during her/his
cradle-to-grave career, it will be raised to participate in the rewards and
punishments. Tradition teaches that the bodies of the elect will receive a
dowry of upgrades: clarity, agility, subtlety, and impassibility. Convinced
that grace builds on nature, some of Scotus' predecessors sought to explain
the dowry in terms of infused habits. For Scotus, metaphysics constrains,
insofar as accidents can be infused into a subject only if it is essentially such
as to be able to receive accidents of that kind, and no subject has a passive
capacity to receive accidents that are formally incompatible with what is
essential to it. If Aristotelian science sets the defaults for what is essential to
human bodies and for soul–body relations, the infused quality strategy can
work for only some dowry features but not others.

---

[23] *Lect.* II, dd. 30–32, q. 4, nn. 32, 34 (Vat XIX, 299–300).
[24] *Lect.* II, d. 29, q. un., n. 18 (Vat XIX, 288); *Lect.* II, dd. 30–32, q. 4, n. 53 (Vat. XIX, 307).
[25] Ibid., nn. 11, 18 (Vat. XIX, 285, 288).   [26] Ibid., n. 14 (Vat XIX, 287).

Thus, Scotus understands *clarity* to be apt coloration, which he is perfectly happy to say involves infused qualities.[27] Likewise, *agility* can be partly explained in terms of an intensification of the soul's natural power to move its body and partly in terms of impediment-removing accidental changes (such as the replacement of heavy bodily humors with lighter ones).[28] But where Aristotelian defaults identify what is essential to soul–body interactions, it would be absurd to suppose that anything could be done to give *post-mortem* souls omnipotent control over their *post-mortem* bodies. If the elect in heaven will move wherever and however they want to, this will not be because a human intellectual soul suited to a human body suddenly has power to make it fly, but because God has adopted a general policy for the heavenly state to move the elect soul's body according to its wishes.[29]

Tradition likewise tells how glorified heavenly bodies will be *subtle* in the sense of simultaneously occupying the same place as another body is occupying (think of the risen Christ passing through closed doors). Scotus explains that this is metaphysically possible only because the quantitative dimensions of the one body are not *formally* but only *virtually* incompossible with those of another. Normally and naturally, a body's quantitative dimensions *cause* it to fill a place in such a way that it cannot be simultaneously occupied by others. God will have to obstruct such natural causal consequences to allow two bodies to occupy the same place at the same time.[30]

Finally, *impassibility* cannot be explained by appeal to supernaturally infused qualities either. Human bodies are composites of prime matter and substantial form(s). Prime matter is essentially in potency with respect to any form it lacks but could naturally receive. Its being actually subject to one does not take away its potency to receive others and so does not remove the composite's susceptibility to corruption. Like other animal bodies, human bodies are heterogenous. By their very natures, the elements from which they are composed have contrary qualities, and the elemental qualities are contrary by their very natures. All of these internal causes of corruption will be present in resurrected as much as *ante-mortem* bodies. The perpetual preservation of resurrected bodies will have to be explained by an external cause: viz., God acts according to a general

[27] *Ord.* IV, d. 49, q. 15, nn. 2, 5 (Wad. X, 606–607; Vivès XXI, 495, 500).
[28] *Ord.* IV, d. 49, q. 14, nn. 6–7, 9, 11 (Wad. X, 595–598; Vivès XXI, 477–479, 489–490).
[29] Ibid., n. 11 (Wad. X, 598; Vivès XXI, 489–490).
[30] *Ord.* IV, d. 49, q. 16, n. 19 (Wad. X, 551; Vivès XXI, 519–520).

policy for the *post-mortem* state to obstruct the natural activities of corrupting causes.[31]

II.4   The indignities of the damned

The tradition that the damned were forever tormented by hell fire was difficult to interpret philosophically. For one thing, immaterial beings—the fallen angels and separated human souls (between death and resurrection)—were held to be tormented in the flames. But immaterial beings have no passive capacity to be corrupted by corporeal fire, and corporeal fire has no active capacity to undo them. Scotus holds that the damned as much as the elect are eventually resurrected to metaphysical completeness. And human bodies do have a natural capacity to be corrupted by fire. Only a certain degree of heat is formally compatible with a body fit for animation. Still, further heating will eventually reduce the body to ashes. So, even if the resurrected damned could undergo sensory suffering from the damage inflicted on the body by the fire, this could not naturally go on forever because the human body would naturally be consumed by the fire in short order.

II.4.1   Hellfire torment for spirits

If fallen angels and separated souls are tormented in the flames, it must be that the hellfire somehow causes or at least occasions mental anguish. Scotus agrees with Aquinas: it can't be that the spirits mistakenly believe that the fire will hurt them. They should be metaphysically astute enough to know better. If God caused them to hold this false belief, God would be a deceiver.[32] Scotus rejects Henry of Ghent's suggestion that a supernatural habit is infused to make spirits capable of being acted upon in the relevant way by a corporeal agent such as fire.[33] Scotus contends: either the habit is corporeal, in which case the spirit has no passive capacity to receive it, or it is spiritual and would not make a spirit the kind of thing that could be acted upon in the relevant way by fire. Scotus accuses Henry of misunderstanding the role of habits. What of itself has no power to act or to be acted upon by agents of a certain kind cannot acquire such power through habits. Rather habits only augment or facilitate the exercise of powers already possessed.[34]

---

[31] *Ord.* IV, d. 49, q. 13, nn. 2–3, 9 (Wad X, 578, 587; Vivès XXI, 448–449, 464).
[32] *Ord.* IV, d. 44, p. 2, q. 1, nn. 70–72, 83–86 (Vat. XIV, 110–112, 115–116).
[33] Ibid., nn. 73–76 (Vat. XIV, 112–113).   [34] Ibid., n. 75 (Vat. XIV, 112–113).

Scotus distinguishes between sensory sorrow (*dolor*), which is a passion of the sensory appetite, and intellectual distress (*tristitia*), which is found in the will. Sensory sorrow is not found in angels. It is not found in separate souls either because while the intellectual soul houses the formal principle of sensory functions, it is not the whole sensory power. Rather, the composite of intellectual soul and mixed body is. Accordingly, it is the composite, not the intellectual soul alone, that is the subject of cognitive and appetitive sensory functions.[35]

By contrast, the subject of intellectual distress is the will, and such distress is naturally consequent upon the apprehension of something that appears contrary to the individual's well-being.[36] If it seems unreasonable that intellectual distress in damned angels and separate souls should be based on a false belief about the natural causal propensities of immaterial beings and fire, what other perceived disadvantage could underlie it? Scotus recognizes two. First, the spirit is forcibly detained in the flames. This is not disadvantageous because being detained in the fire is contrary to a spirit's natural place, because—unlike the elements—spirits don't have natural places.[37] Rather it must be that the spirit hates being in the flames and hates the fact that God detains it in the flames, so that it cannot freely go elsewhere.[38] God is the *efficient* cause of its detention, and fire is only the *formal* cause and so is an instrument of Divine torment.[39]

Second, the spirit's intellect is determined to perpetual and intense consideration of fire as an object. The spirit perceives this as disadvantageous because fire is not a suitable object of prolonged attention in an intellect that prefers delightful objects and different ones at different times. Knowing that it is doomed to pay attention to this unattractive object in perpetuity, the spirit hates the situation, and this gives rise to intellectual distress.[40] Here fire is a partial efficient cause of the intellect's apprehension of fire as an object, but God is the principal cause of the intellect's being involuntarily detained in an intense consideration of the fire.[41] Because freedom to think about what it likes is more important to the spirit than freedom to move from one place to another, the spirit hates the thought-control more and so feels more intellectual distress over it.[42]

---

[35] Ibid., nn. 80–82 (Vat. XIV, 114).   [36] Ibid., n. 83 (Vat. XIV, 115).
[37] Ibid., nn. 85–86 (Vat. XIV, 115–116).   [38] Ibid., nn. 87–91 (Vat. XIV, 116–117).
[39] Ibid., n. 88 (Vat. XIV, 116).   [40] Ibid., n. 95 (Vat. XIV, 118–119).
[41] Ibid., nn. 67–69 (Vat. XIV, 110).   [42] Ibid., nn. 100–101 (Vat. XIV, 120).

II.4.2   Hellfire torment for resurrected human beings

Scotus recognizes that fire present to a corruptible substance animated by
the sensory soul can have two sorts of effects: real and univocal versus
intentional and equivocal. After judgment, since the human body is
essentially corruptible, fire present to it would be able to produce effects
of both sorts. Nevertheless, Scotus contends that neither effect essentially
depends on the other, and it would be absolutely possible for one effect to
occur without the other, whether by Divine power or because of some
created obstacles.[43] Moreover, real change does not produce sensory
sorrow because sensory sorrow is caused by the sensory apprehension of
the disagreeable object, and the object qua object causes an intentional
change (i.e., causes the sensory power to have it as an intentional object).
The intentional change is both necessary and sufficient. But a real change
in the body cannot produce sensory sorrow apart from an intentional
change.[44]

Everyone agrees that in the resurrection Divine power miraculously
obstructs the internal causes of bodily destruction. But the question here
is: how does God use fire to torment the resurrected damned without their
bodies burning up first? For Scotus, there is no question here of infused
qualities or habits doing any work. The explanation of these indignities has
to be external in the form of Divine obstruction of created causes. One
way would be for God to co-operate with the fire only in the production of
its intentional effect and not in the production of its real effect. Since
sensory sorrow is not *formally* incompatible with soundness of body, the
only other miracle required would be for God to obstruct sensory sorrow's
efficient causal action to produce corruptive effects in the body.[45] The
highest degree of heat fire can produce in human bodies is formally
incompatible with the proportions presupposed for animation, but sensory
apprehension of the highest degree of heat (an intentional change) is not
formally incompatible with the body's survival.[46]

Another way would be for God to co-operate with the fire in introducing real heat into the body but obstruct the fire from producing a degree of
heat that would be formally incompatible with the constitution of the
body. This way God would not co-operate with the fire for its whole effect.
Yet another way, God could co-operate with the fire for its full effect—for
a degree of heat formally incompossible with the constitution of the mixed

---

[43] *Ord.* IV, d. 44, p. 2, q. 2, nn. 125–127 (Vat. XIV, 126–127).
[44] Ibid., nn. 128–131 (Vat. XIV, 127).   [45] Ibid., n. 138 (Vat. XIV, 130).
[46] Ibid., n. 139 (Vat. XIV, 130–131).

body so that the constitution of the mixed body would be destroyed and yet miraculously conserve its life.[47] Scotus thinks that there is no way to prove which it is.[48] But Scotus prefers the first because he reckons it will involve fewer miracles, and—where the damned are concerned—miracles should not be multiplied beyond necessity.[49]

III   WILL-POWER AS CROWNING DIGNITY

For Scotus, the dignity of human beings *ex puris naturalibus* is rooted in the will. Like Peter John Olivi[50] before him, Scotus takes the distinction between *natural* power and *voluntary* power to be metaphysically fundamental. Two features of natural power are important here. [i] First, natural powers are *deterministic*. A natural power P is power for an object O in circumstances C, only if an agent with power P acts to the limit of that power to produce O in C. If the power were not sufficient, always or for the most part, to produce O in C, that power would not count as power for O in C. [ii] Second, natural inclinations built into a thing aim at individual or species perfection, i.e., natural inclinations are for those conditions and function that make a thing an optimal specimen of its kind.

By contrast, [not-i] *the will is a self-determining power for opposites without succession*. Scotus explains that good is the proper object of willing and evil the proper object of nilling, i.e., something can be willed only insofar as it is thought of as good and nilled only insofar as it is thought of as evil. But over and above its orientation toward its object, the will includes *executive* power, which determines itself to choose or not to choose, to will O in C or to will against O in C or simply not to will O in C. The will does not always act to the limit of its power. In whatever circumstance (apart from Divine determination), a created will is *power for action or inaction*: power to act and power not to act, but not power to act and not to act both at once. Moreover, will-power is a *power for opposite objects*: power to produce O in C and power not to produce O in C, although not power to produce both O and not-O in C at once. Scotus goes further. Will-power is not simply *power for opposites in succession*: power to produce O in C at T1 and power not to produce O in C at T2. Will-power is *power for opposites without succession*. Following Olivi[51] and

---

[47] Ibid., nn. 143–144 (Vat. XIV, 131–132).   [48] Ibid., n. 142 (Vat. 131).
[49] Ibid., n. 133 (Vat. XIV, 128).   [50] Olivi, *In II Sent.,* q. 57 (Quaracchi II, 305–394).
[51] Olivi, *In II Sent.*, q. 57 (Quaracchi II, 348–352).

Henry of Ghent,[52] Scotus maintains that although the will wills O in C at T, the will as naturally prior to its act is still power at T not to will O in C at T and power at T to nill O in C at T. Scotus' thought is that acting at T does not take away the will's efficient causal power not to act at T. Willing O in C at T does not take away the will's efficient causal power for not-willing O in C at T, or the will's efficient causal power for nilling O in C at T. Just because the will is acting it doesn't mean that it doesn't have all of the efficient causal power it had before.[53]

For Scotus as for Olivi[54] and Henry,[55] *such self-determination is necessary for making the agent's actions its own.* Natural agents might seem to be self-determined insofar as they act out of built-in powers and natural inclinations: e.g., the heavy earthen object seems to move itself down toward its natural place. Scotus denies that this is the correct interpretation, both because natural agents get their powers from the causes that bring them into being, and because the powers they thereby receive are deterministic in that—barring obstructions—they always act to their limit to produce their effects in relevant circumstances. Of course, created intellectual agents—human souls and angels—also get their essential powers from what produces them in existence—viz., God. But there is still a way for them to *own* their actions, over and above essentially having a formal functional principle, a passive power to receive volitions. The will-power of humans and angels includes executive power to control its action or inaction as well as the intentional direction of any of its acts.

[not-ii] For Scotus, it is important for will-power to be *self-determining*, because it is also power to be *self-transcending*. From an Aristotelian point of view, *everything* is endowed with natural inclinations toward its own perfection. If earth has a natural inclination to go down and fire to go up, animals also have natural appetites for their own survival and functional flourishing. Intellectual natures are no exception. Scotus appropriates Anselm's label: the will is essentially possessed of an *affectio commodi* or natural inclination to the agent's own (individual or species) advantage, a natural inclination to seek what is good for itself *(bonum sibi)*. Will-power is distinctive among appetitive powers in that it is also essential to the will to have an *affectio iustitiae*, an inclination to love things for their own sake because of their own intrinsic value (as *bona in se*). Because there are goods

[52] Henry of Ghent, *Quodl.* X, q. 9 (*Opera omnia* XIV, 244–245).
[53] Scotus, *QMet.* IX, q. 15, nn. 20–34 (OPh IV, 680–684).
[54] Olivi, *Sent.* II, q. 57 c. and ad 22 (Quaracchi II, 317–323, 330, 368–369); q. 58, ad 14 (Quaracchi II, 437–438).
[55] Henry of Ghent, *Quodl.* XIII, q. 11, ad 2 (Opera omnia XVIII, 97–104).

other than myself that are equal to myself (other human beings) and goods other than myself that are more worthy than myself (e.g., the common good and God), the native *affectio iustitiae* endows the will with a capacity for self-transcendence.[56]

The *affectio commodi* is a natural inclination like the sensory appetites: if it were the only inclination of intellectual appetite, it would—like the sensory appetites—act deterministically to urge the will to go for maximal apparent advantage. If the will had only the *affectio commodi*, a power for opposites would be pointless. But the power of self-determination and the *affectio iustitiae* belong together because otherwise the agent would not *own* its just acts in a way that would make them imputable to the agent itself.[57]

This dual dignity—the capacity for self-determination and the capacity for self-transcendence—is what turns human beings into *moral agents*.[58] Once again, natural appetites exercise their causality by natural necessity. But the will is a power for opposites that requires to be regulated by the right rule. In morals, the proximate rule is right reason, the deliverances of the agent's own correct practical reasoning. Where right reason under-determines, the Divine will is the higher rule. If Scotus holds that the will is the primary locus of moral evaluation (e.g., its choice to give alms), the external act (e.g., the actual giving of alms) is subject to its own, not simply derivative, moral evaluation. Right reason dictates not only when and how it is appropriate to will, but when and how it is appropriate for the external act to be performed (e.g., that alms are to be given to worthy beggars, privately rather than ostentatiously, with gratitude to God rather than condescension). So via hylomorphic composition, the intellectual soul lifts up the merely vital or corporeal to the level of acts worthy of moral evaluation.[59] Moreover, this dignity applies to human beings *ex puris naturalibus*. Both the capacity for and obligation to manifest heroic virtue that lays down life for others even without hope of eternal life, it is possessed by pagans as well as Christians (by Socrates as much as St. Francis). Once again, unbelief and lack of sacramental participation do not and cannot erode the essential powers of human beings.[60]

---

[56] Scotus, *Ord.* III, d. 26, q. un., n. 110 (Vat. X, 35–36).
[57] *Ord.* II, d. 39, qq. 1–2, nn. 22–23 (Vat. VIII, 463); *Ord.* III, d. 17, q. un., nn. 9–15 (Vat. IX, 565–568); *Ord.* III, d. 26, q. un., n. 110 (Vat. X, 35–36); *Ord.* IV, d. 49, qq. 9–10, nn. 2–8; (Wad. X, 505–514; Vivès XXI, 330–333). See also Wolter 1972.
[58] See Boler 1990, 1993.
[59] Scotus, *Quodl.*, q. 18, nn. 2–16 (Wad. XII, 475–486; Vivès XXVI, 228–249).
[60] *Lect.* II, d. 27, q. 7, nn. 18–19 (Vat. XIX, 278).

IV THE INTELLECTUAL SOUL: SUPERNATURAL GIFTS AND STARTLING CAPACITIES!

Natural dignity pertains to human being because of what it is in itself. For Scotus, this is presupposed and yet almost nothing in relation to the honors God confers.

IV.1 Extravagant initiatives

Scotus explains: God's act of creation is motivated by God's friendship-love *(amor amicitiae)* for the Divine essence, a love of the Divine essence because of its own intrinsic worth (as a *bonum in se*) and for its own sake. Such friendship-love is not jealous, but so loves as to desire other co-lovers for the beloved. For Scotus, God's primary goal in creation is to expand the Trinitarian circle of co-lovers of the Divine essence. In particular, God wants to include a creature who would love the Divine essence as much as any creature possibly could. Metaphysics constrains: what rocks and trees and cows are essentially makes them ineligible. Metaphysics makes it conditionally necessary that God looks to intellectual creatures to accomplish this purpose. Scotus tells us that out of all possible intellectual creatures, God elected the human soul of Christ for this role. A created intellectual nature who loved God as much as any creature possibly could would imitate the Divine will in loving the Divine essence by friendship-love, and so would be non-jealous and desire other created co-lovers. God therefore elects not only the soul of Christ but also other human souls and angels and predestines them to beatific vision—to intellectual intuitive cognition and everlasting enjoyment of the Divine essence.

Natural kinds form an excellence hierarchy—what Scotus calls "an essential order of eminence"—in which, for any pair of creatable natures, one is more excellent than the other.[61] Intellectual natures (angels and humans) are more excellent than any non-intellectual natures. Even so, every creatable natural kind is finite and so only finitely lovable, whereas the Divine essence as infinite is the most eminent being. There is nothing about what intellectual creatures are intrinsically (even when they are perfect specimens) that would make them worthy of Divine favor, much less of inclusion in the Trinitarian friendship circle. Scotus' God wills "wedding garments" to suit the elect for such high society. God gratuitously creates statutory categories of worth by freely and contingently

[61] *DPP*, c. 3, nn. 35, 39, 44 (Kluxen, 44, 48, 54; Wolter, n. 3.25, p. 57; n. 3.38, p. 61; n. 3.52, p. 67).

establishing laws that stipulate the conditions under which intellectual creatures will count as worthy of Divine acceptance and/or eternal life. God wills infused habits for the elect (original justice before the fall, infused grace/charity after the fall) to make them acceptable and dignify their finite and temporal actions with eternal significance. For Christ, the predestined head of the community of created co-lovers, God wills, not only maximal grace/charity, beatific vision and enjoyment, and many remarkable "upgrades," but also hypostatic union. *The greatest dignity of human nature is that it has been freely and contingently assumed by God the Son!*[62]

Distinctive of Scotus' theology is his insistence that in the order of Divine purposes, predestination and election are naturally prior to the permission of sin.[63] One metaphysical consequence is that sin does not influence which souls exist so that no one owes her/his existence to Adam's fall.[64] Since sin *does* affect who mates with whom, Scotus infers that the same individual could have had different parents.[65] Since—apart from sin—male and female would exist in equal numbers, yet they do not now exist in equal numbers, Scotus concludes that some individuals of one gender must be able to exist and be of the opposite gender. He remarks that this should not be so metaphysically startling because Aristotelian science treats gender as an accident![66]

IV.2   *The adequate object of the human intellect*

Grace discloses nature. When it comes to the adequate object of the human intellect, Scotus refuses to settle for Aristotelian defaults. Aristotelian cognitive psychology infers from the observed regularity—that cradle-to-grave human cognition begins with the senses—that the human intellect depends on sorted sense-image to supply the materials from which to abstract intelligible contents. Scotus reads Aquinas as taking this mode of cognitive psychological processing to be *essential* to the human condition and so as identifying the adequate object of the human intellect with

[62] *Ord.* III, d. 4, q. un., n. 47 (Vat. IX, 215–216); *Ord.* III, d. 7, n. 58 (Vat. IX, 284–285). Cf. *Rep. Par.* III, d. 7, q. 4, in *Ioannis Duns Scoti Doctoris Mariani Theologiae Marianae Elementa* (ed. Balić, 14–15); *Rep. Barcin.* III, d. 2, q. 3, in *Ioannis Duns Scoti Doctoris Mariani Theologiae Marianae Elementa* (ed. Balić, 182–184). See also *Ord.* III, d. 32. q. un., n. 21 (Vat. X, 136–137).
[63] *Ord.* I, d. 41, q. u.n, nn. 45–46 (Vat. VI, 332–334); *Ord.* III, d. 7, q. 3, nn. 60–61 (Vat. IX, 286–287); *Rep. Barcin.* III, d. 2, q. 3 in *Ioannis Duns Scoti Doctoris Mariani Theologiae Marianae Elementa* (ed. Balić, 183).
[64] *Lect.* II, d. 20, q. 2, nn. 21–22 (Vat. XIX, 195–196).   [65] Ibid., n. 30 (Vat. XIX, 197–198).
[66] Ibid., n. 31 (Vat. XIX, 198).

the quiddities of material things. Doesn't Aquinas reason that—because all of our *ante-mortem* concepts are proper to material thing—we are able to conceive of immaterial things (e.g., God and the angels) only analogically? Scotus mostly agrees that this is the way the human intellect functions *ante-mortem* (I say *mostly* because Scotus agrees with Augustine that we are directly aware of our own mental acts). He even concedes that the scientific case is strong enough that unaided natural reason could be led to Aquinas' purported conclusion.[67] But where this issue is concerned, natural reason is not unaided. The doctrine of creation tells us that the elect are predestined to an intellectual intuitive cognition of the Divine essence. For Scotus, metaphysics constrains: this could be so, only if the human intellect has essentially a passive capacity for receiving such an act. Metaphysics constrains again: powers are essentially defined by their adequate objects. Powers are essentially capable of receiving only those acts whose objects are subsumed under the power's adequate object. Light and color are the adequate object of vision. Since sound is not a species of light or color, visual power cannot directly perceive sound. Scotus takes it for granted: the intellectual power that the soul will have in the life to come is the same one that it has now. If so, the quiddities of material things cannot be its adequate object because God is an immaterial being and the Divine essence is not a material quiddity! Scotus concludes that the adequate object of human intellectual power must be the same as that of other intellectual beings (i.e., God and the angels): viz., being in general.[68]

Aquinas, of course, agreed that the elect will have an intuitive cognition of the Divine essence in the life to come. Aquinas recognized this mode of understanding as supernatural and moved to account for it by appealing to the *lumen gloriae*, a supernatural disposition that exceeds any and every natural faculty.[69] Scotus protests that the metaphysical job of habits is to enable powers to achieve their adequate objects promptly and delightfully. It is metaphysically impossible for any habit—whether acquired or super-naturally infused—to expand the adequate object of a power or to alter the fundamental mode of its functioning. The only alternative would be for God to provide the human intellectual soul with a new cognitive power

---

[67] *Quodl.*, q. 14, n. 12 (Wad. XII, 373; Vivès XXVI, 47). See Wolter 1949.
[68] *Lect.* I, d. 3, p. 1, qq. 1–2, nn. 92–110 (Vat XVI, 259–265); *Ord.* I, d. 3, p. 1, q. 3, nn. 137–151 (Vat III, 85–94); *Quodl.*, q.14, nn. 11–12 (Wad. XII, 272; Vivès XXVI, 40, 46–47).
[69] Thomas Aquinas, *In IV Sent.* d. 49, q. 2, a.6 and a. 7 (Parma VII, 1208, 1210–1211).

(analogous to awarding us a sixth sense)—a proposal which Scotus mentions only to dismiss out of hand.[70]

If the adequate object of the human intellect is being in general, however, Scotus has some further explaining to do. Intellectual thought is a natural process; intellect and objects function as Aristotelian natural causes that always act to the limit of their powers to produce their effects. If immaterial beings as much as material beings fall under the adequate object of our intellect, then why don't they act on our intellects to give us experiences of immaterial objects here and now? For Scotus, the only explanation is external: Divine wisdom has fixed some law for this present state.[71] As to what considerations might have weighed with Divine wisdom, Scotus has two suggestions. Perhaps God wanted to honor our natural hylomorphic composition with a season of coordination between our intellectual and sensory functioning. Alternatively, perhaps Divine obstruction of human natural capacities for direct cognition of immaterial things is a punitive consequence of Adam's fall.[72]

IV.3 How lower than the angels?

Reflection on the supernatural dignities awarded to Christ reveals still more about the natural dignity of essential human capacities. Scotus' estimate of God's primary reason for creation is startling—to include in the Trinitarian friendship circle a creature who loves the Divine essence as much as any creature could. But Divine election of the soul of Christ might seem, not merely surprising, but utterly unreasonable. Doesn't Hebrews 2:7 declare: human being is a little lower than the angels? In Scotus' language, in the essential order of eminence in which—for any pair of natures—one is more excellent than the other and God is the most eminent being, angelic natures come higher, have more dignity than human nature. Would Divine preference for the human soul of Christ not show bad taste? Worse still, wouldn't the higher nature have more excellent powers than the lower nature? Wouldn't angelic intellects be capable of clearer vision, angelic wills of more perfect love than any human soul?[73] In short, isn't it metaphysically impossible for the human soul of Christ to fulfill such a calling? Scripture and tradition say "no." Medieval

[70] Duns Scotus, *Ord.* I, d. 3, p. 1, q. 3, n. 114 (Vat. III, 71).
[71] *Ord.*, Prol., p. 1, q. un., nn. 29, 61–62 (Vat. I, 17–18, 37–38).
[72] Ibid., n. 37 (Vat I, 21); *Ord.* I, d. 3, p. 1, q. 3, n. 187 (Vat. III, 113–114); *Ord.* IV, d. 45, q. 1, n. 25 (Vat. XIV, 143).
[73] *Ord.* III, d. 13, qq. 1–4, n. 2 (Vat IX, 385).

Christology insists that throughout its existence, the human soul of Christ has the maximum degree of infused grace, the most perfect vision, and the most perfect act of enjoyment (fruition) of the Divine essence. Explaining how this can be leads Scotus to further surprising estimates of natural human powers.

One tempting solution appealed to hypostatic union: whereas angelic natures excel human natures in themselves, hypostatic union more than makes up for this difference by flooding the human soul of Christ with enhanced powers. Like Bonaventure, Scotus adamantly rejects this position. Certainly, being the Divine Word's human soul is an honor. Metaphysically, however, hypostatic union is merely a real relation of dependence on the Divine Word, an accident that inheres in the human nature (or perhaps several real relations inhering in the various components of human nature) as in a subject. Metaphysics teaches: a subject is naturally prior to whatever inheres in it and so is whatever it essentially is prior to such inherence. In itself, hypostatic union can no more expand the essential capacities of its subject than any other inherent accident or infused qualities can.[74] Scotus adds: even if this *were* possible, it would do little to rationalize God's original choice, since God could have infused such qualities into an angel, or assumed an angelic nature instead, or as well.[75]

Scotus' own instinct is to *contest the inference from "more excellent nature" to "more excellent powers" to "more excellent acts."* Yes, angelic nature is more excellent than human nature, and angelic subjects of thought and choice are more excellent than the human soul (which is only a fragment of a nature). But Scotus maintains, controversially, that intellects and wills are, with respect to their acts (acts of understanding and volitions, respectively), at once passive receiving subjects and (at least partial) active causes. Scotus proposes that human intellectual souls are not inferior but rather equal to angels so far as the *passive* receptive power is concerned, and that human acts of intellect (will) are of the same species as angelic acts of intellect (will). But angels exceed human intellectual souls so far as their *active* power is concerned.[76] Since such receptive and active powers are essential to the the intellectual substances in question, this equality in passive receptive power and differential with respect to active power are

---

[74] *Ord.* III, d. 12, q. u., n. 13 (Vat. IX, 383); *Ord.* III, d. 13, qq. 1–4, nn. 57, 69–70 (Vat. IX, 408, 412–413).

[75] *Ord.* III, d. 13, q. 1–4, nn. 3–4, 7, 58 (Vat. IX, 385–387, 408).

[76] Ibid., nn. 21, 79–81 (Vat. IX, 391, 416–418); *Ord.* III, d. 14, q. 4, n. 126 (Vat. IX, 474).

naturally consequent upon the essences of angels and human souls, respectively.

IV.3.1 *Maximal infused grace?*

Grace/charity is an infused quality. God is its total active cause; angels and human souls are passive receivers. To convince us that angels and humans do not relevantly differ in their passive capacities to receive grace, Scotus surveys several metaphysical principles about how a subject's passive receptive capacities might or might not be limited. First, he considers:

> [P1] If [a] a subject X is receptive of a suitable accident F that comes in degrees, and [b] the subject is not determined of itself to some of these degrees, then [c] X can of itself receive any degree of F.

For example, [a] water is—unlike the human soul—a subject that can receive heat. But intense heat evaporates water (in primitive chemistry, changes it into air) because [b] the very nature of water sets a limit to how intense a degree of heat it can receive. [P1] says that if the nature of the subject sets no such limit, then the subject can receive any degree because one degree would be no more formally incompatible with it than any other.[77] Where supernatural qualities producible only by Divine voluntary action are concerned, natures can set up barriers to receiving that quality at all: rocks and trees and cows are not the right kinds of thing to receive grace. But given that intellectual nature *is* the right sort to receive *that kind* of accident, nothing in angelic or human nature could set any limit on *how much* grace it could receive because *nature* does not determine itself to one degree rather than another of a *supernatural* quality.[78]

Even among natural qualities, the appropriate receptive base (what makes the subject a metaphysically appropriate receiver of such qualities) is not always restricted to a single natural kind or species. Rather, Scotus maintains:

> [P2] if X and Y are related to an accident F according to the same receptive base *(ratio receptivi)*, any differences in species between X and Y are irrelevant to their respective capacities to receive F.

Different receptive bases (e.g., bodies and immaterial intelligences) are required for different kinds of accidents (e.g., for colors and for thoughts). But sometimes the same receptive base can exist in things of different kinds. For example, a stone and a piece of wood can both be white. The

---

[77] *Ord.* III, d. 13, qq. 1–4, n. 46 (Vat. IX, 402–403).   [78] Ibid., nn. 59–60, 73 (Vat IX, 409, 414).

fact that stone and wood are of different natural kinds is irrelevant to their receptive capacity for whiteness.[79]

Scotus then adds the premiss:

> [P3] if S and S* are accidents of the same species, then their receptive base will be the same.

Since grace/charity is a form of the same kind whatever the receiving subject,[80] the receptive base is the same in angels and humans, despite the fact that angels and humans themselves differ in species. The receptive base would be the generic property of being an intellectual nature that essentially includes will-power—a property that human souls and angels share.[81]

Theological consensus had it that grace comes in degrees. Scotus aligns with those who say that there is a maximum degree.[82] If so, reason would recommend: it is better to confer maximal grace on someone than on no one.[83] So far as God's absolute power is concerned, God could confer maximal grace on more than one intellectual creature. Scotus explains that God gives "grace without measure" to only one because monarchical organization of the Church is preferable![84] God reserves this dignity for the human soul of Christ instead of the highest angel because Christ descends from Adam and so is a fitting channel of grace for Adam's race. By contrast, angels do not come in families. God infuses each angel with a lower degree of grace directly.[85] Scotus adds: God wills hypostatic union for Christ's human nature, not only to honor Christ but also to save angelic face—so that angels, in being subordinate to Christ as head, will not be subordinate to a person who is merely human!

IV.3.2   Maximally perfect vision of the word?

Scotus affirms that it is possible for the human soul of Christ to be perfected by a maximally perfect vision of the Word. Christ's human intellect is the receptive basis for such an act, and this receptive capacity pertains to human soul essentially and so prior to its reception of any inherent form or habit.[86] By [P1]–[P3], there is no difference between the receptive capacity of Christ's intellect and that of angels when it comes to a

---

[79] Ibid., n. 47 (Vat. IX, 403–404).   [80] Ibid., n. 70 (Vat. IX, 412–413).
[81] Ibid., n. 47 (Vat. IX, 403–404).   [82] Ibid., n. 30 (Vat. IX, 394–395).
[83] Ibid., n. 54 (Vat. IX, 406–407).   [84] Ibid., nn. 52–53 (Vat. IX, 406).
[85] Ibid., n. 78 (Vat. IX, 416).   [86] Ibid., nn. 18, 27 (Vat. IX, 428, 432).

vision of the Divine essence freely produced by God acting alone as its efficient cause.[87]

IV.3.3 Maximally perfect fruition?

Consideration of maximal grace/charity and beatific vision led Scotus to claim that the human soul's natural *receptive* capacity, both will (of grace/charity) and intellect (of beatific vision), is equal to that of the angels. For the same reasons, so far as natural receptive capacity is concerned, God could act alone to cause an act of maximally perfect fruition in any human soul[88] and therefore in the human soul of Christ.[89] But what about the will's *active* power to produce such an act of fruition?

Scotus' view is that human souls have less active power than angels, and human wills have less active power than angelic wills. Given an intuitive cognition of the Divine essence and general Divine concurrence, Christ's human will could act alone to cause an act of fruition,[90] but for a perfect act of fruition, it would need the added efficient causal power of maximal grace/charity. The active power of angelic wills *could* be likewise supplemented to enable them to produce an act of maximally perfect fruition. In fact, however, God chooses not to confer as much grace on angelic wills as on the human soul of Christ so that Christ's human will together with maximal grace has more efficient causal power to produce an act of fruition than angelic wills with lower degrees of grace.[91] Of course, both grace and the created will are secondary causes of the act of fruition, and God can act alone to supply the efficient causality of any secondary cause. So it is metaphysically possible not only for God to act alone to produce the act of fruition but also for God to act together with the created will and without grace to produce it.

Depending on the natural-power differential, God's grace distribution policies might explain how Christ's human soul has the most efficient causal power to put into an act of fruition and so *de facto* has an act of fruition more perfect than that of any other intelligent creature. But it does not seem to show how Christ's human will together with grace can elicit the maximum possible act of enjoyment. For enjoyment is a will-act. If angelic will-power plus maximal grace is greater than human will-power plus maximal grace, it would seem that the upgraded angelic power would be able to produce a more perfect act of enjoyment than the upgraded

---

[87] Ibid., n. 21 (Vat. IX, 429).   [88] Ibid., n. 91 (Vat. IX, 420–421).
[89] Ibid., n. 81 (Vat. IX, 417–418).   [90] Ibid., n. 84 (Vat. XIX, 418–419).
[91] Ibid., n. 81 (Vat. IX, 417–418).

human soul could. Since enjoyment just *is* a will-act, it would seem that the most perfect degree of enjoyment possible for a creature could not be actively produced by any human will plus maximal grace. Since angels and humans are equal in passive receptive power, the human will would still be able to receive such an act, but would not be able to elicit it, unless God acted together with the human will and maximal grace to take up the causal slack.

IV.4   Infinite capacity?

Tradition hands it down that the human soul of Christ throughout its existence *does* and the human souls of the elect *will* see not only the Divine Word, but all things in the Divine Word. Scotus distinguishes between *extensional* and *intensional* infinity. Intensive actuality is a measure of metaphysical eminence. God alone is intensively infinite; creatures are intensively finite by nature. But the range of creatables (common natures and individuals) known by the Divine Word is extensionally infinite (there are infinitely many of them). Metaphysics challenges: how can either the intensively infinite (= God) or the extensionally infinite (= all creatables) be seen by the acts of *any* finite cognitive powers, whether human or angelic?

For Scotus, the obvious move is to *deny that infinity in the object (whether extensional or intensional) implies intensive infinity in the cognitive act or power.* The human soul's act of seeing God is an intensively finite quality that is produced in an intensively finite intellect that—because its adequate object is being in general—has the passive capacity to receive an act of cognizing any being.[92] As above (see Sections IV.3.1 and IV.3.2), no infused habits are needed to make the created intellect receptive enough, and no infused light is required to make the object intelligible enough. The created intellect itself is essentially receptive, and the Divine essence is maximally intelligible. As an omnipotent voluntary cause, the Divine essence is the perfect motive power and acts immediately on created intellects to produce such acts.[93]

But what about the *extensional* infinity of objects that would seem to be involved in seeing all things in the Divine Word? Scotus flirts with the view that the soul of Christ actually sees everything the Divine Word sees, and does so by a simultaneously inhering actual infinity of distinct acts.[94]

---

[92] *Ord.* III, d. 14, qq. 1–2, n. 59 (Vat. IX, 449).   [93] Ibid., n. 25–27 (Vat. IX, 431–432).
[94] Ibid., n. 69 (Vat. IX, 452–453).

Since all intellects have being in general as their adequate object, for *each* being, they are able to receive an act of understanding it. Perhaps seeing red and seeing green are incompossible acts. But where intellectual acts of understanding beings are concerned, no pair of these acts is incompossible with each other. Scotus reasons, if there is a passive capacity for each and for any two, there is a *passive* capacity for receiving all simultaneously.[95]

Scotus teeter-totters about whether to assign the human intellect *active* power at a given time to elicit each of infinitely many cognitive acts at that time. After all, Scotus does insist that powers are naturally prior to their acts in such a way that eliciting one at a given time does not take away the power at that time for eliciting another at that time.[96] Nevertheless, because any finite power has an adequate effect such that it cannot simultaneously cause more effects of that type, no created intellect would be able to elicit them all simultaneously.[97] On this view, the human soul would be able to receive infinitely many acts of cognizing all possible creatures, but would lack power to elicit (be an active cause of) all of the infinitely many at once.

Attractive as Scotus finds this last position, he recognizes that it flies in the face not only of conventional wisdom that a finite subject cannot have infinite receptive capacity but also of the Aristotelian prohibition against a simultaneously existing actual infinity of really distinct things.[98] His alternative suggestion reverts to the more customary view that the single act through which Christ or the blessed see the Word habituates them toward knowing those things that shine in the Word. Nevertheless, as finite powers they never see infinitely many simultaneously with perfect attention, but only some appropriate finite number.[99]

V SUMMING THE SURPRISES

It is time to draw Scotus' results together.

V.1 *Natural dignities*

Scotus has no doubts: human nature is rational animality. In assessing its natural dignity, he lets Aristotelian science set the defaults on animality: humans are by nature mortal and by nature beset with conflicting

---

[95] Ibid., n. 61 (Vat. IX, 450–451).   [96] Ibid., n. 72 (Vat. IX, 453–454).
[97] Ibid., n. 74 (Vat. IX, 454).   [98] Ibid., n. 69 (Vat. IX, 452–453).
[99] Ibid., nn. 68, 76–79 (Vat. IX, 452, 454–456).

appetites. In gaging our rational nature, however, Scotus looks to Christ: "praise him too much rather than too little,"[100] but let what Christ's human nature actually is set the standard for what is metaphysically possible for us all. The resulting picture is distinctive.

(1)   First, Scotus nuances comparisons between humans and angels. While angelic natures are more excellent than human natures, and angelic intellects and wills are more excellent than human ones with respect to their *active* powers, their *passive* receptive powers do not differ in species and neither do their acts.

(2)   Second, Scotus follows Peter John Olivi and Henry of Ghent in making will-power the glory of human nature and echoes their understanding of it. For Scotus, the created will is not just intellectual appetite, an *affectio commodi* operating deterministically and aimed at individual or species perfection (at *bona sibi*), but a self-determining power for opposites without succession. Moreover, where Anselm sees the *affectio iustitiae*, the inclination to love things for their own intrinsic worth (as *bona in se*), as a *donum superadditum* bestowed at creation and lost in the fall and gradually restored via sacramental participation, Scotus insists that the *affectio iustitiae* is essential to and so inalienable from the human will because (as above) the scope of a power is essential to it and cannot be expanded by any *dona superaddita*. What the will essentially is, endows intelligent creatures with the capacity for self-transcendence and makes their actions morally appraisable.

(3)   Third, it pertains to the human will essentially to have the capacity to receive maximal grace and maximal fruition and to include active power to cause—given object-presence and Divine concurrence—an act of fruition; and (allegedly) to include active power to cooperate with maximal grace to elicit an act of maximal fruition.

(4)   Fourth, despite the human intellect's cradle-to-grave functional coordination with the senses, its eternal destiny identifies its adequate object as being in general and shows it to be essentially receptive of beatific vision and of act(s) of seeing all creatables (an extensional infinity of them) in the Word—if not by infinitely many acts simultaneously, then by a single act that furnishes a habit by means of which the intellect can from time to time elicit one or more acts of understanding finitely many distinctly. Soteriology *shows* the human

---

[100]   Ibid., n. 53 (Vat. IX, 406).

intellect to have such capacities and to have them *essentially*. Human nature would have them whether or not any human being ever actually saw God.

V.2 Supernatural dignities

[1] For Scotus, supernatural dignities begin with predestination to beatific vision and enjoyment of the Divine essence. [2] For the human soul of Christ, they continue with hypostatic union. [3] In every state, there are supernatural helps to bring the elect to their goal. In Eden, there was infused original justice on the inside to make the will's control of sensory appetites easier, optimal climate, and the tree of life on the outside to make death optional. After the fall but under grace, there is infused grace/charity which functions causally like acquired habits, not to determine, but to make it easier for the will to impose rational priorities on sensory appetites and choose the right thing. In heaven, infused grace/charity also adds efficient causal power to the will in eliciting an act of fruition. In heaven, the bodies of the elect will also be infused with optimal coloration. Some heavy humors will be replaced with lighter ones, and the will's natural power for moving its body will be intensified.

[4] Divine policies also dignify jurisprudentially, first and foremost by creating the statutory category of worth. Nothing about what any creature is naturally or essentially is intrinsically worthy of Divine favor, much less of being included in the Trinitarian friendship circle. Free and contingent Divine legislation lays it down that finite intelligent creatures infused with finite qualities—whether original justice in Eden or grace/charity after the fall—are to be counted *prima facie* worthy of eternal life (of being included in the Trinitarian friendship circle); and their acts are deemed meritorious (*prima facie* deserving of eternal reward). Divine legislation also establishes sacramental systems for grace distribution in this present life.

[5] Grace does not always build on nature. Sometimes grace obstructs nature. Divine policies for the systematic obstruction of natural causes vary from state to state. In this present age, God interferes with natural human intellectual functioning by systematically preventing immaterial things from acting on human intellects. In consequence, cradle-to-grave human understanding largely relies on sense images from which it abstracts intelligible content. Whether this policy is motivated by Divine desire to coordinate human intellectual and sensory functions or to punish Adam's race, this restriction will be lifted at death when separated souls will

be allowed their full cognitive range.[101] Further systematic obstructions
are involved in the body's dowry, where subtlety and impassibility
are concerned.

V.3   Remarkable upshot

Scotus is called "the Subtle Doctor" because of his formidable capacities
for meticulous analysis and ingenious argumentation. Against Henry of
Ghent's theory of Divine illumination, Scotus vigorously defends the
Aristotelian sufficiency of natural powers for natural functioning. Yet, for
Scotus, the biggest consequence of Adam's fall may well be Divine
obstruction of our intellectual functions, which forces us to Aristotelian
indirection in doing science. If God did not interfere, the natures of things
would act directly on our intellects to produce intuitive cognitions of them
as well as of their individuators. We would have an easy time of abstracting
quidditative concepts of real essences from our immediate experience of
the things themselves. As it is, we have to rely on constructed concepts
(as Locke and Berkeley would later say, relative ideas: e.g., the powers and
the nature that account for why these functions and features regularly go
together) abstracted from our experience of accidents.

By contrast, Adam's fall leaves our will-power—with its inalienable
affectio iustitiae—in admirable condition. True, the loss of original justice
means that we "feel the pain" when we deny our sensory appetites their
objects. But this is nothing a robust determination to follow right reason
and Divine commands cannot decide to bear. Given Divine legislation, we
are also fully competent in this cradle-to-grave lifetime to earn merit.

Should we conclude that Scotus cares more about morals and merit than
about science? On balance, I don't think so. Scotus is characterizing both
faculties as he thinks he actually finds them. He takes experience as a datum
to be accounted for, just as much as Aristotle and any Enlightenment
philosopher would.

---

[101] *Ord.* IV, d. 45, q. 2, nn. 62–74 (Vat. XIV, 156–162).

CHAPTER 7

Duns Scotus on matter and form

Cecilia Trifogli

INTRODUCTION

Matter and form are the fundamental ingredients of the Aristotelian physical world. The relevant objects of this world are of many different kinds. They include things such as (i) earth, water, air, fire (the so-called elements), (ii) wood, iron, bronze (non-living mixed bodies), and (iii) plants, animals, and human beings (living bodies). All this variety of things have a common ontological structure: they are material substances, that is, compounds of matter and form (hylomorphic compounds). Thus, matter and form are thought of as parts or components of material substances. They are parts of a special kind, though. Robert Pasnau calls them 'metaphysical parts' and contrasts them with integral parts.[1] Matter and form are called 'metaphysical parts' because they are parts that only a metaphysical investigation rather than empirical methods can reveal. Indeed, theoretical assumptions about the change of a substance and its identity are those that mostly reveal its hylomorphic composition. Integral parts by contrast are parts in the ordinary sense of being extended parts. Any material substance is a body, that is, a thing endowed with three-dimensional extension, and therefore, it has integral parts; for example, branches and leaves are integral parts of a plant. For an Aristotelian, however, the ultimate components of a material substance are its metaphysical parts and not its integral parts. For integral parts are themselves compounds of matter and form. For example, both a whole lump of bronze and any of its integral parts, however small, are compounds of matter and form, whereas the matter and form of the whole bronze and of any of its parts are not themselves compounds of more basic entities.

The status of fundamental constituents of the physical world that Aristotle ascribes to matter and form was tacitly accepted by medieval

---

[1] Pasnau 2011: 6–11.

Aristotelians who did not consider any significant alternatives to Aristotle's hylomorphic model. There was also substantial agreement about some general motivations for positing matter and form as fundamental constituents of the physical world. Still, a great variety of issues internal to hylomorphism were raised and hotly discussed.[2] Scotus is arguably the medieval philosopher who gave the most sophisticated contribution to these discussions.[3]

In this chapter, I present Scotus's views on four major issues in the medieval debate about hylomorphism: (1) the existence of matter; (2) the nature of matter; (3) the plurality of forms and (4) the hylomorphic composition of living substances.[4]

I   THE EXISTENCE OF MATTER

Like the great majority of medieval philosophers, Scotus maintains that the strongest argument for the existence of matter is the argument from change: it is because the substances of the physical world are subject to change that they contain matter as one of their components. Scotus, however, does not take this common argument for granted. He is aware that it is open to objections and produces forceful additional arguments in its defence. In doing so, he engages in a subtle discussion about the distinction between physical change and creation from nothing.[5]

The argument from change for the existence of matter is based on the distinctive property of matter of being the persistent subject of a substantial change, that is, what remains throughout a change from a substance to a substance of another kind, being first under one of the two opposite forms involved in such a change and then under the other. For example, in the case of a change from water into air, the persistent subject would be something that persists throughout the whole process in which water is transformed into air, and it is under the form of water at the beginning of this process and under the form of air at the end of it. The

[2] For a concise outline of some major themes of the scholastic debate, see Pasnau 2010.
[3] On this assessment of Scotus's contribution, see Ward 2014: 2.
[4] My presentation of Scotus's views is based on the following primary sources: *Lect.* II, d. 12, q. un., "Utrum in substantia generabili et corruptibili sit aliqua entitas positiva distincta a forma quae dicatur esse materia" (Vat. XIX, 69–101) for sections I and II about matter; *Ord.* IV, d. 11, p. 1, a. 2, q. 1, "Utrum panis convertatur in corpus Christi in Eucharistia" (Vat. XII, 205–270) and *QMet.* VII, q. 20 "Utrum partes organicae animalis habeant distinctas formas substantiales specie differentes" (OPh IV, 381–394) for Sections III and IV about form.
[5] On Scotus's discussion of the existence of matter, see also Cross 1998: 13–16; Pasnau 2011: 27–29; Ward 2014: 8–18.

crucial point of the argument is then to prove that in a substantial change there is such a persistent subject. Scotus's formulation of this standard argument is as follows:

> The first claim (i.e., that matter exists) is proved by the argument of the Philosopher,[6] which is more effective than the other arguments (although some people disregard it). His argument goes as follows: (i) Every natural agent requires something passive on which the agent acts (this is evident to the senses); (ii) that passive thing on which the agent acts is changed from one opposite to the other opposite; (iii) but one of the opposites does not become the other opposite in such a way that nothing common to each of them remains (e.g., whiteness does not become blackness). (iv) Therefore, just as in an accidental change the agent that changes something moves it from one opposite to the other opposite, in such a way that it remains the same under each of the opposites, so in a generation, the agent of generation must change something from a form to another form in such a way that it remains the same under each of the two forms. That thing is said to be matter.[7]

The first premise (i) of Scotus's argument is a claim about the way in which a natural agent acts in order to bring about a change. It is clearly meant to contrast the action of a natural agent from a divine action of creation from nothing. A natural agent acts on something, that is, it requires a thing on which it acts. For example, when a natural agent like fire produces a change of water into air, it does so by acting on water, which is then the patient in this change, whereas God can produce air starting from neither water nor any other substance, but simply from nothing.

Given this initial premise, one would expect that Scotus argued for the existence of matter as a persisting substrate of substantial changes by showing that matter so understood is required to preserve the 'naturality' of such changes and distinguish them from productions of things out of nothing. However, this is not exactly the line of argument that Scotus further develops. The connection between the natural character of

---

[6] Aristotle, *Phys.* I, 7, 190a13–21.

[7] Duns Scotus, *Lect.* II, d. 12, q. un., n. 11 (Vat. XIX, 72–73): "Primum ostenditur per rationem Philosophi, quae efficacior est aliis (licet quidam eam contemnant). Formatur eius ratio sic: omne agens naturale requirit passum in quod agens agit (hoc patet ad sensum); illud passum, in quod agens agit, transmutatur ab opposito in oppositum; hoc oppositum non fit illud oppositum, ita quod nihil commune remaneat utrique (sicut albedo non fit nigredo); sicut igitur in transmutatione accidentali transmutans aliquid movet illud ab opposito in oppositum, manens idem sub utroque oppositorum, ita oportet in generatione quod generans transmutet aliquid a forma in formam, manens idem sub utraque; illud dicitur esse materia."

substantial changes and the existence of a persisting substrate of them remains implicit.

Another line of argument instead appears, one based on an analogy between accidental changes (i.e., changes relative to accidental properties of a substance) and substantial changes (i.e., changes relative to the substances themselves). Both kinds of change are changes between opposites and more specifically between opposite forms: accidental forms, like whiteness and blackness, in an accidental change, and substantial forms, like the form of water and that of air, in a substantial change. A change, however, is not simply a succession of opposite forms, but a succession of opposite forms in a subject. In Scotus's example, it is not the case that whiteness becomes blackness in the sense that whiteness as such comes to be from blackness as such but rather that a white thing comes to be from a black thing, that is, whiteness comes to exist in a subject starting from a subject in which blackness exists. Thus, a change involves not only opposite forms but also a subject. Furthermore, in an accidental change, the subject persists throughout the change: for example, it is one and the same thing that is first black and then white, that is, one and the same subject in which blackness and whiteness exist in succession. In Aristotelian terms, the subject of an accidental change is a substance and this change is a variation in the accidental forms of a substance; but accidental forms do not affect the identity of a substance so that the substance persists throughout any of its accidental changes. The crucial assumption in Scotus's argument is that this account of change as involving a persisting subject is valid for substantial change too: just as in an accidental change, the subject persists throughout the change and takes on opposite forms, similarly in a substantial change there is a subject that persists throughout the change and takes on opposite substantial forms. For example, in the substantial change from water to air, there is a subject that persists throughout this change and is first under the form of water and then under the form of air. Such a persisting subject is matter, as Scotus states in concluding the argument from change.

The assumption of a persisting subject in a substantial change is not as evident and uncontroversial as it would appear from Scotus's argument. Scotus himself admits that it is not universally accepted. He presents an objection to it reflecting the view of some of his contemporaries.[8] The objection says that the analogy between accidental change and substantial change on which Scotus's argument relies is wrong because nothing

---

[8] Ibid., n. 12 (Vat. XIX, 73).

persists throughout a substantial change; rather, the whole initial substance is transformed into the whole final substance. For example, when water is transformed into air, water as a whole, that is, each of its components (both the subject and its substantial form) ceases to exist and air as a whole comes to be from it so that no subject persists throughout this change. Something totally new comes to be as a result of a substantial change.

A serious problem with the view that nothing persists throughout a substantial change is that of saving the assumption that such a change is of a different kind from a divine act of creation out of nothing. These philosophers address this problem by pointing out that the sentence 'something is produced from nothing' is ambiguous because the term 'nothing' can refer either to the starting point of the production or to components or parts of the thing produced so that the sentence can be understood either in the sense that

(1)   An agent starts to produce something absolutely from nothing, that is, *nothing absolutely* is the starting point of the action

or in the sense that

(2)   *Nothing* (no component) *of the thing produced* exists at the starting point of its action.

Sense (1) is stronger than (2): (1) implies (2) but the converse implication is not valid. In our example, the production of air starting from water is not a case of production from nothing in sense (1) because there is something, namely, water, from which this production starts, but in the view defended by these philosophers that nothing persists through this change, it is a case of production from nothing in sense (2). According to these philosophers, the difference between God and a natural agent then is that God can produce something from nothing in both sense (1) and sense (2) but a natural agent can do this only in sense (2), and this is what happens in a substantial change.[9] This distinction also suggests why these philosophers think that the argument from change presented above is not conclusive. The initial premise (i) about the way a natural agent acts should be interpreted as the negation of (1)—i.e., there is something that is the starting point of the action of a natural agent—but the conclusion reached by the argument is the denial of (2), i.e., there is something of the thing produced that exists at the starting point of the action of a natural

---

[9]   Ibid., n. 14 (Vat. XIX, 73).

agent. Thus, the argument ultimately relies on the invalid inference from (2) to (1).

Scotus agrees with these philosophers that the claim that only God can produce something from nothing is to be understood in sense (1). However, he objects to the distinction between (1) and (2) by arguing that the two readings are equivalent. It is not only the case that (1) implies (2), but also the converse implication from (2) to (1) holds in the case of a natural agent so that if a natural agent could produce something from nothing of the thing produced then it could also produce it from nothing at all. There is an extra premise that is needed to make the inference from (2) to (1) a valid one. This premise says is that

> (P) If an agent can produce an effect E as a whole, then it can also produce it in the absence of anything that weakens its productive power.[10]

And, in Scotus's view, the fact that there is a thing on which an agent starts to act to produce another thing is a factor that hinders and weakens its action. His argument for this claim is that the initial thing from which an action starts is contrary to that produced by the agent with its action so that the agent must corrupt the contrary initial thing in order to effect the change, and this is something that weakens that agent's active power. Therefore, if an agent can produce an effect E as a whole (2), then by (P), it can also produce E starting from nothing (1).

Principle (P) seems sound, but its application to the case of a natural agent is not so evident as Scotus thinks it is. The assumption that the existence of something as the starting point of the action of the natural agent is an obstacle to its action is not convincing. One could object that the presence of a starting point is not a hindrance but a requisite of the action of the natural agent. This agent cannot act unless there is something presupposed by its action, and therefore, it is rather the absence of this thing that would hinder its action and not its presence. Scotus's appeal to the notion that the initial thing is contrary to that produced by the agent in support of the claim that the presence of this thing hinders the action of the agent does not seem very helpful either. For, in Aristotle's physics, it is

---

[10] Ibid., n. 15 (Vat. XIX, 73–74): "Contra: agens quod habet in virtute sua totum effectum, non minus potest producere amoto quocumque quo posito magis debilitatur virtus eius quam fortificetur; sed per te generans habet in virtute sua activa totum effectum, quia nihil eius praesupponit in instanti generationis; igitur generans potest producere genitum amoto quocumque quo posito magis debilitatur virtus eius quam fortificetur. Per actionem autem in contrarium corrumpendum, debilitatur virtus eius activa et non fortificatur; igitur agens naturale amoto quocumque passo potest producere effectum."

an essential feature of a natural change that it is between contraries, and therefore it is an essential feature of a natural agent of such a change that its action starts with the corruption of a contrary. Scotus, however, does not consider this possible line of attack to his reply.

II THE NATURE OF MATTER

Scotus thinks that the property of matter of being the persisting subject in a substantial change not only provides the strongest argument for the existence of matter but also contains clear indications about its nature.[11] In our example of a change from water to air, since matter persists throughout this change whereas the form of water and that of air do not (the first passes away so that it does not exist at the end of the change, and the second comes to be so that it does not exist at the beginning of the change) and these are the only two forms involved in this change, matter must be an entity distinct from any forms: (i) neither itself a form nor containing a form as one of its components. (ii) It must, however, be an entity capable of receiving any forms, that is, a subject of forms. (iii) But since matter remains one and the same entity under different forms, the identity of matter cannot depend on the forms it receives, that is, matter must be an entity in its own right independently of any forms.[12] In Scotus's words, matter is a 'positive entity distinct from a form.'[13]

Matter is commonly characterized as a being in potency, and conditions (i) and (ii) are those condensed under this common description: matter is a being in potency in the sense that matter is something that lacks any forms and is in potency to receiving any forms. Scotus thinks, however, that it is crucial that condition (iii) too be included in the characterization of matter. The being in potency of matter must be such that it is compatible with its being a positive entity in its own right, apart from any forms. To make his point clear, he appeals to a distinction between two notions of being in potency, i.e., being in potency objectively and being in potency subjectively:

> For something is said to be in potency in two ways. In one way because it is the terminus of a potency, i.e., that toward which a potency is directed— and this thing is said to be objectively in potency (just as we say that the Antichrist is now in potency and similarly the whiteness that has to be

---

[11] On Scotus's discussion of the nature of matter, see also Cross 1998: 17–33; Ward 2014: 27–40.
[12] Duns Scotus, *Lect.* II, d. 12, q. un., nn. 52–53 (Vat. XIX, 89–90).
[13] Ibid., n. 1 (Vat. XIX, 60).

generated). In another way, something is said to be in potency as the subject of a potency, that is, that in which there is a potency—and in this way something is said to be subjectively in potency, because it is in potency to something else by which, however, it is not yet perfected (as a surface that has to become white).[14]

Scotus's distinction between objective and subjective potency is well illustrated by the example of the surface and its whiteness. Suppose that a surface is now black but will be painted white. The relevant potency in this example is the potency of a surface to whiteness. In Scotus's words, whiteness is the terminus of the potency, i.e., the entity to which the potency is directed, whereas the surface is the subject of this potency, i.e., the entity in which the potency to whiteness exists. 'Being in potency' can be truly predicated both of the whiteness and of the surface, but in different senses: the surface is a being in subjective potency, that is, the subject of the potency, whereas the whiteness is in objective potency, that is, the terminus of the potency.

What is important for Scotus to stress with this distinction is that the terminus of a potency and its subject have different ontological statuses. The terminus of a potency or what is in objective potency is an item that does not exist: it can exist or will exist but does not yet exist; instead, the subject of the potency or what is in potency subjectively is an item that already exists, although it can still acquire some properties. Applying this distinction to the case of matter, Scotus concludes:

> Therefore, matter is a being in potency in the second way, that is, as some positive being which is by nature capable of receiving an act and is a being in potency to all the acts that can receive. And in this way matter is a being in potency to a greater extent than the subject of an accident because matter has in itself less actuality and is capable of a greater actuality.[15]

It is only subjective potency that is compatible with the status of matter of being a positive entity. For matter is an entity in its own right independently of any forms of which it is receptive just as a subject of accidents is

---

[14] Ibid., n. 30 (Vat. XIX. 80): "Nam aliquid dicitur esse in potentia dupliciter: uno modo, quia est terminus potentiae, sive ad quod est potentia,—et istud dicitur esse in potentia obiective (sicut Antichristus modo dicitur esse in potentia, et similiter albedo generanda); alio modo, dicitur aliquid esse in potentia ut subiectum potentiale sive in quo est potentia,—et sic dicitur aliquid esse in potentia subiective, quia est in potentia ad aliud, quo tamen nondum perficitur (ut superficies dealbanda)."

[15] Ibid., n. 37 (Vat. XIX, 82): "Est igitur ens in potentia secundo modo, sicut aliquod ens positivum, quod natum est recipere actum et est ens in potentia ad omnes actus quod potest recipere. Et sic est magis ens in potentia quam subiectum accidentis, quia minus in se habens actualitatis et maioris actualitatis capax". See also ibid., n. 42 (Vat. XIX, 84–85).

an entity in its own right independently of the accidental forms of which it is receptive (e.g., the surface with respect to the colours). Thus, the difference between the two kinds of subject is not a difference in kinds of potentiality, that is, it is not the case that a subject of accidents is in subjective potency while matter is in objective potency. The difference is only one of degrees of subjective potentiality: the potentiality of matter is greater than that of a subject of accidents. The gradation in potentiality— as Scotus explains—is determined by an inverse gradation in the actuality associated with it: the substantial forms of which matter is receptive are more 'actual' or give 'more actuality' than the accidental forms of which a subject of accidents is receptive. Indeed, substantial forms are responsible for the kind of thing that something is whereas accidental forms are only responsible for non-essential/extrinsic properties of a thing.

A serious problem in Scotus's account of matter as being in subjective potency is that it seems to ascribe incompatible properties to matter. Matter as a positive entity must be something of itself actual in the sense of something that actually exists; but being actual presupposes having a form or being a form, whereas matter is absolutely formless. Thus, while a surface is something of itself actual because it has its own form apart from those of which it is receptive (e.g., it is a two-dimensional extension), matter does not qualify for being something of itself actual because it does not have its own form.

The crucial assumption from which this problem originates is the association of actuality with form so that being actual is equivalent to having a form. This assumption is the cornerstone of Aquinas's view on the nature of matter:

> Everything that is in act either is an act itself or is a potency that participates in an act. But being an act is repugnant to the *ratio* of matter, which according to its own *ratio* is a being in potency. It follows, therefore, that matter can only be in act in so far as it participates in an act. But the act participated by matter is nothing else but a form so that the claims 'matter exists in act' and 'matter has a form' are equivalent.[16]

---

[16] Thomas Aquinas, *Quaest. de quolibet* III, q. 1, a. 1 "Utrum Deus possit facere quod materia sit sine forma" (Leon. XXV.2, 242, ll. 53–62): "Omne enim quod est actu, uel est ipse actus, uel est potencia participans actum; esse autem actum repugnat rationi materie, que secundum propriam rationem est ens in potencia; relinquitur ergo quod non possit esse in actu nisi in quantum participat actum. Actus autem participatus a materia nichil est aliud quam forma; unde idem est dictu, materiam esse in actu et materiam habere formam." On Aquinas's view on matter, see Wippel 2000: 312–327.

Scotus finds that Aquinas's equivalence between existing in act and having a form is not sound, since it implies that matter is not something real. In his interpretation, Aquinas gives to matter the ontological status of something in objective potency, that is, of something in potency to existence, and thus of a non-being, like the whiteness to be generated in a black surface. But this is inconsistent with a number of positive properties that Aquinas himself ascribes to matter, like being the subject of a substantial change.[17] Even more fundamentally, Aquinas's position does not save the common assumption that material substances are composite entities. In Scotus's understanding, this requires that both components of a material substance are genuine entities in their own right, whereas Aquinas's account reduces its material component to a non-being.[18]

Despite its serious problems, Aquinas's equivalence between the existing in act of matter and its having a form has a strong intuitive appeal in that it is based on the common characterization of form as the act of matter. If form is the act of matter, doesn't it follow that for matter to exist in act is for matter to have a form? Scotus maintains that this conclusion does not follow. The reason for this is that the term 'act' is used in different senses when we say that form is the act of matter and when we say that matter exists in act:

> If you ask whether matter must be said to be an act or not, I reply that I do not want to discuss about names. For if act takes its name from 'to act', then matter is not an act in that way. I say, however, that matter is some true reality, which produces something one when it is joined to the actuality of a form. Thus, if act and potency are taken insofar as they divide being, in this way everything which has its own entity outside its cause is said to be an act, and in this way matter, being a principle and a cause of a thing, is said to be a being in act. But if potency is taken as a principle distinct from the act that a form confers, in this way matter is said to be a potency (and this is the way in which Aristotle speaks about act in *Metaphysics* VII and VIII). For in this way act is distinguished from that which receives the act. And in this way matter is not an act because it is a principle receptive of act and as such must be free of every act.[19]

---

[17] Duns Scotus, *Lect.* II, d. 12, q. un., nn. 31–36 (Vat. XIX, 80–82).

[18] Ibid., n. 49 (Vat. XIX, 88).

[19] Ibid., n. 38 (Vat. XIX, 82): "Si autem quaeras an debeat dici actus aut non, dico quod nolo de nomine disputare. Si enim actus dicatur ab 'agere', sic non est actus. Sed dico quod materia est aliqua realitas vera, quae cum realitate formae facit unum. Unde si actus et potentia accipiantur prout dividunt ens, sic actus dicitur omne illud quod habet entitatem suam extra causam suam,—et sic materia, cum sit principium et causa rei, dicitur ens in actu; si autem accipiatur potentia ut est principium distinctum contra actum informantem,—sic materia dicitur esse potentia (et sic loquitur Philosophus de actu VII et VIII *Metaphysicae*): sic enim actus distinguitur contra illud

Thus, with the claim that matter exists in act we mean that matter is something that actually exists rather than something that is in potency to existence. But this kind of actuality intrinsic to matter as actual being is not that conferred to it by a form. Matter is indeed of itself formless. Matter, however, has its own formless actuality. Because of this formless actuality, matter is something positive, and in particular, the subject of the potentiality (subjective potency) to substantial forms. Thus, a composite substance is not a composite of something purely potential and something actual, as in Aquinas's view. Rather, it is a composite of two items that are both true realities and thus both actual, but their respective actualities are of distinct kinds.

III   PLURALITY OF FORMS

While Scotus departs from Aquinas in maintaining that form is not the only actual component in a material substance, he agrees with Aquinas and the other medieval philosophers about the kind of actuality associated to form. According to this common view, a form confers actuality to a substance in the sense that it is responsible either for the kind of thing that a substance is—for its very nature—or for some of its contingent properties. In Aristotelian terms, a form responsible for the nature itself of a substance is called 'substantial form' while a form responsible for a contingent property of it is called 'accidental form'. For example, the soul is a substantial form of a human being because it is responsible for its essential nature of rational animal, whereas the colour of its hair is an accidental form. This common view about form and the distinction between the two kinds of form are well grounded in Aristotle's metaphysics. There is a distinctively medieval controversy, however, about the number of substantial forms in a substance. While the plurality of accidental forms in a substance is commonly admitted—in our example of a human being, the accidental form responsible for the colour of the hair is not the same as that responsible for its being curly—the question of whether there is only one substantial form in a given substance or more than one is matter of great debate. Aquinas is a strong supporter of the unitarian view. He maintains that in every composite substance—from the most simple, i.e., an element, to the most complex, i.e., a human being—

quod recipit actum,—et sic materia non est actus, quia est principium receptivum actus; tale autem oportet esse denudatum ab omni actu."

there is only one substantial form.[20] Scotus defends the possibility of a plurality of substantial forms against Aquinas's attack. He argues that Aquinas's unitarian view is based on wrong assumptions about hylomorphic compounds, and that there is actually a class of substances, namely, the living substances, with more than one substantial form.[21] This section is devoted to Scotus's reply to Aquinas's unitarian view, while the next one to his pluralist account of living substances.

Aquinas's most powerful line of argument in favour of the unitarian position appeals to a fundamental feature of a material substance on which there is universal agreement, namely, that of being something with a strong unity: something per se one, in medieval terminology. The basic idea here is that a material substance is a composite entity having prime matter and substantial form as its components, but it is not simply the aggregate of its components; rather, it is one thing resulting from them. The strong unity of a substance is commonly contrasted with the weak unity of an accidental compound, that is, an entity composed of a substance and an accidental form of it, for example, the compound of a human being and the colour of her hair: this is not one thing, but the aggregate of two things. It is also commonly assumed that the difference between the strong unity of a material substance and the weak unity of an accidental compound derives from the nature of their respective components. In particular, a substantial form is the kind of thing that can be a component of something per se one, while an accidental form can only be a component of something accidentally one. For Aquinas, however, there is a crucial condition that a substantial form must satisfy in order to be a component of something per se one: it must be itself one. As Aquinas puts it, a substance is per se one because its substantial form is one so that the existence of more than one substantial form in a substance would be incompatible with its per se unity. He illustrates this claim with the example of a human being. If three distinct souls—a vegetative soul, a sensitive soul, and a rational soul—were responsible for the nature of a rational animal, then a human being would not be per se one, since these three forms could not combine to produce something per se one.[22]

The intuition of Aquinas here is that the per se unity of a composite substance requires that this substance has only one actual or actualizing component. Thus, the fact that in a composite substance there is (prime)

<hr/>

[20] On Aquinas's view, see Wippel 2000: 327–351.
[21] On Scotus's view, see also Cross 1998: 47–76; Ward 2014: 76–109.
[22] Thomas Aquinas, *Summa theologiae* I, q. 76, a. 3 c.

matter as a component in addition to a substantial form does not spoil its per se unity because, according to Aquinas, matter is absolute potentiality with no actuality of its own. Furthermore, when it is joined to any substantial form, matter becomes completely actual so that no potentiality is left from the union of matter and form. In other words, the actuality conferred by a substantial form does not admit of degrees of completeness. Thus, a composite substance has an absolute unity because its two metaphysical constituents are such that matter is purely potential and its substantial form fully actualizes the potentiality of matter. Accordingly, if a thing composed of matter and a substantial form were to acquire another form, then this thing and that form could not combine in a further thing with absolute unity, because unlike matter, the thing on which this additional form supervenes is something already fully actual, that is, an actual substance.

Scotus thinks that Aquinas's account of the unity of a composite substance is wrong. The most serious problem with it is the assumption that there must be only one component of such a substance that is responsible for its being or actuality. This assumption, in Scotus's view, does not save the status of a composite entity of such a substance and reduces it to a simple entity, an entity with only one component. Appealing to the distinction between simple and composite entities, Scotus points out that it is generally agreed that both a simple entity like an intelligence (i.e., a pure form) and a composite entity like a material substance are one entity so that per se unity is ascribed not only to simple entities but also to composite ones. But if it is commonly conceded that an entity with distinct components has per se unity and so is one being, then it should also be conceded that its being is composed of the beings corresponding to its components. The components of a composite entity are indeed themselves entities and therefore each of them has its own being, and each contributes to the being of the whole.[23] Thus, according to Scotus, Aquinas's account of the unity of a composite substance does

---

[23] Scotus, *Ord.* IV, d. 11, p. 1, a. 2, q. 1, nn. 249–251 (Vat. XII, 255): "Ad rationes igitur pro prima opinione. Ad primam concedo primam propositionem, quod "unius entis est unum 'esse'"; sed secunda, scilicet quod "unum 'esse' requirit tantum unam formam", neganda est, accipiendo 'esse' uniformiter in maiore et minore: sicut enim ens et unum dividuntur in simplex et compositum, ita 'esse' et 'unum esse', distinguntur in 'esse' tale et tale; ergo 'esse' per se unum non determinat sibi 'esse' simpliciter, sicut nec aliquod divisum determinat sibi praecise alterum dividentium. Isto modo totius compositi est unum 'esse', et tamen includit multa 'esse' partialia, sicut 'totum' est unum ens et tamen multas partiales entitates habet et includit ... hoc modo 'esse' totius compositi includit 'esse' omnium partium, et includit multa 'esse' partialia multarum partium vel formarum, sicut totum ens ex multis formis includit illas entitates partiales".

not work even in the case of a substance with only one substantial form because the matter of such a substance contributes its own being to the whole distinct from the being of its substantial form so that its being is actually a composite of two partial beings.

According to Scotus, therefore, a sound account of the unity of a composite substance, instead of reducing its being to a simple one, should acknowledge that its being is composite. The relevant questions to be answered then become: 'What are the conditions that the partial beings of a composite substance must satisfy for that substance to be per se one?' and: 'How can such conditions be satisfied in a substance with more than one substantial form?'. Scotus's answer to these questions goes as follows. Consider first the case of a substance with only one substantial form F in addition to matter M. What makes this substance one is not, as Aquinas thinks, the condition that matter does not contribute its own being, but the condition that the being contributed by matter is in potency to form F. Thus, both M and F have their own beings, but their beings are such that one is potential to the other. Scotus's idea is that this potency-act model can be extended to the case of a pluri-formed composite. So suppose now that a substance is composed of matter M and two substantial forms F1 and F2. With the example of a human being, suppose that F1 is the form of the body and F2 is the soul. This substance has per se unity provided that it can be decomposed into two essential parts that are related as potency to act. The two parts would be (i) that composed of matter M and form F1 and (ii) and that consisting of form F2. And just like matter M is in potency to F1 so the composite of M and F1 is in potency to F2. With our example, the composite of matter and the form of a body is a body potentially alive, a body in potency to be made actually alive by a soul-form F2. Thus, in reply to Aquinas's claim that the being of a composite substance derives from a single form, Scotus says:

> But if one gives importance to the words, I concede that the total being of the whole composite is principally in virtue of one form, and that form is the one in virtue of which the whole composite is this being, and this is the last form supervening on all the preceding ones. In this way the whole composite is divided into two essential parts, that is, into its proper act, that is, the last form, in virtue of which it is what it is, and into the proper potency with respect to that act, which potency includes first matter with all the preceding forms. In this way I concede that that total being is completed by one form, which gives the whole what it is, but it does not follow from this that exactly one form is included in the whole or that in the whole many forms are not included, but not as specifically constituting that

composite, but as things included in the potential aspect of this composite.[24]

The crucial assumption in Scotus's account of the unity of a pluri-formed composite is that substantial forms can be ordered in such a way that one is in potency to the other. Being substantial forms, they are all responsible, in some degree, for the specific being of the substance to which they belong, but they are ordered in a hierarchy such that all of them except the last only partially actualize the specific being of a substance and only the last one brings it to completion. The contrast with Aquinas is worth being made explicit. Aquinas assumes that there cannot be substantial forms that contribute only partially to the specific being of a substance because it is in the very nature of a substantial form that it is responsible for its whole specific being. Therefore, once a substantial form comes to exist in matter, the resulting compound is a substance in its own right, in its complete specific being. Any other form coming to exist in this compound would have the status of an accidental form, being a form that supervenes on a complete substance and so could only be responsible for some accidental property of it. As Aquinas puts it, a plurality of substantial forms leads to deny the ground for the distinction between substantial and accidental forms. For Scotus, on the contrary, it is not an essential feature of a substantial form that it is responsible for the whole specific being of a substance so that there can be substantial forms that only partially contribute to it, and therefore, there can be more than one such form in a given substance.

IV THE HYLOMORPHIC COMPOSITION OF LIVING SUBSTANCES

Living substances include plants, non-rational animals, and rational animals, i.e., human beings. Being alive is posited as an essential feature of these substances, and therefore, it is accounted for by a substantial form, which, following Aristotle, medieval philosophers identify with the soul.

---

[24] Ibid., nn. 252–253 (Vat. XII, 255–256): "Si tamen omnino fiat vis in verbo, concedo quod totale 'esse' totius compositi est principaliter per formam unam, et illa est forma, qua totum compositum est 'hoc ens'; illa autem est ultima, adveniens omnibus praecedentibus; et hoc modo totum compositum dividitur in duas partes essentiales: in actum proprium, scilicet in ultimam formam, qua est illud quod est,—et in propriam potentiam illius actus, quae includit materiam primam cum omnibus formis praecedentibus. Et isto modo concedo quod 'esse' istud totale est completive ab una forma, quae dat toti illud quod est; sed ex hoc non sequitur quod in toto includatur praecise una forma vel quin in toto includantur plures formae non tamquam specifice constituentes illud compositum, sed tamquam quaedam inclusa in potentiali istius compositi".

Thus, in the Aristotelian tradition, it is commonly agreed that the soul is a substantial form of a living substance. The controversial question is whether the soul is the only substantial form of such a substance. While Aquinas insists that for living substances too the unitarian model applies, Scotus, and with him many other scholastic philosophers, maintains that this is exactly the class of substances for which the unitarian model is inadequate and a pluralist model instead holds. In his view:

> universally in every animate thing it is necessary to posit that form in virtue of which it is a body, distinct from that in virtue of which it is animate.[25]

Scotus's point can be expanded as follows. A living substance is a body of a special kind: a living body. Accordingly, there are two relevant kinds of essential properties of a living substance, that is, those relative to its being a body and those relative to its being alive. Contrary to what Aquinas thinks, it is not the case that both these properties can be accounted for by just one substantial form, namely, the soul. Rather, its soul is responsible for its being alive, but it is not also responsible for its being a body. What makes it a body is a substantial form distinct from the soul, the so-called form of the body. For example, it is the form of the body that is responsible for the existence of a bodily organ, like an eye, and it is the soul that is responsible for its vital function, for example, for the visual power of an eye. Later in this section, we shall see something more about Scotus's view on the form of the body. Let us first understand why Scotus thinks that we need to posit the form of the body in addition to the soul.

His strongest argument is that such an additional form is necessary to give an adequate account of the kind of change that the death of a living substance involves. When Socrates dies, for example, what is left is his corpse. The intuitive view that Scotus wants to defend is that the corpse of Socrates is actually the body of Socrates so that the body of Socrates remains the same in the passage from life to death: it is the same body that is first alive and then dead. The identity of the body through death, however, requires that there is a form of the body distinct from the soul. For the body remains the same insofar as the substantial form that is responsible for its being a body persists; but the soul does not persist through death, given that the body is no longer alive; therefore, it cannot be the soul that is responsible for its being a body, and so there must be

---

[25] Ibid., n. 280 (Vat. XII, 265): "... universaliter in quolibet animato necesse est ponere formam illam —qua corpus est corpus—aliam ab illa qua est animatum".

another form that is responsible for this.[26] Equivalently, if the soul is the only substantial form in Socrates, what persists in the passage from life to death is only the prime matter of Socrates but not also his body; the corpse of Socrates is not the body of Socrates but a body totally different from the body of Socrates, given that the only component that the two bodies share is prime matter. Thus, a unitarian cannot save the intuitive view that the body of a living substance persists through death.

More generally, a unitarian cannot save the common intuition that a living substance is a composite of body and soul as two distinct components. Indeed, Aquinas admits that this common intuition is wrong. Instead, for him, the correct view about the decomposition of a living substance is that this is a decomposition into prime matter and the soul so that there is no body independently of the soul, given that it is the soul itself that in virtue of which the body is the body, and hence a living body.[27]

Furthermore, a unitarian is forced to postulate a substantial form that is newly produced at Socrates's death, the substantial form responsible for the kind of body that Socrates's corpse is, but—as Scotus argues—a unitarian cannot give a satisfactory account of the coming into being of such a form. For, in the unitarian view, the agent responsible for the death of a living body is also responsible for the production of the form of the corpse; but while it is perfectly plausible that agents of very different kinds can produce death, that is, remove the soul from the body, it is not plausible at all that such different agents can produce completely similar forms of the corpse. With Scotus's example, the corpse of a cow killed with a knife and that of a cow killed by drowning are very similar; how then is it possible that the agents producing the two corpses—the knife and water— are so dissimilar? A unitarian does not have a good answer to this question, according to Scotus.[28]

Which are exactly the substantial forms in a living substance, according to Scotus? The passage quoted above seems to suggest that there are two such forms: one in virtue of which a living substance is a body, that is, the form of the body, and the other in virtue of which it is living, that is, the

---

[26] Ibid.: "... forma animae non manente, corpus manet. Et ideo universaliter in quolibet animato necesse est ponere formam illam—qua corpus est corpus—aliam ab illa qua est animatum. ... Unde corpus, quod est altera pars <i.e., compositi>, manens quidem in suo 'esse' proprio sine anima, habet per consequens formam qua est corpus isto modo, et non habet animam—et ita illa forma necessario est alia ab anima."

[27] Thomas Aquinas, *Summa theologiae* I, q. 76, a. 4, especially arg. 1 et ad 1.

[28] Duns Scotus, *Ord.* IV, d. 11, p. 1, a. 2, q. 1, nn. 225–226 (Vat. XII, 246–247).

soul. This is not, however, Scotus's considered view. More precisely, he adopts a unitarian view about the soul, that is, he assumes that the animating form or soul is only one form in all kinds of living substance so that even in the case of a human being there is only one form responsible for all its vital operations (vegetative, sensitive, and rational). He supports, however, a pluralist view about the form of the body: there is not only one substantial form in virtue of which the body of a living substance is the body it is. For the body of a living substance is a highly complex one, containing many specifically different organic parts, for example, flesh, bones, heart, liver, lungs, eyes, and so on. And Scotus finds it odd that just one form could be responsible for this great variety of organic parts.[29] He thinks that we should rather posit that each organic part has its own substantial form distinct from that of any other organic part so that, for example, the form in virtue of which the heart is the organic part it is is different from the form in virtue of which the lever is the organic part it is.[30] This pluralist view also finds strong support in the fact that different organs have different existential careers. For example, the fact that in the formation of the embryo, the heart is the first organ to be produced can easily be explained if one assumes that the form responsible for the identity of the heart is distinct from that of any other organ.[31] Similarly, the fact that in the corpse, bones persist much longer than the flesh can easily be explained if one assumes that the form responsible for the identity of bones is distinct from the form responsible for the identity of the flesh.[32]

What is then the form of the body to which Scotus refers in the passage quoted above and in many other occasions? Is it just the collection of the substantial forms of the organs? Or is it rather another bodily form that supervenes on the collection of organs?[33] Scotus does not devote to these questions the attention they would have deserved and leaves them without an explicit answer. It is not surprising that his scattered remarks on this topic have given rise to diverging interpretations. According to one of them, that of Richard Cross, there is a form of the body over and above the forms of the organs;[34] according to the other one, that of Thomas Ward, there is not such a form so that the forms of the organs are entirely responsible for the body of a living substance.[35]

---

[29] Duns Scotus, *QMet.* VII, q. 20, n. 31 (OPh IV, 387).   [30] Ibid., n. 11 (OPh IV, 382).
[31] Ibid., n. 38 (OPh IV, 389–390).   [32] Ibid., n. 15 (OPh IV, 383).
[33] For Scotus's formulation of these alternatives, see ibid., n. 19 (OPh IV, 383–384).
[34] Cross 1998: 68–71.   [35] Ward 2014: 90–93.

CHAPTER 8

Duns Scotus, intuitionism, and the third sense of 'natural law'

Thomas Williams

In this chapter, I'm assuming the truth of my radically voluntarist reading of Scotus with respect to the moral law: that is, that God is free with respect to all contingent practical principles and that there is no explanation for what God wills with respect to those principles in terms of God's nature, our nature, or anything else.[1] Proceeding from that assumption, then, my question is this: How, for Scotus, do we know the truth of practical principles? Necessary practical principles are easy: they are necessary in virtue of their terms, so all we need in order to see their truth is to understand their terms. But contingent practical principles are difficult. If I am right about how they get their truth value—in virtue of the divine will alone—there seems to be no obvious way for us to know them. We cannot know them by inference from any facts about God, for they do not follow from any facts about God; we cannot know them by inference from any facts about human nature, for they do not follow from any facts about human nature. Though they are not strictly speaking brute facts, since they do have an explanation (the divine will), they are brute-with-respect-to-us; for we cannot read the mind of God, and so we have no way of knowing directly whether that in virtue of which true contingent practical principles are true in fact obtains or not. We could know, it seems, only indirectly, by report: that is, by revelation.

It's important to acknowledge from the outset that there is no explicit discussion of this question anywhere in Scotus. So any possible answer to the question "How, according to Scotus, do we know the truth of contingent practical principles?" will lack textual support in one obvious sense.

---

[1] I have a whole raft of new and better arguments for that claim in a chapter entitled "God and the Moral Law," which I will include in a book (now in progress) on Scotus's ethics; but for the time being, see in particular Williams 1998a. Authors who find a much less radical voluntarism in Scotus include Wolter 2015; Ingham 2001; and Borland and Hillman 2017.

But I think this lack of textual support is not, in itself, an objection to any particular account of how we know contingent practical principles. For Scotus clearly thinks we *do* know contingent practical principles, and it is reasonable to ask on his behalf *how* we know them. If we can identify a means by which we know them that is (a) consistent with what Scotus says about the relationship of the moral law to the divine will and to human nature, (b) consistent with what Scotus says more generally about our knowledge of contingent truths, and (c) consistent with Scotus's actual argumentative practice in dealing with contingent practical principles, we will have as much as we can expect.

My claim is that Scotus is, and must be, an intuitionist about contingent practical principles. First, a bit of terminological clarification. "Moral intuitionism" names both a normative view and a meta-ethical view. The normative view is that there is a plurality of irreducible *prima facie* duties; the meta-ethical view is that moral truths (or moral properties, or whatever) are known by intuition, that is, immediately and non-inferentially. The intuitionism I am concerned with here is the meta-ethical view. Such meta-ethical intuitionism (intuitionism with respect to moral epistemology) can be either generalist or particularist: generalist if what we are said to know by intuition is general moral truths (e.g., "Murder is not to be done," "Promises are to be kept"), particularist if what we are said to know is particular moral truths (e.g., "This act is not to be done," "This state of affairs is good"). Scotus's moral intuitionism is generalist, not particularist. For Scotus holds that we derive conclusions about the rightness of particular acts by reasoning from intuitively known practical principles by way of a practical syllogism.

My argument for the claim that Scotus is an intuitionist about contingent practical principles proceeds in three stages. First, I argue that what Scotus says about the relationship of the moral law to the divine will and to human nature rules out any account on which moral truths can somehow be "read off" God's nature, our nature, or the notion of the final end, happiness. Second, I show that Scotus recognizes epistemically immediate contingent propositions, so there is theoretical room in Scotus's account of knowledge for the kind of intuitionism that I say characterizes our knowledge of contingent practical principles. Third, I show that Scotus's actual argumentative practice is consistent with his being an intuitionist. In that context, I draw out what, as far as I can tell, is a hitherto unnoticed third sense of 'natural law' in Scotus. This sense of 'natural law', frequently used but never explicitly defined, makes Scotus's commitment to moral intuitionism very clear.

The first two stages of the argument develop ideas I have written about before,[2] and I will accordingly dispatch them as briefly as possible so that I can get to the third stage, which is new and (I think) the most compelling part of the argument.

I THE MORAL LAW AND KNOWLEDGE OF CONTINGENT PRACTICAL PROPOSITIONS

First, I argue that what Scotus says about the relationship of the moral law to the divine will and to human nature rules out any account on which moral truths can somehow be "read off" God's nature, our nature, or the notion of the final end, happiness. The connection between Scotus's account of the contingent part of the moral law and the view that we cannot know contingent practical truths by argument is quite straightforward. Scotus argues that the contingent part of the moral law is freely determined by the divine will. And he understands 'freely' here in a strong sense:

> Suppose you ask why the divine will is determined to this contradictory rather than that. I reply: "It is characteristic of the improperly educated to seek causes and a demonstration for everything"—so says Aristotle in *Metaphysics* IV [1006a5–8]—"for there is no demonstration of a principle of demonstration." *That the will wills this* is immediate, such that there is no intermediate cause between the will and what it wills, in the same way that *heat heats* is immediate (though the latter case is a matter of what is natural, whereas the former is a matter of freedom). Consequently, there is no cause of why the will wills this other than the fact that will is will, just as there is no cause of why heat heats other than the fact that heat is heat. For there is no prior cause. (*Ord.* I, d. 8, p. 2, q. un., n. 299; Vat. IV, 324–325)

So God's willing in one way rather than another does not follow from any prior truths; the proposition "God wills P" is, if it is contingent, not merely contingent but immediate. Consequently, we know in advance that any argument purporting to establish the truth of a contingent moral proposition will be invalid. For example, there is no cause of its being the case that murder is prohibited other than the fact that God willed to prohibit murder. An argument purporting to show some other cause, some reason for that prohibition besides God's will, must be invalid. For its conclusion,

---

[2] In Williams 1997. Some of the language in Sections I and II of this chapter is borrowed from that earlier paper. To avoid extensive redundancy, I have recapitulated the argument of that paper as briefly as I can; I have also responded to further discussion of these issues in the secondary literature over the last 20 years.

that murder is wrong, does not in fact follow from any other propositions whatsoever.

Now it might be thought that I have moved a bit too fast here. There are, after all, entailment relations among various contingent propositions. So I have to qualify my claim that any contingent proposition about what God wills must be not merely contingent but immediate. After all, "God wills that there be horses" and "God wills that there be animals" are both contingent, but the former entails the latter, and the latter is (or at least might be) known on the basis of the former. "God wills that there be animals" therefore seems to be contingent but not immediate.

So perhaps the contingent propositions of the moral law follow from some other contingent propositions. The obvious place to look is at human nature. Perhaps the contingent part of the moral law follows from facts about human nature. Since it is contingent that beings with human nature exist, the moral law that prescribes the behavior that is fitting (or proscribes the behavior that is unfitting) for such beings is likewise contingent. And on this view, one would still be able to say that the moral law depends essentially on the divine will since the existence of human beings depends essentially on the divine will. But we would be able to read the moral law off human nature, and the arbitrariness that my more radical reading of Scotus's voluntarism attributes to the contingent part of the moral law is avoided.[3]

The arguments for attributing such a view to Scotus deserve extensive attention of a kind that I cannot give them here, since I am focusing on Scotus's moral epistemology rather than on the foundation of his normative ethics; so I shall simply (and, I admit, unsatisfyingly) state briefly the reasons that I continue to insist on a more voluntarist reading. When Scotus discusses the dependence of practical principles on the divine will, he always states his view in the starkest way possible: every contingent practical principle has its truth solely from the divine will. It is clear that, for example, "Adultery is not to be committed" is contingently true; there is never any hint that "If human beings exist, adultery is not to be committed" is necessarily true. Moreover, it seems to me impossible to square this less radical reading of Scotus's voluntarism with his discussions of dispensation from the moral law and the distinction between God's absolute power and God's ordained power.[4] Finally, as I argue in the third

---

[3] For such an argument, see especially Wolter (ed. and trans.) 1987: 25–30.
[4] For a brief but compelling discussion of this, see Hagedorn 2019: 63–66.

section of this paper, Scotus's actual argumentative practice reflects the kind of voluntarism I attribute to him, not this more modest form.

Another genus of attempts to mitigate the contingency-to-the-point-of arbitrariness that I attribute to the moral law on Scotus's view comprises arguments that some aspect of the *divine* nature limits God's creative choice. The favorite divine attributes in this context have been God's justice,[5] his rationality,[6] and (more recently) his aesthetic sensibilities[7] (for lack of a better expression). Briefly to these: Scotus explicitly flat-out denies that God's justice constrains his activity of moral legislation.[8] The only sort of rationality that constrains God is instrumental. Yes, one who wills the end must will the means: but there is no end God must will, apart from himself, and no creaturely means is necessary for that end. The attempt to use the rationality of God's will to argue against my account rests on a gross equivocation: 'rational' for us is an approval term whose contrast terms are 'arbitrary', 'capricious', 'mad', and the like; but for Scotus, it's a term with purely descriptive content. It means "capable, synchronically, of opposite acts," and rationality in that sense clearly does not constrain the divine will—quite the opposite, in fact.[9] As for God's aesthetic sensibilities, the claim that the "consonance" of the contingent part of the moral law with the necessary part bespeaks a kind of aesthetic fittingness that gives God a reason to command as he does is without foundation in the texts of Scotus. Scotus uses *consonans* to indicate logical compatibility, not aesthetic harmony.[10] And even if Scotus did have such divine aesthetic sensibilities in his system, they would be unavailing for our present purposes, since (a) there's no reason to suppose we can do the divine mind-reading necessary to read the moral law off God's aesthetic preferences and (b) since the contingent part of the moral law is just that, contingent, either God's aesthetic sensibilities aren't a necessary feature of his nature or his aesthetic sensibilities don't pick out (that is, entail) a unique set of moral truths; either way, we're again left unable to read off the moral law from the facts available to us by natural reason.

---

[5] For defenses of such an argument, see Wolter (ed. and trans.) 1987: 11–16, and Ingham 2001: 197–200.

[6] For defenses of such an argument, see Wolter (ed. and trans.) 1987: 16–24, and Ingham 2001: 187–197.

[7] For defenses of such an argument, see Bychkov 2014 and Cross 2012b.

[8] See Williams 2000: 171–189.   [9] See Williams 2000: 189–198 and Williams 2009: 9–11.

[10] On this point see Steele 2016.

II   EPISTEMICALLY IMMEDIATE
CONTINGENT PROPOSITIONS

Having argued that Scotus's account of the moral law rules out any explanation of our knowledge of contingent practical principles according to which we can "read off" such principles from facts about God or about us, I now argue that there is theoretical room in Scotus's account of knowledge for the kind of intuitionism that must characterize our knowledge of contingent moral propositions. Scotus recognizes the existence of contingent truths that are immediate, that is, not derived from any logically prior truths. Indeed, he insists that there must be such truths: "otherwise there would be an infinite regress in contingent truths, or else something contingent would follow from a necessary cause—either of which is impossible."[11] Now we need to distinguish here between two sorts of immediate contingent truths. I shall call them metaphysically immediate and epistemically immediate. Metaphysically immediate contingent truths are those for which there is no further explanation at all; they are the sorts of truths we might be inclined to call "brute facts"—not merely brute relative to other facts, but absolutely brute, as we might say. Scotus's favorite examples of such truths are, not surprisingly, facts about the divine will.

> Among contingent truths there is a first that is immediate and nonetheless contingent, since it is not traced to a necessary truth (for a contingent truth does not follow from a necessary truth). And therefore in this case one must stop with "The will of God wills this," which is contingent and yet immediate, since there is no other cause, logically prior to the will, of why the will wills this and not something else.[12]

This sort of immediacy, however, is not characteristic of the contingent part of the moral law. There is a "logically prior" cause—the divine will itself—that explains why the moral law is what it is.

The moral law is therefore not metaphysically but epistemically immediate. That is, while the fact that murder is wrong depends upon and is in some sense explained by the fact that God wills that murder be wrong, our knowledge that murder is wrong does not depend upon our knowledge that God wills that murder be wrong. Scotus certainly recognizes contingent truths that are immediate in this epistemic sense: for example, "I am

---

[11] *Ord.* I, d. 3, p. 1, q. 4, n. 238 (Vat. III, 145). See also *Ord.* prol., p. 3, qq. 1–3, n. 169 (Vat. I, 112–113), and *Ord.* I, d. 8, p. 2, q, un., n. 300 (Vat. IV, 325).

[12] *Ord.* I, d. 8, p. 2, q. un., n. 300 (Vat. IV, 325).

awake" and "I am understanding."[13] Clearly such facts as "I am understanding" and "I am awake" are not absolutely brute or metaphysically immediate, but they are epistemically immediate. I do not know that I am awake on the basis of any logically prior facts, although no doubt there are logically prior facts.

The contingent truths of the moral law are epistemically immediate in just this way. Although they depend on logically prior facts, they are not known on the basis of any logically prior facts. They can therefore function as "principles of demonstration" for which there is in turn no demonstration,[14] as unargued-for starting points for argument. They are, in words from Saint Paul that Scotus quotes in several places, "written on our hearts."[15] We can assume that they were written there by God who created us with moral intuitions to suit the moral order he freely and contingently created.

III INTUITIONISM AND SCOTUS'S ARGUMENTATIVE PRACTICE

Having now shown that there is room in Scotus's thought for knowledge of epistemically immediate contingent propositions, I turn to my central point. What I mean to show here is that Scotus's actual argumentative practice reflects a conviction that practical principles are known immediately. There is both a negative and a positive side to this case. The negative side is that Scotus does not in fact seek to establish any contingent practical principle by arguing from facts about God or human nature and indeed rejects such attempts at arguing for contingent practical principles. The positive side is that Scotus helps himself to practical principles in just the way that an intuitionist does (and must). In the course of making the positive case, I uncover a hitherto unnoticed third sense of 'natural law' to which Scotus frequently appeals in his treatment of particular moral issues. This third sense of 'natural law' makes it clear that for Scotus the natural law is as much an epistemic notion as it is a normative notion.

A full-blown defense of the negative case would require an exhaustive look at all of Scotus's argumentation concerning contingent practical principles, which is obviously not feasible here. Instead, I look at a fairly typical example of such argumentation and then examine some purported

---

[13] *Ord.* I, d. 3, p. 1, q. 4, nn. 238–239 (Vat. III, 144–146).   [14] Ibid.
[15] Romans 2:15, quoted at *Ord.* prol., p. 2, q. un., n. 108 (Vat. I, 70); II, d. 28, q. un., n. 27 (Vat. VIII, 303); III, d. 37, q. un., n. 42 (Vat. X, 290); and IV, d. 3, q. 4, n. 147 (Vat. XI, 202).

counterexamples to my claims raised by Thomas Ward in "A Most Mitigated Friar."[16]

As an example of the way in which Scotus analyzes purported arguments for moral truths, consider his discussion of lying.[17] Scotus considers three philosophical arguments for the claim that lying is always wrong. The first argument, drawn from William of Auxerre, would, if successful, show that the prohibition against lying belongs to the necessary part of the moral law: "Some say that lying is necessarily a sin because it necessarily turns one away from God, who is truth, and a lie is contrary to truth."[18] Scotus replies that "a lie is not opposed immediately to the first Truth, but rather to the truth of some particular thing about which the liar is speaking. So just as badness opposed to some particular created good does not necessarily turn someone away from the first uncreated Good, neither does falsity opposed to any truth unconnected with the first Truth [necessarily] turn someone away from the first Truth."[19] Only acts that necessarily turn someone away from God are necessarily prohibited, and so the prohibition against lies is contingent.

But our question here all along has been about the contingent part of the moral law, so Scotus's rejection of William of Auxerre's argument merely establishes that the prohibition of lying belongs to the part of the moral law with which we are concerned. The second argument, drawn from Aquinas, proceeds from an account of the structure of moral acts that Scotus also accepts and argues that lying is generically bad. Aquinas and Scotus agree that an act is generically bad when it has an unsuitable object or matter;[20] they also agree that no particular act that is generically bad can ever be good (whereas a particular act that is generically good can be bad if some feature of the act other than its object is bad). They disagree, however, about whether the object of a lie—namely, something the speaker believes to be false—is unsuitable in such a way as to making lying generically bad and therefore never permissible. Aquinas thinks it is;[21] Scotus thinks it is not.

Scotus's chief objection to the argument involves an analogy with murder. In Aquinas's view, the analysis of the structure of the acts of lying and murder are parallel, and both have inappropriate objects and are accordingly generically bad:

---

[16] Ward 2019.   [17] Here I expand upon my treatment of this discussion in Williams 1997.
[18] *Ord.* III, d. 38, q. un., n. 14 (Vat. X, 298).
[19] *Ord.* III, d. 38, q. un., n. 15 (Vat. X, 298). The edition's text is manifestly incorrect here; for the correction, see *John Duns Scotus: Selected Writings on Ethics*, 261, n. 9.
[20] For Aquinas, see *Summa theologiae* I–II.18.2; for Scotus, see *Ord.* II, d. 7, q. un., n. 29 (Vat. VIII, 89).
[21] *Summa theologiae* II–II, q. 110, aa. 1 and 3.

Act	Object	Character of object	Moral status of act
speech	something believed to be false	inappropriate	generically bad
killing	an innocent human being[22]	inappropriate	generically bad

Scotus argues, however, that an innocent human being is not in fact an inappropriate object for an act of killing, because

> it can become licit to kill [an innocent] human being, for example, if God revoked the commandment "You shall not kill" (as was said in the previous question [d. 37 n. 13])—and not merely licit, but meritorious, for example, if God commanded someone to kill, as he commanded Abraham concerning Isaac.[23]

Now the harm done to one's neighbor by depriving him of a true opinion or inducing a false opinion is clearly less grave than the harm done to him by depriving him of bodily life altogether—"indeed," Scotus says, "there is scarcely a comparison."[24] So if the killing of an innocent human being can be licit, it is even more obvious that the utterance of something the speaker believes to be false can be licit.

Puzzlingly, Thomas Ward takes this argument to be a point in favor of his view that Scotus does sometimes offer arguments for contingent moral truths:

> While it is indeed a sobering thought that God could make some killing, or lying, permissible or even obligatory, it simply does not follow from this possibility that natural laws against killing and lying obtain in the first place through a divine command. Indeed, later in the same passage, Scotus implies that killing is worse than lying for reasons that do not have to do with divine will . . . Scotus here makes clear that the persuasive power of his example depends on murder being much worse than lying.[25]

First, the claim that the commandments against killing and lying obtain only by divine command is not meant to follow directly from the claim that God could make some killing and lying permissible or even obligatory. What supports the stronger claim is Scotus's reference to the discussion of the Decalogue in the preceding question. There Scotus argues that only acts with an immediate relation to the divine nature are necessarily good or bad. If an act has such a relation, it is easy enough to see how the act is right or wrong in itself. For example, perjury involves an immediate

---

[22] Scotus ups the stakes a bit by describing the person killed not merely as "innocent" but also as "useful to the commonwealth."
[23] *Ord.* III, d. 38, q. un., n. 17 (Vat. X, 299–300).   [24] Ibid.   [25] Ward 2019: 398.

relation to God, since Scotus understands perjury as the deliberate act of swearing *by God* to something one disbelieves or doubts. Such an act clearly involves irreverence to God, which cannot be licit. But if an act lacks an immediate relation to the divine nature, its rightness or wrongness is subject to God's will. There is, as Scotus argued in his reply to William of Auxerre, no immediate connection between particular truths or falsehoods and the divine nature. God was therefore free to establish a moral order in which things believed to be false were a licit matter for speech.

Moreover, in his discussion of the Decalogue Scotus refers us to two other discussions that provide the theoretical background for his account of the contingency of the commandments of the second table: his denial of practical cognition in God (*Ord.* prol., p. 5, qq. 1–2, n. 333; Vat. I, 218) and his insistence that God's will is not determined necessarily to anything other than himself (*Ord.* I, d. 2, p. 1, qq. 1–2, nn. 79–81; Vat. II, 176–177). Both passages—along with other passages[26] that apply those discussions explicitly to the modal status of moral truths—make it clear that the second-table commandments obtain only because God wills that they obtain.[27]

Nor does Scotus's comparison of the relative gravity of lying and murder tend at all to suggest that Scotus thinks one can reason from facts about human nature to contingent moral truths. Given the kinds of things we are, of course it is worse for us to lose our life than to lose a true belief; our natures determine what contributes to our flourishing and what is detrimental to it. But Scotus could hardly be more emphatic that natural goodness and badness have no necessary significance for moral rightness and wrongness. God need not prescribe what is naturally good; he need not prohibit what is naturally bad. We cannot reason from the fact that something is good for our neighbor to the conclusion that we ought to promote or preserve it. In fact, even if we are allowed to assume the requirement to love our neighbor, we *still* cannot derive the claim that "one must will-against killing him (with respect to the good of his person) and that one must will-against committing adultery (with respect to the good of the person married to him), and that one must will-against stealing (with respect to the goods of fortune that he has at his disposal)."[28] Natural

[26] For example, *Ord.* I, d. 8, p. 1, q. un., n. 273 (Vat. IV, 307), and d. 38, q. un., n. 4 (Vat. VI, 303–304); *Rep.* I-A, d. 38, qq. 1–2, nn. 37–38 (Wolter and Bychkov II, 457–458).
[27] I make these arguments at length in "God and the Moral Law."
[28] *Ord.* III, d. 37, q. un., n. 36 (Vat. X, 288–289).

goodness shapes the moral law only to the extent that God wills accordingly.

Scotus offers a third argument for the wrongness of lying, drawn from Bonaventure, who argues that lying by its nature involves an evil intention, the intention to deceive. Therefore, any lie will be circumstantially bad, since it is directed to a morally illicit end. Although Scotus offers no refutation of this argument, at least four considerations make it clear that he must reject it. First, the same kind of objection Scotus raises against Aquinas's argument works equally well against Bonaventure's: God is free not to prohibit deception, and he is free to permit or even to command deception. Second, in discussing famous lies from Scripture, Scotus is willing to admit that there are cases in which someone deliberately tells a falsehood with the intention to deceive and yet is not held guilty of sin; so we can be certain that Bonaventure's account of what makes lying sinful cannot be correct. Third, the only "proof" of the wrongness of lying that Scotus endorses is the appeal to revelation: "without exception every such lie told deliberately is a mortal sin, for it is prohibited without qualification by the commandment, 'You shall not speak false testimony against your neighbor.'"[29] And fourth, the distinction Scotus makes between lies that are mortally sinful and those that are not has to do, not with whether they involve the intention to deceive, but with whether they do harm. And as the analogy with murder makes clear, the prohibition against doing harm is contingent in such a way that one could not come to know by any chain of reasoning that such a prohibition is in force.

In short, no facts about human nature, divine nature, particular people, or particular situations constrain God's contingent and sovereign willing of the moral law. There is no intermediary, so to speak, between God's will and the contingent part of the moral law. So there is nowhere for natural reasoning to get started in formulating any sort of discursive justification for a contingent moral truth. It cannot start from God's will itself, since God's will is not accessible to natural reason. It cannot start from anywhere else, because there is no road from anywhere else—that is, from any of the facts that *are* accessible to natural reason—to any contingent moral truth.

Thomas Ward objects that my conclusion here is much too strong, because Scotus does in fact offer "secular" arguments—that is, arguments not depending on any revealed premises—for the goodness of sexual intercourse and of marriage.[30] So let's look at those arguments and see what they tell us.

---

[29] *Ord.* III, d. 38, q. un., n. 23 (Vat. X, 303–304).   [30] Ward 2019: 395–398.

The arguments about sexual intercourse are found in *Ordinatio* IV, d. 26. The two "secular" arguments are as follows:

(1) For a human being to preserve his own species is not more contrary to right reason or to natural inclination than for any other animal to preserve its species; indeed, the more perfect a species is, the more this accords with inclination. And a species cannot be preserved in a regular way otherwise than by procreation.

(2) Even if human beings were immortal, it would still be suitable for them, in keeping with a correct natural inclination, to share their species in the way that would be possible for them, namely, by procreation.[31]

Both arguments appeal to natural inclination: the principle, presumably, is that what is in accord with natural inclination is suitable (*conveniens*). The first argument also appeals to the notion of right reason: it is not more contrary to right reason for human beings to procreate than for any other animal to procreate. Both the negative character of this appeal to right reason (it is *not contrary* to right reason) and its extension to the other animals deserve brief comment. Its negative character may not mean anything much; Scotus doesn't always express himself economically, and so his formulation could well be a clumsy way of saying that it is in accord with reason. The extension of the principle to other animals is puzzling, however; surely we cannot say that any behavior of animals either accords or does not accord with right reason, for other animals lack reason altogether. It would be human reason, not animal reason, that rightly judges that animal procreation is a suitable thing: suitable because it accords with natural inclination, and suitable also because the preservation of a species is itself suitable, and "a species cannot be preserved in a regular way otherwise than by procreation."

From these two arguments (and two other arguments that depend explicitly on "things believed") Scotus is willing to conclude only that the act of procreation is not intrinsically—that is, generically—bad. The remaining possibilities are that it is intrinsically generically good or that it is not intrinsically good but is capable of being morally good because it is characterized by correct circumstances. It is not intrinsically good, Scotus argues, because its object is not "intrinsically worthy of being willed." Only God is such an object, because only God is the ultimate end. By contrast, "the good thing that is the object of the act of procreating or of willing to

---

[31] *Ord.* IV, d. 26, q. un., n. 13 (Vat. XIII, 339).

procreate offspring is not the ultimate end, but merely something ordered, or capable of being ordered, to the ultimate end."[32]

The only remaining possibility, then, is that the act is not intrinsically good but is capable of being morally good when it is characterized by correct circumstances. The first circumstance (not just for this act, but for any act) is the end. Scotus describes the correct end of this act as follows: "willing to procreate offspring *to be brought up religiously in order to expand the worship of God*" (*Ord.* IV, d. 26, q. un., n. 19; Vat. XIII, 340). Scotus's secular argument for this conclusion is extraordinarily brief and unsatisfying:[33] "This is proved by reason: the end of human beings is perfect human activity, as we read in *Ethics* I and X; therefore, it is for the sake of this end that a given person ought to will to have offspring" (*Ord.* IV, d. 26, q. un., n. 20; Vat. XIII, 341). The connection between the quite general notion of "perfect human activity" and the very particular end of bringing up children religiously in order to expand the worship of God is not further elucidated, and it is hardly self-evident. And the other circumstances that Scotus goes on to detail—"that this act ought to be of determinate persons" (*Ord.* IV, d. 26, q. un., n. 23; Vat. XIII, 341–342), "that it is honorable for these persons to be obligated to one another in an indissoluble bond" (*Ord.* IV, d. 26, q. un., n. 29; Vat. XIII, 343)—are derived from this end. So it is important to reflect on how Scotus might suppose that he is justified by reason in identifying this end as the one in virtue of which the act of procreation accords with right reason.

Here we can only speculate. One is initially tempted to think that Scotus is leaning on the love of God as an intrinsically good act. Having children in order to bring them up religiously in order to expand the worship of God would, on this reading, be justified precisely because it is a manifestation of love of God. But this won't do. If this end were straightforwardly equivalent to, or at least redescribable as, loving God, the act would be generically good, as love of God is generically good; but Scotus denies that the act of procreation is generically good. Nor can Scotus be thinking that perfect human activity *requires* that people get married and procreate, since he of course recognizes celibacy as licit. So perhaps the thought is something like this: procreation for the sake of bringing up

---

[32] *Ord.* IV, d. 26, q. un., n. 16 (Vat. XIII, 340).
[33] Cf. Ward 2019: 395: "The secular argument for the requirement of this circumstance is convoluted." But it isn't convoluted; it's just bad, or (to be charitable) enthymematic. I quote the argument in full.

children religiously is *one* way of engaging in perfect human activity; procreation for any other reason is not; so this end (and no other) is a good-making circumstance for the act *procreating offspring*.

What, then, is the justification for the claim that this end (and no other) is a good-making circumstance for that act? Scotus offers two, the first relying on "things believed" (*Ord.* IV, d. 26, q. un., n. 21; Vat. XIII, 341) and the second appealing to authority. So he has no secular argument for the claim, and indeed it is only the appeal to authority that gives him precisely the claim that he wants:

> This is confirmed through Augustine, *On Genesis* IX: "Not all who have offspring have the good of offspring, since it is not the offspring themselves who are said to be the good of offspring, but rather the hope or desire by which one seeks offspring so that they may be instructed in religion."[34]

Ultimately, then, Scotus offers no secular argument for the goodness of procreation. The middle term (so to speak) of the argument he does give— namely, that procreating for the sake of giving one's offspring a religious education and thereby expanding the worship of God is a form or manifestation of perfect human activity—is something Scotus professes to know only on the basis of faith and authority.

Scotus identifies two further good-making circumstances of the act of procreation. (The end is, as Scotus consistently maintains, the first circumstance after the object,[35] so these further good-making circumstances presuppose that the act has the right end; if the act lacks the right end, these other circumstances cannot make the act good.) The first is that it be "of determinate persons" (*Ord.* IV, d. 26, q. un., n. 23; Vat. XIII, 341–342), that is, of one man and one woman; the second is that these persons are "obligated to one another in an indissoluble bond for this end" (*Ord.* IV, d. 26, q. un., n. 29; Vat. XIII, 343). Scotus acknowledges that the first of these is not "proved by natural reason to be unqualifiedly necessary, in such a way that its opposite would be repugnant to natural and manifest reason" (*Ord.* IV, d. 26, q. un., n. 28; Vat. XIII, 343); he likewise says that the second "could not be proved manifestly by natural reason" to be "unqualifiedly necessary" (*Ord.* IV, d. 26, q. un., n. 30;

---

[34] *Ord.* IV, d. 26, q. un., n. 22 (Vat. XIII, 341). Though there is something a bit like this in *De Genesi ad litteram* IX, 7, and Richard Middleton (who is apparently Scotus's source here) attributes these words to Augustine in his commentary on the *Sentences* (IV, d. 31, princ. 1, q. 3 in corp.), the quotation actually derives from Peter Lombard, *Sent.* IV, d. 31, c. 2, n. 4 (II, 444).

[35] See *Ord.* prol., p. 5, qq. 1–2, n. 251, n. 362 (Vat. I, 169); I, d. 48, q. un., n. 5 (Vat. VI, 388–389); II, d. 40, q. un., 10–11 (Vat. VIII, 470); *Quodl.*, q. 18, n. 6 (Vivès XXVI, 236–237); English translation in John Duns Scotus, *God and Creatures*, n. 18 (Alluntis and Wolter, 403).

Vat. XIII, 343–344). The best we can say is that it is "honorable (*honestum*) for persons belonging to the Church to be determinately conjoined one with another for this act" (*Ord.* IV, d. 26, q. un., n. 28; Vat. XIII, 343) and "that it is honorable and consonant with a natural reason that a man and woman should be under such an obligation [i.e., that of indissoluble monogamous marriage] for the sake of such an end" (*Ord.* IV, d. 26, q. un., n. 30; Vat. XIII, 343–344).

So Ward errs in thinking that Scotus uses "arguments drawn from natural reason, reflecting on natural goodness and badness in human action, to derive conclusions about how we ought morally to act."[36] Only if the circumstances that make for natural goodness were "unqualifiedly necessary, in such a way that [their] opposite would be repugnant to natural and manifest reason," would natural reason be able to establish conclusions about what is morally required. But those circumstances are not unqualifiedly necessary. They are "consonant"—that is, consistent, compossible—with self-evident principles and conclusions that follow demonstratively from such principles, in other words, with the natural law in the strict sense (n. 31). But then their opposites are likewise consonant with such principles and conclusions: otherwise, the goodness of a properly circumstanced act of procreation *would be* unqualifiedly necessary.

So the question recurs: what, if anything, does this "consonance" really come to? Does it constrain, or at least guide, the deliverances of reason? Consonance by itself does not seem to do the right kind of work, since consonance, as Scotus uses the term, falls short of entailment. But it is important that Scotus does not here say merely that the goodness of procreation is consonant with the natural law in the strict sense: he says that it is *evidently* consonant with the natural law in the strict sense and therefore belongs to the natural law in some looser sense (ibid., n. 31; Vat. XIII, 344). I propose that it is not mere consonance, but the *evidentness* of that consonance, that Scotus is appealing to here. Consonance is a logical notion, evidentness an epistemic notion. Accordingly, I shall argue that what unites the notion of natural law in its strict and looser senses for Scotus is the epistemic status of the principles that belong to natural law. They are the principles that we know intuitively.

From the evidence presented so far, the claim that belonging to the natural law is a matter of epistemic status is at best tenuously supported. But a look at references to natural law in Book IV of the *Ordinatio* shows Scotus making extensive use of this epistemic notion of natural law.

---

[36] Ward 2019: 395.

Thus at *Ord.* IV, prol., n. 11 (Vat. XI, 3), when he is setting out the organizational scheme of Book IV of the *Sentences*, we find Scotus saying that the Master will deal with "the principal sacrament of the Mosaic law" and then consider "what corresponded to it in the law of nature," meaning, in the time before any law had been given. He speaks in several places of the age or era (*tempus*) of the law of nature. For example, he says that "we do not read of any sacrament instituted by God in the age of the law of nature" (*Ord.* IV, d. 1, p. 2, q. 2, n. 218; Vat. XI, 77).[37] In one question he asks "whether there was any sacrament corresponding to circumcision in the age of the law of nature" (*Ord.* IV, d. 1, p. 4, incidentalis q. 2, n. 385; Vat. XI, 138), and in his reply he uses several variations on the phrase: "during the age of that law of nature" (*pro tempore illius legis naturae*, ibid., n. 391; Vat. XI, 139),[38] "in the age of the law of nature" (*in tempore legis naturae*, ibid., n. 392; Vat. XI, 139), "during that age" (*pro tempore illo*, n. 395, ibid., Vat. XI, 140), and even "in the law of nature" (*in lege naturae*, ibid., n. 396; Vat. XI, 141).

The last example is drawn from the claim that it is possible that some form of sacrifice was instituted as a sacrament by God in the law of nature, so there the expression might refer not to the era (though that still seems the most natural reading in context) but to the obligations that held during that era. That is, it is possible that God instituted some sacrifice as a sacrament as one of the obligations that held during the period when no law had been given. Certainly, this second meaning is another way in which Scotus speaks of the "law of nature:" "Hence those things that belonged to the law of nature were also to be observed by Moses until the giving of the Law on Mount Sinai" (*Ord.* IV, d. 3, q. 4, n. 203; Vat. XI, 222).

What are we to make of this third sense (or these third and fourth senses) of 'natural law'? Scotus seems to accept a normative and an epistemic claim about the natural law in whatever sense. The normative

---

[37] This is language from an argument that Scotus rejects, but he does not reject the language of *pro tempore legis naturae* for the age in which no law had been given. One sees a similar pattern in *Ord.* IV, d. 3, q. 4, n. 156 (Vat. XI, 205): "And if the question is what remedy for original sin there was for the young children of the Jews from the Passion until the proclamation of the Gospel, it is said [by Richard Middleton] that it was not circumcision but the faith of the parents, as in the age of the law of nature"; Scotus rejects the argument, but for reasons that do not tell against this use of the expression *tempore legis naturae*, which indeed he uses *in propria persona* a little later in the question.

[38] Paris, Bibliothèque nationale de France, ms. lat. 15854 (=Q), which I tend to follow for reasons given in the introduction to Williams 2018, omits the demonstrative; this omission makes for a better and more consistent reading, but the substantive point is not affected if we simply follow the edition.

claim (uninterestingly enough) is that whatever belongs to the natural law ought to be observed; the epistemic claim is that whatever belongs to the natural law can be known independently of revelation because it is "written inwardly on the heart." It is by this epistemic criterion that natural law is distinguished from positive law, which of course also ought to be observed:

> On the basis of [Jesus'] statement [in John 15:22, "If I had not come and spoken to them, they would not have sin"] I accept the following proposition: "no one is bound by any divine precept unless it is promulgated by someone suitable and authoritative or by truthful report and the testimony of good people that everyone ought rationally to believe"; and I understand this to apply to positive law, which is not known inwardly in the heart." (*Ord.*, IV, d. 3, q. 4, n. 147; Vat. XI, 202)

The commandments of the second table are known inwardly in the heart, as Scotus says explicitly in *Ord.* III, d. 37, q. un., n. 42 (Vat. X, 290). Whether the other obligations that obtain during the era of the law of nature—such as, perhaps, the obligation to offer some sort of sacrifice—are likewise known inwardly in the heart is not entirely clear.[39] If they are, we have a unifying or core sense that unites all three notions of 'natural law': they are the obligations that are known intuitively whether because they are self-evident or follow from what is self-evident (natural law in the strict sense) or because they are evidently consonant with such truths (natural law in the broad sense) or because they are simply, in some way, evident (natural law in this underdeveloped third sense).

---

[39] Scotus talks of God as *instituting* some sacrament in the time of the natural law. Institution sounds like positive law, and positive laws, as we have seen, are not written inwardly on the heart.

CHAPTER 9

The bounds of sense: adequacy and abstraction in the later works of Duns Scotus

Wouter Goris

The doctrine of the first adequate object of the intellect has been discussed controversially by scholars of the work of Duns Scotus. Against its philosophical interpretation by Honnefelder, Dumont, and Aertsen, who relate the doctrine to the foundation of metaphysics in the univocal concept of 'being',[1] the representatives of the French tradition, including Gilson, Bérubé, Bazán, and Demange, argue that, since Scotus holds that only the theologian can have knowledge of the first adequate object of the intellect, he upholds a theological anchoring of metaphysics.[2] By advancing the thesis of the non-existence of the adequate object, Demange even claims that Scotus gradually abandons the view that there is an adequate object of the human intellect altogether.[3] Demange's claim matches with hitherto unnoticed suggestions by Francis of Mayronis and Peter Thomae that Duns Scotus would still allow for an adequate object of the human intellect but only to please the *vulgus*.[4]

---

[1] See Honnefelder 1989; Dumont 1998b; Aertsen 2012.

[2] See Gilson 1937; Gilson 1952; Bérubé 1983: 140–141; Bazán 2001; Demange 2007. Bazán brilliantly ironizes his own point by claiming: "If we were to follow Scotus' premises, it seems that we would be forced to conclude that only a theologian could have been able to write the 'Critique of Pure Reason'" (Bazán 2001: 209–210). Without agreeing on the overall conclusion of these interpretations, I want to stress the innovative character and the methodological significance of their analyses: the developmental account introduced by Bérubé, the contextualization of the limits of metaphysics by Scotus's noetics and anthropology by Bazán, and more fundamentally the contextualization of philosophical theory through epistemological practises by Demange. The importance of Gilson's studies requires no comment.

[3] Demange 2007; see Goris 2018.

[4] See Petrus Thomae, *Reportatio* I, d. 3, q. 1 (Biblioteca Apostolica Vaticana, ms. Vat. lat. 1106, ff. 116v–117r): "... in principio quaestionis ubi <Doctor> loquitur secundum intentionem suam dicit quod nullum potest poni obiectum primum intellectus nostri habens primitatem virtualitatis respectu omnium per se intelligibilium, licet infra volens satisfacere vulgo assignaverit ens primum eius obiectum ex eo quod in ipso occurrit duplex primitas, scilicet communitatis et virtualitatis ...; ne igitur videretur potentia remanere sine obiecto primo dixit hoc volendo satisfacere vulgo quod ens erat eius obiectum primum, sed a proposito dicit quod nullum potest sibi assignari, quia si esset obiectum eius primum aut esset primum secundum primitatem virtualitatis aut secundum primitatem communitatis; sed nullo istorum modorum est primum respectu omnium per se

In this contribution, I propose an interpretation of the doctrine of the first adequate object of the human intellect that pays special attention to its status as the product of abstraction. It is remarkable—and at the same time somewhat puzzling—that, in the course of his development, Duns Scotus seems to adopt the very position he sets out to combat initially, viz., the position (which he ascribes to Aristotle and Thomas Aquinas) that the 'essence of material things' (*quiditas rei materialis*) is the first object proper to the human intellect. As is well known, Scotus argues in the *Ordinatio* both as a theologian and as a philosopher against this position.[5] The three arguments by which he refutes the position of Aristotle and Aquinas from a philosophical point of view focus on (i) the natural desire for knowledge of the immaterial substances as the drive to human fulfilment and (ii) the requirement to provide the human intellect with an adequate object ample enough to explain its aspirations in the realm of metaphysics, thus ruling out (iii) that the intellect has a first object less general than 'being'.[6] Scotus, who explicitly construes this philosophical refutation by speaking of the potency "from the nature of the potency," will later on deny the philosopher exactly such a perspective.

The question is, therefore, to know whether Duns Scotus modifies his appreciation of the doctrine of the first adequate object of the intellect as a *philosophical* doctrine. And we will see that its status as the product of abstraction plays a pivotal role in this regard. The available textual evidence indeed shows that Scotus revised his doctrine of the adequate object of the intellect over the course of his intellectual development. It also shows, however, that across those stages Scotus still provided the intellect with a proper, adequate object. What is at stake in Scotus's doctrinal revision is not the issue whether the human intellect has an adequate object; rather, it is whether it is up to the philosopher or the theologian to decide what exactly the adequate object of the intellect is. In this sense, Scotus came to qualify his original position that the philosopher has full access to such

intelligibilium." The same claim is made by Franciscus de Mayronis, *In Sent.* I (redactio 'ab oriente'), d. 3, q. un., a. 7 (Biblioteca Apostolica Vaticana, ms. Vat. lat. 896, f. 15va): "Ideo videtur hic Doctor noster voluisse satisfacere vulgo." Thanks to Garrett Smith for drawing my attention to these passages; note their difference from Demange's claim of the non-existence of the adequate object of the intellect, which is less concerned with the all-too-great scope of the intellect (see below, nt. 35) than with the restriction of our knowledge to 'limited being' in the present life (see below, nt. 39).

[5] See Honnefelder 1989: 63–71; Aertsen 2005a; Aertsen 2005b.

[6] See *Ord.* I, d. 3, p. 1, q. 3, nn. 116–118 (Vat. III, 72–73); the first argument is already part of the first version of Scotus's third question on the second book of the *Metaphysics*. See *QMet.*, q. 2–3, nn. 27–28 (OP IV, 208–209). By contrast, the argumentative strategy associated with the other two objections, viz., the relation between the knowledge of 'being' and the possibility of metaphysics, seems to be added later: see ibid., n. 93 (OP IV, 227–228).

knowledge. This reorientation is motivated—and best explained, as we shall argue—by Scotus's adoption of a distinction originally formulated by William of Ware.

I DUPLEX OBIECTUM NATURALE

Scotus's *Lectura* and *Ordinatio* start with the same objection. If a potency has something common as its first natural object, it can by nature arrive at every *per se* object contained under that first object. Now, since the first natural object of our intellect is 'being'—*qua* 'being' Scotus adds, to make the link with the subject of metaphysics explicit—our intellect could by nature arrive at the metaphysical knowledge of every being, with the undesirable effect of rendering supernatural theology superfluous.[7]

By reducing the argument to the following structure, we will identify elements that are amenable to alternative evaluations.

Major   Every potency that has something common as its first object can by
            nature exercise an act toward everything contained, as a natural
            per se object, under this first object.
Minor   The first natural object of the intellect is 'being in common', viz.,
            'being as being'.
Conclusion Hence, our intellect can naturally know every being.

Duns Scotus evolves in the way he addresses the underlying equivocation. The *Lectura* briefly disambiguates two senses of a 'natural object'. One has to distinguish between the object to which the potency is naturally inclined (the *obiectum inclinabile*), and the object by which the potency is naturally moved (the *obiectum motivum*), for the intellect is naturally inclined to, but not naturally moved by, every object contained under 'being'.[8] One could surmise that in the more extensive treatment of the *Ordinatio*,[9] Scotus repeats the initial distinction of the *Lectura* and subsequently rejects it. But that is not correct. Scotus actually challenges

---

[7] *Lect., prol.*, q. 1, n. 1 (Vat. XVI, 1) and *Ord., prol.*, p. 1, q. un., n. 1 (Vat. I, 1). See Bérubé 1983: 129ff.; Bazán 2001: 204ff. A masterly introduction to the encompassing problematics is offered in Boulnois 1998.
[8] *Lect., prol.*, q. 1, n. 49 (Vat. XVI, 21).
[9] *Ord., prol.*, p. 1, q. un., nn. 90–92 (Vat. I, 54–57). Bérubé correctly stresses the late dating and the game-changing character of the distinction between the *obiectum attingibile* and *inclinabile*, while maintaining that Scotus would have held throughout his career that the sensible quiddity is the moving object of the intellect in the present state; see Bérubé 1983: 140.

the solution that William of Ware gives to the same objection. Whereas William makes a distinction between the *obiectum attingibile* and the *obiectum inclinabile* in order to deny the major premise of the argument while conceding its minor, Scotus adopts this distinction but objects to the use that Ware makes of it.[10]

The discussion with William of Ware is relevant to Scotus's notion of a first adequate object, as its subsequent steps show. (i) Already in the formulation of the objection itself, both in the *Lectura* and in the *Ordinatio*, the first natural object of a potency is characterized by its adequacy. If the *ratio* of its first object, viz. the *ratio* of 'being', were to be found in something the potency cannot attain, the object would not be adequate to the potency, but rather exceed it. (ii) The notion of adequacy returns in Scotus's formulation of Ware's solution, viz., that it would be enough to deny the major premise for the *obiectum attingibile* in order to block the conclusion about what is naturally attainable. Indeed, Ware asserts that the first object, since it is adequate to the potency, is something common abstracted from all things the potency is able to operate upon.[11] But it is not necessary that if the intellect naturally understands such a common abstracted object, it naturally understands everything contained under it. Hence, Ware accepts the minor premise that 'being' is the first natural object of the intellect but rejects the major premise that the intellect naturally attains everything contained under it. (iii) Scotus objects to Ware's solution that it refutes itself. One cannot at the same time affirm that 'being' is an adequate object that can be naturally attained and deny that everything contained under it can be naturally attained; for the latter would imply that it is not the adequate object, but rather that something less common under it is the adequate object of the intellect. (iv) Scotus concludes that Ware's argument is marred by a fallacy. Although 'being' as something conceived in a single act is naturally intelligible,[12] 'being' is not the first object that can be naturally attained, for as it is a first object, viz.,

---

[10] There is more to say about William of Ware's refutation of the objection in the second question of the prologue of his *Sentences* commentary and of Scotus's rendering of it; I deal with the former elsewhere in a forthcoming study on Scotus's doctrine of the first adequate object of the intellect and confine myself at present to the latter. The evident indication that Scotus discusses a rival position in the *Ordinatio*, viz. the "per ipsum" in n. 91, is misconstrued as a reference to Henry of Ghent by the Vatican editors; Bargius and Lychetus correctly identify William of Ware as Scotus's actual opponent.

[11] *Ord., prol.*, p. 1, q. un., n. 90 (Vat. I, 54): "... obiectum primum est adaequatum potentiae, et ideo abstractum ab omnibus illis circa quae potest potentia operari."

[12] Ibid., n. 91 (Vat. I, 55–56): "... ens ut est quid intelligibile uno actu (sicut homo est intelligibilis una intellectione) sit naturaliter intelligibile (illa enim unica intellectio entis ut unius obiecti est naturalis) ... antecedens est verum ut ens est unum singulare intelligibile."

as included in every *per se* object, it is naturally attainable only if every *per se* object is naturally attainable. (v) Hence, Scotus's own response to the objection follows a different path and rejects the minor of the argument: 'being' is not a first natural object in the sense that it is naturally attainable, but only as that to which the potency is naturally inclined. Not only does Scotus read in this way Avicenna's claim that 'being' is first impressed in the mind, referring the reader to the third distinction of the first book of the *Ordinatio* for a discussion of what actually is the first object that is naturally attainable, but he also quotes Anselm to deny that we have any potency that is by itself sufficient to act. Accordingly, it would not be inappropriate for a potency to be naturally ordered to an object that it cannot naturally attain by natural causes.[13]

To summarize, Scotus's distinction between the *obiectum attingibile* and the *obiectum inclinabile* in his reply to the opening objection and the corresponding discussion of the position of William of Ware in the *Ordinatio* have implications for the doctrine of the first adequate object. Scotus's claim is that the first natural object is adequate in the sense that it is something common abstracted from all things the potency is able to operate upon. On the one hand, therefore, 'being' is naturally intelligible as something conceived in a single act (*unum singulare intelligibile*) and is the first natural object to which the intellect is naturally inclined. On the other hand, 'being' is not a first natural object of the intellect in the sense that it would be naturally attainable. That would require that every *per se* object of the intellect was naturally attainable. This is not the case, however, because of the intellect's reliance on abstraction. But what exactly is the role and place of abstraction here? As we shall see, Scotus evaluates the following four claims, which presuppose that, in the absence of direct intellectual intuition under the present condition, we only have knowledge *a posteriori* of our intellect and its cognitive capacities.

- Knowledge of the *per se* objects of the intellect comes about naturally by abstraction from the senses.
- Knowledge of the first adequate object comes about by abstraction of something that is common to all *per se* objects of the intellect.

---

[13] This conception of a power that is directed of itself alone to something that it cannot attain on its own is at odds with the Aristotelian notion of a natural power to which Scotus recurs in his refutation of Aquinas in the third distinction of the first book of the *Ordinatio*; consequently, Scotus dismisses the relevant objection as begging the question (see infra, n. 25, and *Rep.* IV A, d. 49, q. 7).

- Knowledge of the first object adequate to the intellect's capacities in this life comes about by abstraction of something that is common to all the *per se* objects of which the intellect can attain knowledge by abstraction from the senses.
- Knowledge of the first object adequate to the intellect's capacities considered under the aspect of the nature of the potency comes about by abstraction of something common to all the *per se* objects that the intellect is naturally inclined to cognize.

II QUIDITAS REI SENSIBILIS

Other passages in the *Ordinatio* help to trace the effects of Scotus's discussion with William of Ware on his notion of a first adequate object. After presenting the opening objection I have mentioned above, Scotus adds further detail to his claim that in this life we do not know 'being' as a first natural object of the intellect in the sense that it would be naturally attainable.

In the context of the controversy between philosophers and theologians in the opening question of the *Ordinatio*, heralded by its first objection, Scotus introduces the philosophers' claim that because of the perfection of nature, no supernatural perfection is necessary. One famous argument in favor of this claim asserts that whoever can naturally understand a principle can naturally understand the conclusions virtually included in that principle; therefore, since we naturally understand the first principles of the intellect, which virtually include all its conclusions, we can naturally know all scientifically knowable conclusions.[14] In reaction to this argument, Scotus suggests that the position of the philosophers cannot be refuted on the basis of natural reason, but only by arguments based on belief. Against the arguments he advances, he subsequently raises *instantiae* and then responds to them. A further famous counter-argument to Scotus's own view is such an *instantia*. In order to ascertain that natural reason has distinct knowledge of human beings' final end, viz. intellectual knowledge of God, the objection argues that it is naturally knowable that the first object of the intellect is 'being' as Avicenna holds; therefore, since it is naturally knowable that the *ratio* of 'being' is most perfectly instantiated in God, and the end of every potency is the most perfect *per se* object contained under its first object, it follows that the human intellect has

---

[14] *Ord., prol.*, p. 1, q. un., nn. 9–11 (Vat. I, 7–8).

natural knowledge of God. The argument is corroborated by additional arguments that the intellect is naturally able to know both its first object and the most perfect *per se* object contained under it.[15]

It sometimes proves difficult—*pace* Gilson—to distinguish Scotus's own position from the arguments he presents in favor of the position of the philosophers. But, here at least, Scotus is clear in his denial: he refers to the third distinction of the first book of the *Ordinatio* to explain that, in this life, we have no natural knowledge of our intellect and what is contained under its first object; we only know what is intelligible for us under a general *ratio* that can be abstracted from sensibles.[16] Hence, Scotus denies the very assumption made by the *instantia*. It is incorrect to say that we naturally know that 'being' in its indifference towards the sensible and the insensible, is the first object of the intellect. Avicenna erred in this regard, inadvertently undermining philosophical rigor by religious belief—Scotus tacitly reproduces Averroes's criticism here, but to the opposite effect— when he inferred that, since the separate soul has intellectual knowledge of the divine essence in itself, immaterial substance must be contained under the first object of the intellect. If, however, Aristotle is here described as the better philosopher, since he defended that the first object of our intellect is the quiddity abstracted from sensibles,[17] the point is not that Scotus accepts his position *tout court*, but that he judges it to be the position better argued on the basis of natural reason alone.

Evidently, such a restriction of the first object of the intellect to what can be abstracted from sense cognition reproduces the very position that Scotus's theory of the first adequate object of the intellect originally intended to refute: the doctrine he attributes to both Aristotle and Aquinas, viz. that the *quiditas rei materialis* is the first known object proper to the human intellect.[18] Scotus now even defends this doctrine against

---

[15] Ibid., nn. 24–25 (Vat. I, 15–16). The objection touches upon an important strand in Scotus's reflection on the first adequate object, viz. the power's fulfillment by an act turned towards the most perfect *per se* object contained under its first adequate object, in the case of the adequacy by commonness—for in the case of the adequacy by virtuality, the adequate object is itself necessarily the most perfect object. See *Lect.* I, d. 3, p. 1, q. 1–2, n. 130 (Vat. XVI, 276; see also *Ord.* I, d. 3, p. 1, q. 1–2, n. 103, Vat. III, 65–66); *Lect.* III, d. 27, q. un., n. 12 (Vat. XXI, 203; see also *Ord.* III, d. 27, q. un., n. 30, Vat. X, 58–59): "omnis potentia habens aliquod obiectum commune adaequatum nata est habere actum perfectissimum circa supremum contentum sub eo in quo omnia includuntur." *Rep.* I-A, d. 1, q. un., nn. 8 and 16 (Wolter and Bychkov, 90 and 93) articulates the issue in systematic connection with the final section of the *Sentences*, viz. Rep. IV-A, d. 49, q. 7; see infra, n. 43.

[16] *Ord.*, *prol.*, p. 1, q. un., n. 29 (Vat. I, 17).   [17] Ibid., n. 33 (Vat. I, 19–20).

[18] In the *Lectura*, Scotus objects to Aristotle with philosophical arguments and reproaches Aquinas as a theologian for holding a position that flatly denies the beatific vision; the *Ordinatio* reproduces the

elements of his own criticism, when he adds in a later addition (a so-called *extra*) that if the material quiddity is said to be the first adequate object of the intellect, one can still account for knowledge of the immaterial substance; the range of a potency, he suggests, is not necessarily restricted to what is virtually or formally contained under its adequate object.[19] And to the objection that, if we do not know what the first object of the intellect is, we could not tell what is intelligible at all, Scotus answers that we do not have sufficient knowledge of the soul and its potencies in this life to know *on account of the nature of the potency* what is contained under its first object; if we know that the potency has certain objects, it is because we perceive that they are attained (*attingi*) by its act.[20]

To summarize, from the absence of the soul's direct intuition of itself in this life, Scotus infers the abstractive character of the first object of the intellect, which is to say that we are informed about the scope of what the intellect can grasp only insofar as we have actual access to intelligible objects. Therefore, what the first naturally attainable object of the intellect is *on account of the nature of the potency* cannot be decided upon by purely natural means. Philosophy, however, can correctly identify the first adequate object of the intellect *under present conditions*, viz., as restricted by the bounds of sense. It is a matter of good philosophy, therefore, to reject overestimations of the scope of philosophical cognition that would leave no room for a theologian's account of what the first adequate object of the intellect actually is—even if the theologian's account is without demonstrative force for a philosopher, who has no reason to differentiate between the potency's nature and its present conditions.

same argument (see supra, n. 6), while inserting doctrinal elements running counter to it. In reaction to the position that "obiectum intellectus coniuncti est quiditas rei materialis propter proportionem intellectus ad obiectum," the *Reportatio* states: "licet conclusio in se sit tolerabilis, sed deductio de proportione non." (*Rep.* I-A, d. 3, q. 1, n. 17; Wolter and Bychkov, 190) The same holds for the *Quodlibet* (see infra, n. 39).

[19] *Ord., prol.*, p. 1, q. un., n. 33 (Vat. I, 20, ll. 14–22): "Sed si ad hoc opponitur quod, si quiditas materialis sit primum et adaequatum obiectum potentiae intellectivae, quod intellectus intelligere non poterit aliquid de substantiis separatis, quia obiectum adaequatum vel virtualiter vel formaliter includit omne illud in quod potest potentia ferri; sed quiditas materialis nec virtualiter nec formaliter continet substantias separatas, ergo etc. – dico quod assumptum non est verum, quia quinque sensibilia communia, puta numerus, figura, etc., sentiuntur sensu visus per se, quae nec formaliter nec virtualiter continentur sub colore vel luce; sufficit enim aliqua continentia concomitantiae." Scotus here appeals to elements elsewhere discussed in the context of the "aequivocatio de primo obiecto et per se ipsius potentiae." See *Lect.* II, d. 9, q. 1–2, nn. 115–116 (Vat. XIX, 52–53); *Ord.* II, d. 9, q. 1–2, nn. 124–125 (Vat. VIII, 195–196); see also *QMet.*, IX, q. 5, n. 30 (OP IV, 570).

[20] *Ord., prol.*, p. 1, q. un., n. 38 (Vat. I, 21–22). Although the intellect has necessarily certain cognition of its own acts in this life (cf. *Ord.* I, d. 3, p. 1, q. 4, nn. 228–229 and nn. 238–239; Vat III, 137–138 and 144–146), it has no intuitive cognition of itself as a power and of the soul.

III   UNUM INTELLIGIBILE: BEING AS THE SUBJECT OF METAPHYSICS

At several places in the opening question of the *Ordinatio*, Duns Scotus has occasion to refer to his commentary on the third distinction of the first book of the *Sentences*. In each case, he postpones his discussion of the restrictions imposed on intellectual cognition in the present life. This is interesting, for —as we have already pointed out—the discussion of the first adequate object of the intellect was originally meant to determine what knowledge the intellect is capable of *independently of its present conditions*. Hence, one might want to assume that all passages in this discussion that now assign a first adequate object to the intellect *in the present life* postdate Scotus's discussion with the position of William of Ware.[21] This is especially evident in the case of a later addition (again a so-called *extra*) presumably occasioned by the criticism that Henry of Harclay gave of the way in which Scotus rejected Aquinas's position on the first adequate object of the intellect.[22]

In his critique of Scotus's original rebuttal of the position ascribed to Aristotle and Aquinas, Henry of Harclay differentiates a *twofold adequate object*, distinguishing between the scope of our intellect's cognition in this life and the one pertaining to the nature of the potency as such. Scotus's *extra* suggests that such a distinction between adequate objects of the intellect was raised by the worry that natural reason might not be able to prove that the human intellect has an adequate object that surpasses the scope of our intellect's cognition in this life. Harclay's criticism accordingly targets Scotus's originally optimistic claim that both theological and phil-osophical arguments prove that the human intellect is not restricted by nature to cognition of essences abstracted from material things.

In his *extra*, Scotus addresses Harclay's criticism step by step and observes that Harclay agrees with the position of Aristotle and Aquinas

---

[21] A similar ambivalence characterizes the famous *dubitatio de primo obiecto intellectus pro statu isto* in the *Ordinatio*, where Scotus presents the *quiditas rei sensibilis* as the first adequate object, *in ratione motivi*, of the intellect *pro statu isto*, while denying that a particular state of a power has proper bearing on its first adequate object; see *Ord.* I, d. 3, p. 1, q. 3, nn. 185–188 (Vat. III, 112–115).

[22] Cf. *Ord.* I, d. 3, p. 1, q. 3, nn. 123–124 (Vat. III, 76–77). Just like in the case of William of Ware, I discuss Scotus's encounter with the position of Henry of Harclay only as that position is presented in the text. My more extensive discussion elsewhere addresses, apart from the identification of 'articulus' with 'Arcelinus', the absence of the doctrine ascribed here to Harclay in the relevant section in his *Sentences* commentary; see again my forthcoming study on Scotus's doctrine of the first adequate object of the intellect. Here it may suffice to note that 'Arcelinus', which is a variant spelling forthcoming of 'Harclay', was rendered by the Assisi scribe as 'articulus'. For the numerous variations on 'Harclay' see the *Ratio criticae editionis operum I. D. Scoti* (Vat. I, 160–161, especially 160, n. 2) and the ulterior discussion in *Adnotationes* (Vat. IV, 1*–39*).

regarding the adequate object of the intellect in the present life, but disagrees regarding the adequate object that belongs to the intellect by the nature of the potency. If natural reason cannot prove that, by the nature of the potency, the intellect has an adequate object that exceeds its adequate object in this life, then Scotus's objections against the position of Aristotle are rendered unsubstantial. Of course, the objections against Aquinas, the theologian, remain valid.

Harclay's agreement with the position of Aristotle and Aquinas stems from a more specific rendering of the position involved, making the "quiddity (or essence) of sensible things" (*quiditas rei sensibilis*, instead of *quiditas rei materialis*) the adequate object of the intellect in this life. This specification allows for cognition derived from the sensible, yet not arrived at by the senses themselves. Although the intellect depends on input from the senses in this life, its knowledge is not restricted to what the senses themselves apprehend, for the intellect grasps universal content that is essentially or virtually included in the *phantasma* (viz., in the object of the highest sensitive power), among which is the highest essentially included the concept of being. The adequate object assigned to the intellect in this life hence acknowledges the range of universal content essentially and virtually implied in sense cognition, and thereby identifies the proper foundation of metaphysical cognition in this life, the concept of 'being'.[23]

If Harclay agrees with Aristotle and Aquinas regarding the adequate object of the intellect in the present life, he disagrees with them as to the adequate object that belongs to the intellect by the nature of the potency. For Harclay holds that nothing less universal than 'being' can be the adequate object that belongs to the intellect by the nature of the potency, and accordingly distinguishes the latter from the 'quiddity of sensible things' as the adequate object of the intellect in the present life, a distinction that Aristotle (and Aquinas) did not make. A question then arises about the status of this distinction, if Aristotle (and Aquinas) did not accept it. The three arguments with which Scotus had refuted Aristotle are compromised if natural reason cannot prove that something more

---

[23] *Ord.* I, d. 3, p. 1, q. 3, n. 123 (Vat. III, 76): "Concordant hic Aristoteles et Arcelinus (*ed.* articulus), quod quiditas rei sensibilis est nunc obiectum adaequatum, intelligendo 'sensibilis' proprie, vel inclusi essentialiter vel virtualiter in sensibili ... Non igitur nunc est adaequatum obiectum eius quod supremae sensitivae, quia intelligit omne inclusum in sensibili essentialiter, usque ad ens, sub qua indifferentia nullo modo sensus cognoscit,—et etiam inclusum virtualiter, ut relationes, quod non sensus."

universal than the 'quiddity of sensible things' is the adequate object that belongs to the intellect by the nature of the power.[24] Scotus, who leaves the issue unresolved whether or not natural reason can prove this, subsequently recants his arguments against Aristotle.

After having described the partial agreement and disagreement between Harclay and Aristotle regarding the adequate object(s) of the intellect, Scotus draws some consequences from the suggestion that natural reason cannot prove that nothing less universal than 'being' is the adequate object that belongs to the intellect by the nature of the potency. He recasts, one after the other, his own three objections against the *philosophical* claim that the 'quiddity of material things' is the first adequate object of the intellect. The first objection, which argued that a natural desire cannot be in vain, is rejected by Scotus as simply begging the question.[25] The second and third objections are reputedly similar and Scotus answers them in the same vein. The issue here is the possibility of metaphysics. Scotus already accepted Harclay's argument that the adequate object of the intellect in this life, which covers all universal content essentially and virtually implied in sensitive cognition, includes the concept of 'being' as the foundation of metaphysical cognition in this life. Hence, the sheer possibility of metaphysics is not an argument for assigning an adequate object to the intellect in this life that is more encompassing than the 'quiddity of sensible things'. Scotus proves the point by distinguishing between the concept of 'being' as it is the subject of metaphysics and the concept of 'being' as it would be the first adequate object of the intellect. Upon the presupposition that the 'quiddity of sensible things' is the first adequate object of the intellect in this life, metaphysics as a science is possible for us, since the concept of 'being', as "one intelligible," is essentially contained in this first adequate object. Yet the knowledge of 'being' at which we arrive in this way does not necessitate us to redefine the adequate object of the intellect in this life in such a way that nothing less universal than 'being' would be the adequate object. For if 'being' were the first adequate object of the intellect in this life, it would not be such as one most universal intelligible apart from all other intelligibles, but rather as containing everything intelligible indifferently. The implication of the latter would be, Scotus specifies, that everything contained under 'being' could be understood by us in this life, which is not the case. Therefore, 'being' is not the first adequate object of the intellect in this life, although the subject of

---

[24] See supra, n. 6.   [25] *Ord.* I, d. 3, p. 1, q. 3, n. 123 (Vat. III, 76).

metaphysics, the knowledge of which is accessible to us in this life, is "being as being."[26]

To summarize: In his defense of the possibility of metaphysics under present conditions, Scotus abandons the identification of the subject of metaphysics with the first adequate object of the intellect. He assigns a universal scope to the subject of metaphysics that he denies to the first object of the intellect, albeit not in the same sense. In his discussion with Harclay, Scotus draws the consequences of the distinction he made earlier in his discussion with William of Ware, viz. the distinction between 'being' as "one intelligible," which is naturally attainable, and 'being' as the "first object," which is not naturally attainable, since not everything contained under it is naturally attainable. That distinction has now become an indication of the distinction between the first adequate objects of the intellect under present conditions and by the nature of the potency.

IV   IACET IN DEPOSITO

Several additions to the third distinction of the first book of the *Ordinatio* indicate how Duns Scotus planned to restructure his entire investigation of the first adequate object of the intellect. One such addition still announces to further subdivide—into five questions—the discussion, which started off with three questions in the *Lectura* and took on four questions in the edited version of the *Ordinatio*.[27] Another, later addition "extra de manu sua" draws the solemn conclusion from the complication that presented itself to Scotus: since the first object of the intellect is only manifest on

---

[26] Ibid., n. 77 (Vat. III, 77): "Ad secundum: ens ut est 'quoddam unum intelligibile' continetur sub quiditate sensibili, supra exposita. – Alia, de metaphysica, probat quod ens ut 'hoc intelligibile' intelligitur a nobis, sed si esset primum obiectum, hoc esset secundum totam indifferentiam ad omnia in quibus salvatur, non ut aliquod unum intelligibile in se, – et quidlibet illius indifferentiae posset intelligi. Ideo non est obiectum adaequatum pro nunc. ... Ens enim in quantum ens, communius est quocumque alio conceptu primae intentionis (secunda intentio non est primum obiectum), et sic intelligitur nulla contractione omnino cointellecta – nec habitudine ad sensibile, nec quacumque." For Scotus on metaphysics *pro statu isto*, in relation to his theory of cognition, see Pini 2008; Pini 2014. Pini shows, based on the *Metaphysics* commentary, how the univocity of the concept of 'being' makes it possible for our impaired cognitive capacities to gain access to substances or the essences of material things in the present life, thus grounding the possibility of metaphysical knowledge of 'being' despite the sensory limits of cognition. This perspective agrees with Scotus's later accommodation of the position of Harclay, namely with his accepting a metaphysical knowledge of 'being' that is essentially included in the sensible.

[27] *Ord.* I, d. 3, p. 1, q. 3, n. 1 (Vat. III, ll. 14–22). There is, however, evidence suggesting that the addition reflects an actual phase of the text transmission. Versions of the *tabula Scoti* in *Sentences* commentaries like the one of Harclay (Biblioteca Apostolica Vaticana, ms. Vat. lat. 13687, f. 98ra) show that the division in five questions was current and authoritative; the Vatican edition moved its traces to the apparatus.

account of the *per se* objects known by its acts and is not adequate by virtuality, but, at least in this life, by the commonness of a univocal concept alone,[28] Scotus concludes that "this whole third question," which deals with the first adequate object of the intellect, now "rests in the archive (*iacet in deposito*)."[29]

After these two additions, or perhaps even in between them, Scotus's Parisian lecture on the *Sentences* takes place.[30] The Parisian lecture certainly postdates the first addition to the *Ordinatio* just mentioned, which announces an even more detailed discussion of the first adequate object of the intellect, for the *Reportatio* precisely omits the discussion of "the whole third question." In the second addition to the *Ordinatio*, Scotus announces that he intends to do so, or—if we date this *extra* after the Parisian lecture, as I am inclined to do—tells us why he did so.

The suppression of the discussion of the first adequate object of the intellect in its proper place in the third distinction in the first book of the *Reportatio Parisiensis* resembles the aftermath of demolition with remains scattered over the periphery. We encounter those remains in the revised Prologue, in an additional question in distinction 35 of the first book, and in an additional question to distinction 24 of the second book—all of these revisions have become necessary because of the suppression of the discussion of the first adequate object of the intellect in its proper place in the third distinction in the first book of the *Reportatio Parisiensis*.

Two aspects stand out in the way the Parisian lecture's revised Prologue discusses the first adequate object of the intellect: first, its recasting of the distinction between two types of adequacy, namely the adequacy of commonness and of virtuality; second, its answer to the opening objection in the *Lectura* and the *Ordinatio*, which we now find elsewhere because of the reorganization of the Prologue's questions. To start with the latter: the objection is part of a different argumentative strategy here,[31] for the issue of the first adequate object is now used to argue for the necessity of a supernatural perfection of the intellect. Scotus infers from the adequacy of

---

[28] For the distinction between adequacy by virtuality and by commonness, see *Lect.* I, d. 3, p. 1, q. 1–2, n. 90 (Vat. XVI, 259); *Ord.* I, d. 3, p. 1, q. 3, nn. 127–129 (Vat., III, 79–81); *Rep.* I-A, *prol.*, q. 1, nn. 25–26 (Wolter and Bychkov, 8); *Rep.* I-A, d. 35, q. 2, nn. 83–88 (Wolter and Bychkov, 375–378; see also *Quodl.*, q. 5, Vivès XXV, 213); *QDA*, q. 21, n. 6 (OP V, 205–206).

[29] *Ord.* I, d. 3, p. 1, q. 3, n. 24, adn. (*Scotus extra*) ad l. 19 (Vat. III, 15–17), esp.: "Aliter, quia 'per se obiectum' manifestum est ex actibus potentiae; primum autem obiectum concluditur ex multis 'per se obiectis'" (Vat. III, 17, ll. 11–12).

[30] For the *status quaestionis* with regard to the *Reportatio Parisiensis*, see the special issue: Goris and Honnefelder 2018, especially the groundbreaking essay Dumont 2018.

[31] See *Rep.* I-A, prol., q. 3, n. 209 (Wolter and Bychkov, 74) and its answer at n. 228 (Wolter and Bychkov, 80).

'being' as the first object of the intellect that the divine essence is a *per se* object and hence knowable, although we cannot arrive at such knowledge by natural means alone; hence the urge for a supernatural perfection.[32]

Scotus's distinction between the adequacy of commonness and the adequacy of virtuality, which results from the inclusion of the first two modes of *per se* predication in the primacy of adequacy as defined in *APost* I, 4–5, is used to respond to the revised version of the same objection in the first question of the Prologue of the *Reportatio Parisiensis*. If it is objected that the subject of a science as the first object of the corresponding habitus is to be adequate by commonness, just like the underlying potency, Scotus answers that the subject of a science, unlike the first adequate object of a potency, is only adequate by virtuality, not by commonness. In his explanation of the distinction between both types of adequacy, Scotus emphasizes that in the case of the adequacy by commonness the *per se* objects of the potency have motive force independent of the first adequate object, because the fact that the first object is adequately common to the potency is only manifest on the basis of the abstraction from its *per se* objects.[33]

In the same vein, Scotus contrasts the first object of the human intellect as imperfect and as the mere product of abstraction to the perfect adequacy of the divine essence which itself virtually contains everything knowable in *Rep.* I-A, d. 35, and *Rep.* II-A, d. 24. In *Rep.* I-A, d. 35, Scotus denies that some common aspect could be the first adequate object of the divine intellect. His argument is that such a common aspect is abstracted from many instances, in such a way that everything contained under it must be able to move the power as a *per se* object; but it would be derogatory for the divine intellect to be affected by inferior objects—which led Aristotle to understand the absolute as *noêsis noêseôs*.[34] If it is an indication of imperfection that no single *per se* object is adequate to the created intellect since it can be affected by every being, in reality this is a "perfection compensating an imperfection," because in this way the intellect exceeds the sensitive potencies. In *Rep.* II-A, d. 24, Scotus replaces the distinction between formal and material objects with one between the adequate object of a potency and its *per se* objects, by arguing that the adequate object is something common abstracted from the *per se* objects, which alone are real. Only organic potencies are distinguished by their adequate objects;

---

[32] Ibid., n. 222 (Wolter and Bychkov, 78). It is an important confirmation of the argument that we are developing here that the altered argumentative strategy defines the question "Utrum natura humana sit natura infima capax beatitudinis" (*Ord.* IV, d. 49, q. 7), omitted in the Vatican edition of the *Ordinatio* because it was imported from the *Reportatio*.

[33] Ibid., q. 1, nn. 23–26 (Wolter and Bychkov, 7–8).

[34] *Rep.* I–A, d. 35, q. 2, n. 83 (Wolter and Bychkov, 375–376).

the immaterial potencies, i.e. intellect and will, share the same adequate object, viz. "the whole of being." If one asserts the univocity of the concept of 'being', an adequate object can be assigned to the intellect, viz. 'being', which is abstracted from every *per se* object of the intellect that is apprehended by itself; if there is no single aspect common to all *per se* objects of the intellect, the very absence of an adequate object can be seen as a perfection of a potency thus unlimited.[35]

To summarize, what occasioned the suppression of the discussion of the first adequate object of the intellect in its proper place in the third distinction in the first book of the *Reportatio Parisiensis* is reflected in the fragmentary treatments that replaced the discussion missing from the third distinction. The point of those new, fragmentary treatments is to recognize that natural reason only knows its first object inasmuch as it has access to *per se* objects, viz. to the *obiectum naturale attingibile*. Preponderant now is the imperfect, i.e. abstractive, character of the first adequate object by commonness. This indicates that Scotus focuses on the first adequate object of the intellect in this life and has no further use for the first adequate object of the intellect on account of the nature of the potency—which was the original use of the expression "adequate object of the intellect." In other words: the distinction between the adequacy of commonness and the adequacy of virtuality is interpreted in a new way in light of the opposition between human and divine cognition, which replaces the distinction—itself already the product of a revision of the original notion of a first adequate object, as we have seen—between two senses of the first adequate object of the human intellect, in this life and by the nature of the potency.

V   ENS LIMITATUM

The fourteenth question of the *Quodlibet* nevertheless bears witness to Scotus's principal adherence to the differentiation of the first adequate object of the human intellect in this life and by the nature of the potency, despite its absence in the *Reportatio Parisiensis*. *Pace* Demange, it would be incorrect, therefore, to attribute to Scotus a flat denial that the human intellect has a first adequate object at all. Scotus certainly evolved with regard to the issue of what the first adequate object of the human intellect is, but not in the sense that he came to abandon or renounce an adequate object in the case of the human intellect. Scotus rather revised his position on the status of the knowledge necessary to determine what the first

[35] *Rep.* II-A, d. 24, q. un., ad 2 (Vivès XXIII, 115–116) and its variants (see Goris 2018: 446–455 and 463–469).

adequate object of the human intellect is. The question, therefore, is not whether the human intellect has a first object that is adequate to it, but who has such insight into the nature of the intellectual potency as to be able to decide upon what its adequate object is.

This being said, the fourteenth question of the *Quodlibet* is remarkable for its explicit limitation of the first adequate object of the human intellect in this life. Indeed, the whole setting of the question attests to Scotus's growing lack of interest for the question of what the first adequate object of the human intellect is by the nature of the potency—in this regard, the human intellect agrees with the angelic intellect in having 'being' as its first adequate object. The whole focus is—just like in the *Reportatio Parisiensis*—on the issue of the first adequate object of the human intellect in this life. This issue is settled with recourse to William of Ware's contrast between the *obiectum inclinabile* and the *obiectum attingibile* because the first object adequate to the human intellect becomes known by its abstraction from the *per se* objects to which it is common.[36]

One final time, the issue in the relevant section of the fourteenth question of the *Quodlibet* is the same as in the opening objection of the *Lectura* and the *Ordinatio*.[37] How to explain that the human intellect does not have immediate cognitive access to the divine essence, although the divine essence is a *per se* object contained under its adequate object? Scotus distinguishes the *obiectum primum naturale* into an *obiectum attingibile* and an *obiectum inclinabile* to suggest that, independently of its *status*, the intellect always has "limited being" as its first natural object in the sense of an *obiectum attingibile*, whereas the *obiectum inclinabile* is 'being' in its analogical or univocal commonness.[38]

---

[36] *Pace* Bérubé, who holds that in the fourteenth question of the *Quodlibet* Scotus suppressed the primacy of commonness and the abstractive character of the first adequate object in favor of the primacy of virtuality (Bérubé 1983: 142).

[37] It is important to emphasize that the passages discussed below are taken from the second article of the question, which inquires about human cognition of God in this life, in the sense of perfect immediate cognition "qua attingitur obiectum sub perfecta ratione suae cognoscibilitatis, hoc est, per se propria et distincta." That there is imperfect cognition, in the sense of cognition "qua attingitur tantum per accidens, vel tantum in aliquo conceptu communi vel confuso," is not disputed: "dico quod quodcumque transcendens per abstractionem a creatura cognita, potest in sua indifferentia intelligi, et tunc concipitur Deus quasi confuse, sicut animali intellecto homo intelligitur. Sed si tale transcendens in communi intelligitur sub ratione alicuius specialioris perfectionis, puta summum vel primum vel infinitum, iam habetur conceptus sic Deo proprius, quod nulli alii convenit." (*Quodl.*, q. 14, art. 1; Vivès XXVI, 5–6).

[38] *Quodl.*, q. 14, art. 2 (Vivès XXVI, 40): "Diceretur quod obiectum primum naturale potest dupliciter intelligi: uno modo, ad quod potentia inclinatur; alio modo, ad quod potentia potest naturaliter attingere, scilicet ex concursu causarum naturalium; ens in sua communitate, sive sit univocationis sive analogiae, non curo modo, etsi ponatur obiectum adaequatum cuiuscumque intellectus creati, loquendo de obiecto adaequato primo modo, non tamen de obiecto adaequato secundo modo, immo sic pro quocumque statu, cuiuscumque intellectus creati praecise, ens

In discussion with Aquinas, Scotus concedes that in this life the first adequate object of the intellect, taken as an *obiectum attingibile*, is the *quiditas rei sensibilis*, although on account of the nature of the potency it is the same as the object of the angelic intellect, viz. 'being'. This cannot be denied by a theologian, Scotus says. But the philosopher is bound to mistakenly identify the adequate object of the intellect in this life as the first adequate object "as such."[39]

Scotus advances a philosopher's arguments claiming that 'being', as it is indifferent to the sensible and the insensible, is the first natural object, not in the unproblematic sense of an *obiectum inclinabile*, but in the problematic sense of an *obiectum attingibile*. The refutation of these arguments, however, does not mean that *ens limitatum* is the first adequate object of the intellect "as such." Scotus had already conceded that a more restricted version of the 'quiddity of the material things', viz. the *quiditas rei sensibilis* (in accordance with the exact formulation of the two passages in the Prologue and in the third distinction of the first book of the *Ordinatio* that we discussed previously), is the first adequate object of the intellect in the sense of an *obiectum attingibile* in this life.[40] Hence, just as was observed in the Prologue of the *Ordinatio*, according to the fourteenth question of the *Quodlibet* it can be proved to (and by) the philosopher that the adequate object of the created intellect attainable in this life is not 'being', but 'limited being' or the 'quiddity of sensible being'. However, by natural reason alone one cannot prove that 'being' is the first attainable object of the intellectual potency as such. Accordingly, Scotus denies, at the end of his development, that the philosopher has access to the knowledge that 'being' is the first natural attainable object, adequate to the intellect on account of the nature of the potency "as such."

To summarize: The fourteenth question of Scotus's *Quodlibet* presents an integral recapitulation of the various specifications and variations of the original doctrine of the first adequate object of the intellect described in the previous sections. The main issue in the question is what knowledge

---

limitatum est obiectum adaequatum, quia praecise illud potest attingi virtute causae naturaliter motivae intellectus."

[39] Ibid. (Vivès XXVI, 46–47): "Dico igitur quod obiectum naturale, hoc est, naturaliter attingibile adaequatum intellectui nostro, etsi pro statu isto sit quiditas rei materialis, vel forte adhuc specialius, quiditas rei sensibilis, intelligendo non de sensibili proprie solum, sed etiam de incluso essentialiter vel virtualiter sensibili; tamen obiectum adaequatum intellectui nostro ex natura potentiae non est aliquid specialius obiecto intellectus angelici, quia quidquid potest intelligi ab uno, et ab alio. Et hoc saltem concedere debet theologus, qui ponit istum statum non esse naturalem. ... Tamen philosophus, qui statum istum diceret simpliciter naturalem homini, nec alium expertus erat, nec ratione cogente conclusit, diceret forte illud esse obiectum adaequatum intellectus humani simpliciter ex naturalibus potentiae, quod percepit sibi esse adaequatum pro statu isto."

[40] See above, n. 17–19 and 23.

the intellectual acts available to human beings give them of their *per se* objects, which is, at least according to Scotus, the only viable way to address the first adequate object as a natural attainable object.[41] The first object naturally attainable in this life is the 'quiddity of sensible beings' such as it gives rise to all universal content included virtually or essentially in 'sensible being', up to the concept of 'being'. As we have seen in Scotus's discussion with Harclay, this recognition invalidates the second and third objections against the position of Aristotle and Aquinas that the 'quiddity of material things' is the first adequate object of the intellect. It is no mere coincidence, therefore, that the fourteenth question of the *Quodlibet* omits these very objections (which Scotus at first thought would convince a philosopher) in its criticism of the position of Aristotle and Aquinas, and now focuses on the implicit denial of the beatific vision instead—a problem for the theologian only.

VI CONCLUSION

In answering the question of whether Duns Scotus modifies his appreciation of the doctrine of the first adequate object of the intellect as a *philosophical* doctrine, we have paid attention to its status as the product of abstraction, which Scotus discusses especially in his later texts. (i) Abstraction first became the focus of Scotus's attention in the distinction between the *obiectum attingibile* and the *obiectum inclinabile* that he adopted from William of Ware: the first adequate object is something common abstracted from all things the potency is able to operate upon. Although 'being' is naturally intelligible as something conceived in a single act, and it is the first natural object to which the intellect is naturally inclined, it is not a first natural object of the intellect in the sense that it would be naturally attainable. For the intellect does not have access to everything contained under 'being', but only to certain *per se* objects by way of abstraction. Hence, the first adequate object of the intellect is something common that is predicated only of *per se* objects that are naturally attainable. (ii) The insight into the abstractive character of the first adequate object, which Scotus infers from the absence of the soul's direct intuition of itself in this life, induces him to revise his criticism of the position of Aristotle (and Aquinas) that the quiddity abstracted from sensibles is the first object of our intellect. This position is now deemed to do justice to the perspective proper to natural reason, since under present conditions we only know what is intelligible for us under a general *ratio*,

[41] See above, n. 20.

such as the one that can be abstracted from sensibles. This insight hence assumes a positive character, as it blocks any overestimation of the range of philosophical cognition that excludes the theologian's account of what the first adequate object of the intellect is on account of the nature of the potency. (iii) Scotus revises his initial criticism of the philosophical account of the quiddity abstracted from sensibles as the first adequate object of our intellect. The first argument articulating the natural desire for knowledge is rejected as begging the question; what is attainable is not made known by what is desired, but vice versa. The second and third arguments articulating the need to account for the possibility of metaphysics are answered by conceding that 'being' as "one intelligible", is naturally attainable as essentially contained in the first adequate object of the intellect under present conditions. (iv) The abstractive character of the first object of the human intellect, which was introduced to characterize the first adequate object of our intellect in this life in contrast to its first adequate object by the nature of the potency, assumes a new role in the *Reportatio Parisiensis*, where it serves to characterize the first adequate common object of the human intellect in contrast to the first object of the divine intellect, which is adequate by virtuality. Growing stress on the imperfection involved in the abstractive character of the first object of the human intellect—useful to show the perfection of divine cognition—leads Scotus to the insight that the *per se* objects of the human intellect have motive force independently of the first adequate common object, which is now itself qualified as abstracted from its *per se* objects, which alone are real. Admittedly, the fact that there is no single *per se* object that is adequate to the created intellect is an indication of the created intellect's imperfection. But since the created intellect can be affected by every being, the same phenomenon can be interpreted as a "perfection compensating an imperfection," because in this way the intellect exceeds the sensitive potencies. (v) The fourteenth question of Scotus's *Quodlibet* inquires what knowledge the intellectual acts available to human beings give of their *per se* objects. This is an abstractive account, which is the only viable way to address the first adequate object in lack of the soul's direct intuition of itself in this life. By granting that the first object naturally attainable in this life is the 'quiddity of sensible being', which gives rise to all universal content included virtually or essentially in sensible being up to the concept of 'being' the *Quodlibet* omits the very objections, which Scotus at first (when criticizing the positions of Aristotle and Aquinas) thought would convince a philosopher. Now the focus is rather on the implicit denial of the beatific vision as a theologian's problem.

Returning to our opening question, we may conclude that the distinction of two senses of a first natural object, which Scotus adopts from William of Ware, is at the heart of the development of Scotus's doctrine of the first adequate object of the intellect. This is true not only in the sense that the *obiectum naturale attingibile* is restricted to limited being, or even to the *quiditas rei sensibilis*, but also in the hitherto somewhat neglected, yet equally important sense that 'being' is, already under the present conditions, the *obiectum naturale inclinabile*. This is crucial for assessing the philosophical character (warranted by the fact that the *obiectum naturale inclinabile* is a *natural* object) of major elements of the doctrine of the first adequate object of the intellect. For it is on this basis that Scotus assigns *throughout his career* an identical (*idem re et ratione*) adequate object to the two immaterial potencies of the soul, i.e. intellect and will.[42] It is also on this basis that he invests human beings with a natural inclination toward their own perfection.[43] And it is, finally, on this same basis that Scotus can conceive of intellect and will as *perfectiones simpliciter*, which underlies both his philosophical doctrine of creation and the normative analysis of thought and human agency.[44] We have to conclude, therefore, that Scotus's doctrine of the first adequate object of the intellect is first and foremost a *philosophical* doctrine, and that in his later works, this philosophical character is preserved even when certain qualitative insights are reserved for the theologian.[45]

---

[42] See apart from passages of the *Rep.* II-A, d. 24 (discussed in Goris 2018): *Lect.* I, d. 3, p. 1, q. 1–2, n. 141 (Vat. XVI, 279–280); *Ord.* I, d. 3, p. 1, q. 3, nn. 177–181 (Vat. III, 108–109); *QDA*, q. 20, n. 20 (OP V, 203–204); *QMet.*, q. 5, nn. 24–35 (OP IV, 567–572).

[43] See *Ord.* IV, d. 49, q. 8 (Vivès XXI, 303–316) *Rep.* IV-A, d. 49, q. 7 (Vivès, XXIV, 653–657).

[44] See *Rep.* I-A, d. 35, q. 1 and d. 45, q. 1–2 (Wolter and Bychkov, 351–371 and 541–558); *DPP* c. 4, concl. 3ff. (Wolter, 79–81); *et passim*. See furthermore the *adnotatio Scoti* discussing the opinion of "Arcelinus" that "intellectus secundum rationem suam propriam et formalem, videlicet secundum quam distinguitur a voluntate, est perfectio simpliciter" (*Ord.* I, d. 8, p. 1, q. 4, n. 185; Vat. IV, 253–256); and this passage connecting the notion of a *perfectio simpliciter* with that of transcendentality (which is standard doctrine, of course: *Lect.* I, d. 8 and Ord. I, d. 8): *Lect.* III d. 32 q. un., n. 15 (Vat. XXI, 256). See Wolter 1946: 162–175; Hoeres 1962; Honnefelder 2012: 73–88.

[45] The present contribution has benefited from critical comments by Stephen Dumont, Ludger Honnefelder, Giorgio Pini, and Garrett Smith for which I am grateful.

CHAPTER 10

Before univocity: Duns Scotus's rejection of analogy

Giorgio Pini

Duns Scotus's view that being is a univocal concept—undoubtedly one of his most famous and controversial positions—is a view about the way we think and talk about the world. Its gist is that, when we think about something as a being, we do so by virtue of just one type-concept, no matter what kind of thing we are thinking about—whether an infinite entity like God, a finite object like a creature, a substance or an accident.[1] To this claim about the way we think there corresponds a claim about the way we talk about the world: the term 'being' has one and the same meaning when used to refer to God or creatures, substances or accidents.[2] Since this view tells us something about the way we think and talk about the world but nothing about the way the world is, it is not, strictly speaking, a metaphysical view, even though Scotus held that both metaphysics and theology as currently practiced are possible only if we assume that the concept of being is univocal.[3]

As is well known, Scotus formulated this view in opposition to Henry of Ghent's claim that to think about something real as a being is always to think about a certain thing in a specific way, i.e. by virtue of a concept targeted precisely at it. Accordingly, Henry held that when we think about God and creatures as beings, we do so by way of two separate concepts,

---

[1] *Lect.* I, d. 3, p. 1, q. 1–2, nn. 21–34 (Vat. XVI, 232–237); *Lect.* I, d. 8, p. 1, q. 3, nn. 60–81 (Vat. XVII, 20–28); *Ord.* I, d. 3, p. 1, q. 1–2, nn. 26–55 (Vat. III, 18–38); *Ord.* I, d. 8, p. 1, q. 3, nn. 51–79 (Vat. IV, 173–189); *Rep.* I-A, d. 3, q. 1, nn. 28–40 (Wolter and Bychkov I, 193–196). See also *Coll. Ox.* q. 4 (Alliney and Fedeli, 35–48); *Coll. Par.* 13 (= Balić 24; Vivès V, 199–204); *QDA*, q. 21, nn. 25–37 (OPh V, 218–224).

[2] I am using the term 'meaning' in a generic way. The technical notion is that of 'signification', which I will introduce below. The view that being is univocal can also be formulated in terms of predication: the concept of being and the corresponding term 'being' are predicated of anything (except other transcendental concepts and ultimate differentiae) in the same way (which was usually called 'in quid' to contrast it with denominative or in quale predication).

[3] *Lect.* I, d. 3, p. 1, q. 1–2, nn. 110–113 (Vat. XVI, 265–267). See Pini 2010.

one pertaining to God, the other one pertaining to creatures. Similarly, when we think about creatures, we do so by way of ten different concepts, one corresponding to each of the ten Aristotelian categories.[4] Indeed, any time we believe that we are thinking about different kinds of things by way of one concept of being, we are illicitly mixing up concepts that, although superficially similar, are nevertheless distinct from one another.[5]

Interpreters have not failed to note that Scotus seems to pay little or no attention to what was by far the most common way of describing the nature of being in circulation in the late thirteenth and early fourteenth century, namely that being is actually a cluster of concepts, some of which are more fundamental than other ones.[6] The standard way of presenting that view—which boasted direct Aristotelian ancestry[7]—was that the term 'being' is said in many ways but all those ways are referred to a core sense so that 'being' means some things (i.e. God and substances) primarily and other things (i.e. creatures and accidents) secondarily. This is of course the view that being is neither univocal nor equivocal but analogous. Following the most recent literature, I will call this view 'semantic analogy' to stress that it is a theory about the way the term 'being' signifies. But we should not forget that to that semantic claim there correspond two other claims, one about the way concepts are related to one other and, even more fundamentally, another claim about the way things in reality are ordered to one other as prior (God and substances) and posterior (creatures and accidents). Both medieval authors and their modern interpreters are usually aware that these three claims, although related, are distinct from one another. Specifically, the semantic claim about the meaning of the term 'being' is related to but distinct from the so-called metaphysical analogy, which concerns the way things are related to each other in the world.[8]

---

[4] Henry of Ghent, *Summa*, a. 21, q. 2 (Badius I, ff. 123vE–125vV). See Dumont 1998a; Dumont 1998b; Boulnois 1999, 265–291.

[5] Henry of Ghent, *Summa*, a. 21, q. 2, ad 3 (Badius, I, ff. 124vP–125rS). The view that the allegedly univocal concept of being is actually the confusion between two similar concepts was also held by Simon of Faversham as well as by some anonymous arts masters active in Paris in the 1270s, who attributed that confusion to Plato. It is not clear if those masters were influenced by Henry of Ghent or the other way around. See Donati 2003: 93–95.

[6] For the views of some of Scotus's followers, who variously tried to fill this alleged gap in their master's position, see Garreth Smith's contribution to this volume. On thirteenth-century theories of analogy, see Ashworth 1991; Ashworth 1992. In general on medieval theories of analogy, see Ashworth 2008.

[7] Aristotle, *Met.* IV, 2, 1003a33–b10.

[8] On the distinction between the semantic and the metaphysical approach to analogy, see Pini 2002b: 39–42, 46–49, 51–73; Donati 2003: 69–70; Ashworth 2013: 232.

Semantic analogy was endorsed, in one version or another, by the majority of Scotus's contemporaries, including his own target, Henry of Ghent.[9] So why did Scotus, in his standard presentation of the view that being is a univocal concept, seems to pay no attention to it? My suggestion is that Scotus had already ruled it out as a viable option elsewhere. He was not alone in that respect: his rejection of semantic analogy was a trait he shared with several authors active in Oxford in the second half of the thirteenth century.

Scotus's arguments against semantic analogy, even though not ignored by his interpreters, have not been subjected to the close scrutiny they deserve.[10] The focus of those arguments is the way the term 'being' signifies substance and accidents, not the way it signifies God and creatures. Accordingly, in what follows I will focus mostly on the case of substance and accidents. The main reason for the relative neglect of Scotus's arguments against semantic analogy, I believe, is that they are found exclusively in his early works, notably in some of his questions on Aristotle. Nevertheless, I think it would be a mistake to downplay the importance of Scotus's position on semantic analogy when we come to assess his later views on being. Independently of whether one regards Scotus's arguments as successful or not, they should be considered as a necessary preface to his famous doctrine of the univocity of the concept of being.

This chapter has three parts of different lengths. First, I consider the historical context in which Scotus developed his rejection of semantic analogy. Second, I turn to Scotus's two arguments against semantic analogy. Third, I conclude by considering what Scotus's arguments tell us about his approach to metaphysics in general.

I TWO APPROACHES TO ANALOGY

Scotus's rejection of semantic analogy can be better appreciated once it is considered in its historical context. In the last decades of the thirteenth century, there were two main approaches to analogy with regard to the term 'being'. The first approach was predominant in thinkers active in Paris. The second approach was common in Oxford. I will call the first approach the 'continental tradition' and the second approach the 'English

---

[9] Henry of Ghent, *Summa quaest. ord.*, a. 21, q. 2 (Badius, 2, f. 124rI–vL).
[10] These arguments are considered in Prentice 1968. For more recent but rather short treatments, see Boulnois 1999: 243–249; Pini 2002b: 52–57; Ashworth 2013: 236–238.

tradition'. While the English tradition seemed to have been unknown in Paris, there were some exponents of the continental tradition in Oxford.[11]

Those two approaches differed for deep philosophical reasons concerning the relationship between semantics (i.e. the way words signify) and metaphysics (i.e. the way things are in the world). The best way to introduce the contrast between those two traditions is probably to consider the different ways they dealt with a specific problem posed by Aristotle's works.

As is well known, in the first lines of the *Categories* Aristotle introduces two relations: synonymy (which, following the Latin tradition, I will call 'univocity') and homonymy (which, again following the Latin tradition, I will call 'equivocity').[12] Both relationships involve three kinds of items: linguistic terms, accounts or definitions (*logoi* in Greek, *rationes* in Boethius's translation), and things. Univocity holds when two or more things are called the same way and share the same account or definition. So in the case of univocity, we have one term, one account, and many things. For example, 'human being' is a term said of both you and me according to the same account or definition of human being. It follows that you and I are said to be human beings univocally. By contrast, equivocity holds when two or more things are called the same way but do not share an account or definition. So in the case of equivocity, we have one term, many accounts, and many things. For example, 'bank' is a term said of two things, namely the land alongside a river and a financial establishment, but not according to the same account or definition. It follows that the land alongside a river and a financial establishment are called 'bank' equivocally.

In the Middle Ages, univocity and equivocity were commonly regarded as semantic relations, namely relations involving words and their

---

[11] In what follows, I rely on Donati 2003, Donati 2012, and Donati 2014. Both the continental and the English tradition came in several varieties. Here I will only sketch the common traits of those two traditions. Also, even though thirteenth-century authors were familiar with different kinds of analogy, I will focus only on the one involving primary and secondary signification of different things. On the different classifications of analogy, see Ashworth 1992: 119–122; Boulnois 1999: 239–249; Donati 2003: 67–68; Ashworth 2013: 231–236. Finally, I am leaving aside a minority view that developed at Paris toward the end of the thirteenth century, according to which 'being' signifies only one account (*ratio*), which nevertheless pertains to different things in different degrees. That view was defended by an anonymous commentator on Aristotle's *Sophistical Refutations* and, a little later and with different arguments, by Radulphus Brito. See Donati 2003: 98–111, and Donati 2013. Scotus considered and rejected it in *QSE*, q. 15, nn. 5–12 (OPh II, 332–335). Like Donati (and unlike Ashworth), I think that textual evidence strongly indicates that the arguments I will consider are directed not against the one *ratio* view but against the many *rationes* view. See Ashworth 2013: 236.

[12] Aristotle, *Cat.*, 1, 1a1–12. See Ashworth 1992, 100–105.

meanings. Specifically, the semantic relation that was invoked here was signification.[13] Signification was taken to be a relation between two items: the first item is said to be the sign of or to "signify" the second item; conversely, the second item is said to be "signified" by the first item. Something is the sign of something else when it makes somebody think of what it is a sign of. For example, the word 'water' signifies water because it makes those who hear that word (and know English) think about water— more precisely, it causes in their minds the thought of water. I will refer to the thought a word causes in a hearer's mind as the concept through which or by virtue of which that word signifies what it does. Accordingly, the *Categories* passage on univocity and equivocity was commonly interpreted as making claims about the way words signify things through concepts, where the Aristotelian "accounts" or "definitions" (*logoi*) were usually interpreted as conceptual items (*rationes*).[14]

At first sight, the two semantic relations introduced in the *Categories* are exhaustive. Signification occurs either through one or through more than one concept: a certain word makes me think either of one sort of thing or of different sorts of things. It is well known, however, that elsewhere Aristotle considers terms like 'healthy' and claims that those terms are said in many ways but all those ways are related to a core case.[15] Since, according to Aristotle, 'being' behaves in that respect like 'healthy', this class of terms—which came to be known as 'analogous'—became the object of special attention in the later Middle Ages.[16]

Now the question is: where should terms like 'being' and 'healthy' be placed with reference to the distinction between univocity and equivocity drawn in the *Categories*? It is when answering this question that the supporters of the continental and of the English tradition differed.

The authors belonging to the continental tradition held that analogy falls in between equivocity and univocity. Like equivocal terms, analogous terms such as 'healthy' and 'being' signify many things through many

---

[13] For a short treatment of the notion of signification, see Ashworth 1991, 43–50.

[14] On the different meanings of the term *ratio*, see Ashworth 1992, 105. Scotus clearly takes *ratio* as a conceptual item in *QSE*, q. 15, n. 18 (OPh II, 337).

[15] Aristotle, *Met.* 4.2 1003a33–b10.

[16] Aubenque 1989; de Libera 1989; Ashworth 1992: 107–109. Sometimes (for example in Aquinas, *In Met.*, IV, lect. 1, nn. 535–543 [Cathala and Spiazzi, 151–152]) it was held that 'healthy' and 'being' behaved similarly in every respect. Other times (for example in Aquinas, *In I Sent.*, d. 19, q. 5, a. 2, ad 1 [Mandonnet, 492]) it was held that 'being' and 'healthy' belonged to two distinct kinds of analogous terms. Even in the latter treatments, however, it was agreed that terms like 'healthy' and 'being' behaved similarly in some important respects, insofar as both of them signify one thing primarily and other things secondarily. See Ashworth 1992: 123–124; Donati 2003: 66–67, 75–76, 87, 105–106.

concepts. But unlike what happens in the case of equivocal terms such as 'bank', the things signified by terms such as 'healthy' and 'being' are related to each other: your healthy diet is related to your health as one of its causes and your healthy complexion is related to your health as one of its signs. Sometimes, these authors said that terms such as 'healthy' and 'being' signify what they do through concepts or accounts that are partly the same and partly different. They are partly the same because the accounts of all dependent items contain a reference to the core case. They are partly different because each of those accounts expresses a different relation to the core case (e.g., being a cause of health or being a sign of health).[17]

So according to this view, an analogous term (a) signifies many things through many concepts; (b) signifies some of those things primarily and others secondarily. Specifically with regard to the term 'being' as said of substances and accidents, the relation holding among things (say, you as a substance and your intelligence as one of your qualities) was taken to be mirrored by a parallel relation holding among the way we think about such things: I can conceive of your intelligence as a being only by referring it to you as one of your properties. In turn, the relations holding among things and concepts were taken to be mirrored by the way the term 'being' signifies: 'being' signifies substances like you primarily and accidents like your intelligence secondarily.[18]

Given the parallelism between the ways things are, the ways they are conceived, and the ways words signify them, the authors belonging to the continental tradition held that it is possible to follow the path from things to words through concepts in the reverse order and start from the way words signify to reconstruct the way things are related to one other in

---

[17] Aquinas, *ST* I, 13, 5. See Ashworth 1992: 124. Aquinas's point was followed by many other authors in the continental tradition.

[18] The main elements of the continental tradition can be found in the different treatments of analogy given by Aquinas, specifically in *In I Sent.*, d. 19, q. 5, a. 2, ad 1 (Mandonnet, 492), *Summa theologiae* I, 13, 3; *Summa theologiae* I, 13, 5; *ST* I, 13, 6; and *In Met.*, IV, lect. 1, nn. 535–543 (Cathala and Spiazzi, 151–152). This tradition was developed by a number of thinkers writing after Aquinas and influenced by him, including Peter of Auvergne, Godfrey of Fontaines, and several anonymous commentators on Aristotle. See Pini 2002b: 39–42; and especially Donati 2003: 81–98 (note in particular the texts she quotes at p. 86). For two presentations of this position, see Peter of Auvergne, *QMet.* IV, q. 2, (Monahan 1955, 159–161); Godfrey of Fontaines, *Quodl.* III, q. 1 (de Wulf and Pelzer, 163). As I mentioned, here I focus on the case of 'being' said of substances and accidents. It should be noted that the case of 'healthy' and the the case of 'being' as said of God and creatures are more complicated: see Ashworth 1992: 124–126, as well as what I will say below. The close relationship between the way words signify (*modi significandi*), the way we conceive of things (*modi intelligendi*), and the way things are (*modi essendi*) is usually associated with authors belonging to the so-called modist tradition, on which see Marmo 1994: 139–159.

reality. If a word signifies several things according to two unrelated accounts—as the word 'bank' signifies the side of a river and a financial establishment—we can infer that the things signified by that word have essences of different kinds. By contrast, if a word signifies several things according to the same account, we can usually infer that the things signified by that word share some or even all of their essential characteristics. Finally, if a word signifies several things according to a relation of priority and posteriority (or, as it was sometimes said, according to accounts or concepts that are partly the same and partly different), we can infer that the things signified by that word are related to each other according to real relations of priority and posteriority, i.e., that some things are dependent on others in important respects.

So the basic assumption of the continental tradition was that, as a general rule, semantics tracks metaphysics. Accordingly, if you had asked a continental author whose task it is to consider analogous terms, he would have answered that it is a task shared by logicians (who consider the way words signify) and metaphysicians (who consider the way things are).

By contrast, the authors belonging to the English tradition held that the difference between what Aristotle says in the *Categories* on univocity and equivocity and what he says in the *Metaphysics* on words said in many ways with reference to one core meaning indicates a division of labor between logicians, on the one hand, and, on the other hand, metaphysicians and natural philosophers. Logicians look at how many concepts or accounts a word is associated with. If a word signifies many things through one concept, logicians classify that word as univocal. By contrast, if a word signifies many things through many concepts, logicians classify that word as equivocal. No intermediate case is possible. That is Aristotle's approach in the *Categories*. By contrast, real philosophers—i.e. natural philosophers and metaphysicians—are interested not in the number of concepts associated with a word but in the way things are related to one another in reality. If the things signified by a word are related to each other by real relations of dependence, real philosophers classify that word as 'analogous'. Consequently, authors belonging to the English tradition held that words like 'healthy' and 'being' are equivocal for logicians, because they have many accounts, but analogous for real philosophers, because the things signified by those words are linked to one other by real relations of dependence.[19]

---

[19] The main elements of this tradition can be found in a series of English authors writing in the second half of the thirteenth century, including Godfrey of Aspall, Richard of Clive, John Dinsdale,

So whereas authors in the continental tradition stressed the parallelism between ways of signifying and ways of conceiving, on the one hand, and, on the other hand, ways of being, authors belonging to the English tradition denied that it made sense to talk of any such parallelism. But an important complication should be mentioned: authors working in the continental tradition were aware that in a few cases the correlation they stressed between modes of signifying, modes of thinking, and modes of being broke down. Specifically, Aquinas (who can be considered as the typical representative of the continental tradition) identified two problematic situations.

The first problematic situation occurs when what is prior in reality is not prior (i.e. first known) to us.[20] For example, we can conceive of God as being, good, etc. only after we have acquired the concepts of being, good, etc. from creatures. Accordingly, it seems that in the case of features applied to both God and creatures the way we conceive of them is the reverse of the way those features are related to one other in reality: we first think of creatures as beings and only afterward do we think of God as being, but in fact a creature's being is dependent on God's being. Since the way words signify things parallels the way we think of those things, it seems that some words (such as the word 'being' when said of God and creatures) should signify primarily what in reality is posterior.[21] Even in those cases, however, Aquinas held that signification eventually realigns with the real order obtaining in reality. For he distinguished two ways words can be considered: first, with regard to what they were originally intended to signify *(quantum ad impositionem nominis)*; second, with regard to the actual order obtaining among the things signified *(quantum ad rem significatam per nomen)*. I take that the point of introducing this distinction was not just to separate the historically contingent way words came to be associated with certain things from the actual order obtaining among things in reality. If that were the whole point of the distinction, Aquinas would just be restating the original problem, namely that there is a contrast between what is prior in reality and what is prior to us. Rather, I believe that Aquinas's point was to imply that, once we come to grasp the

---

William of Chelvestun, William Bonkes and a number of anonymous Aristotelian commentators. See Donati 2003: 71–81; Donati 2014. According to the evidence currently at our disposal, it seems that the English tradition died out after Thomas Wylton at the beginning of the fourteenth century.

[20] Aristotle, *APo.* I, 2, 71b33–72a4.

[21] Thomas Aquinas, *Summa theologiae* I, 13, 6. Aquinas considers the term 'healthy' sometimes as similar to 'being' said of God and creatures *(Summa contra gentiles* I, 34) other times as similar to 'being' as said of substance and accident *(Summa theologiae* I, 13, 6, arg. 3 and ad 3).

actual order of priority and posteriority obtaining among things, our way of thinking about those things changes, and so the order of priority and posteriority in a word's signification shifts. So when words such as 'being', 'good', etc. are first used, they are meant to signify creatures, and so they do—they make people think about creatures. But once we come to realize that being and good in creatures are dependent on God's being and goodness, the words 'being' and 'good' make us think primarily about God and only secondarily about creatures. (Remember that the medieval notion of signification is always relative to a cognizer: for a word to signify something is for it to cause a certain concept in the hearer's mind.)[22]

The second problematic situation to which Aquinas called attention concerns some generic terms such as 'body'.[23] When one focuses merely on signification, 'body' must be considered as a univocal term, because it signifies any body according to one concept or account: no matter what kind of body you are thinking about, it is something extended in three dimensions. So according to the logician, who considers the way words signify, 'body' is a univocal term. But when one focuses on the things signified by the term 'body', it turns out that there are two different kinds of bodies, i.e. heavenly and sublunar. Those two kinds of bodies differ in essence from one another and accordingly have different essential properties, for heavenly bodies are incorruptible while sublunar bodies are subject to generation and corruption. Accordingly, the natural philosopher and the metaphysician, who look at the way things are in reality, consider the term 'body' not as univocal but as equivocal. Nevertheless, both Aquinas and his continental followers took cases such as that of the term 'body' as marginal. As such, those cases were not considered to be sufficient to cast any serious doubt on the close link holding between semantics and metaphysics in all other cases: as a rule, the parallelism between semantics and metaphysics held, and the few cases where that parallelism fails to obtain should be flagged and set aside as exceptions.

The authors belonging to the English tradition appear to have been influenced by Aquinas's remarks on the term 'body'. But unlike their continental counterparts, they did not consider it as a deviant case. Rather, they held that it pointed to a more general phenomenon. In their opinion, the distinction between the logical and the metaphysical approach should be extended to words such as 'being'. More specifically, some (even

[22] *Summa theologiae* I, 13, 3; I, 13, 6. See Ashworth 1992: 124–126.
[23] Aquinas, *In I Sent.*, d. 19, q. 5, a. 2, ad 1 (Mandonnet, 492). See Maurer 1955; Donati 2003: 68; Ashworth 2013: 231–232.

if not all) authors belonging to the English tradition appear to have combined their claim that 'being' is equivocal for the logician and analogous for the metaphysician with an explicit rejection of the view that words such as 'being' signify one thing primarily and other things secondarily, i.e. what is now known as 'semantic analogy'. This is what we find in John of Dinsdale, an author active in the Oxford arts faculty in the early 1280s.[24] Even though Dinsdale does not seem to give much of an argument and leaves some room for an alternative approach, his insight is that the way linguistic terms signify does not reflect the order of priority and posteriority holding among things. Accordingly, analogy does not concern primarily the way words signify (what Dinsdale, following the tradition, calls *analogia ex voce*). Strictly speaking, analogy is a real relation of dependence holding among things in the world.[25] Accordingly, Dinsdale's view is characterized by a divorce between semantics and metaphysics, which mirrors the distinction between Aristotle's *Categories* and *Metaphysics*. The idea is that we cannot figure out the way things are in the world merely by looking at the way words signify. Semantics does *not* track metaphysics.

It would be a mistake to dismiss the English approach to analogy as a marginal position. That we might be tempted to do so is due, I believe, only to the importance that the continental approach to analogy has assumed for us, mostly because of the role of Aquinas in that tradition. Between the thirteenth and fourteenth century, however, things must have appeared different, especially for authors active in England. Indeed, in the first years of the fourteenth century Thomas Wylton described the English approach to analogy as the "common view"—obviously, common not in Paris but in Oxford, where Wylton was then writing.[26]

Scotus was a typical exponent of the English tradition on analogy. In his early philosophical works, up to the first draft of his *Questions on the Metaphysics*, he held just what Wylton called the 'common view', namely that being is equivocal for the logician and analogous for the

---

[24] Donati 2013: 180–182.

[25] Dinsdale, *QMet.*, f. 61ra (in Donati 2013: 181–182, n. 12): ". . . analogia est principaliter ex parte rei et non ex parte vocis. Aliqua enim est proprietas quae per prius convenit uni rei quam alteri, sed nulla est proprietas quae magis conveniat substantiae vocis quam alii. Et ideo in re est ordo principaliter et non ex parte vocis."

[26] Thomas Wylton, *Quaest. super Phys.*, I, q. 13 (Schmaus, 15): "Tenendo ergo viam communem dico, quod ens est aequivocum quantum ad logicum, analogum tamen quantum ad naturalem vel metaphysicum." See Donati 2013: 79. As Donati indicates, Wylton wrote his commentary probably before 1304.

metaphysician.[27] By the time Scotus turned to theology, he argued for the univocity of being but he did not give up the twofold approach to being characteristic of the English tradition, which contrasts the consideration of the logician with that of the metaphysician. Accordingly, in his theological works, Scotus held that being is univocal for the logician and analogous for the metaphysician.[28] The division of labor between logic and metaphysics was a key presupposition of his new view that being is univocal just as it was a key presupposition of his previous view that being is equivocal. In line with his English background, Scotus presented the univocity of being as a view concerning the way we think and talk about the world, not as a view about the way the world is. He also linked his view on the distinction between the logical and the metaphysical approach to a criticism of semantic analogy, just as John Dinsdale had done before him. Unlike Dinsdale, however, Scotus gave some detailed arguments to support his view. It is to those arguments that I now turn.

II SCOTUS'S ARGUMENTS AGAINST SEMANTIC ANALOGY

Scotus dealt extensively with semantic analogy in two of his philosophical works: in question 4 of his *Questions on Aristotle's Categories* (on whether being is univocal to the ten categories) and in question 15 of his *Questions on Aristotle's Sophistical Refutations* (on whether it is possible for some words to signify one thing primarily and other things secondarily). In both places, Scotus argued that semantic analogy should be rejected both in general and specifically in the case of the term 'being'.[29] In what follows, I will make use of both works to reconstruct his position.

As I mentioned above, the view that Scotus rejected includes two claims: an analogous term (a) signifies many things through many concepts; (b) signifies some of those things primarily and others secondarily. In order to show that semantic analogy must be rejected, Scotus assumed the first claim, namely, that we are dealing with terms that signify many things

[27] Duns Scotus, *QPraed.*, q. 4, n. 37 (OPh I, 285); *QSE*, q. 15, n. 20 (OPh II, 337–338); *QMet.* IV, q. 1, n. 70 (OPh III, 315–316). See Pini 2002b: 68–69. For the two drafts of *QMet.* IV, q. 1, see Pini 2005.

[28] Duns Scotus, *Lect.* 1, d. 3, p. 1, q. 1–2, n. 117 (Vat. XVI, 268); *Ord.* I, d. 3, p. 1, q. 1–2, n. 163 (Vat. III, 100–101). See Pini 2002b: 69–73.

[29] Duns Scotus, *QPraed.*, q. 4 (OPh I, 273–292); *QSE*, q. 15 (OPh II, 331–339). In both questions, Scotus also considers and rejects the view that 'being' signifies only one account/concept (*ratio*), which nevertheless pertains to the things signified in different degrees. As I mentioned above in note 11, I will leave that aside and focus on Scotus's treatment of the more common view that 'being' signifies one thing primarily and other things secondarily through *different* accounts/concepts.

through many concepts, and rejected the second one. He argued that it is impossible for any term signifying many things through many concepts to signify some of those things primarily and other things secondarily.

When presenting semantic analogy in his *Questions on Aristotle's Sophistical Refutations*, Scotus highlighted its supporters' assumption that modes of being are mirrored by modes of conceiving, which in turn are mirrored by modes of signifying:

> ... one can say that some things do not have an order to each other, and some do. If those things that do not have a relation to each other are signified by a word, they are signified purely equivocally. But those things that do have a relation to each other will be signified in the mode of priority and posteriority. For conceiving follows being, just as signifying <follows> conceiving. From the fact that there is an order of priority and posteriority in reality, it follows that there will be an order or priority and posteriority in signifying.[30]

Scotus raised two arguments against this view. He presented the first argument both in question 4 of his *Quaestiones on Aristotle's Categories* and in his question 15 of his *Questions on Aristotle's Sophistical Refutations*.[31] Here is how he formulated this argument in his *Questions on Aristotle's Categories*

> The second type of analogy given above [e.g., the analogy by which a term signifies one thing primarily and other things secondarily according to different accounts] seems to be impossible, for it can happen that one is unaware of what is simply prior when the name is imposed on what is posterior, for what is simply posterior can be first for us, and thus will be understood first, and signified first. If therefore this word is afterward imposed on what is simply first, it is clear that it will <not>[32] signify secondarily that on which it was first imposed because it once signified it primarily, therefore <it will> always <signify it primarily>. For after a word has been imposed, it will not change with respect to signifying that on which it was imposed, and so the order of things does not entail any order in the signification of words.[33]

---

[30] Duns Scotus, *QSE*, q. 15, n. 2 (OPh II, 331–332). The English translation is taken from Ashworth 2013: 242, with a few modifications. Scotus presents the same view in *QPraed.*, q. 4, n. 28 (OPh I, 281).

[31] Duns Scotus, *QPraed.*, q. 4, n. 32 (OPh I, 282–283); *QSE*, q. 15, n. 1 (OPh II, 331), where it is given as an argument *quod non*.

[32] As Ashworth indicates, *non*—present in some manuscripts but left out by the editors—has clearly to be supplied.

[33] Duns Scotus, *QPraed.*, q. 4, n. 32 (OPh I, 282–283). The English translation is taken from Ashworth 2013: 239–240.

Remember that the position Scotus intended to reject posits a parallel-ism between ways of being, ways of conceiving, and ways of signifying. What Scotus found problematic was the relationship between ways of being and ways of conceiving.[34] For it is a fact that sometimes we happen to know first what is posterior in reality. This point (backed by Aristotle's distinction between what is prior by nature and what is prior to us)[35] is confirmed by frequent experience. In the current environment, we must reconstruct the structure of the world from what is cognitively more accessible to us but sometimes explanatorily dependent on what is cogni-tively less accessible to us. In those cases (which are far from being rare), the order of discovery and the order of explanation come apart. Given the assumed parallelism between ways of conceiving and ways of signifying, any time something is cognized first, it is named and signified first, even though it might be explanatorily dependent on a thing that is cognized only afterward.

As I mentioned above, Aquinas was well aware of this problem. He held, however, that even in cases where there is a contrast between order of signifying and conceiving, on the one hand, and order of being, on the other hand, we come eventually to realign the order of signification with the order of things by distinguishing the historical way we came to know a certain aspect of reality from the correct signification of a word. As I mentioned above, I believe that this amounts to positing that the signification of words shifts once we realize that what is first known to us is actually dependent on something else that, although not first known to us, is nevertheless prior in reality.[36] By contrast, Scotus denied that, when we come to realize that what is prior to us is *not* what is prior in reality, there can occur a change in the signification of words. Rather, the word we have been using (say, 'being') still signifies primarily what it first signified, even though that thing turns out to be dependent on something we come to know and refer to afterward. That this is the case is due to a principle that Scotus here mentioned and that was commonly assumed in his times: once a word is imposed to signify something primarily, it will always signify that thing primarily.[37] This principle has some plausibility. Consider the following example. The word 'water' was initially used to refer to the transparent liquid we drink. When people became aware of its

---

[34] Scotus will raise issues against the relationship between ways of conceiving and ways of signifying in *Lect.* I, d. 22, q. un., n. 2 (Vat. XVII, 301); *Ord.* I, d. 22, q. un., n. 4 (Vat. V, 343); *Rep.* I–A, d. 22, q. un., nn. 22–23 (Wolter and Bychkov, II, 7–9). See Ashworth 1980; Boulnois 1995.

[35] Aristotle, *APo.* I, 2, 71b33–72a4.

[36] Thomas Aquinas, *Summa theologiae*, I, 13, 6. See above, note 22.   [37] See Ashworth 2013: 224.

chemical composition, they realized that the water we drink is mostly H_2O, even though it is not *just* H_2O, for it also includes several minerals. As a result, H_2O was also called 'water'. So let us say that H_2O (which came to be called 'water' relatively late) is in reality prior to the liquid we drink (which also includes other stuff in addition to H_2O and was called 'water' well before H_2O came to be called 'water'). Still, when 'water' came to signify H_2O, it was not the case that the word 'water' came to refer primarily to H_2O and secondarily to the liquid we drink. Once the word 'water' was used to refer to the liquid we drink, it kept its original meaning as its primary meaning, even when people came to have a better understanding of its actual composition. Incidentally, cases of change of meanings are not a counterexample to this principle, because they would count as cases where a second, separate act of name-giving has occurred. Consequently, Scotus seems to be entitled to draw the conclusion that the discovery of the actual order obtaining among things does not cause a change in the way words signify.

Scotus's second argument against semantic analogy appears in the solution to q. 15 of his *Questions on Aristotle's Sophistical Refutations*. Like the argument I have just considered, this new argument focuses on the problematic interface between the structure of the world and the way we become aware of it. But while the first argument was based on a contingent characteristic of the way our intellect works in our current environment, Scotus's second argument focuses on the nature of our intellect and its proper way of operating. Consequently, the second argument cuts deeper than the first one. It is also more complicated.

The argument proceeds in two stages. In the first stage, Scotus proves a general thesis about signification, namely that any given signifying word signifies through a concept that is both distinct from the concept through which something else is signified and determinate to the specific thing that is signified by that word. I will call this the 'distinct and determinate signification thesis'. In the second stage, Scotus argues that the distinct and determinate signification thesis rules out the possibility of semantic analogy.

Here is how Scotus formulates the first stage of this argument:

> In reply to the question, one should say that so far as the signifying word is concerned, it is not possible for a word to signify one thing primarily and another secondarily, for to signify is to represent something to the intellect. Thus what is signified is first conceived by the intellect. But everything that is conceived by the intellect is conceived under a distinct and determinate concept, because the intellect is a certain act, and thus what it conceives, it

distinguishes from another thing. Therefore everything that is signified is signified under a distinct and determinate concept.[38]

In this passage, Scotus demonstrates the distinct and determinate signification thesis in several steps. He starts with a definition of 'to signify'. To signify is "to represent something to the intellect." Remember that signification is a relation between a sign and what is signified in relation to somebody. So for a word to signify a certain thing is for that word to cause the concept of that thing in the intellect of the one who hears and understands that word. In his definition, Scotus stresses that signification presupposes the hearer's *prior* acquaintance with the object: it is not just a matter of presenting, it is a case of *re*-presenting something to the intellect. This allows Scotus to shift the focus from signification to the way the intellect works.

The next step is the most important and also the most obscure in the first stage of the argument. Scotus makes a claim about the nature of the intellect ("the intellect is a certain act") and from this he derives a claim about the way the intellect works (i.e. the intellect conceives what it does by way of distinct and determinate concepts). It is difficult to see what Scotus might have in mind when he says that the intellect is a certain act. My suggestion is that he means that it is in the intellect's very nature to carry out an activity, namely to think: an intellect that does what it is supposed to do is an intellect that thinks. By contrast, consider prime matter: it is in prime matter's nature to exercise no activity and to be potential with respect to the exercise of any activity; if prime matter exercised a specific activity, it would not be a prime matter anymore.

So much for the claim that the intellect is an act. Now any act is an act of a certain kind (*quidam actus*), as opposed to potencies, which might be indeterminate to different outputs (as the case of prime matter makes clear). For example, if I am actually singing, I am singing something specific, no matter how badly. Similarly, if I am thinking, I am thinking about something specific, no matter how confusedly—it is impossible to have a thought and not to think about one thing or another. But if I am thinking about a certain thing, I am not thinking about a different thing—I am picking out or distinguishing what I am thinking about from among other things.

Accordingly, my tentative reconstruction of this step in Scotus's argument is that (i) the intellect's very nature is to think, (ii) to think is to think

---

[38] Duns Scotus, *QSE*, q. 15, n. 17 (OPh II, 336). The English translation is taken from Ashworth 2013: 245, with a few modifications.

about something, (iii) to think about something is to distinguish what is being thought about from other objects.

The last step in the first stage of Scotus's argument is less complicated. Given the close relationship between signifying and conceiving, Scotus concludes that, just as any time something is conceived it is conceived by virtue of a distinct and determinate concept, so any time something is signified it is signified by virtue of a distinct and determinate concept. For example, just as the concept *cat* picks out cats rather than dogs, so the word 'cat' signifies cats, not dogs.[39]

I think that Scous would not deny that we are often unable to tell what specific kind of thing we are thinking or talking about—quite often, we think and speak about things in a confused way. His point, however, is that, no matter how vague is the concept by which I am thinking about what I am thinking about, that concept allows me to pick out what I am thinking about by distinguishing it from something else (about which I am *not* thinking).

In the second stage of his argument Scotus shows that the distinct and determinate thesis is incompatible with the possibility of semantic analogy:

> If, therefore, an analogical word or utterance is imposed on diverse <things>, it is necessary for it to be imposed on them under a distinct and determinate concept. If therefore an analogical word is imposed on diverse things under different concepts, it is necessary that it represent them equally so far as the signifying word is considered. Hence there can be an analogy in reality, but in a signifying word, no priority or posteriority can occur. For there is some property which belongs more properly to one thing than to another, but there is no property which belongs more properly than another to the substance of a word.[40]

In this passage, Scotus reasons that the distinct and determinate signification thesis entails that a word signifies all the things it does—i.e. it presents those things to the intellect—*equally*. This seems to be correct. The distinct and determinate signification thesis states that any time a word signifies a certain thing, it signifies that thing through a concept that

---

[39] Scotus goes on to illustrate his conclusion with a reference to prime matter, which, even though potential at the highest degree, it is nevertheless cognized (and presumably signified) in a determinate and distinct way. This example is supposed to stress that the fact that any thought of the intellect is a determinate thought (namely, it is about a certain object and not another one) depends on the nature of the intellect, not on the nature of the object—what I am thinking about might well be indeterminate, nevertheless my thought is not indeterminate to being about what it is.

[40] Duns Scotus, *QSE*, q. 15, n. 18 (OPh II, 336). The English translation is taken from Ashworth 2013: 245–246, with a few modifications.

picks out that thing from among other things. Since this is a general thesis
about signification, it applies to each and every case in which something is
signified by a word. It follows that, if a word signifies different things
through different concepts, each of those things is signified through a
concept that distinguishes that thing from among other things, i.e. a
distinct and determinate concept. Take for example the term 'healthy',
which signifies the state of your body, your diet, and your complexion.
The word 'healthy' signifies each of those things in a distinct and determined way. When the word 'healthy' signifies the state of your body, it
signifies it—not your diet or your complexion. And when the word
'healthy' signifies your diet, it signifies your diet—not the state of your
body or your complexion. Similarly, the term 'being' signifies substances
through a concept that pertains to substances and only to substances and it
signifies qualities through a concept that pertains to qualities and only to
qualities.[41] What is ruled out is that terms such as 'being' signify some
things secondarily—say, a quality—by virtue of signifying another thing
primarily—namely, the substance in which that quality inheres. Rather,
qualities are signified through a concept that is distinct from the concept of
substance. It is true that qualities depend on substances. But the distinct
and determinate signification thesis rules out that the real dependence
holding among things might be reflected in the way words signify. As
Scotus says, "in a signifying word no priority or posteriority can occur."
Now semantic analogy is supposed to occur when a word signifies many
things, one of which is signified primarily and other ones secondarily. It
follows that semantic analogy is impossible. In the next sentence, Scotus
reiterates his point: it is possible for a property to pertain more or less to
different *things*, but it is impossible for a property (I take that Scotus is here
thinking specifically of the property of signifying a determinate thing) to
pertain to a word considered as such (i.e. a certain sound or string of
letters) more than another property does. Take again the term 'healthy'. It
is impossible for the property of signifying an animal as healthy to pertain
to the sound or the string of letters *healthy* more than the property of
signifying a diet as a cause of health does, because that is just how sounds
and strings of letters work as signs of other things.

There seems to be an obvious objection to this line of reasoning. The
concept of healthy when applied to a diet contains a reference to the

[41] It should be remembered that at this stage Scotus holds that 'being' is equivocal for the logician and
analogous for the metaphysician, so to the term 'being' there correspond as many concepts as there
are categories.

animal's health: a diet is conceived as healthy because it is conceived as causing health in an animal. Similarly, the concept of being when applied to an accident, say a quality, contains a reference to a substance: a quality is conceived as a being because it is conceived as depending on a substance. There seems to be no reason why this feature about the way we conceive things signified by terms such as 'healthy' and 'being' should not be carried over by the signification of those terms. Accordingly, terms such as 'healthy' and 'being' do seem to signify one thing primarily and other ones secondarily, after all. Against this objection, Scotus grants that a reference to a core case (say, to substance) might be contained in our concepts and definitions of the other cases (say, of accidents). What matters, however, is not that some of the concepts through which supposedly analogous terms signify contain a reference to a core thing. Although true, this is irrelevant. Rather, what matters is that those concepts are still distinct from one another. For example, when I think about a diet as healthy, it is true that the concept *healthy* in my mind is that of the cause of the animal's health, and so it contains a reference to the core case signified by the term 'healthy'. But it is still a fact that the concept of a diet as the cause of the animal's health is a concept distinct from the concept of the animal's health. Similarly, when I think about a quality as a being, I might well have in my mind the concept of a quality as dependent on a substance. Still, that concept is distinct from the concept of a substance: when I think about a quality as a being, what I am thinking about—what the concept *being* picks out in that case—is a quality and just a quality, I am not also thinking about a substance. This is reflected in the way words signify. When 'being' signifies a quality, it picks out a quality and only a quality, it does not pick out a substance primarily and a quality secondarily.[42]

Scotus's key point in this argument is that the intellect works in a discrete way, by picking things out by way of determinate concepts. Because of the close relationship between conceiving and signifying, the intellect's way of working is transferred to the way words signify. In order to get a correct understanding of this argument, I think that it is important to stress two things. First, Scotus's argument is directed against the view that terms such as 'being' and 'healthy' signify what they do through *many* concepts. Second, Scotus focuses on simple acts of the intellect. To that extent, the concepts through which terms signify are simple concepts, as

---

[42] Duns Scotus, *QSE*, q. 15, n. 25 (OPh II, 339). The same point is made more explicitly by an anonymous English author quoted in Donati 2013: 192, n. 145.

opposed to propositional acts and acts of reasoning. Note that this is what the supporters of semantic analogy held. They claimed that words such as 'healthy' and 'being' signify many related things by way of different and related concepts, but that each of those concepts is simple, i.e. it is grasped by the intellect when the intellect carries out a simple act of thinking. For example, when I hear the word 'healthy' said of a diet, that word causes in my intellect the concept *being the cause of an animal's health*. Even though that concept has a certain complexity (for it can be analyzed into the concept of a cause and the concept of an animal's health), it is still such that it can be grasped by a simple act of thinking. So Scotus seems to be entitled to restrict his attention to simple concepts.

III   HOW NOT TO DO METAPHYSICS

The analysis of Scotus's two arguments against semantic analogy has brought to light some important aspects of his conception of how metaphysics should and should not be done. The first argument focuses on the contingent but frequent mismatch between what is prior in reality and what is prior to us. Scotus stresses the deep implications of this distinction when it comes to assessing the possibility of making inferences about reality from the signification of words. The second argument is based on the insight that simple acts of thinking are not well suited to capturing the way those essences are related to each other. Since the way words signify depends on the way our intellect grasps things by a simple act of thinking (also called 'acts of apprehension'), it follows that we cannot figure out the complex ways things are related to one another through the analysis of the signification of words. From both arguments, we can conclude that Scotus holds that the semantics of simple terms tells us something important about the way we conceive the world but cannot be taken as a reliable guide to the way the world is unless it is complemented with complex arguments concerning the way real essences are related to and interact with each other.[43]

---

[43] I presented versions of this paper in workshops at the University of Geneva, Brooklyn (Cornell Summer Colloquium in Medieval Philosophy), and London (Notre Dame Summer Aristotelian Workshop). I thank the organizers of those events and their participants for their questions and suggestions.

CHAPTER 11

Analogy after Duns Scotus: the role of the *analogia entis* in the Scotist metaphysics at Barcelona, 1320–1330

Garrett R. Smith

The analogy of being (*analogia entis*), a notion derived from various texts of Aristotle subjected to further elaboration in the Greek, Arabic, and Latin commentary traditions, continues to inspire contemporary critics and defenders.[1] Today almost exclusively associated with Thomas Aquinas, the doctrine of the analogy of being was nevertheless almost universally held during the medieval period. This doctrine is supposed to mediate between the competing claims of divine simplicity and the need for theology and metaphysics to have scientific status. It also safeguards the distinction between the creator and creation. The reason for this is that analogy is a mean between the extremes of univocity and equivocity. If being and the pure perfections (goodness, wisdom, etc.) were said univocally of God and creatures, then they would have these realities in common outside the soul, thus compromising the creature–creator distinction. If being and the pure perfections were said equivocally of God, then all natural knowledge of God and being would be impossible. The analogy of being provides enough difference between the analogates to preserve divine transcendence, but enough unity to allow for some natural knowledge of God.

The term *analogia entis,* however, has a variety of meanings, owing to the varied sources that influenced its development. The ultimate source was Aristotle, who, in the *Categories*, classified terms as either equivocal or univocal, with no apparent medium, whereas in the *Metaphysics* he said that "being is said in many ways," primarily in reference to substance (Latin: *ad unum*), secondarily in reference to accidents. This primary and secondary predication (*per prius et posterius*) of being was further developed

---

[1] It should be noted that, though some have claimed that Thomas de Vio Cajetan (1469–1534) coined the technical term 'analogia entis', the term has a more ancient pedigree, dating to at least as early as Albertus Magnus. For the claim that 'analogia entis' originates with Cajetan, see Terán-Dutari 1970; Betz 2019: 87. For the term in Albert, see Salas 2013: 611 n. 2. On the development of the analogy of being, see Ashworth 2008; Lonfat 2004; de Libera 1989.

by the Arabic commentary tradition, where it was seen as located between pure equivocity and univocity, and it found its way into the writings of Thomas Aquinas.[2] Boethius, in his commentary on the *Categories*, followed the exhaustive division into equivocals and univocals, classifying the prior and posterior predication of the *Metaphysics* as a kind of equivocity.[3] During the thirteenth century, there were distinctive approaches to analogy at Paris and Oxford.[4] At Paris, thinkers held that there were relations of dependence, participation, and causality that obtained outside the soul between substance and accidents, God and creatures, and that these relations were reflected on the level of concepts as well. Thus 'being' is said *per prius et posterius* of God and creatures, that is, primarily of God and secondarily of creatures. At Oxford, though the relations outside the soul between substance and accidents, God and creatures, were also thought to be analogical, on the level of concepts it was argued that they were equivocal. In brief, at both universities thinkers agreed that outside the soul there obtained "real" or "metaphysical" analogy, but at Paris, thinkers held that within the soul the concepts derived from the world also stood in a relation of analogy, whereas at Oxford it was thought that on the level concepts such relations were equivocal.

John Duns Scotus was one of the first thirteenth-century thinkers who defended the univocity of being.[5] Educated at Oxford, he initially held the common Oxonian view that being was analogical outside the soul and equivocal on the level of concepts. His eventual innovation lay in substituting conceptual univocity for conceptual equivocity.[6] Thus even in his late works in which he holds univocity, it is clear that he still holds metaphysical analogy (the order between things standing in an analogical

---

[2] See, for example, Thomas Aquinas, *Summa contra gentiles* I, c. 34 (Leon. XIII, 103–104).

[3] Boethius, *In Cat.* I (PL LXIV, col. 166B). On Boethius' classification, see Ashworth 2008, 22–25, and for comments on Averroes' classification, ibid., 29

[4] On the common opinions at Oxford and Paris, see Donati 2003; Pini 2005: 80–84; and Pini's contribution to the present volume.

[5] It is worth noting that, as Ashworth 2008: 27, reports, the univocity of being was defended in the twelfth century; Alexander Nequam even claimed it was the common opinion of the masters.

[6] On Scotus' shift to univocity, see Pini 2005. It should be noted that such a shift to univocity required an evolution in the notion of univocity itself, from the notion that univocal concepts correspond with a reality in things outside the soul, to the notion that univocity could be a feature of concepts alone. With this in mind, compare Duns Scotus, *QPraed.* q. 7, n. 9 (OPh I, 309): "Sed cum omni univoco correspondeat in re aliqua unitas—aliter accidenti et substantiae esset aliquod univocum—, dubium est quid sit illud unum in re a quo sumitur univocatio generis," with *Ord.* I, d. 8, p. 1, q. 3, n. 82 and nn. 137–150 (Vat. IV, 190 and 221–227).

relation Scotus calls *attributio*).[7] But what about a conceptual analogy? Here even specialists are in dispute.[8] Certainly, there are a number of texts that indicate that he holds conceptual analogy, even though he would reject the most common Parisian formulation of it, namely, the predication of being *per prius et posterius*.[9] This is because there is no medium between univocity and equivocity on the level of concepts; a concept either has the same content as another and thus is univocal, or it is equivocal.[10] But nevertheless Scotus does claim that God can be conceived via analogical concepts, describing the concept of God as "entirely other than that which is said of a creature;"[11] this description is fully compatible with the Boethian classification of analogy under equivocity. For Scotus, concepts have unity; univocal concepts have a higher degree, equivocal concepts a lower degree, yet we can form complex concepts containing both degrees of unity. In other words, univocal concepts and analogical–equivocal concepts are compatible.[12] Thus we can form concepts of God and creatures according to their relations of dependence or the notion of exceeding and exceeded; these concepts stand in an analogical relation, the relation of *attributio*. But we can also abstract the common concept of being that is univocal to each concept proper to God or creatures. For Scotus, then, conceptual analogy and univocity are compatible. Scotus did not, however, explain in any great detail how analogy (*attributio*) was to be incorporated into his theory of univocity.

---

[7] Cf. Duns Scotus, *Ord.* I d. 3 p. 1 q. 3, n. 163 (Vat. III, 100–101). On the relation between analogy and *attributio*, see Donati 2003: 65–66; Ashworth 2008, 28–31. It was an element of both Thomas Aquinas's and Henry of Ghent's theories of analogy, as can be seen from Porro 2019.

[8] For the claim that Scotus holds conceptual analogy, see Cross 2012a; Dumont 2003: 307; Porro 2019: 283–284; Smith 2019: 643–651. For the opposing claim, see Giorgio Pini's contribution to the present volume; Marrone 2001, vol. 2, 524.

[9] On Scotus' later theory of analogy, see Smith 2019.

[10] Cf. Duns Scotus, *Ord.* I, d. 8, p. 1, q. 3, n. 88 (Vat. IV, 195): "... quantumcumque illud quod concipitur sit secundum attributionem vel ordinem in diversis, si tamen conceptus de se unus est ita quod non habet aliam rationem secundum quam dicitur de hoc et de illo, ille conceptus est univocus." The point is that if the same *ratio* is present in both analogates, it will be said univocally, not analogically.

[11] Duns Scotus, *Ord.* I, d. 3, p. 1, q. 1–2, n. 26 (Vat. III, 18): "... dico quod non tantum in conceptu analogo conceptui creaturae concipitur Deus, scilicet qui omnino sit alius ab illo qui de creatura dicitur, sed in conceptu aliquo univoco sibi et creaturae." This text itself modifies the parallel statement in the earlier *Lectura* I, d. 3, p. 1, q. 1–2, n. 21 (Vat. XVI, 232): "... est dicendum ... quod non concipitur Deus in conceptu communi analogo sibi et creaturae, sed in conceptu communi univoco sibi et creaturae ..."

[12] Cf. Duns Scotus, *Ord.* I, d. 8, p. 1, q. 3, n. 83 (Vat. IV, 191): "... concedo quod unitas attributionis non ponit unitatem univocationis, et tamen cum ista unitate attributionis stat unitas univocationis ... in proposito, quod in ratione entis, in qua est unitas attributionis, attributa habeant unitatem univocationis ..." For analysis of this passage, see Smith 2019: 647–650.

This failure or lack of interest in analogy on the part of Scotus has had negative consequences for his modern reception. The reason for this is that today, as Cyril O'Regan puts it, "the major signature of Christian metaphysics turns out to be analogy. Scotus, who supports the univocity of being, is consigned to the dark past and with him the rationalism and essentialism that it supports and that supports it."[13] Indeed, Scotus' alleged rejection of the analogy of being is supposed to be a turning point in the history of Western thought, initiating a period of decline.[14] In light of Scotus' "failure," however, and in order to retrieve the Scotist doctrine of the *analogia entis* for contemporary philosophers and theologians, I turn not to the writings of Duns Scotus himself but to three of his followers who extended the Scotistic doctrine of univocity to incorporate the analogy of being. These followers are Aufredo Gonteri, Peter of Navarre, and Peter Thomae.[15] All of them taught at the Franciscan *studium generale* at Barcelona during the 1320s. In particular, we shall examine their definitions of analogy and whether they view the analogy of being as compatible with the univocity of being.

A turn to Barcelona requires explanation. Scotus' importance as one of the first to defend the univocity of being is well established. But why consider the views of his followers, whose reception and reformulation of his views could obscure the complexity of Scotus' own positions?[16] One reason to consider the thinkers active in Barcelona is that they all had privileged access to the thought of Duns Scotus. Scotus' own position with respect to univocity underwent significant development, and the complexity of this development has bedeviled his modern interpreters for decades. Some elements of his theory, such as whether being is the object of the intellect, seem to have been under constant reconsideration, rendering his overall theory unstable.[17] The Barcelona Franciscans were in a unique position, however, because at that time Scotus' autograph material still survived. Thus Peter Thomae cites autograph manuscripts of Scotus, as well as scraps of parchment (*cedulae*) containing arguments that Scotus

[13] O'Regan 2015: 612.
[14] For discussion of this evaluation of univocity, see Horan 2014. For a detailed study of Scotus' role in the historiography of philosophy, see Pomplun 2016.
[15] There was also a fourth Franciscan active in Barcelona during this time, Guillelmus de Rubione, but I omit discussion of his views given that on the issue of analogy he simply paraphrases Walter Chatton's theory of the same. Cf. William of Rubio, *In Sent.* I, d. 3, q. 3, a. 2 (Badius, f. 84rb–va) and Walter Chatton, *Lect.* I, d. 3, q. 2, a. 2 (Wey and Etzkorn, 90–91).
[16] For reflections on this point, see Pini 2010: 512–515.
[17] On this topic, see the contribution of Wouter Goris in the present volume.

inserted into manuscripts of his works.[18] He also advanced the intriguing claim that part of Scotus' theory of the object of the intellect had been developed simply to satisfy the masses, raising the possibility of an esoteric teaching of Scotus.[19] Aufredo Gonteri, whose name appears on the Adhesion list of 1303 as a resident of the Franciscan convent at Paris, knew Scotus personally and by his own account had heard Scotus lecture for a long time.[20] He also knew Scotus' writings intimately, for he pointed out a false report (*reportatio*) of Scotus' lectures on book III of the *Sentences*.[21] Peter of Navarre refers to a debate Scotus held, probably at Paris while lecturing on book II d. 24, on the univocity of being, which has escaped modern scholarly attention.[22] Another reason to consider the views of the Barcelona Franciscans is that these thinkers, as well as a few others from the same decade, were read into the following centuries, which looked back upon the decade of the 1320s as particularly significant. It is

---

[18] For these citations, see Schabel and Smith 2012: 382, n. 82.

[19] For this claim, see Petrus Thomae, *Rep.* I, d. 3, q. 1, a. 2 (Città del Vaticano, Biblioteca Apostolica Vaticana, ms. Vat. lat. 1106, ff. 116v–117r): "... dicit Doctor quod ens virtualiter includit proprias passiones et ultimas differentias, ita quod illa quibus ens non est univocum includuntur virtualiter in illis quibus ens est univocum, omnia tamen genera, species et individua et partes omnes essentiales generum includunt ens quidditative ... tamen in principio quaestionis, ubi loquitur secundum intentionem suam, dicit quod nullum potest poni obiectum primum intellectus nostri habens primitatem virtu<alita>tis respectu omnium per se intelligibilium, licet infra, volens satisfacere vulgo, assignaverit ens primum eius obiectum, ex eo quod in ipso occurrit duplex primitas, scilicet communitatis et virtualitatis, nam omne per se intelligibile aut includit essentialiter rationem entis, sicut sunt univoca entis, vel continetur virtualiter in includente essentialiter rationem entis, ut ultimae differentiae et eius passiones, ut dictum est, quae virtualiter includuntur in includentibus quidditative rationem entis. Ne igitur videretur potentia remanente sine obiecto primo, dixit hoc volendo satisfacere vulgo quod ens erat eius obiectum primum, sed a proposito dicit quod nullum potest sibi assignari, quia si esset obiectum eius primum, aut esset primum secundum primitatem virtualitatis aut secundum primitatem communitatis; sed nullo istorum modorum est primum respectu omnium per se intelligibilium. ... Quantum ad tertium, quod est utrum potentia intellectiva nostra habeat aliquod obiectum commune sibi adaequatum, dicit hic Doctor volendo satisfacere vulgo, et ne potentia remaneat sine obiecto, quod ens est eius obiectum primum, quia in ipso occurrit duplex primitas praedicta ..."

[20] For the Adhesion list, see Courtenay 2011. Gonteri's name is on p. 221. For his claim to have heard Scotus lecture, see Aufredus Gonteri, *Lect.*, prol., q. 6, quoted in Duba, Friedman, and Schabel 2010: 315: "... venerabilem doctorem et fratrem Iohannem Scotum, quem pro posse quasi ubique sequor, quia ipsum diu audivi..."

[21] Cf. Aufredo Gonteri, *Lect.*, prol., q. 14, quoted in Duba, Friedman, and Schabel 2010: 316: "... notitia scientifica tollat necessitatem habendi fidem de eadem veritate, non tamen est ei compossibilis, ut patet ex dictis supra, licet in quadam falsa reportatione III d. 24 videatur dicere oppositum."

[22] Cf. Petrus de Navarra, *In Sent.* I, d. 8, q. 6 (Sagües Azcona, I, 361): "Et ista est opinio Scoti non solum in primo sed in secundo libro (quaestione de superiori et inferiori portione) ubi respondet ad aliquas rationes quae fuerunt factae, illo anno quo ipse legebat, contra eum." For more on this text, see n. 49.

during this decade that Scotism emerged as a distinct movement in the schools and universities of Europe. The early period of reception of Scotus' views on univocity and analogy, from 1308 to 1320, was characterized by internal Franciscan critiques inspired by defenders of Henry of Ghent. But once these were dispensed with, the great theorists of analogy and univocity, namely the Barcelona Franciscans and a few others, such as Antonius Andreae and Franciscus de Mayronis, began to extend Scotus' insights to new problems and develop comprehensive systems. Moreover, it is they who first engaged the Thomist version of the *analogia entis*. Aquinas and Scotus are difficult to compare on the issue of univocity, since Scotus uses a completely different definition of univocity than does Thomas, rendering it hard to see whether their positions are compatible or not.[23] The Barcelona Franciscans, however, use a definition of univocity closer to Aquinas' own usage than to that of Scotus. A final reason to consider the present group of thinkers is that they developed unique theories of analogy. Unfortunately, however, few works of our Barcelona authors were printed. As a result, the native Scotist tradition of analogy developed by these figures, particularly Peter Thomae, was lost. Indeed, later generations of Scotists took their point of departure from Cajetan, analyzing his views and rejecting them by reference to the text of Scotus. According to the seventeenth-century Scotist Bartolomeo Mastri, for example, "the ancient scholastics wrote little about analogy" and the modern debates over analogy were all the result of Cajetan's inept attempt to classify and codify the *analogia entis*.[24]

I   AUFREDUS GONTERI

Our first Scotist is Aufredo Gonteri.[25] A Breton in origin, he lectured on the *Sentences* at Barcelona in 1322, though book I of these lectures, the typical place where univocity of being is discussed, does not survive.[26]

---

[23] On this point, see Giorgio Pini's contribution to the present volume, and Smith 2019: 641–643. For a recent comparison of Aquinas, Henry, and Scotus, see Porro 2019.

[24] For these comments of Mastri and his theory of analogy, see Smith 2019: 667–671.

[25] On the life and works of Aufredo Gonteri, see Duba, Friedman, and Schabel 2010; Schabel and Smith 2012: 372–380; Smith 2018: 79–88.

[26] Gonteri does refer to his Barcelona 1322 lecture on book I in his Barcelona 1322 lecture on book II in terms that suggest the accounts of univocity were identical in the Barcelona 1322 and Paris 1325 versions. Cf. *Ord.* II, d. 12, q. 5 (Wrocław, Biblioteka uniwerstytecka, ms. I F 184, f. 510rb): "Ad secundum de analogia dico quod duplex est analogia inter aliqua: una est analogia inter aliqua in quibus non invenitur aliquid eiusdem rationis, sicut patet in exemplo adducto de sano, et in talibus verum est quod adducitur; alio modo est analogia inter aliqua quae tamen participant aliquid eiusdem rationis in eis, tamen participatum secundum prius et posterius, sicut patet de speciebus

He later lectured again at Paris in 1325, becoming a Master of Theology around this time, and it is these later lectures, existing in a heavily revised state, that contain his views on univocity.[27] He does not explicitly set out to reconcile the analogy of being with univocity. What he does is attempt to define some of the basic terms in the debate, namely, the notions of concept, unity of a concept, univocal concept, and finally analogical concept.[28] But it is clear from his definitions that he sees analogy and univocity as compatible; the issue is rather to prove the univocity of being.

Gonteri holds a version of univocity close to Scotus' own. His discussion centers around the defense of two *conclusiones*:[29]

C1: the intellect can acquire naturally a concept of being that is one, univocal and common with respect to God and creatures.

C2: the concept of being so common is not one by a unity of confusion, lacking a distinct *ratio*, as Peter Auriol argued, but has a determinate and distinct *ratio*.

In support of C1 Gonteri deploys a version of Scotus' argument from the certain and doubtful concept (reformulated to meet the critique of Peter Auriol), Scotus' argument from the impossibility of knowing God in the wayfaring state of life, and the arguments from pure perfections and the notion of comparison.[30]

Gonteri's views on the definition of univocity itself are also close to Scotus. Like Scotus, Gonteri holds that univocity is a feature of concepts, indeed, it is a kind of unity that concepts have. Attempting to harmonize Scotus' definition of univocity with his distinction between *in quid* and *in quale* predication, Gonteri divides univocal concepts into two kinds: one that is distinguished against equivocal concepts and one that is distinguished against denominative concepts.[31] The first kind of univocity is quidditative, the first mode of Aristotelian per se predication, and Scotus' *in quid* predication. Gonteri classifies both the Aristotelian definition of

---

eiusdem generis in quibus proprie non fit comparatio, quia iuxta genera latent aequivocationes, ut dicitur VII *Physicorum*, et in talibus non est verum quod assumitur, quia cum unitate talis analogiae potest stare unitas univocationis, cum non sint incompossibiles unitates sed disparatae, sicut alias declaravi de univocatione entis primo libro d. 3." I owe this reference to Alessandro de Pascalis. (Note that Wrocław, Biblioteka uniwerstytecka, ms. I F 184 is sometimes cited in the literature as ms. I F 184.)

[27] For the edition of this text, see Smith 2018: 92–170.
[28] Aufredo Gonteri, *Lect.* I, d. 3, q. 2, a. 1 (Smith, 94–97).
[29] Aufredo Gonteri, *Lect.* I, d. 3, q. 2, a. 2, n. 16–17 (Smith, 97–98).
[30] Cf. Aufredo Gonteri, *Lect.* I, d. 3, q. 2, a. 2 (Smith, 97–106).
[31] Cf. Aufredo Gonteri, *Lect.* I, d. 3, q. 2, a. 1, n. 13 (Smith, 96).

univocity and Scotus' two criteria for identifying univocal concepts as examples of this first mode of univocity.[32] The Aristotelian definition is that
univocals are those that have a name and a definition in common. Scotus'
criteria for univocal concepts are (1) that the unity of a univocal concept is
sufficient so that affirming something and denying something of the same
results in a contradiction and (2) that a univocal concept can serve as the
middle term of a syllogism and unite the extremes without a fallacy of
equivocation.[33] The Aristotelian definition and Scotus' conditions sit uneasily
together, however, because the Aristotelian definition could also be applied to
things, whereas the Scotist criteria apply only to concepts.[34] The second kind
of univocity is that which is distinguished against denominative concepts,
which corresponds to the notion of *in quale* predication in Scotus' thought.
For example, the color white in the concrete is said of Socrates denomina-
tively, since it is an accidental modification of Socrates, whereas the color
white in the abstract is said quidditatively of a concrete case of whiteness.

Gonteri also holds that the analogy of being and univocity are compatible. Like Scotus, Gonteri admits of both metaphysical analogy and
conceptual analogy. Glossing a passage from Scotus, Gonteri argues that
from the perspective of the natural philosopher being is analogical, since
the natural philosopher studies real natures that stand in a relation of
attribution. But such analogy does not prohibit univocity, for one can
abstract a common concept of being univocal to substance and accident, as
well as to God and creatures, from the special concepts of substance and
accident, which stand in the relation of attribution.[35] Thus univocity and
metaphysical analogy are compatible.

---

[32] For the Aristotelian definition, see *Cat.* 1, 1a7–15.

[33] For Scotus' description of univocal concepts, see *Ord.* I, d. 3, p. 1, q. 1–2, n. 26 (Vat. III, 18). For a
stronger interpretation of these criteria, according to which they are necessary and sufficient
conditions for univocal concepts, see Cross 2005: 251. Interestingly, the criteria are absent from
Scotus' other discussions of univocity; they are inserted in a second hand in the margin of the
Lectura, but the editors deemed the insertion inauthentic. Cf. *Lect.* I, d. 3, p. 1, q. 1–2, n. 21 (Vat.
XVI, 232). Scotus deployed the first criterion as an argument for univocity in his *QDA*. Cf. *QDA*,
q. 21, n. 27 (OPh V, 219): "Item, omnis ille conceptus qui sufficit ad contradictionem est univocus,
quia contradictio est affirmatio et negatio circa idem univocum—hic enim non est contradictio:
canis currit, canis non currit; sed conceptus entis sufficit ad contradictionem secundum
Philosophum VIII *Metaphysicae*—immo prima contradictio est formata de ente, sicut de quolibet
esse vel non esse; igitur, etc." On the dating of the *QDA*, see most recently Stephen D. Dumont's
essay on Scotus' life in the present volume.

[34] On the application of the Aristotelian definitions to things as well as words, see Ashworth 1992:
97–98; Pini 2002a: 171–175.

[35] Aufredo Gonteri, *Lect.* I, d. 3, q. 4, a. 2, n. 49 (Smith, 163–164): "Modo dico quod secundum
considerationem philosophi naturalis considerantis naturas et rationes speciales substantiae et
accidentis ens analogice dicitur de eis, cum ista tamen analogia ex parte rei stat univocatio in
conceptu communi uno quo formaliter conveniunt. ... Omnes igitur auctoritates philosophorum

Conceptual analogy and univocity are also compatible, once various kinds of analogy are distinguished. Gonteri classifies analogous concepts as midway between equivocal and univocal concepts, a claim that is closer to Thomas Aquinas, Henry of Ghent, and Averroes than to Duns Scotus and Boethius.[36] The reason Gonteri is able to support this claim is that, unlike Scotus, Gonteri offered a definition of analogy. According to Gonteri, an analogous concept is "that by which some things are conceived by one name at the same time according to a relation of one to another or both to some third."[37] Analogous concepts can be midway between univocal and equivocal concepts because of the relation between the analogous concepts. Equivocal concepts have a name but no relation or order between them, whereas univocal concepts are said in exactly the same way. Attempting to clarify the matter, Gonteri distinguishes two kinds of analogy.[38] The first kind of analogy posits multiple things agreeing in a name, but having diverse notions or definitions that are nevertheless ordered to each other or to some third notion or definition. Gonteri offers here the classic example of health: 'health' is said of an animal, food, and urine in different ways (formally, effectively, and significatively, relationally) according to diverse notions (*rationes*).[39] This kind of analogy matches that of Thomas Aquinas. Aquinas had also posited two kinds of analogy, both explained by the example of health, namely, one kind in which many names are said of one, or one name is said of another. In both cases, there is a difference of *ratio* for Aquinas.[40] Gonteri's second kind of analogy is between things

de hac materia sic exponi possunt quod pro tanto dicunt ens dici aequivoce vel analogice propter diversitatem naturarum substantiae et accidentis, quarum una secundum se totam habet attributionem ad aliam cum qua manet univocus conceptus abstrahibilis ab eis." *Ibid.* n. 52: "Ad auctoritatem Philosophi et Commentatoris in IV *Metaphysicae* dico quod in ente est analogia ex natura rei, licet cum ea stet unitas univocationis in conceptu communi, quia sunt unitates ordinatae diversarum rationum, quia accidens et substantia formaliter sunt entia." For the text in Scotus, see *Ord.* I, d. 3, p. 1, q. 3, nn. 162–163 (Vat. III, 100–101).

[36] Aufredo Gonteri, *Lect.* I, d. 3, q. 2, a. 1, n. 15 (Smith, 96): "Ulterius sciendum est quod conceptus analogus est medius inter conceptum univocum et aequivocum..."

[37] Aufredo Gonteri, *Lect.* I, d. 3, q. 2, a. 1, n. 14 (Smith, 96): "... et est conceptus analogus ille quo aliqua concipiuntur uno nomine simul secundum quandam habitudinem unius ad aliud vel amborum ad aliquod tertium."

[38] Aufredo Gonteri, *Lect.* I, d. 3, q. 2, a. 1, n. 14 (Smith, 96–97). For discussion of Gonteri's theory of analogy, see Smith 2018: 68–69.

[39] Aufredo Gonteri, *Lect.* I, d. 3, q. 2, a. 1, n. 14 (Smith, 96–97): "Sciendum tamen quod analogia est duplex: quaedam proprie dicta quae est inter plura convenientia uno nomine quae sunt diversarum rationum habentia habitudinem unius ad alterum vel aliorum ad tertium, sicut hoc nomen 'sanum' dicitur de sano in animali et in cibo et in urina analogice, ut dicitur IV *Metaphysicae*, quia sanitas formaliter est in animali, in urina significative, in cibo supposita virtute nutritiva effective, et ita non secundum eandem rationem."

[40] Cf. Thomas de Aquino, *Summa theologiae* I, q. 13, a. 5 (Leon. IV, 146–147).

having a common name and a formal notion that is univocally common to them; but the analogates participate in the formal notion in varying degrees, namely according to the prior and posterior, and the more and less. Gonteri's example for this kind of analogy is that of several species in the same genus, and an equivocal cause and its effects.[41] These examples are less helpful than those for the first mode of analogy. Though there is supposed to be a univocal formal notion, such does not seem to be the case for an equivocal cause and its effects. Moreover, as Gonteri himself points out, according to Aristotle there are equivocations that are hidden in the genus.

Armed with his distinction between the two modes of analogy, Gonteri is able to reconcile analogy with univocity. Of the two kinds of analogy, only the second is compatible with the univocity of being. Glossing a text of Scotus that we briefly considered above, Gonteri argues that both analogical concepts and univocal concepts posit different degrees of unity that are formally distinct from each other.[42] The model for the relation between analogical and univocal concepts is a genus and its species. A genus and a species each posit a degree of unity. A genus has a weaker unity than does a species, and yet their respective unities are compatible since two things that are one in species will also be one in their genus. Without giving an argument to support the analogy, Gonteri claims that analogical and univocal concepts function in the same way as the concepts of a genus and a species. Thus analogical concepts posit a weaker unity than do univocal concepts, but both unities are compatible. That is, what Gonteri calls the 'special concepts', the concepts that are proper to God and proper to creatures respectively, are in analogical relation to each other, but nevertheless from the concept of a creature that stands in an

---

[41] Aufredo Gonteri, *Lect.* I, d. 3, q. 2, a. 1, n. 14 (Smith, 97): "Alia est analogia inter aliqua in uno nomine quae conveniunt in una ratione formali univoca in eis reperta, tamen in participando illam rationem secundum magis et minus, prius et posterius, attenditur analogia, et illo modo inter species eiusdem generis est aequivocatio et analogia secundum Philosophum VII *Physicorum*, quia ut dicitur ibi, iuxta genera latent multae aequivocationes, et talis analogia semper est inter causas aequivocas et suos effectus."

[42] Aufredo Gonteri, *Lect.* I, d. 3, q. 2, a. 1, n. 14 (Smith, 97): "Modo prima unitas conceptus analogi excludit unitatem univocationis ab illis inter quae est, sed secunda unitas conceptus analogi, licet sit alia formaliter ab unitate univocationis et ab ea disparata et minor ea, eam tamen non excludit, immo stat cum ea, nec eam distrahit, licet enim sola unitas analogiae non ponat unitatem univocationis proprie dictam, sicut nec sola unitas generis ponit unitatem specificam inter aliqua, quia minor unitas non ponit maiorem ... tamen unitas analogiae non necessario excludit unitatem univocationis proprie dictam ab illis inter quae est, immo stat cum ea, sicut et unitas generis stat cum unitate specifica qua aliqua sunt unum in genere et unum in specie concretive, licet haec unitas generis sit alia formaliter ab unitate specifica abstractive ..." For the parallel passage in Scotus, see *Ord.* I, d. 8, p. 1, q. 3, n. 83 (Vat. IV, 191–192).

analogical relation to the concept of God the concept of being can be abstracted. The special concept (for example, "finite being" or "infinite being") has within itself both the weak unity of analogy and the strong unity of univocity.

Gonteri's contribution to the present debate largely serves to point to the original texts of Scotus that Gonteri follows, with some connections drawn that are missing in the texts themselves, such as the claim that the proper concepts of God and creatures are analogically related.[43] Thus Gonteri and Scotus both hold that univocity is a feature of concepts only, without a corresponding reality outside the soul. But Gonteri does not only paraphrase Scotus' text. He also attempts to add features of the Parisian tradition to the Scotistic theory of univocity. The most noticeable is the attempt to pair Scotus' criteria or description of univocal concepts with the Aristotelian definition of univocity widely in use. Gonteri also reintroduced the notion of *per prius et posterius* predication, which had been rejected by Scotus in his early logical writings.

II PETRUS DE NAVARRA

Peter of Navarre (or Atarrabia) first appears in 1317 as provincial of the Franciscan province of Aragon.[44] He lectured on the *Sentences* between 1320 and 1323, in all likelihood at the Franciscan *studium generale* in Barcelona. These lectures are probably from around 1323 since he is believed to have attacked Aufredo Gonteri.

Unlike Aufredo Gonteri, Peter of Navarre explicitly set out to reconcile the competing claims of those holding analogy of being and those holding univocity of being.[45] In his question on univocity he supplied arguments from both sides of the debate before offering his own solution. The side opposing univocity he described as holding the "common opinion," which maintains that being does not have a concept that is univocal to God and creatures or substance and accidents, but rather the concept of being primarily signifies God and secondarily creatures, primarily substance

---

[43] Another connection that Gonteri draws is between the univocal concept of being, the object of the intellect, and the subject of metaphysics. Gonteri identifies all three, though there is no text in Scotus' works that does so. Cf. Aufredo Gonteri, *Lect.* I, d. 3, q. 2, a. 2, n. 42 (Smith, 105): "Confirmatur, quia ens est primum obiectum intellectus secundum rationem entis secundum Avicennam I *Metaphysicae* suae, et de hoc postea dicetur, et est obiectum unius scientiae, scilicet metaphysicae, ut dicitur in principio IV *Metaphysicae*; ergo habet unam rationem communem secundum quam est obiectum."

[44] On the life and works of Peter of Navarre (or Atarrabia), see Schabel and Smith 2012: 380–381.

[45] Cf. Petrus de Navarra, *Scriptum* I, d. 3, p. 1, q. 1 (Sagües Azcona, I, 183–194).

and secondarily accidents. In support of this position, Peter reports five arguments: the first is from the *Summa* of Thomas Aquinas, the remaining ones are from Henry of Ghent. The third argument is Henry's claim that the unity of attribution is repugnant to the unity of univocity, which had inspired Scotus' attempt at reconciling his position with analogy.[46] The four arguments on behalf of the univocity of being are all paraphrased from Scotus' *Ordinatio*.

Peter's own position in the face of the two opposing positions is an attempt at reconciliation. According to Peter, the two groups of thinkers do not actually disagree, at least the main exponents of each opinion do not.[47] In order to reconcile (*ad concordandum*) them, Peter proposes a division within the notion of univocity. This division does not involve Scotus' own definition of a univocal concept in *Ordinatio* I d. 3, that is the two criteria discussed above. For Peter of Navarre, these criteria serve as an argument for the univocity of being.[48] Instead, Peter takes his point of departure from some replies to objections found in *Ordinatio* I d. 8 and what appears to be the remnants of a debate over the univocity of being that survives only in the *Additiones secundi libri* d. 24, which were compiled by William of Alnwick from Scotus' lectures at Oxford and Paris. Scotus probably held the debate at Paris as part of his lectures on the *Sentences*.[49]

Peter of Navarre divides the notion of univocity in two. According to Peter, there are two kinds of univocal concepts: one in which there is a unity of indifference with respect to that to which it is common and a unity of indifference in the mode of conceiving (*modus concipiendi*), and a second kind of univocal concept that consists only in a unity of an indifference in the mode of conceiving.[50] The first kind of univocity is

---

[46] Petrus de Navarra, *Scriptum* I, d. 3, p. 1, q. 1, a. 1, n. 8 (Sagüés Azcona I, 185): "Tertia: quae habent unitatem attributionis non univocantur sed magis sunt analoga; sed Deus et creatura, substantia et accidens habent unitatem attributionis; ergo etc."

[47] Ibid., n. 21 (Sagüés Azcona I, 189–190): "... dico quod, quantum mihi videtur, primi et secundi non discordant in re (loquor de principalibus doctoribus qui praedictas opiniones posuerunt; si aliqui alii declaraverunt aliter, non curo)." Here I take "si" from the apparatus criticus of the edition.

[48] Cf. ibid., n. 19 (ed. Sagüés Azcona I, 189): "Dicunt ergo isti quod ens est univocum ad omnia entia, quia alias in omni syllogismo esset fallacia aequivocationis et numquam esset aliqua vera contradictio."

[49] Note that Dumont argues that the text in the *Ordinatio* is an objection by Scotus and thus does not represent his position, whereas I argue against this. Cf. Dumont 1995b: 144; *Petri Thomae Quaestiones de ente* (Smith, lxxviii). For Peter of Navarre's reference to the Parisian debate over univocity, see above n. 22; for commentary on the same, see Goris 2018: 455–463. On the *Additiones secundi libri*, see Dumont 2018: 410–424.

[50] Petrus de Navarra, *Scriptum* I, d. 3, p. 1, q. 1, a. 3, nn. 21–22 (Sagüés Azcona I, 189): "Ad concordandam igitur utramque opinionem est sciendum quod conceptus univocus accipitur

univocity proper, the kind normally employed by the philosophical tradition and applied to genus and species, universals and categories. It has two elements, the unity of indifference and unity of a mode of conception. Peter identifies the unity of indifference as an Avicennian-Scotistic common nature, that is, the unity of a quiddity as such that is less than numerical. According to Peter, there is a real similitude between different individuals of a species, all of which agree in the common nature.[51] The second kind of univocity does not have the real similitude of the *univocata*, that is, that which agrees in the univocal notion. It is a unity only of a mode of conception. The unity here is supplied by the intellect, not by things having an agreement outside the soul. Peter's example is the description "some human being" (*aliquis homo*). This description is common to all individual humans, but it is not a real unity.[52]

Armed with his distinction between the two types of univocity, Peter of Navarre argues that both sides are right, but that they are talking past each other. Thus he agrees with the arguments of Thomas Aquinas and Henry of Ghent against the univocity of being, in the sense that Peter thinks they are attacking only the first sense of univocity. If being were univocal in the first sense, then being would be a genus and there would be a real similitude between God and creatures, with the resulting problem for divine simplicity that God would agree in some reality with creatures and not agree in another reality, and thus he would be complex.[53] Thus the first group of thinkers was right to deny univocity, but they did not deny the second sense. Peter of Navarre concedes that being is univocal in the second sense of univocity, and he claims that this is what Scotus meant when he argued for the univocity of being, and it is only to this sense of

---

duplicter. Uno modo accipitur conceptus univocus alicuius ex unitate et indifferentia eorum quibus est commune et modi concipiendi. Et isto modo est univocatio proprie dicta, et de tali ut plurimum loquuntur philosophi, et isto modo genus et species dicuntur univoca et alia universalia et etiam praedicamenta. . . . Alio modo accipitur conceptus univocus tantummodo ex indifferentia modi concipiendi."

[51] Petrus de Navarra, *Scriptum* I, d. 8, q. 6, nn. 147–148 (Sagües Azcona I, 360).

[52] Petrus de Navarra, *Scriptum* I, d. 3, p. 1, q. 1, n. 21 (Sagües Azcona I, 190): "Alio modo accipitur conceptus univocus tantummodo ex indifferentia modi concipiendi. Exemplum: aliquis homo est individuum vagum, commune, univocum omnibus individuis hominis sub differentiis individualibus; sed individuis, ut sic, nihil est commune nisi ex modo concipiendi. Hoc autem univocum non est universale reale, sed est commune tantum communitate rationis et modi concipiendi . . ."

[53] Ibid., n. 23 (Sagües Azcona I, 190): "Ad propositum ergo applicando: accipiendo univocationem primo modo, ens non est univocum, quia tunc esset genus, nec esset verum dictum Philosophi, I *Physicorum* . . . nec dictum IV *Metaphysicae*. . . . Et istud concludunt efficaciter rationes adductae pro prima opinione; et credo quod est impossibile quod ens sic sit univocum, quia Deus et creatura se totis distinguuntur; alias Deus non esset simpliciter simplex."

being that Scotus' criteria for univocal concepts apply. Being is univocal in the sense that the intellect conceives beings or things under an indifference that it itself supplies. The indifference is the product of an act of the intellect and there is no real similitude outside the soul on which it is based.[54] Peter of Navarre concludes that in fact no one had defended the first sense of univocity, not even Scotus. But not all had denied the second sense; indeed, Henry of Ghent and Thomas Aquinas importantly had not done so.

Unlike Gonteri, then, who had proposed a distinction between analogical concepts in order to reconcile the loose collection of theories of analogy with Scotistic univocity, Peter of Navarre proposed a distinction between univocal concepts. The point of the distinction is to allow both Thomas Aquinas' and Henry's arguments against univocity to hold and Scotus' arguments for univocity. Thus it is clear that neither Peter of Navarre nor Aufredo Gonteri denies what might be called the analogical worldview or metaphysical analogy, and the Scotist credentials of both authors are beyond dispute. Both authors, however, are dependent on various texts of Duns Scotus and those of the defenders of analogy. It was left to Peter Thomae to move beyond the textual dependence on Scotus and reconceive the debate.

III PETRUS THOMAE

Peter Thomae was a resident of the Franciscan convent at Barcelona from around 1303 to the late 1320s.[55] He later served John XXII in Avignon as penitentiary and abbreviator but fell out of favor under Benedict XII. Accused of necromancy, he died in the papal prison in 1340.

Peter discussed the relation between analogy and univocity in several works, the most important being his *Reportatio*, from around 1323–1324, and his *Quaestiones de ente*, from around 1325.[56] The *De ente* is the longest

---

[54] Ibid., n. 24 (Sagûes Azcona I, 191): "Accipiendo vero univocationem secundo modo, scilicet quae accipitur ex indifferentia modi concipiendi, dico quod ens est univocum Deo et creaturae, substantiae et accidenti, quia intellectus noster concipit entia sub indifferentia, non quod ista indifferentia sit ex parte rei vel rerum, sed hoc habet intellectus ex natura sua. Et isto modo ens non est universale reale vel genus, sed dicitur commune tali unitate quae sufficit ad salvandam contradictionem et ad vitandam aequivocationem in medio syllogistico. ... Et hoc modo concludunt omnes rationes adductae secundo. Primo ergo modo omnes negaverunt univocationem entis secundo modo non, ad minus aliqui."

[55] On the life and works of Petrus Thomae, see Schabel and Smith 2012: 381–386; Smith 2010.

[56] The *Reportatio* is unedited. It survives in one manuscript: Città del Vaticano, Biblioteca Apostolica Vaticana, ms. Vat. lat. 1106. For the *De ente*, see *Petri Thomae Quaestiones de ente*.

medieval treatment of the problem of being, and in it, Peter navigates nearly the entirety of the Greek and Arabic tradition as it was known to the Latins, as well as the debate before and after Scotus among the Latin scholastics. In addition to the standard Scholastic authors, such as Thomas Aquinas, Henry of Ghent, and Duns Scotus, Peter also cites and quotes several texts of Richard of Conington, Thomas Rondel, and Peter Auriol that are no longer extant. He also engaged his fellow Franciscans at Barcelona, by attacking Peter of Navarre's theory in both the *Reportatio* and the *De ente*. It is unclear whether he knew of Gonteri's theory. Gonteri had lectured in Barcelona in 1322, but only his lectures from Paris in 1325 survive. He is also close to paraphrasing Scotus rather than developing his own views. In a sense, Peter Thomae expands upon the hints provided by Aufredo Gonteri and Peter of Navarre. As we have seen, Gonteri tried to reconcile univocity and analogy with a distinction between analogical concepts, whereas Peter of Navarre proposed a distinction between univocal concepts. Peter Thomae, however, in both his *Reportatio* and *Quaestiones de ente*, proposes an extensive series of subdivisions within the notions of equivocity, univocity, and analogy.

Peter's discussion of analogy in the *De ente* is found in question 7, a textually intricate composition: the question is divided into two articles, the first of which is a detailed analysis of the positions of Peter Auriol and Gerard of Bologna. The second article has five parts: first Peter lays out distinctions, then he provides descriptions of what he distinguished, third he derives a series of corollaries, fourth he elaborates the degrees of intentions, fifth he examines the compossibility or non-compossibility of various distinctions. For the sake of brevity, we will consider only Peter's definitions of univocity and analogy, their subdivisions, and compatibility.

Peter Thomae does not follow Scotus' two criteria for univocal concepts in his own definition of univocity. As we saw already, Gonteri assimilated Scotus' conditions to Aristotle's definition of univocity. Peter Thomae also returns to Aristotle, ignoring Scotus' criteria altogether in favor of the Aristotelian definition. But he quotes the definition from the commentary of Boethius, which yields an important distinction.[57] Aristotle had defined univocals as those of which a common name is said. Boethius adds that not only are univocals "said of things" but things themselves "are" univocal. According to Peter, the Boethian addition allows for a distinction between univocity according to being (*esse*) and according to speech.[58] But this is

---

[57] Petrus Thomae, *Quaest. de ente*, q. 7, a. 2 (Smith, 154–157).
[58] Petrus Thomae, *Quaest. de ente*, q. 7, a. 2 (Smith, 141).

not to say that Peter Thomae's position approaches that of Peter of Navarre: though he recites Peter of Navarre's opinion at length, Peter Thomae dismisses it on the grounds that, even if it is partly founded on the words of Scotus, it does not hold that the concept of being is a real concept, which Peter Thomae thought he had already proven in a previous question.[59] Peter of Navarre's position then vitiates Scotus' original arguments for univocity, for a real concept is a first intention concept, a concept that arises from sense cognition, and Scotus' original arguments depend on the notion that the concept of being is a real concept.

Not only does Peter define univocity, but he also subdivides it into a series of degrees, corresponding with the levels of the Porphyrian tree of the categories. Thus he does not provide a precise enumeration of these degrees. The first degree of univocity is what pertains to the vague individual, for example, "some human being," which is contracted from the lowest species by means of an indeterminate individual difference, signified by the terms 'someone' or 'a certain one'. The second grade of univocity pertains to the lowest species, the third to the lowest genus, the fourth to the first subalternate genus, and as we ascend the categorical line up to the highest genera, we pass a degree of univocity at every level. The final degree is the highest or most general genus, for example, substance or quality.[60] But, given that Peter defends the univocity of being, he qualifies this claim that the highest degree of univocity is that of the genus with the comment that the absolutely or unqualifiedly (*simpliciter*) highest is the quidditative concept of being. Among the degrees of univocity there is an order of perfection, with the first degree being the most perfect and the last, the quidditative concept of being, the most imperfect. Intermediate degrees are more or less imperfect depending on their distance from the first degree.[61]

Peter defines analogy as obtaining when "the name is common and the *ratio* of the name found in the analogates is the same *per prius et posterius.*" This means that there is a term whose definition remains the same when said of two things, but there is an order among the analogates according to which the term is said of one in a prior sense, of the second in a posterior sense. Peter divides analogy into two kinds, following a "common and ancient distinction." The distinction depends upon whether the analogous notion (*ratio*) is formally present in each of the analogates or only in one of

---

[59] Petrus Thomae, *Quaest. de ente*, q. 11, a. 3 (Smith, 294–295).
[60] Petrus Thomae, *Quaest. de ente*, q. 7, a. 2 (Smith, 149).   [61] Ibid.

them.[62] An example of analogy in which the analogous term is found in both analogates is being as said of substance and accidents: substance is the primary instance of being, it depends on nothing, so being is said in a prior way of substance, whereas accidents are being in a derivative, secondary way and depend upon substance for their being, and so being is said in a posterior way of accidents. But the notion (*ratio*) of being is found in both substance and accidents. Peter's example of the second kind of analogy, in which the analogous term is found in only one analogate, is health, as it is said of an animal and the diet of an animal; diet is a cause of health in an animal, but health is not formally present in diet.

According to Peter Thomae, there are twelve degrees of analogy.[63] These degrees of analogy fall under the "ancient and common distinction." Degrees 1–4 are all analogies in the first sense, for the analogous notion is formally present in both analogates. Degrees 5–12 fall under the second. Most of the examples were widely employed during the thirteenth and fourteenth centuries, many of them are taken from various passages of Aristotle.

1. All analogates formally participate the analogous term or notion, with the relations of prior and posterior, perfect and imperfect, caused and cause; these are said according to the exemplar, efficient and final causes. This degree of analogy is posited for the relation between God and creatures.

2. All analogates formally participate the analogous term or notion with the relations of prior and posterior, etc., but only according to the material cause. This degree of analogy is posited for the relation between substance and accident.

3. The analogates formally participate the analogous only with the relation of perfection/imperfection. This degree of analogy obtains between different categories and can be subdivided according to the number of levels (that is, the genus/species hierarchy) of the categories.

4. All the analogates formally participate the analogous term or notion, but one is prior and per se, the others posterior and through the mediation of the prior. Example: 'transparent' as it is said of its higher and lower analogates.

---

[62] On this widespread distinction, see Ashworth 1992: 126–130.
[63] Petrus Thomae, *Quaest. de ente*, q. 7, a. 2 (Smith, 154–157). Note that Peter also holds metaphysical analogy; see, for example, *Quaest. de ente*, q. 8, a. 1 (Smith, 173): "... inter creaturam et Deum est realis attributio; ergo inter Deum et creaturam est realis unitas attributionis ..." and *Quaest. de ente*, q. 10, a. 1 (Smith, 262–263), where Peter denies that univocity is incompatible with the *analogia entium*.

5. One of the analogates formally participates the analogous, the other is not formally the analogous, but is only so from a relation to the first analogate. Example: 'healthy' said of a person and a diet. This degree of analogy can be subdivided into as many relations as there are to the first analogate. So for the present example of healthy, there can also be relations of causation (*effectivi*), something that causes health, conservation (*conservativi*), and signification (*significativi*).

6. One of the analogates is not said to be such unless by proportion to another. Example: 'point' is called a principle by a proportion to unity.

7. Some things are denominated by one principle in different ways, without formally participating it. Example: various applications of the term 'military' to such things as swords, clothing, horses.

8. A relation of two to two, as in proportions. Example, from Aristotle: as sight is in the body, so the intellect is in the soul.

9. In one analogate there is a thing, in the other a similitude of a thing. Example: *homo verus* and *homo pictus*.

10. The same thing is given distinct names according to prior and posterior senses. Example: a figure drawn on a table is called 'form' because it exists in the mind of the artist who imposed it on a subject, and thus 'form' is said in a prior sense. The figure is also called an image because it represents something, but 'image' is only said in a posterior sense

11. A statement (*dictio*) signifies diverse things in a prior sense and in a posterior sense. Example: 'expedient' signifies the good in prior sense, but it signifies a necessary evil in a posterior sense. Peter also classifies prepositions as indicative of this degree of analogy. Thus the preposition 'in' signifies a relation to a location in a primary sense, and any other meanings are posterior, and the preposition 'according to' primarily signifies a relation to a formal cause and secondarily a relation to an efficient cause.

12. An expression signifies one thing properly and another thing in a transferred sense. Example: 'smile' said of a meadow and a face, or 'to run' said of an animal and a river.[64]

With the various degrees of equivocity (which we have passed over here), univocity, and analogy in mind, Peter offers five conclusions (as was the case with Gonteri, these *conclusiones* are theses that are supported

---

[64] For discussion of these examples, see Ashworth 2007.

by a series of arguments) and four specifications (*specificationes*) to explain the relation between these three notions. It is here that he finally explains to the reader how univocity and analogy are compatible.

C1: true univocity (*unilogia*) can be founded in true equivocity (*aequilogia*).[65]

C2: true univocity and equivocity taken properly are not compatible in the same concept.

C3: true analogy and equivocity taken properly are not compatible with the same concept.

C4: true analogy can be founded in true univocity and contrariwise.

C5: true analogy and univocity are compatible with the same concept.

Specifications:[66]

1. Analogy is only compatible with univocity when the analogates formally participate in the analogous notion or term.

2. Not all grades of analogy are compatible with univocity.

3. Univocity is compatible with analogy in all its degrees except the first two.

4. Univocity has a greater unity than analogy. This means that in the lower levels, where univocity is perfect, there is a threefold unity. This is a unity of voice, concept, and equality of participation. This threefold unity is only in the lowest degree, though Peter notes that some thinkers posit it in the second degree as well. In the degrees of analogy compatible with univocity there is only a twofold unity, that of voice and concept.

C5 is the basic Scotist thesis that analogy and univocity are compatible, shared among the group of Franciscans under consideration here and the Scotist school in general.[67] The specifications explain which degrees of analogy and univocity are compatible in the same concept. From the first specification we learn that only the first four degrees of analogy are candidates for compatibility since it is in these degrees that both the analogates formally contain the analogous notion. From the third

---

[65] Though for reasons of clarity I have not followed Peter's language, in fact he renames the notions of univocity and equivocity. See Petrus Thomae, *Quaest. de ente*, q. 7, a. 2 (Smith, 146–147): "... magis proprie possunt dici 'aequilogia' et 'unilogia' quam 'aequivocatio' et 'univocatio', quae sunt quaedam nomina verbalia, cuius ratio est quia 'aequivocatio' et 'univocatio', cum sint nomina verbalia, magis significant ipsum actum exercitum quam significent ipsas intentiones quarum sunt illae actiones, sicut dicitur ergo 'analogia' et non 'analogatio', ita dicatur 'unilogia' et 'aequilogia'." For the following five conclusions, see ibid. (Smith, 158–161).

[66] Petrus Thomae, *Quaest. de ente*, q. 7, a. 2 (Smith, 164–165).

[67] For the general Scotist claim, see Smith 2019: 655–661.

specification we learn that on the side of univocity, the candidates for compatibility with analogy range from the third degree (the lowest genus) up the categorical line to the highest genus and beyond to the quidditative concept of being. In the final specification, Peter provides a reason why some degrees of analogy and univocity are compatible whereas others are not, namely, the three different kinds of unity possessed by univocal and analogical intentions (*intentiones*). The point of departure is equality of participation, which is found in the lowest two degrees of univocity but not in any degree of analogy since the defining characteristic of analogy is that it obtains where terms are said *per prius et posterius*. Finally, the relevant degree of analogy for the concept that embraces God and creatures is the first.

Peter Thomae's conclusions, specifications, and degrees of intentions, though they are an ingenious and unique contribution to the medieval debate over analogy and univocity, nevertheless do not suffice as an argument. They offer an explanation but not a demonstration; they do not prove that analogy and univocity are compatible in the same concept. For such proof, we must inquire deeper into Peter's discussion of C5, for it is this section of *De ente* question 7 that defends Peter's ultimate position or solution to the question.

Peter defends C5 with five arguments.[68] One is inspired by Scotus' own explanation of how analogy and univocity are compatible, based on the idea that analogy and univocity each posit a distinct degree of unity in a concept, a unity that is non-repugnant.[69] Scotus, followed by Peter Thomae, draws an analogy between the relation of univocity and analogy on the one hand, and the relation of a genus and a species on the other. A genus and a species that is subordinate to it both posit different degrees of unity: a genus encompasses more than a species, so its unity is weaker than that of a species located under it. But individuals of a species possess the unity both of the genus and of the species, even though each has its own degree of unity. Thus the distinct unities brought by univocity and analogy are also compatible in the same concept.

Another argument, likewise dependent on the example of the relation of a genus and a species, holds that the same concept can have both univocates and analogates (that is, referents of both kinds outside the soul), therefore also the same concept can be truly univocal and truly

---

[68] For these arguments, see *Quaest. de ente*, q. 7, a. 2 (Smith, 161–165).

[69] Cf. Petrus Thomae, *Quaest. de ente*, q. 7, a. 2 (Smith, 163 lin. 866–871). For the argument in Scotus, see *Ord.* I, d. 8, p. 1, q. 3, n. 83 (Vat. VIII, 191).

analogical.[70] In proof of the antecedent, Peter offers the example of a genus and species. As was widely accepted, a genus is said univocally, on the authority of Aristotle's *Topics*.[71] Thus, for example, animality is said univocally of its species, such as horse and cat. But the genus is also said analogically, for all the species of a genus stand in a relation of attribution to the first of the genus. Thus, within the concept of a genus, there is both univocity and analogy, the burden of the present question.

Peter Thomae developed the most elaborate account of univocity and analogy of any of the thinkers surveyed here, indeed perhaps the most elaborate from the medieval period. The point of this account was to show that the same concept can be both analogical and univocal. Given that Peter thinks he has proven that certain kinds of analogy are compatible with certain kinds of univocity, and that such compatibility is true of concepts applicable to God and creatures as well as to substance and accidents, he has thus managed to reconcile the new Scotist doctrine of univocity with elements of the analogy of being shared by Parisian thinkers such as Thomas Aquinas and Henry of Ghent, among others.

IV   AN OBJECTION

From the foregoing it is clear that the Barcelona Franciscans attempt to reconcile univocity and analogy by introducing a dizzying array of distinctions between different kinds of concepts.[72] The question then arises, whether we can simply dispense with them and hold a more parsimonious view, perhaps dropping either univocity or analogy entirely. In other words, what motivates the Scotist attempt to unify analogy and univocity?

The answer to this objection is that the thinkers whose views we have reconstructed above were committed to what I have called metaphysical analogy. That is to say, outside the soul, there is a divide between the realms of the created and uncreated, a distinction between the creature and the creator, with the latter transcending completely the former. But creatures are caused by God, sustained by God, participate in God, and are directed to God as their final end. In tandem with a metaphysical analogy, the Barcelona Franciscans also thought that humans could have natural, scientific knowledge of created and uncreated being, and such scientific knowledge provided by theology and metaphysics required

---

[70] Petrus Thomae, *Quaest. de ente*, q. 7, a. 2 (Smith, 161–162).   [71] See *Top.* IV, 5, 127b6.
[72] My reflections here are indebted to JT Paasch and Trent Pomplun.

univocity in concepts. The reason for this is that equivocity is opposed to univocity, and the pure form at least of equivocity vitiates all arguments, rendering them fallacious. Pure univocity cannot capture the relations between God and creatures outside the soul, since God transcends creation, and thus all perfections as found in creation are mixed with limitation and imperfection. Pure equivocity cannot capture these relations either, since it destroys all connections and unity between things. Analogy was often conceived of in Franciscan circles as a Boethian equivocal by design, an equivocal that possessed a higher degree of unity than pure, chance equivocals. Given that it stands midway between pure equivocity and univocity, it could represent the relation of God and the world outside the soul and possessed enough unity of concept that univocal concepts could also be formed from them, sufficient for the sciences of metaphysics and theology. The master of the Barcelona Franciscans, Duns Scotus, had left behind very few remarks on analogy from his mature period, and so to fill in this perceived lack, they drew on elements of the Parisian theory of conceptual analogy, which required a certain number of necessary distinctions and qualifications to be drawn. Having completed them, they had thereby effected a new synthesis of Scotistic metaphysics.

V CONCLUSION

The Franciscans from the *studium generale* at Barcelona hold the general Scotist position that there is metaphysical and conceptual analogy and that these kinds of analogy are compatible with conceptual univocity. Thus contemporary concerns that Scotistic univocity marked the loss or destruction of analogy are unfounded, for even those who knew Scotus personally, such as Aufredo Gonteri, attempted to integrate analogy into what is unquestionably a Scotist metaphysics, even departing from Scotus by reintroducing *per prius et posterius* predication. Moreover, a second departure from Scotus, the abandonment of his definitions of or criteria for univocal concepts marks a point in which all three Barcelona Franciscans moved closer to a view held by Thomas Aquinas, rendering a comparison between their positions and Thomistic metaphysics more profitable than a comparison with the texts of Scotus himself.

Despite their mutual agreement concerning these two points of departure from Scotus, the Barcelona Franciscans differed in their attempts to forge a union between analogy and univocity. Aufredo Gonteri drew a twofold distinction between analogical concepts, one of which is compatible with univocal predication. This distinction perhaps yields too much to the univocal side, since it posits the same *ratio* in both analogates. Peter of Navarre distinguished between two kinds of univocal concepts. This distinction perhaps yields too much to the analogical side, for it is hard to see how being can have a real concept on his view, as Peter Thomae points out. It is Peter Thomae who extensively revised the notions of analogy and univocity in dialogue with the ancient Greek, medieval Arabic, and Latin traditions to develop multiple degrees of analogy and univocity, distinguishing finally a degree in which they are compatible. Indeed, given the depth and scope of his reflections on analogy and univocity, and his knowledge of the previous tradition of reflection on the topic, it is perhaps Peter Thomae who should be regarded as the primary medieval theorist of the *analogia entis*.[73]

---

[73] An earlier version of this essay was presented at the Boston Colloquy in Historical Theology; I thank the participants for their remarks on that occasion. Thanks are also due to Giorgio Pini and Benno van Croesdijk for detailed comments on earlier drafts.

Bibliography

PRIMARY WORKS
WORKS BY DUNS SCOTUS

Duns Scotus, John. *Coll. Ox.* (Alliney and Fedeli) = *Iohannis Duns Scoti Collationes oxonienses.* A cura di Guido Alliney e Marina Fedeli. Firenze: SISMEL – Editioni del Galluzzo, 2016.

Coll. Par. 13 = *Joannis Duns Scoti Collationes,* 13. Opera omnia V, 199–204. Paris: L. Vivès, 1891.

DPP (Kluxen) = Johannes Duns Scotus. *Abhandlung über das Erste Prinzip.* Herausgegeben und übersetzt von Wolfgang Kluxen. Darmstadt: Wissenschaftliche Buchgesellschaft, 1974.

DPP (Wolter) = John Duns Scotus. *A Treatise on God as First Principle.* Translated and Edited with Commentary by Allan B. Wolter. Chicago: Franciscan Herald Press, 1966.

Ioannis Duns Scoti Doctoris Mariani Theologiae Marianae Elementa. Edidit C. Balić. Sibenik: Ex typographia Kačić, 1933.

Lect. I and II (Vat.) = *Ioannis Duns Scoti Lectura in primum et secundum librum Sententiarum.* Studio et cura Commissionis Scotisticae. Opera Omnia XVI–XIX. Civitas Vaticana: Typis Polyglottis Vaticanis, 1960–1993.

Lect. III (Vat.) = *Ioannis Duns Scoti Lectura in tertium librum Sententiarum.* Studio et cura Commissionis Scotisticae. Opera omnia XX–XXI. Civitas Vaticana: Typis Polyglottis Vaticanis, 2003–2004.

Ord. I–IV, d. 49, p. 2, q.un. (Vat.) = *Ioannis Duns Scoti Ordinatio.* Studio et cura Commissionis Scotisticae. Opera omnia I–XIV. Civitas Vaticana: Typis Polyglottis Vaticanis, 1950–2013.

Ord. IV (Vivès) = *Joannis Duns Scoti Quaestiones in quartum librum Sententiarum a distinctione quadragesima nona usque ad quinquagesimam.* Opera omnia XXI. Paris: Vivès, 1894.

Ord. IV (Wad.) = *Joannis Duns Scoti Quaestiones in quartum librum Sententiarum.* Opera omnia X. Lugduni: sumptibus Laurentii Durand, 1639.

QDA (OPh V) = *B. Ioannis Duns Scoti Quaestiones super secundum et tertium De anima.* Ediderunt C. Bazán, K. Emery, R. Green, T. Noone, R. Plevano, and A. Traver. Opera Philosophica V. Washington, DC and St. Bonaventure, NY: The Catholic University of America Press and The Franciscan Institute, 2006.

QMet. (OPh III and IV) = *B. Ioannis Duns Scoti Quaestiones super libros Metaphysicorum Aristotelis. Libri I–V and Libri VI–IX.* Edited by R. Andrews, G. Etzkorn, G. Gál, R. Green, †F. Kelley, †G. Marcil, T. Noone, and R. Wood. Opera Philosophica III and IV. St. Bonaventure, NY: The Franciscan Institute, St. Bonaventure University, 1997.

QPraed. (OPh I) = *B. Ioannis Duns Scoti Quaestiones super Praedicamenta Aristotelis.* Edited by R. Andrews, G. Etzkorn, †G. Gál, R. Green, T. Noone, and R. Wood. Opera Philosophica I, 247–566. St. Bonaventure, NY: The Franciscan Institute, 1999.

QSE (OPh II) = *B. Ioannis Duns Scoti Quaestiones super librum Elenchorum Aristotelis.* Ediderunt R. Andrews, O. Bychkov, S. Ebbesen, G. Etzkorn, †G. Gál, R. Green, T. Noone, R. Plevano, and A. Traver. Opera Philosophica II, 255–566. St. Bonaventure, NY and Washington, DC: The Franciscan Institute, St. Bonaventure University and The Catholic University of America, 2004.

Quodl. (Vivès) = *Joannis Duns Scoti Quaestiones quodlibetales.* Opera omnia XXV and XXVI. Paris: L. Vivès, 1895.

Quodl. (Wad.) = *Joannis Duns Scoti Quaestiones quodlibetales.* Opera omnia XII. Lugduni: sumptibus Laurentii Durand, 1639.

Quodl., q. 16 (Noone and Roberts) = T.B. Noone and H.F. Roberts. "John Duns Scotus' Quodlibet: A Brief Study of the Manuscripts and an Edition of Question 16." In C. Schabel, ed., *Theological Quodlibeta in the Middle Ages. The Fourteenth Century,* 131–198. Leiden and Boston: Brill, 2007.

Rep. I-A (Wolter and Bychkov) = John Duns Scotus. *The Examined Report of the Paris Lecture. Reportatio I-A.* Latin Text and English Translation by A.B. Wolter and O.V. Bychkov. 2 vols. St. Bonaventure, NY: Franciscan Institute Publications, 2004 and 2008.

Rep. I-A, d. 39 (Söder) = J. Söder. *Kontingenz und Wissen: Die Lehre von den futura contingentia bei Johannes Duns Scotus.* Münster: Aschendorff, 1999.

Rep. II-A (Vivès) = *Joannis Duns Scoti Reportata parisiensia. Liber secundus.* Opera omnia XXII, 488–677; XXIII, 1–233. Paris: L. Vivès, 1894.

Rep. IV-A, dd. 1–17 (Bychkov and Pomplun) = John Duns Scotus. *The Report of the Paris Lecture. Reportatio IV-A.* Latin Text and English Translation by O.V. Bychkov and R.T. Pomplun. Parts 1 and 2. St. Bonaventure, NY: Franciscan Institute Publications, 2016.

Rep. IV-A, dd. 18–50 (Vivès) = *Joannis Duns Scoti Reportata parisiensia. Liber quartus a distinctione septima usque ad quadragesimam nonam.* Opera omnia XXIV, 290–688. Paris: L. Vivès, 1894.

English translations

Duns Scotus, John. *On Being and Cognition: Ordinatio I.3.* Translated by John van den Bercken. New York: Fordham University Press, 2016

God and Creatures (Wolter and Alluntis) = John Duns Scotus. *God and Creatures: The Quodlibetal Questions.* Translated by Felix Alluntis and Allan B. Wolter. Princeton, NJ: Princeton University Press, 1975.

Philosophical Writings. Translated by S.B. Wolter. Edinburgh: Nelson, 1962.

Philosophical Writings. Translated by A.B. Wolter. 2nd ed. Indianapolis, IN: Hackett, 1987.

WORKS BY OTHER AUTHORS

Albert the Great. *In II Sent.* (Borgnet) = *B. Alberti Magni Commentarii in II Sententiarum.* In *B. Alberti Magni Opera Omnia.* Cura ac labore Augusti Borgnet. Vol. XXVII. Paris: L. Vivès, 1894.

Anselm. *De libertate arbitrii* (Schmitt) = *Sancti Anselmi Cantuariensis Archiepiscopi De libertate arbitrii.* In *Sancti Anselmi Cantuariensis Archiepiscopi Opera Omnia.* Vol. I, 201–226. Edidit F.S. Schmitt. Edinburgh: Apud Thomam Nelson et filios, 1946.

Monologion (Schmitt) = *Sancti Anselmi Cantuariensis Archiepiscopi Monologion.* In *Sancti Anselmi Cantuariensis Archiepiscopi Opera Omnia.* Vol. I, 1–87. Edidit F.S. Schmitt. Edinburgh: Apud Thomam Nelson et filios, 1946.

Aristotle. *APo.* = *Aristotelis Analytica Posteriora.* In *Aristotelis Analytica Priora et Posteriora,* 114–183. Recensuit brevique adnotatione critica instruxit W.D. Ross. Oxford: Clarendon Press, 1964.

Cat. = *Aristotelis Categoriae.* In *Aristotelis Categoriae et Liber de Interpretatione,* 3–45 Recognovit brevique adnotatione instruxit L. Minio-Paluello. Oxford: Clarendon Press, 1949.

Met. = *Aristotelis Metaphysica.* Recognovit brevique admotatione critica instruxit W. Jaeger. Oxford: Clarendon Press, 1957.

Phys. = *Aristotle's Physics.* A Revised Text with Introduction and Commentary by Sir David Ross. Oxford: Clarendon Press, 1936.

Top. = *Aristotelis Topica.* Edidit D.W. Ross. Oxford: Clarendon Press, 1958.

Aufredus Gonteri. *Lect.* I (Smith) = *Aufredi Gonteri Compilatio lecturae primi Sententiarum,* d. 3, qq. 2–4. Edited by G.R. Smith. In Smith 2018.

Ord. = *Aufredi Gonteri Britonis In I et II libros Sententiarum.* Wroclaw, Biblioteka uniwersytecka, ms. I F 184 (also known as A 211).

Averroes. *In Met.* (Iunt.) = Averroes. *In Metaphysicam.* In *Aristotelis opera cum Averrois commentaria,* 10 vols. Venetiis: apud Iunctas, 1562–1574, Vol. VIII.

Boethius. *In Cat.* (PL LXIV) = *Anicii Manlii Severini Boethii in Categorias Aristotelis libri quatuor.* In *Patrologia Latina.* Edidit J.–P. Migne. Tom. LXIV. Paris: apud Garnier fratres, 1947; reprint Turnhout: Brepols, 1979.

Bonaventure. *In II Sent.* = *S. Bonaventurae Commentaria in quatuor libros Sententiarum Petri Lombardi.* Tom. II. *In secundum librum Sententiarum.* In *Doctoris Seraphici S. Bonaventurae Opera Omnia.* Studio et Cura PP. Collegii S. Bonaventurae. Ad Claras Aquas, 1885.

Burley, Adam and Walter Burley. *Questions on the De Anima of Aristotle.* Edited by Edward A. Synan. Studien und Texte Zur Geistesgeschichte des Mittelalters, Bd. 55. Leiden and New York: Brill, 1997.

Franciscus de Mayronis. *In Sent.* I (redactio 'ab oriente') = *Francisci de Mayronis Opus super primo libro Sententiarum.* Biblioteca Apostolica Vaticana, ms. Vat. lat. 896, ff. 1r–132v.

Francisco Suárez. *Disputationes Metaphysicae* (Berton). In *Francisci Suarez Opera Omnia.* Vol. XXV–XXVI. Edidit C. Berton. Paris: Vivès, 1861; reprint Hildesheim: Olms, 1965.

Giles of Rome. *In II Sent.* (Ziletti) = *Aegidii Romani in Secundum Librum Sententiarum Quaestiones.* Venetiis: ex officina I. Ziletti, 1581.

Godfrey of Fontaines. *Quodl.* III (de Wulf and Pelzer) = *Gaudefridi de Fontibus Quodlibet III.* In *Le quatre premiers Quodlibets de Godefroid de Fontaines* (texte inédit), 156–228. Edité par M. de Wulf et A. Pelzer. Louvain/Paris: Institut supérieur de Philosophie de l'Université/A. Picard & Fils, 1904.

Gonsalvus Hispanus. *Quaestiones disputatae et de Quodlibet.* Bibliotheca Franciscana scholastica Medii Aevi 9. Ad Claras Aquas, Florentiae: ex typographia Collegii S. Bonaventurae, 1935.

Henry of Ghent. *Quodl.* IX (Opera omnia XII) = *Henrici de Gandavo Quodlibet IX.* Edidit R. Macken. In *Henrici de Gandavo Opera omnia* XIII. Leuven: Leuven University Press, 1981.

Quodl. XII (Opera omnia XVI) = *Henrici de Gandavo Quodlibet XII quaestiones 1–30.* Edidit J. Decorte. In *Henrici de Gandavo Opera omnia* XVI. Leuven: Leuven University Press, 1987.

Quodl. XIII (Opera omnia XVIII) = *Henrici de Gandavo Quodlibet XIII.* Edidit J. Decorte. In *Henrici de Gandavo Opera omnia* XVIII. Leuven: Leuven University Press, 1985.

Summa quaest. ord. (Badius) = *Summae Quaestionum Ordinariarum Theologi recepto praeconio Solemnis Henrici a Gandavo.* Paris: in aedibus Iadoci Badii Ascensii, 1520; reprint St. Bonaventure, NY/Louvain/Paderborn: The Franciscan Institute/E. Nauwelaerts/F. Schöningh, 1953.

Summa quaest. ord., art. 41–46 (Opera omnia XXIX) = *Henrici de Gandavo Summa (Quaestiones ordinariae),* art. XLI–XLVI. Edidit L. Hödl. In *Henrici de Gandavo Opera omnia* XXIX. Leuven: Leuven University Press, 1998.

Summa quaest. ord., art. 47–52 (Opera omnia XXX) = *Henrici de Gandavo Summa (Quaestiones Ordinariae).* In *Henrici de Gandavo Opera omnia* XXX. Edidit M. Führer. Leuven: Leuven University Press, 2007.

Liber de causis (Pattin) = A. Pattin. "Le *Liber de Causis.* Edition établie à l'aide de 90 manuscrits avec introduction et notes." *Tijdschrift voor Filosofie* 28 (1966): 90–203.

Molina. *Liberi Arbitrii cum Gratiae Donis, Divina Praescientia, Providentia, Praedestinatione et Reprobatione Concordia* = *Ludovici Molinae Liberi Arbitrii cum Gratiae Donis, Divina Praescientia, Providentia, Praedestinatione et Reprobatione Concordia.* Edidit Johann Rabeneck, S.J. Oniae/Madrid: Collegium Maximum, 1953.

Olivi. *In II Sent.* (Jansen) = Fr. Petrus Iohannis Olivi. *Quaestiones in secundum librum Sententiarum.* Edidit B. Jansen. 3 vols. Ad Claras Aquas: ex Typographia Collegii S. Bonaventurae, 1922–1926.

Peter of Auvergne. *QMet.* (Monahan) = A. Monahan. "Quaestiones in Metaphysicam Petri de Alvernia." In J.R. O'Donnell, ed. *Nine Mediaeval Thinkers: A Collection of Hitherto Unedited Texts,* 145–181. Toronto: Pontifical Institute of Mediaeval Studies, 1955.

Peter Lombard. *Sent.* = *Magistri Petri Lombardi Sententias in IV libri distinctas.* 2 vols. Grottaferrata: Editiones Collegii S. Bonavenuturae ad Claras Aquas, 1971 et 1981.

Petrus de Navarra. *In I Sent.* (Sagües Azcona) = Petrus de Atarrabia sive de Navarra. In *Primum Sententiarum Scriptum.* 2 vols. Edidit Pius Sagües Azcona. Madrid: Consejo Superior de Investigaciones Cientificas, 1974.

Petrus Thomae. *Quaest. de ente* (Smith)= *Petri Thomae Quaestiones de ente.* Edited by G.R. Smith (Petri Thomae Opera II). Leuven: Leuven University Press, 2018.

   Rep. = *Petri Thomae Scriptum super primum Sententiarum.* Biblioteca Apostolica Vaticana, ms. Vat. lat. 1106, ff. 1r–328v.

Philip the Chancellor. *Summa de bono (Wicki)* = *Philippi Cancellarii Parisiensis Summa de Bono.* Edidit N. Wicki. Berne: Francke, 1985.

Richard Middleton. *In Sent.* (Venetiis) = *Richardi de Mediavilla Commentaria super libros Sententiarum.* In *Richardi de Mediavilla Quodlibeta et Commentaria super libros I and II Sententiarum.* 4 vols. Venetiis 1507–1509.

Roger Bacon. *Compendium of the Study of Philosophy.* Edited by Thomas S. Maloney. Auctores Britannici Medii Aevi 32. Oxford: Published for the British Academy by the Oxford University Press, 2018.

Thomas Aquinas. *De Pot.* (Pession) = *S. Thomas Aquinatis Quaestiones disputatae.* 2 vols. Vol. II, pp. 7–276: *De Potentia.* Cura et studio P.M. Pession. Turin: Marrietti, 1965.

   In Met. (Cathala and Spiazzi) = *S. Thomae Aquinatis in duodecim libros Metaphysicorum Aristotelis expositio.* Ediderunt M.-R. Cathala et R.M. Spiazzi. Taurini et Romae: Marietti, 1964.

   In I Sent. (Mandonnet) = Thomas de Aquino. *Scriptum super primum librum Sententiarum.* 2 vols. Edidit P. Mandonnet. Paris: P. Lethielleux, 1929.

   In IV Sent., dd. 23–49 (Parma) = *Sancti Thomae Aquinatis Commentum in quatuor libros Sententiarum Magistri Petri Lombardi.* Vol. 2. In *Sancti Thomae Aquinatis Doctoris Angelici Ordinis Praedicatorum Opera Omnia.* T. VII. Parmae: Typis Petri Fiaccadori, 1857.

   Quaest. de quolibet (Leon.) = *Sancti Thomae de Aquino Quaestiones de quolibet.* Cura et studio Fratrum Praedicatorum. In *Sancti Thomae Aquinatis Opera Omnia.* Tom. XXV.1–2. Romae: Commissio Leonina; Paris: Les éditions du Cerf, 1996.

   Summa contra gentiles (Leon.) = *Sancti Thomae Aquinatis Summa contra Gentiles.* Cura et studio Fratrum Praedicatorum. In *Sancti Thomae Aquinatis Opera Omnia.* Tom. XIII–XV. Romae: Typis Riccardi Garroni, 1918–1930.

   Summa theologiae (Leon.) = *Sancti Thomae Aquinatis Summa Theologiae.* Cura et studio Fratrum Praedicatorum (*Sancti Thomae Aquinatis Opera Omnia.* Tom. IV–XII). Romae: Typis Riccardi Garroni, 1888–1912.

Thomas Wylton. *Quaest. super Phys.* I, q. 13 (Schmaus) = Thomas Wylton. *Quaestiones super Physicam I,* q. 13. In M. Schmaus. *Thomas Wylton als Verfasser eines Kommentars zur Aristotelischen Physik,* 12–33. München: Bayerische Akademie der Wissenschaften 1957.

William Alnwick. *Determinationes* = *Guillelmi Alnwick Determinationes*. Città del Vaticano, Biblioteca Apostolica Vaticana, ms. Pal. Lat. 1805, ff. 1–193.

Quaest. disp. de esse intelligibili et de Quodl. (Ledoux) = *Fr. Guillelmi Alnwick, O.F.M. Quaestiones disputatae de esse intelligibili et de Quodlibet*. Cura P. Athanasii Ledoux, O.F.M. Firenze: Ex Typographia Collegii S. Bonaventurae, 1937.

Walter Chatton. *Lect. I* (Wey and Etzkorn) = Walter Chatton. *Lectura super Sententias: Liber I, Distinctiones 3–7*. Edited by J.C. Wey and G.J. Etzkorn. Toronto: Pontifical Institute of Mediaeval Studies, 2008.

William of Rubio. *In Sent.* (Badius) = *Guillelmi de Rubione in quatuor libros Magistri Sententiarum*. Tom. I. Paris: Badius, 1518.

SECONDARY WORKS

Adams, M. McCord. 2010. "Essential Orders and Sacramental Causality." In M.B. Ingham and O. Bychkov, eds. *John Duns Scotus, Philosopher: Proceedings of the "The Quadruple Congress" on John Duns Scotus*, 191–206. Münster: Aschendorff Verlag.

Aertsen, J.A. 2005a. "Aquinas and the Human Desire for Knowledge." *American Catholic Philosophical Quarterly* 79: 411–430.

2005b. "Hoe kan een theoloog en filosoof zo iets leren? Duns Scotus' kritiek op Thomas van Aquino." *Tijdschrift voor Filosofie* 67: 453–478.

2012. *Medieval Philosophy as Transcendental Thought: From Philip the Chancelor (ca. 1225) to Francisco Suárez*. Leiden: Brill.

Alliney, G. 2005. "La ricezione della teoria scotiana della volontà nell'ambiente teologico parigino (1307–1316)." *Documenti e studi sulla tradizione filosofica medievale* 16: 339–404.

2008. "*Utrum necesse sit voluntatem frui*: Note sul volontarismo francescano inglese del primo Trecento." *Quaestio* 8: 83–138.

2013. "Giovanni di Morrovalle e le *Affectiones* Anselmiane." *Archivum Franciscanum Historicum* 106: 569–84.

Anstey, H., ed. 1868. *Munimenta academica; or, Documents Illustrative of Academic Life and Studies at Oxford*. 2 vols. (Rerum Britannicarum medii aevi scriptores 50). London: Longmans, Green, Reader and Dyer.

Ariew, R. 2000. "Scotists, Scotists, Everywhere." *Intellectual News* 8: 14–21.

Ashworth, E.J. 1980. "'Can I Speak More Clearly than I Understand?' A Problem of Religious Language in Henry of Ghent, Duns Scotus, and Ockham." *Historiographia Linguistica* 7: 29–38.

1991. "Signification and Modes of Signifying in Thirteenth-Century Logic: A Preface to Aquinas on Analogy." *Medieval Philosophy and Theology* 1: 39–67.

1992. "Analogy and Equivocation in Thirteenth-Century Logic: Aquinas in Context." *Mediaeval Studies* 54: 94–135.

2007. "Metaphor and the Logicians from Aristotle to Cajetan." *Vivarium* 45: 311–327.

2008. *Les théories de l'analogie du XIIe au XVIe siècle.* Paris: J. Vrin.

2013. "Analogy and Metaphor from Thomas Aquinas to Duns Scotus and Walter Burley." In C. Bolyard and R. Keele, eds. *Later Medieval Metaphysics: Ontology, Language, and Logic*, 223–48. New York: Fordham University Press.

Aubenque, P. 1989. "Sur la naissance de la doctrine pseudo-aristotélicienne de l'analogie de l'être." *Les études philosophiques* 3/4: 291–304.

Balić, C. 1927. *Les commentaires de Jean Duns Scot sur les quatre livres des Sentences: étude historique et critique.* Louvain: Bureaux de la Revue.

1959. "Henricus de Harcley et Ioannes Duns Scotus." In *Mélanges offerts à Étienne Gilson, de l'Académie française*, 93–121. Paris: Vrin.

1965. "The Life and Works of John Duns Scotus." In J.K. Ryan and B.M. Bonansea, eds. *John Duns Scotus 1265–1965*, 1–27. Washington, DC: The Catholic University of America Press.

Bazán, B.C. 1985. "Les questions disputées, principalement dans les facultés de théologie." In *Les questions disputées et les questions quodlibétiques dans les facultés de théologie, de droit et de médecine*, 15–152. Typologie des sources du Moyen Age occidental; fasc. 44–45. Turnhout, Belgium: Brepols.

2001. "Conceptions of the Agent Intellect and the Limits of Metaphysics." In J.A. Aertsen *et al.*, eds. *Nach der Verurteilung von 1277. Philosophie und Theologie an der Universität von Paris im letzten Viertel des 13. Jahrhunderts: Studien und Texte*, 178–210. Berlin and New York: de Gruyter.

Bérubé, C. 1983. "Jean Duns Scot, critique de l'«Avicennisme augustinisant» sur l'objet de l'intelligence." In C. Bérubé. *De l'homme à Dieu selon Duns Scot, Henri de Gand et Olivi*, 113–146. Roma: Collegio S. Lorenzo.

Betz, J. 2019. "The Analogia entis as a Standard of Catholic Engagement: Erich Przywara's Critique of Phenomenology and Dialectical Theology." *Modern Theology* 35: 81–102.

Boler, J. 1990. "The Moral Psychology of Duns Scotus: Some Preliminary Questions." *Franciscan Studies* 50: 1–56.

1993. "Transcending the Natural: Duns Scotus on the Two Affections of the Will." *American Catholic Philosophical Quarterly* 67: 109–126.

1996. "The Ontological Commitment of Scotus's Account of Potency in his *Questions on the Metaphysics*, Book IX." In Honnefelder, Wood, and Dreyer 1996, 145–160.

Bonansea, B.M. 1983. *Man and His Approach to God in John Duns Scotus.* Lanham, Md: University Press of America.

Borland, T. and A.T. Hillman. 2017. "Scotus and God's Arbitrary Will: A Reassessment." *American Catholic Philosophical Quarterly* 91: 399–429.

Boulnois, O. 1995. "Représentation et noms divins selon Duns Scot." *Documenti e studi sulla tradizione filosofica medievale* 6: 255–80.

1998. *Duns Scot: La rigueur de la charité.* Paris: Cerf.

1999. *Être et représentation. Une généalogie de la métaphysique moderne à l'époque de Duns Scotus (XIIe–XIVe siècle).* Paris: Presses Universitaires de France.

2011. "*Libertas indifferentiae.* Figures de la liberté d'indifférence au moyen âge." In I. Atucha *et al.,* eds. *Mots médiévaux offerts à Ruedi Imbach,* 405–417. Porto: FIDEM.

2014. "'In Harmony with Reason': John Duns Scotus's Theo-aesth/ethics." *Open Theology* 1: 45–55.

Brampton, C.K. 1964. "Duns Scotus at Oxford, 1288–1301." *Franciscan Studies* 24: 5–20.

Bryce, W.M. 1909. *The Scottish Grey Friars.* Edinburgh and London: W. Green and Sons.

Callebaut, A. 1924. "Le B. Jean Duns Scot étudiant à Paris vers 1293–1296." *Archivum Franciscanum Historicum* 17: 3–12.

1928. "Le Bx. Jean Duns Scot à Cambridge vers 1297–1300." *Archivum Franciscanum Historicum* 21 (4): 608–611.

1929. "Les séjours à Paris Du B. J. Duns Scot: son milieu universitaire." *La France Franciscaine* 12: 353–73.

1931. "A propos du Bx. Jean Duns Scot de Littledean. Notes et recherches historiques de 1265 à 1292." *Archivum Franciscanum Historicum* 24: 305–329.

Castagnoli, P. 1931. "Le dispute Quodlibetali di Pietro de Anglia, O. F. M." *Divus Thomas* 34: 413–19.

Cenci, C., and G. Mailleux, eds. 2007. *Constitutiones generales Ordinis Fratrum Minorum I (Saeculum XIII).* Analecta Franciscana 13. Grottaferrata (Roma): Frati editori di Quaracchi.

2010. *Constitutiones generales Ordinis Fratrum Minorum II (Saeculum XIV/1).* Analecta Franciscana 17. Grottaferrata (Roma): Frati editori di Quaracchi.

Cheney, C.R. and M. Jones. 2000. *A Handbook of Dates for Students of British History.* New edition revised by Michael Jones. Guides and Handbooks 4. Cambridge and New York: Cambridge University Press.

Courtenay, W.J. 1978. *Adam Wodeham: An Introduction to His Life and Writings.* Leiden: Brill.

1980. "The Lost Matthew Commentary of Robert Holcot." *Archivum Fratrum Praedicatorum* 50: 103–12.

1987. *Schools & Scholars in Fourteenth-Century England.* Princeton, N.J.: Princeton University Press.

1993. "The Parisian Franciscan Community in 1303." *Franciscan Studies* 53: 157–73.

1995. "Scotus at Paris." In Sileo 1995, Vol. 1, 149–163.

1996. "Between Pope and King: The Parisian Letters of Adhesion of 1303." *Speculum* 71: 577–605.

1999. "Instructional Programme of the Mendicant Convents at Paris in the Early Fourteenth Century." In P. Biller and R.B. Dobson, eds. *The Medieval Church: Universities, Heresy, and the Religious Life: Essays in Honour of Gordon Leff,* 77–92. Studies in Church History. Subsidia 11. Woodbridge,

Suffolk, UK and Rochester, NY: Published for the Ecclesiastical History Society by the Boydell Press.

2011. "Early Scotists at Paris: A Reconsideration." *Franciscan Studies* 69: 175–229.

2012. "Scotus at Paris: Some Reconsiderations." In R. Cross, ed. *The Opera Theologica of John Duns Scotus. Proceedings of The Quadruple Congress on John Duns Scotus Part 2*, 1–19. Archa Verbi Subsidia 4. Münster: Aschendorff Verlag.

2016. "Magisterial Authority, Philosophical Identity, and the Growth of Marian Devotion: The Seals of Parisian Masters, 1190–1308." *Speculum* 91: 63–114.

Cross, R. 1998. *The Physics of Duns Scotus: The Scientific Context of a Theological Vision*. Oxford: Clarendon Press.

1999. *Duns Scotus*. New York and Oxford: Oxford University Press.

2005. *Duns Scotus on God*. Aldershot: Ashgate.

2012a. "Duns Scotus and Analogy: A Brief Note." *The Modern Schoolman* 89: 147–154.

2012b. "Natural Law, Moral Constructivism, and Duns Scotus's Metaethics: The Centrality of Aesthetic Explanation." In J.A. Jacobs, ed. *Reason, Religion, and Natural Law: From Plato to Spinoza*, 175–197. Oxford: Oxford University Press.

2013. "Duns Scotus on Essence and Existence." *Oxford Studies in Medieval Philosophy* 1: 174–202.

2014. *Duns Scotus's Theory of Cognition*. Oxford: Oxford University Press.

2015. "Duns Scotus and Divine Necessity." *Oxford Studies in Medieval Philosophy* 3: 128–144.

de Libera, A. 1989. "Les sources gréco-arabes de la théorie médiévale de l'analogie de l'être." *Les études philosophiques* 3/4: 319–345.

Dekker, E. 1998. "Does Scotus Need Molina? On Divine Foreknowledge and Co-Causality." In E.P. Bos, ed. *John Duns Scotus Renewal of Philosophy*, 101–111. Amsterdam: Rodopi.

Demange, D. 2007. *Jean Duns Scot: La théorie du savoir*. Paris: Vrin.

Denifle, H. and E. Chatelain. 1889. *Chartularium Universitatis parisiensis*. 4 vols. Paris: Ex typis fratrum Delalain.

Docherty, H. 1968. "The Brockie Mss. and Duns Scotus." In *De Doctrina Ioannis Duns Scoti*, Vol. 1, 327–360. Rome: Societas Internationalis Scotistica.

Donati, S. 2003. "La discussione sull'unità del concetto di ente nella tradizione di commento della '*Fisica*': commenti parigini degli anni 1270–1315 ca." In M. Pickavé, ed. *Die Logik des Transzendentalen*. Festschrift für Jan A. Aertsen zum 65. Geburtstag, 60–139. Miscellanea Mediaevalia 30. Berlin and New York: de Gruyter, 2003.

2012. "La doctrine de l'analogie de l'être dans la tradition des commentaires de la *Physique*. Quelques modèles interprétatifs (commentaires de la Faculté des arts, autour de 1250–1300." *Revue Thomiste* 112: 31–59.

2013. "*Apparentia* and *modi essendi* in Radulphus Brito's Doctrine of the Concepts: The Concept of Being." In J. Leth Fink, H. Hansen, and A.M.

Mora-Marquez, eds. *Logic and Language in the Middle Ages: Studies in Honour of Sten Ebbesen*, 337–355. Leiden and Boston: Brill.

2014. "English Commentaries before Scotus. A Case Study: The Discussion on the Unity of Being." In F. Amerini and G. Galluzzo, eds. *A Companion to the Latin Medieval Commentaries on Aristotle's Metaphysics*, 137–207. Leiden and Boston: Brill.

Doucet, V. 1936. "L'oeuvre scolastique de Richard de Conington, O. F. M." *Archivum Franciscanum Historicum* 29: 396–442.

Duba, W.O. 2007. "Continental Franciscan *Quodlibeta* After Scotus." In C. Schabel, ed. *Theological Quodlibeta in the Middle Ages: The Fourteenth Century*, 569–649. Leiden: Brill.

Duba, W.O., R.L. Friedman, and C. Schabel. 2010. "Henry of Harclay and Aufredo Gonteri Brito." In P.W. Rosemann, ed. *Mediaeval Commentaries on the Sentences of Peter Lombard*, Vol. 2, 263–368. Leiden and Boston: Brill.

Duba, W.O. and C. Schabel. 2017. "Remigio, Auriol, Scotus, and the Myth of the Two-Year Sentences Lecture at Paris." *Recherches de théologie et philosophie médiévales* 84: 143–79.

Dumont, S.D. 1988. "The Univocity of the Concept of Being in the Fourteenth Century: II. The 'De ente' of Peter Thomae." *Mediaeval Studies* 50: 188–256.

1995a. "The Origins of Scotus's Theory of Synchronic Contingency." *Modern Schoolman* 72: 149–167.

1995b. "Transcendental Being: Scotus and Scotists." *Topoi* 11: 135–148.

1996. "William of Ware, Richard of Conington, and the Oxford *Collationes* of Duns Scotus." In Honnefelder, Wood, and Dreyer 1996, 59–87.

1998a. "Duns Scotus." In *Routledge Encyclopedia of Philosophy*, Vol. 3, 153–170. London: Routledge.

1998b. "Scotus's Doctrine of Univocity and the Medieval Tradition of Metaphysics." In J.A. Aertsen and A. Speer, eds. *Was ist Philosophie im Mittelalter?* 193–212. Miscellanea Mediaevalia 26. Berlin and New York: de Gruyter.

2001. "Did Scotus Change His Mind on the Will?." In J.A. Aersten, K. Emery, and A. Speer, eds. *After the Condemnation of 1277: Philosophy and Theology at the University of Paris in the Last Quarter of the Thirteenth Century*, 719–794. Miscellanea Mediaevalia 28. Berlin and New York: de Gruyter.

2003. "Henry of Ghent and Duns Scotus." In J. Marenbon, ed. *Medieval Philosophy*, 291–328. London and New York: Routledge, 2003.

2018. "John Duns Scotus's *Reportatio Parisiensis Examinata*: A Mystery Solved." *Recherches de théologie et philosophie médiévales* 85: 337–438.

Effler, R. 1962. *John Duns Scotus and the Principle 'Omne quod movetur ab alio movetur'*. St. Bonaventure, NY: The Franciscan Institute.

Ehrle, F. 1887. "Petrus Johannis Olivi, sein Leben und seine Schriften." *Archiv für Literatur und Kirchen Geschichte des Mittelalters* 3: 377–416.

1892. "Die ältesten Redactionen der Generalconstitutionen des Franziskanerordens." *Archiv für Literatur und Kirchengeschichte des Mittelalters* 6: 1–139

Emden, A.B. 1957–1959. *A Biographical Register of the University of Oxford to 1500*. 3 vols. Oxford: Clarendon Press.

Emery, K. and G.R. Smith. 2014. "The *Quaestio de Formalitatibus* by John Duns Scotus, Sometimes Called the *Logica Scoti*." *Bulletin de philosophie médiévale* 56: 91–182.

Emili, A. 2010. "Minio, Giovanni Di." In *Dizionario Biografico degli Italiani*, Vol. 74, 650–54. Roma: Istituto dell'Enciclopedia Italiana.

Fatigati, M. 2013. "The Causal Role of the Phantasm in Duns Scotus's Cognitive Psychology." Unpublished manuscript.

Flint, T.P. 1998. *Divine Providence: The Molinist Account*. Ithaca: Cornell.

Frank, W.A. 1982. "Duns Scotus' Concept of Willing Freely: What Divine Freedom beyond Choice Teaches Us." *Franciscan Studies* 42: 68–89.

1992. "Duns Scotus on Autonomous Freedom and Divine Co-Causality." *Medieval Philosophy and Theology* 2: 142–164.

Friedberg, E., ed. 1959. *Corpus iuris canonici*. 2 vols. Graz: Akademische Druck-u. Verlagsamstalt.

Frost, G. 2010. "John Duns Scotus on God's Knowledge of Sins: A Test Case for God's Knowledge of Contingents." *Journal of the History of Philosophy* 48: 15–34.

2014. "Peter Olivi's Rejection of God's Concurrence with Secondary Causes." *British Journal for the History of Philosophy* 22: 655–679.

Gibson, S. 1931. *Statuta antiqua Universitatis Oxoniensis*. Oxford: Clarendon Press.

Gilson, E. 1937. "Les seize premier *Theoremata* et la pensée de Duns Scot." *Archives d'histoire doctrinale et littéraire du moyen-âge* 11: 5–86.

1952. *Jean Duns Scot. Introduction à ses positions fondamentales*. Paris: Vrin. (English translation: *John Duns Scotus: Introduction to his Fundamental Positions*. Translated by J. Colbert. New York: Bloomsbury, 2018.)

Glassberger, N. 1887. *Chronica*. Ad Claras Aquas (Quaracchi): Typographia Collegii S. Bonaventurae.

Glorieux, P. 1925. *La littérature quodlibétique de 1260 à 1320*. Belgium: Le Saulchoir Kain.

1933. *Répertoire des maîtres en théologie de Paris au XIIIe siècle*. 2 vols. Etudes de philosophie médiévale 17. Paris: Vrin.

1935. *La littérature quodlibétique II*. Paris: Vrin.

Goris, W. 2018. "Scotus in Paris – On Univocity and the Portions of the Soul," *Recherches de théologie et philosophie médiévales* 85: 439–469.

Goris, W. and L. Honnefelder, eds. 2018. *John Duns Scotus's Reportatio Parisiensis*. *Recherches de théologie et philosophie médiévales* 85: 369–560.

Gorman, M. 1993. "Ontological Priority and John Duns Scotus." *The Philosophical Quarterly* 43 (173): 460–471.

Greenway, D. 1971. "Ely: Bishops." In *Fasti Ecclesiae Anglicanae 1066–1300: Volume 2, Monastic Cathedrals (Northern and Southern Provinces)*, 45–47. London: Institute of Historical Research.

Guillaume de Nangis. 1843. *Chronique latine de Guillaume de Nagis de 1113 à 1300: avec les continuations de cette chronique de 1300 à 1368.* Edited by H. Géraud. Société de l'histoire de France 33. Paris: J. Renouard et cie.

Hagedorn, E.W. 2019. "From Thomas Aquinas to the 1350s." In T. Williams, ed. *The Cambridge Companion to Medieval Ethics*, 55–76. Cambridge: Cambridge University Press.

Hartshorne, C. H. 1862. "Illustrations of Domestic Manners during the Reign of Edward I." *Journal of the British Archaeological Association* 18: 145–52.

Hastings, R. 1890. "The Friars Preachers v. the University, A. D. 1311–1313." In M. Burrows, ed. *Collectanea II.* Oxford Historical Society 16. Oxford: Clarendon Press.

Hauke, H. 1967. *Die Lehre von der Beseligenden Schau nach Nikolaus Trivet.* München: Universität München, Theologische Facultät.

Hechich, B. 1958. *De immaculata conceptione beatae Mariae Virginis secundum Thomam de Sutton et Robertum de Cowton: Textus et doctrina.* Bibliotheca Immaculatae Conceptionis 7. Romae: Academia Mariana Internationalis.

2008. "Il Problema delle 'Reportationes' nell'eredità dottrinale del B. Giovanni Duns Scotus OFM." In M. Carbajo Núñez, ed. *Giovanni Duns Scoto: Studi e ricerche nel VII centenario della sua morte in onore di P. César Saco Alarcón*, 59–129. Roma: Edizioni Antonianum.

Hill, R.M.T. 1975. *The Rolls and Register of Bishop Oliver Sutton, 1280–1299.* Volume VII: *Ordinations May 19, 1290 – September 19, 1299.* Publications of the Lincoln Record Society, Vol. 69. Lincoln: Ruddock and Sons.

Hoeres, W. 1962. *Der Wille als reine Vollkommenheit nach Duns Scotus.* München: Anton Pustet.

Honnefelder, L. 1989. *Ens in quantum ens. Der Begriff des Seienden als solchen als Gegenstand der Metaphysik nach der Lehre des Johannes Duns Scotus.* Münster: Aschendorff.

2005. "Scotus und der Scotismus. Ein Beitrag zur Bedeutung der Schulbildung in der mittelalterlichen Philosophie." In M.J.F.M. Hoenen, J.H.J. Schneider, and G. Wieland, eds. *Philosophy and Learning in the Middle Ages*, 249–262. Education and Society in the Later Middle Ages and Renaissance 6. Leiden/ New Yor/Köln: Brill.

2012. "John Duns Scotus on God's Intellect and Will." In R. Cross, ed. *John Duns Scotus 1308–2008: The Opera Theologica of Scotus*, 73–88. St. Bonaventure, NY: Franciscan Institute Publications.

Honnefelder, L., R. Wood, and M. Dreyer, eds. 1996. *John Duns Scotus: Metaphysics and Ethics.* Leiden: Brill.

Horan, D. P. 2014. *Postmodernity and Univocity: A Critical Account of Radical Orthodoxy and John Duns Scotus.* Minneapolis, MN: Fortress Press.

Incandela J.M. 1992. "Duns Scotus and the Experience of Human Freedom." *The Thomist* 56: 229–256.

Ingham, M.B. 2001. "Letting Scotus Speak for Himself." *Medieval Philosophy and Theology* 10: 173–216.

Jarka-Sellers, H. 1998. "Liber de causis." In *Routledge Encyclopedia of Philosophy*. Taylor and Francis. Retrieved 18 Oct. 2018, from https://www.rep.routledge.com/articles/thematic/liber-de-causis/v-1. doi:10.4324/9780415249126-B069-1.

Keele, R. 2007. "Can God Make a Picasso? William Ockham and Walter Chatton on Divine Power and Real Relations." *Journal of the History of Philosophy* 45: 395–411.

King, P. 1994. "Duns Scotus on the Reality of Self-Change." In M.L. Gill and J.G. Lennox, eds. *Self-Motion: From Aristotle to Newton*, 227–290. Princeton: Princeton University Press.

2003. "Scotus on Metaphysics." In Williams 2003a, 15–68.

2010. "Scotus's Rejection of Anselm: The Two-Wills Theory." In L. Honnefelder *et al.*, eds. *Johannes Duns Scotus 1308–2008: Die philosophischen Perspektiven seines Werkes/Investigations into his Philosophy*, 359–378. Münster: Aschendorff.

Langston, D.C. 1986. *God's Willing Knowledge: The Influence of Scotus's Analysis of Omniscience*. University Park and London: The Pennsylvania State University Press.

1996. "Did Scotus Embrace Anselm's Notion of Freedom?" *Medieval Philosophy and Theology* 5: 145–159.

2010. "*God's Willing Knowledge*, Redux." *Recherches de théologie et philosophie médiévales* 77: 235–282.

Leader, D.R. 1984. "Philosophy at Oxford and Cambridge in the Fifteenth Century." *History of Universities* 4: 25–46.

Leff, G. 1968. *Paris and Oxford Universities in the Thirteenth and Fourteenth Centuries; an Institutional and Intellectual History*. New York: Wiley.

Little, A.G. 1892. *The Grey Friars in Oxford: Part I: A History of Convent; Part II: Biographical Notices of the Friars, Together with Appendices of Original Documents*. Oxford: Printed for the Oxford Historical Society at the Clarendon Press.

1926. "The Franciscan School at Oxford in the Thirteenth Century." *Archivum Franciscanum Historicum* 19: 803–876.

1932. "Chronological Notes on the Life of Duns Scotus," *The English Historical Review* 47: 568–582.

1940. "Theological Schools in Medieval England." *The English Historical Review* 55 (220): 624–630.

1943. *Franciscan Papers, Lists, and Documents*. Publications of the University of Manchester 284. Manchester: Manchester University Press.

Little, A.G. and F. Pelster. 1934. *Oxford Theology and Theologians, c. A.D. 1282–1302*. Oxford Historical Society 96. Oxford: The Clarendon Press for the Oxford Historical Society.

Lonfat, J. 2004. "Archéologie de la notion de l'analogie d'Aristote à Saint Thomas d'Aquin," *Archives d'histoire doctrinale et littéraire du Moyen Age* 71: 35–107.

Longpré, E. 1929a. "L'ordination sacerdotale du Bx. Jean Duns Scot, document du 17 Mars 1291." *Archivum Franciscanum Historicum* 22: 54–62.

1929b. "Nouveaux documents franciscains d'Ecosse," *Archivum Franciscanum Historicum* 22: 588–589.

1935. "Une *Réportation* inédite du B. Duns Scot: le Ms Ripoll 53." In *Geisteswelt des Mittelalters. Studien und Texte*, 974–990. Münster: Aschendorff.

Maierù, A. 1994. *University Training in Medieval Europe*. Education and Society in the Middle Ages and Renaissance 3. Leiden and New York: Brill.

Major, J. 1740. *Historia Majoris Britanniae, tam Angliae quam Scotiae*. Edinburgh: Robertum Fribarnium.

1892. *A History of Greater Britain, as Well England as Scotland*. Translated by Archibald Constable. Edinburgh: T. and A. Constable.

Marcil, G. 1965. "Efficient Causality in the Philosophy of John Duns Scotus." Doctoral dissertation. The Catholic University of America.

Marmo, C. 1994. *Semiotica e linguaggio nella Scolastics. Parigi, Bologna, Erfurt 1270–1330. La semiotica dei Modisti*. Roma: Istituto Storico Italiano per il Medio Evo.

Marrone, S.P. 1996. "Revisiting Duns Scotus and Henry of Ghent on Modality." In Honnefelder, Wood, and Dreyer 1996, 175–189.

2001. *The Light of Thy Countenance: Science and Knowledge of God in the Thirteenth Century*. 2 vols. Leiden, Boston, and Köln: Brill.

Martel, B. 1968. *La psychologie de Gonsalve d'Espagne*. Publications de l'Institut d'études médiévales 21. Montréal/Paris: Institut d'études médiévales/Vrin.

Martin, C.J. 2004. 'Formal Consequence in Scotus and Ockham: Towards an Account of Scotus' Logic.' In O. Boulnois, E. Karger, J.-L. Solère, and G. Sondag, eds. *Duns Scot à Paris: Actes du colloque de Paris, 2–4 Septembre 2002*, 117–150. Turnhout: Brepols.

Maurer, A. 1955. "St. Thomas and the Analogy of Genus," *The New Scholasticism* 29: 127–144.

Moorman, J.R.H. 1952. *The Grey Friars in Cambridge, 1225–1538*. Birkbeck Lectures, 1948–49. Cambridge: Cambridge University Press.

1968. *A History of the Franciscan Order from Its Origins to the Year 1517*. Oxford: Clarendon Press.

O'Regan, C. 2015. "Scotus the Nefarious: Uncovering Genealogical Sophistications." In E.J. Ondrako, ed. *The Newman Scotus Reader: Contexts and Commonalities*, 611–636. New Bedford, MA: Academy of the Immaculate.

Pasnau, R. 2003. "Cognition." In Williams 2003a, 285–311.

2010. "Form and Matter." In R. Pasnau, ed. *The Cambridge History of Medieval Philosophy*, 635–646. Cambridge: Cambridge University Press.

2011. *Metaphysical Themes 1274–1671*. Oxford: Clarendon Press.

Pelster, F. 1922. "Thomas von Sutton O. Pr., Ein Oxforder Verteidiger der Thomistischen Lehre: II. Lehrmethode und Lehrrichtung des Thomas von Sutton." *Zeitschrift für Katholische Theologie* 46: 361–401.

Perler, D. and U. Rudolph. 2000. *Occasionalismus: Theorien der Kausalität im arabisch-islamischen und im Europäischen Denken*. Göttingen: Vandenhoeck und Ruprecht.

Piana, C. 1970. *Chartularium studii Bononiensis S. Francisci (Saec. XIII-XVI)*. Analecta Franciscana 11. Florentiae: ex Typographia Collegii S. Bonaventurae.

Piché, D. 1999. *La condamnation parisienne de 1277: texte latin, traduction, introduction et commentaire*. Paris: Vrin, 1999.

Pini, G. 2002a. *Categories and Logic in Duns Scotus: An Interpretation of Aristotle's Categories in the Late Thirteenth Century*. Leiden: Brill.

2002b. *Scoto e l'analogia: Logica e metafisica nei commenti aristotelici*. Pisa: Pubblicazioni della Classe di Lettere e Filosofia, Scuola Normale Superiore.

2005. "Univocity in Scotus' *Quaestiones super Metaphysicam*: the Solution to a Riddle." *Medioevo* 30: 69–110.

2008. "Scotus on Doing Metaphysics *in statu isto*." In M.B. Ingham and O. Bychkov, eds. *John Duns Scotus, Philosopher*, 29–55. Münster: Aschendorff.

2010. "Scotus's Legacy." In A Speer and D. Wirmer, eds. *1308: Eine Topographie historischer Gleichzeitigkeit*, 486–515. Miscellanea Mediaevalia 35. Berlin and New York: de Gruyter.

2014. "The *Questions on the Metaphysics* by John Duns Scotus: A Vindication of Pure Intellect." In G. Galluzzo and F. Amerini, eds. *A Companion to the Latin Medieval Commentaries to Aristotle's Metaphysics*, 359–384. Leiden: Brill.

Pomplun, R.T. 2016. "John Duns Scotus in the History of Medieval Philosophy from the Sixteenth Century to Étienne Gilson (†1978)." *Bulletin de philosophie médiévale* 58: 355–445.

Porro, P. 2019. "Contro e dentro l'univocità. Le trasformazioni dell'analogia tra Tommaso d'Aquino, Enrico di Gand e Giovanni Duns Scoto." In R. Salis, ed. *La dottrina dell'analogia dell'essere nella 'Metafisica' di Aristotele e i suoi sviluppi nel pensiero tardo-antico e medievale*, 247–286. Padova: Il Poligrafo.

Powicke, F.M. 1931. *The Medieval Books of Merton College*. Oxford: Clarendon Press.

Prentice, R. 1968. "Univocity and Analogy according to Scotus's *Super Libros Elenchorum Aristotelis*." *Archives d'histoire doctrinale et littéraire du Moyen Age* 66: 225–43.

Prestwich, M. 2008. "Kirkby, John (d. 1290), Administrator and Bishop of Ely." In *Oxford Dictionary of National Biography*. Oxford: Oxford University Press.

Quétif, J. and J. Échard. 1719. *Scriptores Ordinis Praedicatorum recensiti notisque historicis et criticis illustrati*. Pari: apud J.-B.-C. Ballard et N. Simart

Rashdall, H. 1942. *The Universities of Europe in the Middle Ages*. New Edition. Edited by F. M. Powicke and A.B. Emden. London and New York: Oxford University Press.

Reichert B.M., ed. 1899. *Acta capitulorum generalium Ordinis Praedicatorum: ab anno 1304 usque ad annum 1378*. Monumenta Ordinis Fratrum Praedicatorum historica 4. Romae: In Domo Generalitia.

Roest, B. 2000. *A History of Franciscan Education (c. 1210–1517)*. Education and Society in the Middle Ages and Renaissance 11. Leiden and Boston: Brill.

2014. *Franciscan Learning, Preaching and Mission C. 1220–1650*. Leiden: Brill.

Salas,V.M. Jr. 2013. "Albert the Great and 'Univocal Analogy'." *American Catholic Philosophical Quarterly* 87: 611–635.

Santogrossi, A. 1993. "Duns Scotus on Potency Opposed to Act in Questions on the Metaphysics." *American Catholic Philosophical Quarterly* 67: 55–76.

Schabel, C., ed. 2006. *Theological Quodlibeta in the Middle Ages*. Vol. 1. Brill's Companions to the Christian Tradition. Leiden and Boston: Brill.

2020. "Ockham, The Principia of Holcot and Wodeham, and The Myth of The Two-Year Sentences Lecture at Oxford." *Recherches de Théologie et Philosophie Médiévales* 81: 59–102.

Schabel, C. and G.R. Smith. 2012. "The Franciscan *studium* in Barcelona in the Early Fourteenth Century." In W.J. Courtenay, K. Emery, and S. Metzger, eds. *Philosophy and Theology in the Studia of the Religious Orders and at Papal and Royal Courts*, 359–392. Turnhout: Brepols, 2012.

Sileo, L., ed. 1995. *Via Scoti: Methodologia ad mentem Joannis Duns Scoti*. Roma: Edizioni Antonianum.

Smith, G.R. 2010. "Bibliotheca manuscripta Petri Thomae." *Bulletin de philosophie médiévale* 52: 161–200.

2018. "Aufredo Gonteri on the Univocity of Being: *Compilatio lecturae primi Sententiarum* distinctio 3 quaestiones 2–4." *Mediaeval Studies* 80: 59–170.

2019. "The Analogy of Being in the Scotist Tradition." *American Catholic Philosophical Quarterly* 93: 633–673.

Schmutz, J. 2002 "L'héritage des Subtils. Cartographie du scotisme au XVIIe siècle." *Les études philosophiques* 1: 51–81.

2008. "Le petit scotisme du Grand Siècle. Étude doctrinale et documentaire sur la philosophie au grand Couvent des Cordeliers de Paris, 1517–1771." *Quaestio* 8: 365–472.

Steele, J. 2016. "Duns Scotus, the Natural Law, and the Irrelevance of Aesthetic Explanation." *Oxford Studies in Medieval Philosophy* 4: 78–99.

Stroick, C. 1974 "Eine Pariser Disputation vom Jahre 1306: Die Verteidigung des Thomistischen Individuationsprinzips gegen Johannes Duns Scotus durch Guillelmus Petri de Godino, O.P." In W.P. Eckart, ed. *Thomas von Aquino: Interpretation und Rezeption: Studien und Texte*, 559–608. Mainz: Matthias-Grünewald.

Sullivan, M. 2010. *The Debate over Spiritual Matter in the Late Thirteenth Century: Gonsalvus Hispanus and the Franciscan Tradition from Bonaventure to Scotus*. Doctoral dissertation. The Catholic University of America.

Terán-Dutari, J. 1970. "Die Geschichte des Terminus 'Analogia Entis' und das Werk Erich Przywaras." *Philosophisches Jahrbuch der Görres-Gesellschaft* 77: 163–179.

Thomas of Eccleston. 1951. *Fratris Thomae vulgo dicti de Eccleston Tractatus de adventu fratrum minorum in Angliam*. Edited by A.G. Little. 1st English edition. Manchester: Manchester University Press.

Thomson, R.M. 2009. *A Descriptive Catalogue of the Medieval Manuscripts of Merton College, Oxford*. Cambridge: D. S. Brewer.

2010. "William Reed, Bishop of Chichester (d. 1385) — Bibliophile?" In G.H. Brown and L. Ehrsam Voigts, eds. *The Study of Medieval Manuscripts of England: Festschrift in Honor of Richard W. Pfaff*, 281–293. Turnhout: Brepols.

Toth, Z. 2017. Medieval Problems of Secondary Causation and Divine Concurrence. Doctoral dissertation. Fordham University.

Vincent, J.A.C., ed. 1893. *Lancashire Lay Subsidies: Being an Examination of the Lay Subsidy Rolls Remaining in the Public Record Office, London: From Henry III. to Charles II.* Vol. I. *Henry III to Edward I (1216–1307).* London: Wyman.

Vos, A. 2019. *John Duns Scotus: A Life.* Kampen: Summum.

Ward, T.M. 2014. *John Duns Scotus on Parts, Wholes, and Hylomorphism.* Leiden: Brill.

2019. "A Most Mitigated Friar: Scotus on Natural Law and Divine Freedom." *American Catholic Philosophical Quarterly* 93: 385–409.

Williams, T. 1997. "Reason, Morality, and Voluntarism in Duns Scotus: A Pseudo-Problem Dissolved." *The Modern Schoolman* 74: 73–94.

1998a. "The Libertarian Foundations of Scotus's Moral Philosophy." *The Thomist* 62: 193–215.

1998b. "The Unmitigated Scotus." *Archiv für Geschichte der Philosophie* 80: 162–181.

2000. "A Most Methodical Lover? On the Rationality of Scotus's God." *Journal of the History of Philosophy* 38: 169–202.

ed. 2003a. *The Cambridge Companion to Duns Scotus.* Cambridge: Cambridge University Press.

2003b. "Introduction: The Life and Works of John Duns the Scot." In T. Williams, ed. *The Cambridge Companion to Duns Scotus,* 1–14. Cambridge: Cambridge University Press.

2009. "The Divine Nature and Scotus's Libertarianism: A Reply to Mary Beth Ingham." Available from http://profthomaswilliams.com/The Divine Nature and Scotus's Libertarianism.pdf.

ed. and trans. 2017. *John Duns Scotus: Selected Writings in Ethics.* Oxford: Oxford University Press.

Willibrord, L. 1931. "B. Ioannes Duns Scotus, Lector Coloniensis," *Collectanea Franciscana Neerlandica* 2: 291–306.

Wippel, J.F. 1981. *The Metaphysical Thought of Godfrey of Fontaines: A Study in Late Thirteenth-Century Philosophy.* Washington, DC: Catholic University of America Press.

2000. *The Metaphysical Thought of Thomas Aquinas: From Finite Being to Uncreated Being.* Washington, DC: The Catholic University of America Press.

Wolf, S. 1980. "Asymmetrical Freedom." *Journal of Philosophy* 77: 151–166.

Wolter, A.B. 1946. *The Transcendentals and Their Function in the Metaphysics of Duns Scotus.* St. Bonaventure, NY: The Franciscan Institute.

1949. "Duns Scotus on the Natural Desire for the Supernatural." *New Scholasticism* 32: 282–317. Reprinted in A.B. Wolter. *The Philosophical Theology of John Duns Scotus,* 125–147. Ithaca, NY: Cornell University Press, 1990.

1972. "The Native Freedom of the Will as a Key to the Ethics of Scotus." In C. Bérubé, ed. *Deus et Homo ad mentem I. Duns Scoti.* Roma: Societas Internationalis Scotistica, 360–370. Reprinted in A.B. Wolter. *The Philosophical Theology of John Duns Scotus,* 148–162. Ithaca, NY: Cornell University Press, 1990.

1990. "Scotus's Paris Lecture on God's Knowledge of Future Events" In A.B. Wolter, *The Philosophical Theology of John Duns Scotus*, 285–333. Ithaca: Cornell University Press.

1993. "Reflections on the Life and Works of Duns-Scotus." *American Catholic Philosophical Quarterly* 67: 1–36.

1994. "Alnwick on Scotus and Divine Concurrence." In W.J. Carroll and J.J. Furlong, eds. *Greek and Medieval Studies in Honor of Leo Sweeney S.J.*, 255–283. New York: P. Lang.

2015. "The Unshredded Scotus." In A.B. Wolter, ed. *The Philosophical Theology of John Duns Scotus*, 241–290. St. Bonaventure, NY: Franciscan Institute Publications.

ed. and trans. 1987. *Duns Scotus on the Will and Morality*. 2nd ed. Washington, DC: Catholic University of America Press.

Xiberta, B.M. 1931. *De scriptoribus scholasticis saeculi XIV ex ordine Carmelitanum*. Louvain: Bureaux de la Revue.

Index

For EU product safety concerns, contact us at Calle de José Abascal, 56–1°,
28003 Madrid, Spain or eugpsr@cambridge.org.

www.ingramcontent.com/pod-product-compliance
Ingram Content Group UK Ltd.
Pitfield, Milton Keynes, MK11 3LW, UK
UKHW020334140625
459647UK00018B/2143

* 9 781108 411387 *